Diaries of a Danish Missionary
Harpoot, 1907–1919

Maria Jacobsen

Diaries of a Danish Missionary
Harpoot, 1907–1919

Translated by Kristen Vind
Edited and with an Introduction by Ara Sarafian

Gomidas Institute Books
Princeton and London

Photocredits: "KMA Collection," Gomidas Institute Archives (UK)

Published by Taderon Press, PO Box 2735, Reading, RG4 8GF,
England, by arrangement with the Gomidas Institute.

Printed and bound in Great Britain by Biddles Ltd., *www.biddles.co.uk*
06 05 04 03 02 01 5 4 3 2 1

ISBN 1-903656-07-9

For inquiries please contact
Gomidas Institute
PO Box 208
Princeton, NJ 08542
USA

Email: books@gomidas.org

On the World Wide Web at *www.gomidas.org*

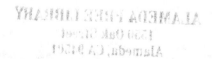

Dedicated by Alma and Varoujan Hovanissian
to the memory of their beloved son
Ara Hovanissian
London 2001

Contents

Introduction

Danish missionaries began working in the Ottoman Empire in the wake of the Armenian massacres of 1895–96, when hundreds of thousands of Armenians were murdered. These killings left much material and spiritual devastation in their wake, including scores of orphaned children. The plight of Ottoman Armenians was widely reported in Europe and in 1898 a Danish missionary movement—Women Missionary Activists (Kvindelige Missions Arbejdere or KMA)—was formed to help victims. The KMA enjoyed the favour of Danish aristocratic circles, as well as the support of the daily newspaper, *Kristeligt Dagblad*.[1] Over the decades the KMA raised thousands of kroners and sent dozens of missionaries for Armenian relief.

The KMA initially operated through Der Deutsche Hilfsbund, the German missionary organization in the Ottoman Empire, but soon established its own institutions and programmes. The first KMA missionary sent to Ottoman Turkey was Christa Hammer, who arrived in the Harpoot-Mezreh area in November 1901. She succeeded in establishing Emaus, a Danish orphanage in Mezreh for Armenian children. Sister Hammer was joined by Christiane Black, and following Hammer's death, Wilhelmine Grynhagen was sent to work there. Maria Jacobsen, also a KMA missionary, was sent to the American hospital in Harpoot in 1907. She soon moved to the new Annie Tracy Riggs Hospital, which opened in Mezreh a year later. Karen Marie Petersen, another Danish missionary, was appointed at Emaus orphanage in 1909. By the beginning of World War I, Maria Jacobsen and Karen Petersen were well-established missionaries in this region.

Armenians in the Harpoot Plain

Harpoot and Mezreh were twin cities situated a few miles apart.[2] The former stood high above the Harpoot plain, while Mezreh, the regional capital, was below, along with sixty-four other Armenian-inhabited villages (see pp. xviii–xix). Around

---

[1.] See introduction to *Maria Jacobsen: Orakroutiun 1907–1919*, transl., ed., and intro. Nerses Pakhdikian and Mihran Simonian (Antelias, Lebanon: Armenian Catholicosate Printing House, 1979), pp. vii–xxi; Libarid Azadian, *Hay Vorpere Medz Yegherni* (Los Angeles, Calif.: Abril, 1995), pp. 179–84.

[2.] Harpoot and Mezreh were both located in the central sub-province (sanjak) of Harpoot, in the province (vilayet) of Mamouret ul-Aziz. Mezreh was the provincial capital and the seat of the governor (vali). The other sub-provinces of Mamouret ul-Aziz were Malatia and Dersim.

40,000 Armenians made up about half of the plain's population.[3] The balance was primarily Kurdish, Turkish, and Assyrian. Armenians were well established and had over sixty churches and eighty schools.[4]

Starting in the nineteenth century, following the development of foreign missionary stations, this area was increasingly linked to the outside world. The American Board of Commissioners for Foreign Missions (ABCFM) had the largest presence with significant investments in schools, orphanages, and hospitals. Euphrates College, which was in Harpoot itself, became particularly well known as an educational centre with several American and European educated teachers and hundreds of students. Der Deutsche Hilfsbund developed an important presence in Mezreh, where it had several schools, orphanages, and a hospital. French Capucin monks and Franciscan sisters also ran several schools and an orphanage in Harpoot and Mezreh. These foreign missions were later joined by American and European consulates, adding to the region's links to the outside world. However, today, most of Harpoot is destroyed, while Mezreh, now called Elazig, remains a regional capital. The former American and European institutions stand no more, and there are no Armenians left to speak of. Even the names of former Armenian-inhabited villages and landmarks have been changed.

The Jacobsen Diaries and the Armenian Genocide

Maria Jacobsen, the author of the present manuscript, was born in Siim (near Horsens), Denmark, in 1882. She came from a devout Protestant family and was a nurse by training. She spent the greater part of her life working for Armenians, first in the Ottoman Empire, and later in Armenian refugee communities in Lebanon.

Throughout her stay in Ottoman Turkey, Maria kept a notebook where she recorded important events in her life. Though she wrote occasionally at first, she began making more regular and detailed entries following the Ottoman mobilization for World War I. She reflected on local conditions and social relations, the impact of the war on missionary activities, as well as on her own work. The single most important subject covered in these diaries, however, became the genocide of Ottoman Armenians.

In 1915 the Harpoot region turned into a theatre of the Armenian Genocide, when the Ottoman government adopted a programme to annihilate Armenians in

---

[3.] According to the 1913 census of the Armenian Patriarchate of Constantinople, the best data we have on Ottoman Armenians to date, 41,173 Armenians were registered in this region and a further 16,643 local Armenians were away in the United States, Russia, and other parts of the Ottoman Empire.

[4.] See Raymond H. Kévorkian and Paul B. Paboudjian, *Les Arméniens dans l'empire ottoman à la veille du génocide* (Paris: Les Editions d'Art et d'Histoire, 1992). For a detailed history of the region, see Vahe Haig, *Kharpert yev Anor Vosgetashte: Houshamadian Azkayin, Badmagan, Mshagouytayin* (New York, 1959).

the empire.[5] Charging Armenian communities with sedition, the Ottoman authorities embarked on what they termed a "deportation programme," which was actually part of the government's genocidal campaign.

In May 1915 Maria Jacobsen began recording specific stages of the genocide of Armenians, starting with the vilification and arrest of Armenians in Harpoot and Mezreh. Soon she was witnessing the passage of convoys of people who were being force marched across the Harpoot plain from further north. The first such convoy was from Erzeroum and indicated what lay ahead for Armenians deported from the Harpoot region.

> They had suffered indescribably on the way from torture, distress, and danger. Many of the men were killed. The women and girls were ravished by soldiers. Many of them are being taken to Turkish and Kurdish homes. They were told they would be going to Harpoot and when, after weeks and months of suffering and danger they reached here, the men and boys who had survived were taken from them and put into prison. This means they will be killed. The women are being kept here for some days and Turkish men come and choose the prettiest women and girls, who are taken home to their harems. The sick who cannot walk are being taken out to the cemetery and left lying there until they die. The rest are being sent on further.[6]

Armenians in Harpoot were treated in a similar fashion and Maria's first record of a local mass murder was the execution of a convoy of 800 people who were murdered near Khankeoy, a Turkish village, a few hours away to the south. Her information came from Melcon Effendi, a local Armenian, who escaped from the carnage. Throughout the summer survivors of other massacres approached Maria for help and informed her of other atrocities.

> As soon as they left the road, they all realized they were going to be killed. Just before evening an order was given to the soldiers to shoot—and this was

---

[5.] For an authoritative contemporary account of the Armenian Genocide, see James Bryce and Arnold Toynbee, *The Treatment of Armenians in the Ottoman Empire, 1915–1916: Documents Presented to Viscount Grey of Fallodon by Viscount Bryce [Uncensored Edition]*, ed. and intro. by Ara Sarafian (Princeton: Gomidas Institute, 2000).

[6.] *Diaries*, 8 July 1915. For additional English language primary accounts of the atrocities committed against Armenians in this region, see the reports filed by Isabelle Harley, Mary W. Riggs, and Ruth Parmelee in James Barton, comp., *"Turkish Atrocities": Statements of American Missionaries on the Destruction of Christian Communities in Ottoman Turkey, 1915–1917*, (Ann Arbor, Mich.: Gomidas Institute, 1998). Also see Tacy Atkinson, *"The German, the Turk and the Devil Made a Triple Alliance": Harpoot Diaries, 1908–1917* (Princeton: Gomidas Institute Books, 2000), pp. 38–39; Henry H. Riggs, *Days of Tragedy in Armenia: Personal Experiences in Harpoot, 1915–1917* (Ann Arbor, Mich.: Gomidas Institute, 1997); Ara Sarafian, comp., *United States Official Documents on the Armenian Genocide*, Vol. 3, *The Central Lands*, (Watertown, Mass.: Armenian Review Books, 1995).

followed by a hail of bullets. But they ran out of ammunition before everyone was killed, so they began slashing with the small axes they carry in their belts, and with bayonets. Suddenly Baron Melcon felt that the rope which bound him was loose, so he jumped up and ran with about 30 others. Most of them were overtaken and shot down. Baron Melcon ran on and on—he did not know where. In the middle of the night he saw some lights and ran in their direction. On the road he saw a Turkish man and asked him what the lights were. The man answered, "Don't you know? It is Mezreh." When he heard the word "Mezreh" he ran as hard as he could and reached our hospital after midnight—completely exhausted and with swollen and bleeding feet. He also appeared quite distracted, and no wonder, with all he had seen. He was hidden here by us, until he could be sent to a more safe place.[7]

Maria's diaries mention a number of mass executions and, significantly, all were organised and took place with official sanction. Foreign nationals were powerless in stopping the carnage, though they did try to intervene with the authorities. The latter, in turn, denied knowledge of such killings, as well as responsibility for them.

Last night about 100 Armenians were sent away from Harpoot, but they reached no further than the spring, two hours walk from the town. Here the soldiers started shooting. A 16 year old boy escaped. He had seen his mother, father, and brother killed. He himself had seven bullet wounds and several bayonet wounds in the back and head. He came to the hospital, where we dressed his wounds and gave him clean clothes."[8]

Sometimes in outlying villages all pretexts of deportations were ignored and people were murdered outright. In the case of Hoiloo, for example, Armenian women and children were simply massacred in their own village. Maria was informed of this episode by a twelve-year-old survivor:

All women were gathered together and killed. The men had been killed earlier. The women were ordered to remove their best clothes, and they were laid on top of each other, two by two, and beheaded. The ones underneath were not all killed the first time and the soldiers shouted to them, "Those of you who are alive—get up. You shall be taken to Mezreh and dealt with there." All who obeyed were killed, but some who lay quite still, as if they were dead, succeeded in escaping later. One of them, a girl of 12 years, came to Mezreh. She had a long and very nasty gaping wound in the neck, which gradually became very infected. Sister Jenny took her in to the Children's Home and every day she is taken to the hospital for treatment.[9]

---

7. *Diaries*, 6 July 1915.

8. *Diaries*, 29 July 1915.

9. *Diaries*, 14 August 1915.

Surviving Victims of the Armenian Genocide

Although the authorities continued to deny the reported killings, the mounting evidence was conclusive. By the end of July 1915 it was clear that the government was conducting a campaign of extermination under the cloak of a deportation programme. "The truth is that the soldiers only go with them [Armenians] to kill the men and the old women, and rob and ravish the young women. Our vilayet is a slaughterhouse. If people from other parts of the country arrive here they are killed."[10]

According to one official Ottoman report, 51,000 Armenians were deported from the province by September 1915, while 4,000 remained hiding in surrounding villages.[11] Most of these 4,000 Armenian survivors were women, orphaned children, and some elderly. There were many more women and children in Muslim households, as well as a handful of men who had renounced their identities as Armenians (by changing their names, converting to Islam, and living under supervision). There was also a scattering of men who had gone into hiding during deportations and massacres, or had deserted from the Ottoman army. All men in the latter category were actively sought out and killed by the government.

While the Ottoman authorities tried to assimilate surviving Armenians into Muslim households or destroy them outright, foreign missionaries attempted to save as many as they could.[12] Missionaries sought the intercession of foreign embassies, pleaded with local authorities for exemptions to "deportations," and offered clandestine relief to survivors wherever possible. With limited resources, they fed a large number of Armenians and waited for a change in fortunes.

Maria's diaries provide an invaluable perspective on this episode of the Armenian Genocide, as thousands of Armenian women and children begged for food and shelter, foraged in refuse tips, and lived in the open—always subject to abuse and murder. Needless to say, the authorities did not provide either food rations or shelter to these Armenians, and missionaries were consistently denied permission to open an orphanage for Armenian children. Survivors had to negotiate between death through privations and murder, or forced absorption into Muslim households.

[10.] *Diaries,* 28 July 1915.

[11.] See [Governor] Sabit Bey to Ministry of Interior (Constantinople), telegram dated Mamuret-ul-Aziz, 18 September 1915, Prime Ministry Ottoman Archives, Istanbul, DH.EUM, 2inci Sb. 68/70.

[12.] See Ara Sarafian, "The Absorption of Armenian Women and Children into Muslim Households as a Structural Component of the Armenian Genocide" in *In God's Name: Genocide and Religion in the Twentieth Century,* ed. Omer Bartov and Phyllis Mack (New York and Oxford: Berghahn Books, 2001), pp. 209–221; Hilmar Kaiser, *At the Crossroads of Der Zor: Death, Survival, and Humanitarian Resistance in Aleppo, 1915–1917* (Princeton: Gomidas Institute Books, 2001).

The continuing war, a poor harvest in 1916—not least because of the destruction of the Armenian peasantry—and the arrival of Muslim refugees from the Russian front exacerbated conditions, especially for Armenians. Furthermore, the United States entry into World War I (April 1917) obliged American missionaries to leave the Ottoman Empire, and their departure had a devastating effect on Armenian relief efforts. Though Maria Jacobsen, a Danish national, remained behind, her resources were exhausted within a few months, and she watched the demise of the people she had been helping. Her diaries are a catalogue of human abuse, misery, and death.

> How many mothers have come with their little child in their arms and begged and beseeched me to have mercy on their child and to give just a piece of bread a day. "Don't give me any" they say, "Only my child, or she will die, and she is all I have left." When I say "No," they cry still more bitterly. ...Then there are others who will not accept "No." They stand talking back, begging and pleading. They kiss my hands and feet. They cannot understand or believe that it is really the truth that there is no money and think I am just being unfair. At long last they go out, disappointed and crying hopelessly, but resolved to come again every day until I give them bread. It is impossible for them, suffering such hunger pangs, to believe and understand, that there is no bread. ...It is misery and endless affliction that has brought these unfortunate people to this point. ...This is what the Turks have longed for and are so glad to see. The Americans, who up to now have sheltered and helped the many poor souls, have now gone, and there is no help coming.[13]

Throughout these difficult times, Maria remained a devout Christian with a deep sense of religious mission. Her diaries are filled with biblical references and some harsh judgements based on her faith. It is this faith which provided her with the fortitude to cope with the developments around her and "to carry out God's work." She remained in the Ottoman Empire during these trying times, though she could easily have returned to Denmark. In one passage, in the midst of all the confusion and carnage, when the Americans were leaving, Maria simply commented, "it is our duty to remain, for how could we go and look for something easier and more comfortable and leave these many poor souls to their fate amongst their enemies."[14] Maria only left the Ottoman Empire when the war was over and Near East Relief workers had come to rehabilitate Armenian communities. Unfortunately, this rehabilitation effort proved to be short lived, as Turkish nationalists regrouped, took over control of the region, and eventually created the modern Turkish Republic in 1923.

---

13. *Diaries,* p. 197.

14. *Diaries,* 11 April 1917.

Editorial Notes

The diaries of Maria Jacobsen have been translated from the original Danish by Sister Kristen Vind and silently edited by the present editor. Editorial notes have been kept to a minimum and the original flow of the Danish text has been kept as far as possible. The Jacobsen diaries were originally written in four books. Readers may consult the original Danish text in Pakhdikian's Armenian edition, which has a facsimile of the original Danish material. All names have been standardized, and there is a glossary and an index of proper nouns appended at the end. The present work includes the photographs which appeared in the original manuscript. All editorial notes appear in brackets.

Finally, we list a number of shortened references Maria makes in her diaries to key people and places. "The Consul" is invariably Leslie A. Davis, the local United States consul; "the Doctor" is the much loved Henry Atkinson, a local American medical missionary; "the Badveli" [reverend] is usually Rev. Vartan Amirkhanian; "Bessie" is Arshaloois Dingilian, the young Armenian girl Maria eventually adopted; "Karen Marie" is Maria's friend and colleague, Karen Marie Petersen. Where Maria makes references to children's homes, one is the Danish "Emaus" orphanage, while the other is the German "Children's Home" which consisted of Pniel, Ebenzer, Elim, and Maranatha (in the German missionary compound in Mezreh). Maria's references to "the Garden" is the summer house a short distance to the north of Harpoot used by American missionaries, and "the College" is the American Euphrates College in Harpoot.

Acknowledgements

Karekin Dickran was instrumental in bringing this project together, and I can not thank him enough for all his contributions. I also wish to acknowledge the late Catholicos Karekin Sarkissian, who originally commissioned this translation, and allowed me to bring it to fruition. The Committee for Recognition of the Armenian Genocide (Armenian Community Council of Great Britain) has been firm in its support, as have numerous friends in Europe and the United States.

ARA SARAFIAN
Reading, Berks.
24 June 2001

Above. American missionary compound, Harpoot.

Below. Mezreh and Harpoot plain are in the foreground. The town of Harpoot is perched on top of the mountains in the distance.

Danish orphanage, Emaus (Mezreh).

Foreign missionaries in Mezreh, 1905. Jenny Jensen, Bødil Bjorh, Wilhelmine Grynhagen, Hansine Marcher, Jensine Ørtz, and Alma Johanson.

Armenian girls at Emaus (Mezreh), 1910.

The distribution of Armenians in the Harpoot plain circa 1915*

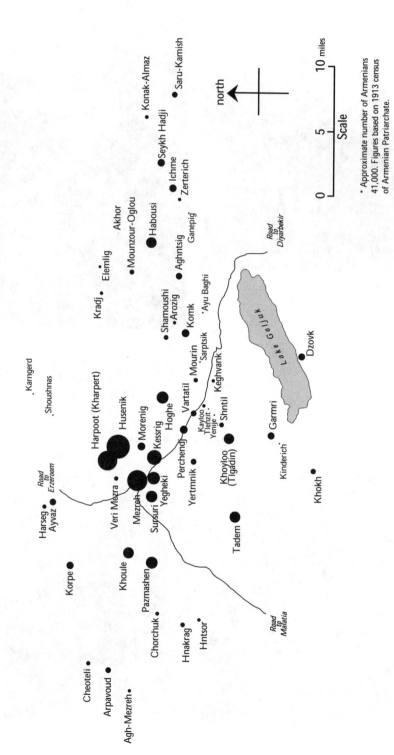

* Approximate number of Armenians 41,000. Figures based on 1913 census of Armenian Patriarchate.

north

Scale

0   5   10 miles

Lake Goljuk

Cheoteli
Arpavoud
Agh-Mezreh

Korpe
Khoule
Pazmashen
Chorchuk
Hnakrag
Hntsor

Harseg
Ayvaz
Veri Mezra
Mezreh
Supsuri
Yegheki
Yertmnik

Karngerd
Shoushnas

Harpoot (Kharpert)
Husenik
Morenig
Kessrig
Hoghe
Perchendj
Vartatil
Mourin
Kayloo
Tenzit
Yenije
Shntil
Keghvank
Sarptsik
Komk
Keghvank

Khoyloo
(Tigadin)
Tadem

Garmri
Kinderich

Khokh

Dzovk

Kradj
Elemlig
Akhor
Mounzour-Oglou
Shamoushi
Arozig
Aghntsig
Ganepig
'Ayu Baghi

Habousi

Ichme
Zerterich
Seykh Hadji

Konak-Almaz
Saru-Kamish

Road to Erzeroom
Road to Malatia
Road to Diyarbekir

The Armenian Population of the Harpoot Region According to the 1913 Census of the Constantinople Patriarchate

Town/village	Population	Households	Churches	Monasteries
Mamuret ul Aziz	4,580	683	5	
Kharpert	4,248	714	6	
Akhor	165	25	1	
Aghouan	400	80	1	
Aghntsig	450	70	1	
Agh-Mezre	125	21	1	
Ayvoz	450	28	--	
Aghvan	100	12	--	
Arozig	140	26	--	
Arpavoud	343	52	1	
Pazmashen	1,450	320	3	
Karngerd	95	25	1	
Kaylou	156	27	1	
Keghvank	108	26	1	
Kradj	130	10	1	
Komk	663	110	1	1
Konak-Almaz	149	22	1	
Tadem	1,300	225	2	1
Yegheki	1,610	253	2	
Yertmnig	365	70	1	
Zartarich	120	13	--	1
Elemlig	86	13	--	
Tlanzig	20	5	1	
Khmriwn	350	40	1	
Ichme	589	60	1	1
Khokh	300	45	1	
Khoyloo	1,201	240	3	1
Khoule	1,278	220	2	1
Tzaroug	131	19	1	
Dzovk	500	93	--	1
Garmri	533	85	2	
Gaban-Maden	265	53	1	
Habousi	1200	180	1	
Husenik	6,090	750	3	
Hnakrag	228	40	2	

Town/village	Population	Households	Churches	Monasteries
Hoghe	1,540	190	1	
Ghourbet Mezre	20	4	--	
Hayelou	45	13	--	
Mourin	200	31	--	
Mouzour Oghlou	250	40	1	
Morenig	660	127	1	
Shamoushi	235	40	1	
Sheykh Hadji	590	72	2	
Chakhlli	17	4	--	
Shntil	245	45	1	
Cheoteli	192	25	1	
Tsor Kegh	160	25	1	
Saru Kamish	346	58	1	
Sursuri	1,366	211	1	1
Sarptsik	149	16	1	
Vzhan	30	5	--	
Vartatil	360	70	1	
Perchendj	681	180	1	
Kessrig	2,280	380	2	1
Keferdiz	400	50	--	
Keorpe	570	102	1	
Hntsor	130	25	1	
Veri Mezre	197	30	1	
Harseg	192	32	1	
Damlou	30	8	--	
Mamash	40	6	--	
Tepekhan	100	25	--	
Gerger-Gargar	450	70	--	
Vahmanoy	173	--	--	
TOTAL**	41,173			

** A further 16,643 local Armenians were registered as working away from this region (mainly in Constantinople, Russia, and the USA)

Diaries of a Danish Missionary
Harpoot, 1907–1919

The lines are fallen unto me in pleasant places. Yea, I have a goodly heritage.

Psalm 16.

At this moment, when a new phase of my life is to begin, I feel prompted to put down some of my experiences and some of my thoughts in this book to enable me to cast back my mind occasionally and review what the Lord has done for me.

[DENMARK] 7 September, 1907. That day is engraved on my mind and it will perhaps always come back to me. It was a day of joy and a day of sorrow at the same time, but I think the joy was stronger. I was now so near the goal I had longed for and striven to achieve. But it was very hard on me when the time came and I had to take leave of my sisters and brothers and also of my dear father. His face was set, and his voice was choked with tears, and it was obvious how he fought with himself not to let me see how hard it was. Then my dear little mother hugged me to her breast as if she could not let me go, but still I had to leave as the train was due shortly. Then again I heard the dear ones say, "God be with you till we meet again," and I was on the train hurrying away. I had taken leave of my dear home. For how long nobody knows, only my Lord and Master.

That night I was in Copenhagen and went to K.M.A.'s Missionary College—my second home. That was the last stage before Armenia.

Then followed some busy weeks with preparations for my departure.

Monday, 16th September. The Reverend Mr. Frantzen had invited me to come together with some friends. We spent a lovely evening talking about Armenia and I think it was enjoyable for many. Before we parted we prayed together and my dear friends placed this calling and me before the Lord.

Tuesday, 19th September. There was a farewell meeting for me at the Y.W.C.A. in the parish of Nathaniel. That was a blessed evening which I shall never forget. The dear young girls, how they all showed me their love and affection. There were flowers all over the place—on all the tables, over the pictures, in fact everywhere. Everyone was there, both from the youth section and the senior section.

We were all seated at the tables, so beautifully decorated, and we started by singing, "Live for Jesus." Then Comtesse Knuth spoke on Isaiah 55-1-3 and pointed out to us that it was a day of joy because we were to take leave of someone about to depart. She then addressed herself especially to me about the goodly heritage I had received from the Lord to be His emissary and bearer of the Gospel, and that I had been given a special talent as a trained nurse.

Then we had coffee and afterwards the young girls performed a poem in song. Then the Reverend Mr. Frantzen presented me, on behalf of the Y.W.C.A., a lovely picture of the wise virgins and reminded me always to watch and pray, Colossians 2-6-7. Some of the younger ones now assigned a passage to me. The Reverend Mr. Tørsleff gave me Psalm 23. He wished that I should always feel "The Lord is my good shepherd," and even if I would suffer want and thirst many times down at the dark river, I should always see that the Lord guided me to the still waters. Mrs. Frantzen gave me the passage, "The Lord is good and his mercy endureth forever."

Miss Marie Grønbech gave me Isaiah 43-1-2. All these passages went straight to my heart. I went home that night with praise in my heart, grateful for all that the Lord had granted me in the dear Y.W.C.A. during the seven years I had been a member.

Tuesday 23rd. I was invited to visit Mrs. Lange together with the board of K.M.A. and some other friends, among them Mrs. Højer from Arabia, Mrs. Bauer from Palestine, Miss Madsen, as well as some former students and all the present students of the Missionary College.

After having spent some time talking together, an opportunity was provided for people to read me passages for the journey. Mrs. Lange had chosen Psalm 18-31-36, and especially impressed upon me that the statutes of the Lord are right, rejoicing to the heart, and that the Lord is a shield to all who put their trust in him.

Mrs. Højer read me a passage from Isaiah (63.9), "In all their affliction He was afflicted, and the angel of His presence saved them." Her own experience had proved this and she wished I would reach the same conclusion. Mrs. Bauer encouraged me always to keep refuge with Jesus in my heart. She said that would help me through all the difficult times which were bound to come. Miss Madsen read me the passage, "If any of you lack wisdom, let him ask of God." She knew I should need much wisdom in those foreign parts and felt the urge to remind me of this gracious promise.

Miss Blædel gave me the passage, II Thess 1-11-12, "That the name of our Lord Jesus Christ may be glorified in you and ye in Him, according to the grace of our God and the Lord Jesus Christ." She said the best thing she could do was to pray to the Lord to consider me worthy of the mission, and that He should be glorified in me and I in Him. Still more of the dear friends spoke and afterwards we prayed together. Now the friends placed the work of the K.M.A. in Armenia, and also the work that I was so soon to begin, as well as myself, before the Lord. It was an enjoyable evening and I truly felt how lovely it is to be admitted to the home of God's children.

Tuesday, 1st October. Then finally it was the day I had looked forward to for so long. At noon Karen-Marie arrived and stayed for the night. That was a great pleasure for me. In the afternoon the Armenia Committee convened and I participated in the prayers. Afterwards Mrs. Lange came up to me and gave me the most lovely fountain pen. I had long wished to have one, but never thought the wish would be fulfilled. This one was a present from the Armenia Committee. Baroness Kurck and Miss Collet gave me a silver chain. Indeed I received many other lovely presents from these dear friends.

All the members of the Armenia Committee were invited to dinner at the Missionary College. We spent an enjoyable time and each received a scriptural passage chosen by Miss Blædel. Mine was St. John 14-29 and Isaiah 60-19. At 7.00 p.m. we all went to the Garison Parish Hall. The meeting started at 7.30 and the hall was almost filled. We first sang, "Et skrig som af nød, fra jorden der lød" [A cry of distress arose from the earth].

Then Miss Collet opened the meeting with prayer and we joined in singing another hymn, "Zion's daughter bow thy ear." Lady Oxholm now spoke about the sufferings of Armenia. Later Baroness Kurck spoke on how prayers are answered. She said that four years ago a minister of the Lord prayed that a nurse be sent out, and at the same time the Lord summoned me, who at that time was serving at the Sundby Hospital. After I had thanked K.M.A. and all my friends for all the love and affection they had shown me, and after I asked them to include me in their prayers, the Reverend Mr. Sorensen spoke on the Word, "I will be gracious to whom I will be gracious, and will show mercy to whom I will show mercy," with special reference to me. He said that the grace of God was the same yesterday, today, tomorrow, and forever. It does not change. Then he ordained me for my mission by laying his hand on my head and praying. A number of friends now assigned passages to me. The Reverend Mr. Frantzen spoke to me on the scriptural passage, "And when they had brought their ships to land, they forsook all, and followed Him." He finally passed on the compliments to the dear Y.W.C.A.

Following the meeting we had tea in the minor hall and I had the opportunity to speak to many friends and take final leave of them.

It was a very blessed evening and I went home, my heart filled with praise and gratitude to my Lord and Master for his wonderful grace in allowing me to go out on his mission. On Wednesday I went to see some of my dear friends for the last time before my departure, and many matters required attention that day.

On Thursday morning there was a letter from Germany saying that I had to be in Berlin on Friday morning. My departure had originally been arranged for Friday morning, but now I had to leave Thursday night. That was a bit of a disappointment, as the time of departure had been announced and many of my friends would come to the station on Friday. But now we got busy packing and arranging the final details.

At lunch I went to see the Reverend Mr. Fibiger and we spent an enjoyable time together. Before I left we prayed and he asked the Lord to be my guide and carry me on his arm when the road became too narrow and difficult. Before I left he said, "So trusting and happy in Jesus' name, onward to Heaven you go, serving the weaker on the way, you and they are brothers to Him, our Father in Heaven lives, He lives." Then we separated, but only to meet again.

In the afternoon my dear Lady Knuth came to bid me farewell. It was so wonderful to feel that she cared for me. Mrs. [blank] came to bid me farewell, as well as Miss Asmussen of Sundby Hospital.

In the afternoon at 5.30 all K.M.A. members and students from the Missionary College met with me at Miss Collet's. When we had eaten we joined in singing the hymn, "Draw me Jesus to Thy bosom" after which we all prayed.

And now the time had come for us to go to the railway station. A crowd of friends had gathered there. As I took leave of all of them, my heart filled with a strange pleasure and peace. When I had ascended the train I found that my dear Miss Blædel was already there, and that was a great comfort. Everybody then joined in the hymn, "God be with you till we meet again." This was the last I heard when the train pulled out from the Copenhagen railway station. Only when I could no longer see them I felt unable to restrain my tears, but then Miss Blædel put her arms around my neck, saying, "God protect thee in thy going out and coming in." That word came to me from the Lord and immediately took a heavy burden off my mind. I could now fare with a light heart. Now the moment had come which I for so long had looked forward to in fear and trepidation. The Lord took away all heavy clouds and granted me to fare with a light heart. That was what I so often had prayed for and my prayers were answered.

On Friday morning Miss Blædel and I arrived at Berlin and after having rested for some hours we went to the railway station to attend to my clothes. Here we met the two German sisters I was to join. We also took a cab and drove around the city to see all the magnificent buildings and monuments. It was all very interesting.

In the evening we prayed together before we went to bed. Miss Blædel then read Psalm 91 and commended me into the hands of my Father.

The next morning, Saturday, we left for the railway station at 8 o'clock and I can remember so clearly the long black train as it came rushing along, and how I had to get on board so hastily before it again pulled out from the station. Then I heard my dear Miss Blædel say, "May the Lord bless you," and the train was again gathering speed. I was now on my way to the country and the mission for which the Lord had prepared me.

It was a wonderful strength the Lord let me have, enabling me to express my praise and thanks at all moments, and even to say to myself, "The lines are fallen unto me in pleasant places. Yea, I have a goodly heritage."

On Tuesday, 29th October, I arrived at Harpoot and I felt with all my heart, the Lord is good and His mercy endureth forever.

I now saw the goal I had so strongly prayed for and longed for in my heart fulfilled, and I could not but fill with thanksgiving because He had induced me to follow my calling and come here. I could only place myself in His hands and pray that He use me as His servant for the glorification of His name and the blessing of souls. That was truly a great day—thanks be to the Lord.

24 December, 1907 (Christmas Eve). So came my first Christmas in this foreign country, away from my dear ones. What a glorious sensation to learn day after day, hour after hour, that the Lord is the same always and everywhere. I have been granted to see also today, and especially this night, that the same joy of Christmas that filled my heart at home has indeed, in even greater measure, filled my heart here.

New Year's Eve, 1908. Mrs. Grynhagen came here today to spend the New Year holidays with me. She is counted among those who take the Lord at his word, trusts Him, expects great works of Him, because He allows us to do so in His name. She is a happy Christian. When it was nearly 12 o'clock we read Psalm 103 together and afterwards we knelt down, thanking the Lord for the immense grace and love He had shown us in the year which had now passed. Then we commended ourselves to Him and His will in the new year. We spent a blessed hour together and entered upon the new year with cheerfulness and hearts full of thanksgiving, because we go with our Saviour and because there is no future without Jesus.

Some months have now passed and we are already in March. We had a cold winter—colder than usual it is said, and I have seen much distress, poverty, and suffering. How it hurts to see these poor and sick people, many even seriously ill. Oh what mercy that I was allowed to come here and work to alleviate some of the serious distress and illness. May I be given the grace to become a blessing here.

16 May, 1908. Since the previous entry I have undertaken a long and very interesting journey and I am now in Aintab. On March 16th I left Harpoot together with Doctor Ward. After three days we arrived at Diarbekir, staying here for one week. It is a very old town, it is said dating from before the birth of Christ. It is surrounded by walls like Jerusalem. From here we went to Mardin where we stayed one month holding a large clinic every day.

Towards the end of April we left and after a four days' journey came to Ourfa, another town dating from before Christ. It was a beautiful town. We stayed with Miss Shattuck. A few days later we left again and came back to Aintab after a journey of 21 days. It was a very difficult journey, but I would not have missed it for anything. We passed through the country proper and had a fine opportunity to see where Turks, Kurds, and the savage Arabs live. They are a truly predatory people. We were surprised over and over again. Oh, how these people are in need of our Lord. They are living like animals. We had many experiences. One night we slept in a tent with horses, camels, and sheep, but everywhere and always our Lord was the same.

19 July. This is the last day of a lovely week. We had a medical conference in which I participated. There were medical missionaries from all of Turkey, Palestine, and Syria. We had some glorious days. The Lord was amongst us and blessed us, and that was evident during each and every meeting. Lord help us win more souls. I see these last few days as a great blessing. In a couple of days I return to Harpoot. Our efforts shall bear fruit.

1 October. Tonight exactly one year ago I was together with my dear friends at the Copenhagen railway station for the last time. And now one year has passed, a wonderful, rich, and blessed year, the happiest in my life. It has been so rich in blessing, and it is all the result of grace. But we have also seen hardship and that is because the Lord wants me to put my faith solely in Him, and He has become even more precious to me and more indispensable. When I am now granted a new year, my heart fills with praise to the Lord and gratitude for the great mercy to be not only His child but also a missionary worker.

It is lovely to serve God, lovely for man and woman. I will make a resolution for this new year, "Serve the Lord with gladness." The Lord is good and His mercy endureth forever. Verily, the lines are fallen unto me in pleasant places, yea, I have a goodly heritage.

20 September, 1908 (Sunday). A long time has now passed since I last wrote in this diary. The reason is not that there has been nothing to write, for every day is full of joy and, I must add, sorrow. So many things make your heart heavy. Particularly when, again and again, one meets the terrible half-heartedness in God's children. Just now I returned from church. A young man delivered his sermon but the spirit was lacking. Everybody takes a strong interest in politics, and this is strongly reflected in the sermons which are dominated by politics. Oh, how we need a spiritual revival bringing life unto the dead, making God's people work for the sanctification of their souls and win souls for the Lord. But even if so many things make one's soul bewail under all that secularity, the happiness is even greater. Oh, what mercy it is to be a child of God and be allowed to serve Him. How I long for the opportunity to lead some of the many who do not know Him as their saviour up to the cross, show them the right road. Indeed, the Lord makes me a winner of souls.

2 May, 1912 (Thursday). IN DENMARK.

So much time has passed since the last peaceful hour with my diary which gives me an opportunity to speak with you. What I have seen during those four years! I have had many blessed hours out there, both with the missionaries and my native friends. How I enjoyed my rewarding work among the sick. What a lovely experience to be allowed to bring some happiness into the lives of poor and lonely people, and bring comfort to the sick, who otherwise would have to lie at home among their ignorant friends and suffer—and even die in many cases—because no one there knows how to help them. When I cast back my mind to the work I was allowed to carry out, my heart fills with gratitude towards the Lord who granted me by His grace to bear some of the burdens in that far country. And a prayer forms in my heart asking forgiveness for all that I failed to do. If the Lord finds me worthy to go out again, I shall do so with joy and gratitude, and with renewed longing to serve Him better than before amongst the sick and poor, lonely and lost.

8 May, 1912 (Tuesday). To think that I am now back in Denmark. When I left and my friends said to me, "Now we hope to see you again in 1912," it seemed so far off in the future, almost unbelievable. Now I am sitting here, and even if the time now and then seemed to pass slowly, the whole period has passed so quickly, almost like a dream. I left Mezreh on 29th March, reached Malatia on Sunday evening and stayed until Monday morning with Miss Ørtz. On Sunday I went to the Protestant church where Dr. Michael preached. Later we paid a visit to Mr. Christoffel, the German missionary who runs a home for the blind. Not only are blind people admitted, but also crippled and mentally retarded people. It was good to see a home for these poor creatures, of which there are many in Turkey. Mostly, they walk around in the streets and live almost like animals. No one cares for them. We left again on Monday morning. We were a party of five. An Armenian doctor, Dr. Michael, who was going to Europe for his holidays; a sister, a lady from Switzerland, who has been head of a Children's Home for boys in Mezreh; Miss Finholdt, who had spent 6 months at the Danish Children's Home in Mezreh; and Miss Karen-Marie Petersen, who joined us in Malatia.

We had quite a lovely journey, first through Asia Minor over high mountains, then across the beautiful green plains. It was indeed a beautiful sight. One day we drove through mountains covered with blue and yellow crocuses, the next day there were irises, and then we saw Christmas roses, big and gorgeous. We could not but exclaim, "Oh, how beautiful." After four days we reached Sivas, a bright town in the mountains. Here the American missionaries gave us an affectionate welcome and insisted that we should stay until Monday, but for several reasons we wanted to reach the coast as soon as possible, and we decided to leave again on Saturday morning. That night we had a warm bath which we enjoyed all the more because we had been travelling for eight days and the inns where we spent the night were not always as clean as they could have been.

Saturday night we reached an inn, known as the Yeni Khan Inn. We stayed here for Sunday, which was Easter Sunday. In the morning we had a small meeting for all in the inn and quite a number turned up. Dr. Michael spoke to them on the significance of Easter. Freedom from sin. In the afternoon we had a small thanksgiving feast. It was a truly peaceful Sunday. On Monday we left again and drove until Friday evening, when we reached Samsoun. In Tokat, two days from Sivas, we went to the Protestant churchyard where the British missionary Henry Martins is buried. He was a missionary in India and there he translated the Bible into three languages. Then he became very ill and on his way home he travelled through Asia Minor but did not get farther than Tokat where he died among strangers and was buried. Friends in Britain put a beautiful stone on his grave to mark the servant of God buried there. The American Mission bought the place, and the churchyard is so well kept as to bear resemblance to a garden with lush vegetation.

We stayed in Samsoun until Sunday at noon. We then embarked on a French steamer for Constantinople, where we arrived on Tuesday morning following quite a lovely voyage, having experienced no gale or other unpleasantness. We should have liked to leave Constantinople on Wednesday but it was impossible to get tickets so we had to stay till Friday evening, but we had no trouble in passing the time. We went to see the largest mosques. I will mention only two of them.

The largest, oldest, and most interesting one is of course the St. Sophia Mosque. It is 1,600 years old and was first a Greek catholic church. But when the holy Moslem war began they took the magnificent building and used it as a mosque. Everything inside the church is made of marble. The huge pillars and the walls are mosaics with ivory inlays. The building accommodates 5,000 people. On the floor there are huge carpets woven in a patterns of small carpets, giving one small prayer rug for each person. On the walls there are five large pictures with the golden names of God, Mohammed, his father-in-law, brother-in-law, and grandchildren. On one wall there was a very old piece of tapestry from Mohammed's grave. One could see that there had been angels, four large cherubims, in the four corners of the ceiling. They had been painted over so as to resemble flowers, but the wings showed. There are big candles where the altar was. The pulpit is used by the Khodja who sits up there every Friday for prayer. It was all very impressive. In various places young men and boys were sitting on the floor on their knees with the Bible, or rather the Koran, in front of them. They were rocking to and fro reading out loud. It gave a very solemn impression in the large room. All the voices were very keen. At the door there are a great many water fountains and here we saw several men preparing themselves for their prayers. They stretched their arms as high up into the air as possible, removed their headgear, and also their socks. Then they washed head, arms, and legs and now they were ready to pray. Many things reveal that it is a very old building. When you enter from the street, you first pass through a large hall from which several doors lead into the church. In front of the doors there are huge, thick, silk tapestries which are very old.

From there we went to Sultan Ahmed's Mosque, which is 300 years old. Before that period it was the sultan's palace. The sultan was also known as the victorious sultan. He was 14 years of age when he became a sultan, his reign covered 14 years, and he went into warfare 14 times, and every time he came out the victor. For that reason this mosque was built for him. It is even more magnificent than the St. Sophia Mosque. A very large room with ample light. The walls are mosaics. There are lots of lamps. On the floors are very valuable carpets reflecting great skill. A Khodja who showed us around showed us a large brown marble slab which had been brought in from Yemen, their sacred place in Mecca. He told us that anybody who suffered from jaundice was cured if he put his hands against the stone. We said to each other, "Imagine this mosque as a Christian church where we could come together and praise the Lord, how lovely that would be." In the centre of the mosque there was a large dais where the Khodjas sat on Fridays for their worship. We entered into conversation with the Khodja guiding us about the war with Italy. His view was that the end of Turkey was near because the people had lost their faith. There was so much infidelity among the Moslems, he was quite convinced that the Christian Jesus would come soon. Those were strange words to hear from a Turk.

[Postcard in diaries. No separate caption.]

Close to the mosque there was a small building, a sepulchral chapel. We went inside and there was Sultan Ahmed's coffin and those of his mother and three wives and 48 children. There were several large caskets with ivory inlays. One contained the Koran, the others various other sacred items. Several prayer chains hung there containing 999 pearls. They had been used by Sultan Ahmed. There was also a large piece of brown silk tapestry, which they told us had been spread over Mohammed's coffin.

On Wednesday 17th April, we went to the bazaar to make various purchases.

In the morning of Thursday, April 18th we went to Bebek to see Robert College from where we had the most lovely view of the Bosporus. We spoke to several of the missionaries.

On Friday 19th April, we packed and went to see the "Selamlik," the Sultan who was coming here to pray at one of the mosques. The day before we had been told that the Italians had attacked at the Dardanelles and people advised us not to leave as they considered it too dangerous, but we left anyway and did not regret it. It was a splendid sight. The soldiers lined the street and played so nicely. The many finely dressed officers on their beautiful horses rode in pairs in a long line before the sultan's carriage. The Sultan looked very grave and sat with his eyes downcast. No wonder, considering what we learned at the time about war and unrest around us. We were happy we had our tickets so we could be sure of getting away in the evening. There were a large number of tourists who now wanted to leave the town, but that was impossible. No steamers could get out of the Bosporus and all seats on the trains had been booked in advance, so they had to wait. In the afternoon we went to see the Dervish dance. It was an appalling sight and that is their manner of worshipping God. They are so pitiable and confused. In the evening of April 19th we left Constantinople. We carried with us a large quantity of clothes for the journey and feared a high charge for it. But the gentleman who received it was somewhat flustered and probably made an error in his calculations. We did not pay very much so we were happy.

On top of that we were taken to a first-class instead of a second-class compartment, and since we were three ladies, we had two compartments, which resulted in Miss Finholdt, the Norwegian lady, being all by herself in one compartment. We had a pleasant time also, because we could stay in the same carriage all the way from Constantinople to Berlin. On the train we met a compatriot, a young engineer who had been engaged in building a cement factory in the vicinity of Constantinople.

Dr. Michael from Mezreh was also on his way to Berlin and he was in the same carriage. He invited us to dinner in the dining car and when we arrived at Budapest, where the train stopped for two hours, Mr. Kristensen took us on a drive around the town. It was certainly beautiful. Straight and wide streets with tall trees on either side. The buildings are all so stylish and clean. The area by the river especially was very beautiful. We went up the mountain by a train. The track was almost vertical. There we saw the Emperor's palace and a fine view over the Danube River.

On Monday April 22nd we reached Berlin. How strange again to be so near one's mother country. In the morning we went shopping and later we had an after-dinner nap. In the afternoon we saw the cathedral.

Tuesday morning, April 23rd, we left Berlin and arrived at Copenhagen in the evening. We really enjoyed travelling home through Denmark. When we caught the first glimpse of Denmark from the steamer a strange feeling came to us, and when we called at Gedser, some little Danish boys were selling flowers. We immediately bought some bouquets and found they were the most beautiful we had ever seen "for they were Danish." Everything looked so homely, the white farms, the lovely Danish woods, and people in the fields. Both men, women, and children waved to us as if to welcome us home. But best of all was the moment when we were received by our dear friends at the new, splendid railway station. Mrs. Oxholm, Mrs. Lange, Miss

Blædel, Miss Fugl, Mrs. Tetens—the brothers and sisters of Karen-Marie, Miss Müller, and Miss Grønbech. No one seemed to have changed. But we did not get much chance to speak to each other before we found ourselves seated in an automobile and rushed through the streets back to Mynstersvej, where we were received by still more K.M.A. ladies. Karen-Marie and I got the very room where we had stayed five years earlier. It was so nicely decorated with flowers, the lovely Danish flowers.

In the afternoon of Wednesday, April 24th, the committee had a meeting and we had an opportunity to see all the ladies of the committee. Several of our friends came and saw us. Wednesday evening Karen-Marie and I visited her sister in Charlottenlund. Thursday, April 25th, we spent unpacking, seeing some friends, and in the evening I went to the Y.W.C.A. in Amager where I spoke to many of my dear young friends.

April 26 (Friday). Miss Blædel's birthday. How lovely to be with her on that day. After my parents, she is the person here on earth I am most fond of. I gave her a Turkish carpet, which I think she liked. In the afternoon many of her friends gathered for a chocolate party and Karen-Marie and I were also there.

In the morning of Saturday, April 27th, I went home to Horsens and I could hardly wait till I was at the railway station. There were my parents and my brothers and sisters, how lovely to see them all again. There was so much to talk about and the days went by quickly. A few days after I had returned home my little sister became ill with influenza, and when her condition improved mother fell ill, and some days later it was my turn. I had a high temperature for several days and the worst thing about it was that, on the day of the Ascension, I was to deliver a speech in Copenhagen at a Foreign Missions gathering. Luckily enough, my temperature fell and I left, but I was far from being well. I arrived safely and the next day I spoke at the May Festival where I saw many of my old friends.

The next day I paid a visit to Doctor Karen Maria Andersen, who said I was to go somewhere to rest. Since there was no vacancy at "Villa Monte" and missionary Joh. Andersen had commented favourably on the rest home Bethania at Masnedsund, I went down there.

I left on May 25th. I was picked up at the railway station by Miss Petersen and was installed in a room facing north. But I did not get much rest. On Friday and Saturday a large number of guests arrived as next Sunday was Whitsun. To my great surprise there was a telephone call from Copenhagen to the effect that there was a letter from Mr. and Mrs. Brown who were in Berlin, saying that they would be in Copenhagen during Monday. But Miss Fugl had called back that we would go to Berlin instead, and now she asked me to be ready to leave together with her on Sunday evening. So we met at Masnedsund. We had a second-class compartment to ourselves and lay down in an effort to sleep. Around 6 o'clock we were in Berlin and immediately we went to the nice large hotel where the Browns stayed. We each had a nice room and I immediately went up to see Mr. and Mrs. Brown.

It was lovely to see the dear friends from Harpoot. They were very surprised to see me wearing a black dress and feared that someone close to me had died. But the reason was the death of our King. After having presented Miss Fugl to them we all went to the dining room to have lunch. In the course of the morning we went for a walk and in the afternoon we went out again together to have a look at the town. But it rained heavily so we did not get far. We went back and spent some pleasant hours together at the hotel. We had much to discuss, as no one of the committee had ever seen any of the missionaries from Harpoot.

When I woke up the next morning I had a severe headache and had to stay in that morning while the others went on a trip with one of Cooks omnibuses to see the town. They returned at noon and I dined with them, but I was still not feeling well, so I had to stay at home again in the afternoon when they went to see the painting exhibition. That night Miss Fugl returned to Copenhagen whereas I stayed on for another five days together with the Browns. These were lovely days and they passed quickly. We had a walk every day and talked about the past and the future. One day Mrs. Brown and I went to see the town by Cooks automobile—a lovely and very interesting trip of three hours. But after having been together for a week we separated and that was sad, as we should probably not meet again in this world. They went to America and did not expect to return to Turkey, as they were both old and not very strong, and it was my hope to go back to Harpoot after my holidays. Mr. Brown saw me to the railway station. Some hours later they departed for America via England. I returned to Bethania and stayed there for three weeks. There were many guests and I did not get much rest. They all knew who I was and asked me about my work, and it often happened that I suddenly found myself surrounded by people asking questions and the result was a long description on my part, often taking several hours. So I did not get much rest, but I met some children of God there who later became some of my most faithful friends. Then at the end of May I left and went to Copenhagen, where I stayed for a few days before I went on to Skælskør to visit Karen-Marie and her parents.

I arrived on June 28th and stayed until July 6th, a nice and lovely time. I spent most of the time in their lovely garden, and went to Kobæk several times to have a swim— those were lovely quiet days. It was so nice to see Karen-Marie, her father, mother, and dear sister. After my visit there, I went home to Horsens on July 6th and stayed for 10 days, but now the time had come for me to leave again. This time I set out on a long trip which I had looked forward to for many, many years. It was to Keswick. So on July 14th I was on the train leaving Horsens at noon, and in Fredericia Miss Collet and Miss Wolff Snedorff joined me. We saw Esbjerg at about 4 o'clock in the afternoon and immediately went on board the steamer where we shared a cabin. The weather was nice and none of us became seasick. We arrived in London at the stipulated time and went by automobile to the China Inland Mission Home where we were welcomed affectionately by Miss Holliday. We had just enough time to change before the bell rang for supper.

When we came into the large dining hall we saw people sitting at the long table, their faces telling many a story of hardship and struggle, but also of victory and joy, and peace that passeth all understanding. There were some young Danish men and women who had spent some months in England and who were now also heading for Keswick. In the autumn they were to go out to our Danish missionary area in China. The next day I joined them on a trip to Kew Gardens, only returning in the evening. The next day Miss Wolff Snedorff and I went to Paternoster Road to do some shopping. When returning we were welcomed on the steps by Baroness Kurck. That was a pleasant surprise, as it was the first time I had seen her since my return. The next morning, July 19th, we all left for Keswick by train at 10 o'clock. When we arrived at the railway station there were two special long trains for the Keswick participants, and they did not stop on the way.

We shared carriages with missionaries from the China Inland Mission and we had a lovely time. We joined in singing and spoke as if it was one long meeting. A Miss Gregg was there who had survived the Boxer Rising in 1900 and she told us much from that time. She won all hearts with her frankness, her joy and strong faith, her deep affection for her Saviour and His mission. There was a dining car and we had our dinner and afternoon tea. In the afternoon we had a visit from the head of "Een for Een Forbundet" (One by One Confederation)—a profound sincere follower of Christ. At 5 o'clock we reached Keswick, a little paradise on earth. Never did I see anything so beautiful, the lovely lakes surrounded by the impressive mountains. The railway station was teeming with people, all radiating happiness: Miss Collet, Miss Wolff Snedorff, two teachers, Misses Ulrich and Vorbech and myself. There were also a Swedish female student and a dear British lady from the China Inland Mission who kept house for us. It was Friday evening and we went to a meeting in one of the tents that night. On Saturday there was a large meeting for all missionaries. We each received a card to wear on the breast and on which to write our name and the country where we operated. We were about 400 missionaries from all parts of the world. Some printed songs were passed around and one had been written particularly for this occasion by Mrs. Head.

On Sunday there were services in the various churches and meetings in the tents and everywhere was crowded. There were two large tents, each could accommodate 6,000. Over the entrance there was a signboard with large letters, "All One in Christ Jesus." Every day when we sat close together, we really felt that the Lord was near. And we did sing, thank the Lord, and pray.

Early Monday the real Convention started. Every morning at 7 o'clock we had prayers and at 10 o'clock bible lessons in both tents. I went to the Eskin Street Tent to Doctor Dixon's bible studies.

At 11.00 there was a meeting where Dr. Griffieth Thomas spoke on the First Epistle of John. I went there too. Then there was a daily meeting at 3.00 p.m. which I always attended, and again in the evening. Just after the evening meeting Miss Wolff Snedorff and I would go down to the square to the open-air meeting.

Among the preachers I heard I was particularly fond of Dr. Griffieth Thomas, Dr. Dixon and the Reverend Stuart Holden, who one afternoon told us about his life in Africa, and we were all enthralled. Again on the last Saturday the South African Mission had invited all missionaries to afternoon tea, and we spent a lovely afternoon together. In the large beautiful room of the hotel, which provided the setting for our meeting, all the small tables were so nicely decorated with flowers and there was a festive atmosphere. After tea and the very pleasant time we spent together, several of the missionaries gave talks, after which we joined in prayer. A photograph was taken of all the missionaries.

[Photograph in diaries. No separate caption.]

We left early Monday and returned to Denmark. We actually made up a small party. Miss Collet, Miss Wolff Snedorff, and Miss Holliday and I went together to Miss Collet's house "Minde" near Lundby on Sealand. Miss Holliday and I had been invited to stay for three weeks. We travelled together with Miss Sophia Rønche, who had returned from China and Miss Mikka Nissen, who has been in England for one year, and finally Dr. Jungersen and his wife, who had also been to Keswick and now returned to Denmark. In the autumn they were to leave for India. I was so happy to get to know them, such wonderful people.

It was a glorious time in Keswick. I had heard so much in advance but it was quite different actually to be there and participate. How comforting to see the many thousands of people, all longing, all harbouring desires of the heart, to see them coming with their bibles and hymn books, all with joy in their eyes. Everywhere we heard thanksgiving and prayers. Apart from that we were in the midst of a piece of lovely nature. The last meeting on Sunday evening was extremely moving. One after another people rose and gave testimony of what the Lord had done for them. Every heart filled with praise and thanksgiving, and that night we did sing. The hymn that appealed most to my feelings was, "Oh, the Deep, Deep Love of Jesus." Never before had I been granted to see so much of his unfathomable love and when we left the tent we joined in singing the hymn, "God Be With You Till We Meet Again" before we separated. We went home laden with rich and precious memories.

[Photograph in diaries. No separate caption.]

Travelling home was not too pleasant. We were very tired and there was a strong wind, so several of us became seasick, but Miss Holliday was the one who suffered most. We were very happy when we saw "Minde" and immediately went to bed where we stayed that day. The next day we all felt better and in the morning Sister Ellen and I drove down to Lundby to pick up Miss Fugl who came to stay with us. Now followed some lovely quiet days. The mornings we spent separately, either out in the corn-field or in the lovely wood. The afternoons we spent together and in the evening we went for a drive. After about two weeks I went to Roskilde and paid a visit to Mr. Smedegaard, a large farmer. Here I stayed for about a week. I had never been there before and they were not personal acquaintances but Mrs. Smedegaard was head of the K.M.A. section and they helped me pass the time. They treated me with such affection and love and I spent some lovely days which I shall always look back on with joy. Also here I came to know some dear children of God. During my stay I delivered a speech at a K.M.A. meeting about my work. There was a large gathering and they listened with attention and interest.

After a stay for about one week I returned to my home where I spent a lovely quiet time in the bosom of my family. I had so often longed to be with my dear ones. Here I stayed for two months, the longest duration I had experienced without breaks.

One night I spoke at a women's meeting. There was a large number of people and I was very happy about this meeting. My sister Betty was away travelling for a month, so father, mother, and my dear sister Anna and I had a very quiet time.

On September 5th Karen-Marie arrived to pay me a visit. She stayed a week and we were very happy about her visit. On Monday, September 9th she and I went to Ejstrup, where we had a meeting in the evening. It was in a rural parish. There were quite a number of people and they seemed to be happy about the meeting. As always I brought along the Armenian costumes and three young people put them on. It was a great success. We spent the night there and left the next morning, first by day coach to Rask Mølle, then by train.

On September 12th Karen-Marie returned to her home and a few days later I went north where I, together with Miss Fugl, was to arrange some meetings. Our first stop was Randers, where we stayed at the hotel and in the evening there was a K.M.A. meeting in the parish hall. Miss Fugl told us about K.M.A.'s work and I about my work in Turkey. The next day we went on to Viborg, where we spent Sunday.

We went to service in the lovely cathedral in the morning and in the evening we had a meeting for K.M.A. in the parish hall. On Monday we left, I heading for [Skive] where I was to speak at a bazaar, both in the afternoon and the evening. I was picked up in Skive by a farmer who took me to his home for dinner and then again to the parish hall, which was packed with people, and here the rector Mr. Jepsen and his wife welcomed me. The meeting started immediately. Afterwards the Rector and his wife invited me home. They lived in an unusual charming rectory, where I stayed for the night. The next morning I went to Skive by coach where I paid a visit to Mr. Jepsen, an Inland missionary, and had dinner. In the afternoon I went by train to Nykøbing Mors to visit my brother Jacob and Mr. Christensen, a manufacturer, whose son is engaged to my sister Betty. I could only stay one day because next morning I had to go on to Hjørring to participate in a K.M.A. meeting in the evening. At the railway station I was received by Miss Louisa Olesen with whom I was to stay. I stayed overnight and the next day Miss Fugl arrived and together we went to Hørmested where we held a K.M.A. meeting in the afternoon. The meeting was held in the home of Mr. Andersen, a farmer. A large number of women were present and after the meeting we had a good dinner. Then, after dinner, we drove to the railway station and now went to Frederikshavn where we stayed with Miss [blank]. She was a very dear lady. This was Saturday evening. On Sunday we had a meeting in the home of the rural dean where we both spoke. After the meeting the dean came up to me with a 10 kroner note for my work. The next day Miss Fugl went to Læsø to hold a meeting there, whereas I went to Sindal to hold a meeting in Rector Larsen's home.

I stayed overnight at the rectory, returned the next day to Frederikshavn, and left in the afternoon for Sæby together with Miss Fugl. We arrived in the evening and stayed with Mr. Myhrmann, a dealer in leather goods. The next day there was a bazaar in the parish hall and I was to speak in the afternoon and again in the evening. It was a large, nice parish hall, decorated so beautifully. There were a large number of children. In the evening the parish hall was packed with grown-up people and I was somewhat nervous at the thought of speaking to so many, but the Lord was with me. In the evening after the meeting some of the important friends met in Myhrmann's home to have coffee, and we did not get to bed until midnight. The next morning I left Sæby at 4 o'clock heading for Horsens and I arrived at 12 o'clock. The next day I went on to Vejle, where I was to participate in the women's meeting lasting for three days. I stayed, together with Baroness Schaffalitzky, Lady Holch, and Miss Fugl, with Mr. Kristiansen, a grocer in Søndergade. The meetings were really pleasant and I met so many friends. After this meeting I went back to Horsens where I stayed for some days.

On October 2nd I went to Copenhagen where a busy period followed. I attended some bible lessons arranged by Skovgaard Petersen, and I participated in a conference for missionaries off foreign duty on the premises of D.M.S. [Danske Missions Selskab or The Danish Missionary Association]. I was very happy about it and got to know some of our Danish missionaries. There were the Reverend Mr. Steinthal with his wife, Mr. L. P. Larsen, Mr. Johan Andersen and his wife, Mr. Heiberg and his wife, and Miss M. Nielsen.

One afternoon we all had coffee at Reverend Busch's. Then the large annual D.M.S. meetings started in Bethesda which also lasted three days and were very interesting.

On the 18th all missionaries had been invited to an evening meeting at Bethesda with the Danish Missionary Council. I was there too and it was a really pleasant evening.

On Sunday, October 20th, Karen-Marie and I went to Elsinore and we immediately went on to the parish hall where we both were to speak. It was a really nice evening and the audience listened with attention. It was a very beautiful drive up there and back through the Danish woods in autumn colours. There was hardly a day on which I did not speak at some meeting. Unfortunately I have forgotten some things but I will note down those I remember:

* an evening in Eliaskirkens Samfund. The place was crowded with people.
* an evening at Mrs. Lange's
* one afternoon at a bazaar in Valby Parish Hall, and another at a bazaar in Hellig-Kors Parish Hall
* several times in Nathanael's Parish
* one day at a bazaar in the Children's Home

In November I had planned to speak one afternoon at a missionary celebration in the Garnison Parish Hall and show slides in the evening, but I felt ill with a severe cold, so Doctor Andersen would not allow me to go, which was a great disappointment to me.

November 6th, my 30th birthday, was a lovely day, 30 years old. Misses Blædel, Fugl and I had lunch together at the office, where the table was decorated with flowers and a small side table was loaded with presents. Flowers, marvellous Danish flowers, were to be found everywhere. Oh, how rich I felt. Presents kept pouring in all day. The ladies of the Armenia Committee and the ladies of Mynstersvej had been invited to lunch and it was a really excellent meal. There was a great surprise just before we sat down to eat. The postman rang the bell and brought me a sealed packet which turned out to contain a watch, presented to me by the missionaries at Harpoot, a very beautiful and fine gold watch with a chain.

In the afternoon I spoke at a bazaar in Vesterbro and in the evening I went to the Y.W.C.A. of Nathaniel Parish. Afterwards, the meeting turned into a social gathering, the coffee tables were decorated and the young members gave me a lovely silver bowl. What faithfulness on the part of the dear young friends. It is so touching to see their love and affection, but I feel so unworthy of it.

In mid-December I went back to Horsens to spend Christmas with my dear family. The last week was very busy but we all managed what we had to do and it was a blessed Christmas. My brother Jacob and my sister's fiancé, Johannes, were also there, so it was a big gathering. Some days after Christmas I went back to Skovgaard to speak at the Christmas celebration of the Y.W.C.A. Sunday between Christmas and New Year [1913] was a busy day. First I spoke to all the Sunday school children, then at the old people's Christmas celebration. When I returned that night I found Miss Blædel ill. She was extremely unwell for some days but then, thank God, her condition soon improved. I was happy to be there as Miss Fugl had left and she would have otherwise been alone with Marie, who then would have had her hands full. At the same time, my little sister Anna became very ill, so I went home as soon as Miss Blædel was better. Anna's condition was then also improving and, naturally, I was very happy. On January 14th I went to Vejle, where I was received at the railway station by Mrs. Jensen, the wife of a chartered surveyor, with whom I stayed. That evening I held a meeting in the parish hall which was almost filled to capacity by men and women. After the meeting some of the friends came home with me and we had coffee. It was 1 o'clock before we got to bed. The next day I was to speak in Vinding Parish Hall and we went there by carriage. When we were under way the carriage broke in two. Luckily enough, no one was injured, but we were of course delayed as another carriage had to be provided. We returned to Vejle after the meeting and the same evening I left for Horsens, where I remained for another three weeks. I spoke on a few occasions and was invited home by people and of course I had to relate my experiences. On February 7th I went to Skælskør to visit Karen-Marie, as the next day was her birthday. It was a really nice day. From early morning congratulations came in a steady stream. She received many flowers. In the afternoon, Karen-Marie and I were busy laying and decorating the table. A large number of Karen-Marie's friends had been invited for the evening. After the meal we spent some pleasant hours together. Naturally, Karen-Marie and I had to tell of our life in Armenia.

The next day we went to Copenhagen together to attend the K.M.A. conference. I got my old room. Karen-Marie stayed at the Missionary College. On that day the guests began to arrive. Miss Soltan and Miss Gregg stayed with Miss Collet. The Missionary College was also full of guests.

Meetings took three days. The two British ladies were the principal speakers. Those were blessed days. The third day was set aside for the Foreign Mission. I also said a few words, especially about the position of women in Turkey.

One afternoon we were invited to Lady Bornemann's, where a number of ladies from the nobility were meeting. Miss Gregg told us about the Boxer Rising. It was a lovely afternoon.

A few days after the conference Doctor K. M. Andersen was asked to come to Mynstersvej to have a look at me. She came on a Sunday and immediately said that I was to go to bed for a prolonged period. During the last few months my health had steadily deteriorated. I was very tired and was always feeling sick and faint. It was now decided that I was to go to Villa Monte on Wednesday.

On Monday Miss Blædel fell ill and Miss Fugl's sister was asked to come and nurse her during her illness. It was somewhat hard for me to leave, knowing the dear Miss Blædel was so unwell, but I had to. Miss Fugl accompanied me to the railway station and I was picked up by carriage at Rungsted. I got a lovely big room on the second floor looking on the Sound. The next morning the cure started. Quiet, no books, no letters, no visitors, in short nothing but rest. It was said that a long period would be required, and I myself expected a couple of months, but it actually came to six. Every two weeks Doctor Andersen came to see me, and it was always a great day. I became so fond of her. After two months I started on massage. Four months later I was allowed to rest in the garden for some hours. During the last month I was permitted to mix with the guests.

It was a very blessed period, with absolutely no contact with people. Alone with the Lord, but it was a rich period, the time was never passing slowly. Here I also made many dear friends. Miss Bjerknes from Norway, Mrs. Kornerup, a dear Christian who six months later was to enter into her Father's joy, and many other dear friends whom I shall always remember. Villa Monte became a second home to me. How nice to be with Augusta Dinesen and Christiane Black, I do not know how to express my gratitude for all the affection they showed me. I also came to know Baroness Schaffalitzky so much better and harbour affectionate feelings for her. I truly enjoyed the lovely garden. I saw it in winter with a white cover, in spring when the small sprouts were coming up, and in summer with all its glory, the little nightingales singing, and the many other small birds hopping from twig to twig. It was a veritable paradise on earth. And all these blessed memories of the glorious home radiating peace, joy, and love, the Lord himself being Alpha and Omega. The lovely garden and scenery will come back to my mind again and again when I am far away and might wish to seek a quiet place for rest and new strength. We must give our thanks to the Lord Himself because He has made His child feel at heart that such places should be found where tired souls can be alone with God and get new strength and thus cope with the troubles of this world.

During my stay at Villa Monte I spoke one night in the month of June at the Y.W.C.A. in Hørsholm. Many young people attended and the Lord was with me, so it went to the heart, and I think several felt encouraged to be workers in His mission.

Then on June 28th I returned to Mynstersvej, Copenhagen, where I and Karen-Marie were to pack some boxes to be sent to Armenia in advance. At the same time, Miss Lauritsen was also packing boxes. She would be leaving for Syria in the autumn.

On July 1st I travelled home again. The first decision had been that I should go somewhere else before going home, but when I promised Doctor Andersen to be careful and rest for four hours a day I was allowed to return home.

On account of my long stay at Villa Monte I missed several events. Early in April my little sister was confirmed. I had been looking forward to it for years, and now I was so near and yet could not participate. In March I was to have participated in the great youth meeting in Herning and spoken at one of the meetings, and in April the plans had included a three week course for missionaries off foreign duty, and in July there was the Nyborg meeting. All of this I failed to attend but the Lord rewarded me doubly during the quiet and deep period at Villa Monte.

How lovely to be back home. We all enjoyed the quiet summer days. On July 24th it was mother's birthday and we experienced a great pleasure as my cousin from America, Elizabeth Frimann, suddenly was at the front door together with my aunt from Herning. It gave my mother a special joy, because she thought her sisters and brothers in America had died, as we had had no news from them for a very long period. Elizabeth stayed with us for some days, but then she had to leave again. A week later she returned and she and mother went to Herning to visit mother's brother.

My sister Betty had gone to Nykøbing to spend five weeks in the home of her fiancé.

One Sunday early in August father, mother, Anna, and I set off for Skanderborg, where we were picked up by my uncle. We then had a ride of a couple of hours in the countryside to a small farm, where we spent the day and returned in the evening.

One day at the beginning of August I received a letter from Miss Louisa Olesen, who stayed at Silkeborg Sanitorium, asking me to visit her, so I went up there and spent a day. I was glad I had been sent to Villa Monte instead of Silkeborg, which had been mentioned as an alternative.

The month of September was the last one at home and quite busy.

One of the first days in the month I went to Randers where I stayed with Doctor Linde. They lived outside the town in a fine villa set in a lovely garden. That evening I spoke at a public meeting in the parish hall. It was packed with people. After the meeting everyone was invited to coffee in the crypt where long tables had been arranged. We were back home at 12.00, it had been such a nice day. The next morning I returned to Horsens but stopped in Lomsberg for some hours in order to visit Maria Braad, an old friend from the Y.W.C.A. in Sundby.

On the second Sunday of September I went to Ring rectory and spoke at the afternoon meeting in the parish hall, which was full of dear faithful friends. After my speech the Reverend Mr. Hansen concluded the meeting and I shall never forget his final words to me, that I might go out with joy, that I might receive so I could give joy and blessing out there. After the meeting we had supper in the rectory and later on they took me to the railway station. What lovely people, how happy I am to know them, and they came to be my friends. Some days later I went to [blank] to hold a meeting. No missionary had ever been there and they were very happy about what they heard.

Now I received so many invitations at home, there was not a day without one, but I had to decline on several occasions, as I did not have the strength to cope with it.

One evening I showed slides to all the children of "Daggry" and they were very grateful. On one of the last few days K.M.A. held a farewell celebration. It was a blessed evening. The large room at the Y.W.C.A. was decorated so nicely and there were long coffee tables. When Miss Hansen had extended her welcome and I had spoken to them about Armenia we sat down at table. The word was given for "free speech," and I received many good wishes.

It was a lovely evening and I was particularly happy for my mother's and my family's sake.

Then came the final days at home with packing and visits, and it was a good thing that those days were so busy as to leave very little time for thinking of the departure until the very last moment. I took leave of my father early in the morning as he had to go, but all the others, my sisters brothers and my mother, saw me to the railway station. There were also some friends. It was particularly difficult to take leave of my mother and my little sister Anna, if only I could have taken them with me. But suddenly the train was hurrying along and I was on my way to my second mother country. I left with gratitude and praise filling my heart. I knew those dear to me were safe in His hands, and I went with Him so I had nothing to fear. I arrived at Copenhagen in the afternoon and now followed some busy days with shopping, packing, and farewell visits.

On Sunday at 6 o'clock I spoke to a large number of schoolboys and after the meeting everyone contributed pictures and books. There were enough pictures to pave the streets of Harpoot.

After this meeting we were all invited to the parish hall where the long coffee tables had been decorated so nicely with flags and flowers. The Armenia Committee was there too. It was a farewell celebration arranged by the Y.W.C.A. As usual, it was a blessed evening, so wonderful to feel the love and affection of the dear young people. Karen-Marie was also there. She and I each received a lovely vase with flowers in the shape of the Danish flag. I also got a flag and Miss Hansen presented me with a small tray with 12 gold pieces for my work. Several of the young girls gave me dolls to take out there. It was a lovely evening. I was given many glorious passages and much proof of the willingness of the young people to support and join in the work.

On Tuesday I spoke in the parish of Sundby.

On Wednesday, October 1st, the Reverend Mr. Fibiger arranged communion for us in the Elijah Church in the afternoon. We were a small flock of K.M.A. friends and a few from the community of the Elijah Church. I shall never forget that day. It was the most blessed hour before my departure. There was a festive atmosphere. Candles were burning, flowers on the altar, the organ playing. And it was so quiet, we felt we were a small flock having a quiet hour with the Saviour himself, and He was with us in the words that we heard, "Arise and eat, because the journey is too great for thee."

On October 3rd, the Committee, Karen-Marie and I were invited to the Reverend Mr. Sørensen's in the evening.

Our suitcases were now packed and the tickets booked. Then on October 4th we had a farewell meeting at the missionary College. First we had dinner at Miss Collet's, and here all the people of Mynstersvej were also present. Baroness Kurck had written a song which we joined in singing. At 8 o'clock all the guests arrived. They were first and foremost all Karen-Marie's and my friends, as well as K.M.A. members, and it proved a very blessed evening. First Mrs. Oxholm spoke on Hebrews 12-1-3 and referred to Jesus as the initiator and perfecter of faith. Then Miss Collet spoke very warmly to us about Jesus' question to Peter—whether he loved Him—and Peter's answer, "Yes Lord, You know I love You." In a like manner we, setting out for the second time, could answer, "Yes, Lord you know I love you."

Karen-Marie and I also spoke of our work and the conditions out there. Then many of our friends assigned passages to us and expressed their good wishes. After the meeting we had tea and I received so very many presents which my friends had brought, and I went from one to the other in taking leave. I was surrounded by friends all the time. It was an exceedingly blessed evening. To my great joy, my friend the Reverend Mr. Fibiger was also there with his family.

In the morning of October 5th Karen-Marie and I went to Johanneskirken to hear the Reverend Mr. Olfert Ricard, and we had dinner with Baroness Schaffalitzky. At 3 o'clock some of our friends came and had coffee, including Misses Møller, Grønbech, Karen-Marie's friends. Karen-Marie and I wore the Armenian costumes and we spoke and sang in Armenian, which was a great success.

Then on Tuesday, October 7th, we had supper for the last time with our beloved Miss Blædel and Miss Fugl. How different from the last time I went out, when I could not get a morsel down. This time I was as unaffected as if I were embarking on a pleasure trip, and again we were having my favourite sweet, "cream horns."

After supper we went to Miss Collet for prayers—or rather, thanksgiving—for our hearts were filled with gratitude because we were again granted to go out there.

We went to the station by taxi where we were soon surrounded by a very large flock of friends coming to say goodbye to us. There we had another proof of the love and affection of our friends. They brought us flowers, chocolate, books, and many other packets and letters that we could open on the train. We had a compartment in a sleeping car to Berlin and our beds were completely covered with parcels. We were carrying the flowers and when we stood at the window waiting for the train to leave, our friends could hardly see anything but flowers. Then they began to sing, "A dwelling secure is Almighty God" and "God be with you till we meet again." While we were listening to the last verse, the train pulled out from the station. The joy was pure, not mingled with tears.

The next morning we were in Berlin at 6.38 and left at 8.36 via Frankfurt on the Oder. We were in Breslau at 2.12, and Kattowitz at 5.45. We reached Cracow at 8.10 and left there by sleeping car. We had a good night's sleep. We could see that we were getting near the Balkan countries. On the horizon there was a huge mountain range and everywhere in front of us were large pumpkin fields. The women were working in their costumes bearing some resemblance to bed jackets, and the men ploughing with oxen were in their costumes with multi-coloured belts. At 10 o'clock we arrived at Zykani where we had to change to another train. A porter helped us with our luggage, but we did not drive more than 10 minutes before we had to bring our luggage out for a customs' check. It all went without trouble however. We were not quite sure if we had got on the right train as people no longer spoke German. There was now no ladies' compartment and we were constantly surrounded by gentlemen asking all sorts of questions.

It was a very tiring journey as our fellow travellers were noisy and kept smoking.

Later in the evening the moon arose and it was a glorious sight when we crossed the Danube River. The train was 1½ hours late, which made me anxious that we would not be in time for the steamer leaving Constantza at 12.00.

However, all went well and it was pleasant to get on board the pretty steamer. We had a cup of tea and a piece of toast, slept well, and got up early the next morning to enjoy the passage of the Bosporus. We did not reach Constantinople, however, until at 2 o'clock.

Friday, the 10th October, 1913. 2.00 p.m. Constantinople. To our great relief, we immediately spotted our hotel guide in the crowd and after a swarm of people had left the ship, we followed our guide to the Customs' House. Here we had to wait for two long hours until our luggage arrived from the ship. We were standing all the time in the midst of a crowd of men shouting and yelling, though it finally came to an end. Unfortunately, it was now too late to see Mr. Peet.

11 October (Saturday). A very busy day. First a trip to Bible House, then shopping and a visit to the steamship office to buy tickets, then home to pack. We had dinner and finally hurried to the harbour with all our things. One hour after we came on board we were told that the steamer would not leave until the next day, and we had a lovely rest.

When we left Constantinople the next day a strong gale was building up, and before long the deck was deserted. Everyone had to take refuge in the cabins and the bells were constantly calling for the assistance of the stewardesses. We were also very sick. Disembarkation at Samsoun was a terrible experience, but we saw that God was with us. There was a violent gale, with large waves, and the boats could not get alongside the steamer as they would crash if the attempt was made. So at the moment when the boat was raised by a wave we had to jump into the boat. It all went well.

In Samsoun we met Miss Lattin who was on her way back to America and Miss Mattoon who had accompanied her. The latter went back to Harpoot with us.

On October 16th we started on the long drive. The first two days were terrible. It had been raining heavily and the roads were completely soaked. We passed through deep holes and over large stones, and on Saturday afternoon we reached Marsovan where we stayed for the Sunday. The two of us, Karen-Marie and I, stayed at Mr. Getschel's, wonderful people. On Sunday we were together with all the missionaries and how lovely it was to get to know them all.

On Monday we went on and reached Sivas on Friday the 24th. We stayed here at Doctor Clark's for the night. The next morning we left again and spent Sunday at an inn, one day's travel from Sivas. We continued on Monday and reached Malatia on Wednesday, where we stayed with Sister Jensine. We remained there on Thursday, packed Karen-Marie's things, and visited the Christoffels.

[Photograph in diaries. No separate caption.]

On Friday morning, October 30th, 1913, we left Malatia. When we reached Komur Khan, that night we were welcomed by Mr. Riggs and his mother, who were on their way to Marsovan. Miss Riggs and Miss Harley were there to meet us and they accompanied us on our way to Harpoot the next morning. It was so lovely to see the dear, dear friends from Harpoot, and it was a happy little flock that gathered in the inn that night for service.

The next morning we left early and at noon we reached Khankeoy where we were welcomed by a large number of friends from Harpoot and Mezreh. We had a meal together in a field. Afterwards we resumed our journey and on the way we met Mrs. Barnum, Mrs. Riggs, and Annie. All of Harpoot Station was out to meet me, and it was lovely to be among the dear friends again that night. It was as if I had returned home.

Karen-Marie stayed in Mezreh where she was to take over the supervision of the Children's Home during the absence of Mrs. Grynhagen. During the first month I stayed with Mrs. Alice Riggs who was alone. My rooms had not yet been put in order, and I spent my first period resting. On the last Thursday of November we held thanksgiving at Consul Masterson's. It was such a nice day. Early in December when Mr. Riggs had returned from Marsovan I moved into my rooms which were situated in Mr. Harvy's home. I had a sitting-room, bedroom, and a clinic.

I now began taking lessons in Turkish. Twice a week I made house calls on Turkish families together with Mrs. Alice Riggs, received Turkish women in my rooms, and treated the sick who came to me. Every morning I went to the schools to see if there were any sick people. If that was the case I would instruct the nurse there as to what had to be done.

On December 24th I went down to Emaus to spend Christmas Eve with Karen-Marie. As soon as I arrived I was told that Jenny was very ill with a high temperature and a confused mind, and there was no one to look after her. Instead of spending the evening together with Karen-Marie and the children I went over to Jenny and spent most of the night with her. On the 25th I returned to Harpoot in the morning to join the missionaries there for the Christmas celebration, this year at Ernest Riggs'. We were all gathered there except for little Annie and her mother. Some days earlier Annie had become very ill. After supper, when we lit the candles on the Christmas tree, she came out of bed for a little while and rested on the settee, but no one was allowed to speak to her. It marred the pleasure which otherwise would have been perfect. Mr. Harry Riggs conducted the Christmas service and many beautiful Christmas hymns were sung.

In the morning of Boxing Day I went back to Mezreh to stay with Sister Jenny until New Year's Eve. She was so much better that she did not require any nurse at night.

I again returned to Harpoot and New Year's Day was busy. Every year on that day we received guests offering their best wishes for the new year. I was together with Mr. Harry Riggs. We received 150 guests that day and in the evening I packed my suitcase for the next day. On January 2nd, we—Mr. H. Riggs and I—were going away on a trip to Palou and Peri. We left Harpoot at 10 o'clock, and reached Sheikh Hadji at 4.30. During the night I stayed with some women, Mr. Riggs was in a separate house. The next morning we left at 9 o'clock, reached the Euphrates at

11.30, and Palou at 4.00 p.m. We were to have stayed with the clergyman, but as they had no more than one small room, we had to live and sleep in the church. The next day, January 4th, Mr. Riggs conducted two services.

We were both exhausted and went to bed early. We had a Monday morning meeting and I spoke on "the open door." I started making house calls. We showed slides in the evening. On Tuesday we had meetings again and I made house calls.

Wednesday we had a meeting for women, then a meeting for church members. Thursday and Friday I made 10 house calls each day—not much responsiveness. Saturday, January 10th, dinner at Manoug Agha's. Examining two new members.

Sunday, January 11th. Morning service. Mr. Riggs spoke on "My relations with Jesus." We had dinner at Kevork Agha's. Mr. Riggs spoke to the Gregorians about Victorious Jesus. In the evening, service with us, christening, and communion.

Monday, January 12th. We went from Palou to Peri over high snow mountains— deep snow. After much danger and trouble we reached the river at about 5 o'clock and we were exhausted. Since there were no keleks as it was late, we had to wade across the river. We reached Badveli Asador's house in Peri at 6 o'clock.

Tuesday, January 13th. I stayed at home, no one to accompany me, and I was very tired. During the week we stayed there I visited 10 houses daily, saw many women, and had a meeting for women in the church. Mr. Riggs delivered a sermon every morning and showed slides of the life of Jesus in the evening. One night it was for Turks—many came.

We were invited to dinner three times. Twice the Kaimakam was there. One day we had 20 courses and finished in one quarter of an hour.

Monday, January 19th. Armenian Christmas. In the morning Mr. Riggs gave a church sermon on the passage, "This is a faithful saying, and worthy of all acceptance, that Christ Jesus came into the world to save sinners, of whom I am chief." Afterwards we took leave of our friends and left Peri at 9 o'clock. We made good speed for it is a two days' journey to Harpoot, but we were home at 6 o'clock in the afternoon, very tired but happy to be back home.

When we returned we learned that Miss Campbell was very ill with typhoid fever. I went down to offer my assistance. On Wednesday January 21st I went down to nurse her at night. I stayed with her for three weeks. It was a very difficult period, her life hung in the balance, but the Lord did hear the many prayers and made her well. After three weeks she was so much better that I was no longer needed during the night, so I went back to Harpoot to have a rest before I was to start on a long journey to Keghi.

On March 3rd it was Annie's birthday, and in the evening we had a birthday party. The next morning Mr. Riggs and I left for Keghi. We rode 12 hours that day and in the evening we arrived at Gulisgaer. It was Armenian but resembled a Kurdish village in every way, savage and ignorant. On Thursday March 10th we travelled for 10 hours across areas with high rocks, deep pools of mud, and at about 2 o'clock we arrived at Tapu. Here a man joined us and we arrived at Kirik Khan in the evening. This was a Kurdish village and they would not accept us. However, they finally did so.

Friday, March 6th. Through deep, deep snow we arrived at the Kurdish village Arkpar in the evening. I did not sleep there either, swarming with fleas, no air, and surrounded by armed Kurds.

Saturday, March 7th. We left through much snow and mud. Reached Temran at 6.00 p.m.

Sunday, March 8th (morning). I went to church wearing our dirty travelling clothes. Our luggage had not arrived yet. My face was swollen and burned by the sun, wind, and snow. We had a women's meeting in the afternoon. The church was almost full. During the 10 days we spent there I visited 10 or 12 homes every day. In the morning and evening I saw and treated many sick people, and handed out drugs. We had three meetings for women, and every time the church was almost full.

Wednesday, March 18th. We went to Keghi, stayed with Harutune Effendi. Here too I immediately began making house calls, every day 12 or more. I saw many sick, crippled, and blind people, and had three meetings for women. The church filled to capacity each time. The women of Keghi were live, warm Christians, and many longed to become soul winners. I became acquainted with a wonderful woman who had not been allowed to go to church for 30 years. Now free, she is happy and radiates quiet peace. She is a pillar in that town. Mr. Riggs was very busy. He held meetings, services, and spoke to individuals. He has great power and his words are very penetrating.

Monday, March 30th. We left Keghi by the same route we had arrived. Instead of snow we now passed through mud. It took four days to get back—lovely to be home again.

On April 8th, Mr. Riggs, Miss Mattoon, and I went to Diarbekir. Mr. Riggs went on horseback and the two of us by carriage. On the first day we reached Kezin Khan, the second we got as far as Arghana, and on the third we reached Diarbekir, where we were received by Badveli Hagop, who also gave us shelter during our stay there which lasted two weeks.

On Sunday we held services, meetings for women, and Sunday school. On weekdays we made house calls. Miss Mattoon took one part of the town, I the other. On some days when we visited Turks, we went together.

During our stay in Diarbekir Mr. John from Mardin came to meet Mr. Sivengood who was to pay a visit to Mardin. Miss Mattoon, Mr. Riggs, some Armenian friends and I twice walked on the walls around Diarbekir. That was very interesting.

On April 29th we returned to Harpoot, and the last two months before the schools were closed were taken up by my usual work among the sick and the Moslems.

Early in July I went to Emaus where I stayed with Karen-Marie for two weeks, and then I returned to Harpoot to help in arranging everything for the Annual Meeting. When I arrived I found that Mrs. Emma Riggs and Miss Riggs had been taken ill. They had been entrusted with preparing the rooms for the guests. So now I was really busy nursing them and seeing to the rooms on top of that. But we succeeded.

All the missionaries moved out of their rooms to let the guests have them. We then lived in tents. On Thursday July 16th they started coming in, the missionaries from Van were the first to arrive. There were Dr. Ussher, his son Nevile, Miss Rogers, Miss McLaren. The next day we saw Dr. Hamilton, Miss Trowbridge, Miss Norton, Dr. Smith and his wife with their lovely little boy Arthur, from Aintab.

Mr. and Mrs. Maynard, their two sons Richard and Robert, and Miss Uline. From Mardin came Mr. Emrich and his son Duncan, Mrs. and Miss Dewey, Miss Norton and Miss Fenenga. From Ezeroum came Mr. Stapleton and Miss Sherman.

Friday, July 17th. The medical conference started. We met at Doctor Atkinson's. In the morning the various reports were read. In the afternoon the native doctors were invited, and we had several talks by the various doctors.

Saturday, July 18th. The conference continued until 5 o'clock in the afternoon. That night the last of our guests arrived.

Sunday, July 19th. In the morning our Annual Meeting was initiated with a service held on the verandah. Mr. Pierce spoke on the sick at the pool of Bethesda. Especially the words, "there is no one to help me down," and then on "the power of God." It was a very blessed service. We felt that God was near.

In the evening we had a "roll call meeting," at which each of the missionaries present said a few words, and the missionaries staying at the various stations had sent a few paragraphs which were read aloud.

Monday morning, the 20th. The daily meetings now began and continued until Friday July 31st. Every morning we had business meetings and negotiations, and in the afternoon from 2-4 o'clock there were meetings which were opened by different missionaries. The subjects focused on "how to approach the true spirit in our work." Those were blessed hours and I am sure they will lend inspiration to our future work. The governing opinion at the meeting was that the time has come for us to concentrate all our efforts and time on the work for the Moslems. The doors are open and we must enter. A request was made for 19 new missionaries to be sent out as soon as possible in order that this new work might be taken up. It was a very solemn moment when, on the last evening of the meeting, we all stood and listened to Mr. Riggs as he read aloud a resolution which we all included in our prayers.

Every morning and every afternoon we started with a service of 30 minutes. We spent many a blessed, peaceful hour together.

One afternoon the German missionaries and the Armenian priests and teachers had been invited. That day we discussed the open doors to the Moslems.

On the second Sunday Mr. E. Riggs spoke on Exodus 33-15, the word of Moses to the Lord, "If thy presence go not with me, carry us not up hence." Subject, "The awareness of the nearness of God."

In the evening we had communion and Mr. H. Riggs delivered a sermon on Colossians 1-27 "Christ in you, the hope of glory." Is Christ in us, living in us? Then we shall be victorious. It was a very peaceful hour.

All One in Jesus Christ. Missionaries from Eastern Turkey Mission at the Annual Meeting in Harpoot in the summer of 1914.

On the last Sunday Mr. Emrich preached and in the evening we had a meeting at which we discussed our work among the Moslems.

At meal times we changed seats so as to be with the different friends several times. Tea was served in the garden every afternoon at 4 o'clock and afterwards we separated, some to play tennis, others croquet. Some, or rather a majority, gathered in small committee meetings.

Twice we had our meals all together in the garden and Mr. H. Riggs sent up a large balloon which he had made himself. It was very successful.

One night we had a concert and we sang many very beautiful hymns and songs, also solos and part-singing.

One night we all made an excursion to the ice cave, where we had supper. Afterwards we rode back while the moon was shining

Monday, August 3rd. Now the friends began to go back to their separate stations. It was a lovely time, so nice to get to know so many friends. This Annual Meeting reminded me so strongly of Keswick in 1912. It was a sanctifying meeting from beginning to end.

Much more could be said about the meetings and the various missionaries if space permitted, but the headline for it all was, "All one in Jesus Christ"

In the morning of August 3rd I went down to Mezreh to make preparations together with Karen-Marie for our journey to Geoljuk which was to start on Wednesday the 5th. But on my way there I learnt that Germany and Russia were at war, and also Austria and Serbia. Turkey was mobilising and had called up all men between 20 and 45 years of age, including here in Harpoot and Mezreh. If they failed to come forward in the course of 10 days they would be killed.

I did not believe it, there were so many rumours. But when I came down to Emaus I found that it was really true. Karen-Marie was beside herself with sorrow. Together we went to the hospital to telephone Harpoot and hear their opinion. It was decided that we were to wait as there was so much unrest and everyone was feeling fear and trepidation. We waited until Thursday, but the situation did not improve. It got worse day by day and it was decided that we were not to go to Geoljuk as the missionaries of Harpoot thought that thousands of Turks and Kurds would take refuge in the mountains and they would be followed by soldiers. So we stayed. On Friday I went back to Harpoot, and now a hard and difficult period has followed. Mezreh and Husenik were filled with Turks, Kurds, and Armenians who had been captured. Food was in short supply, and there was no accommodation for the many people, so the government has now taken over the Turkish, French, and German schools. This school, intended for 80 and at the most 100 pupils, is now packed with 1,000 men. It is like a swarm of flies. There is no food. They only get one small loaf a day of which a man eats two with his meal. There is no bedding and the soldiers walk from house to house to collect blankets, but there are not enough for everyone to have his own, far from it. They do not have any form of uniform, but walk about in their white shalvars, loose shirts, and bright red or light blue small coats. Everything is rotten among them, and it almost broke our hearts when we had to let our friends, the Armenian men, go. How appalling to think that chaste young Christian men had to live among thousands of these brutal and wild people who are worse than animals in their life and lust. The missionaries in Harpoot did what they could. Every day they went to the Vali and the Bingbashi and spoke to them, because the law says that all teachers of the Illahi schools are exempted, and it looked as if they were to go free. But no, this is Turkey, and the law is like a mould which is changed several times a day. The law saying that teachers were exempted was changed, so now they were to be sent to a military academy in Constantinople for training as officers. Poor fellows, they had to go, and several of them were not strong. At home they have wives, old parents, and children, but there was nothing for it, they had to go otherwise they would be hanged. So they left and none of them expected to return. They walked towards an open grave, for epidemics are raging among the soldiers on account of the poor sanitary conditions. In the autumn, for instance, 25,000 soldiers died of typhoid fever in the course of a few months and nothing was done about it.

How often we wished we could have taken their place. I think it would have been easier. In such times of distress we really feel how near we are to our Armenian brothers and sisters.

On Sundays Mr. H. Riggs walks among the soldiers and speaks to them. He cannot have a proper service as these people are unaccustomed to sit listening. He walks about followed by an officer and talks to them about God, about being faithful, living a chaste life, being good to each other. Again and again they shout after him, "Go to the Bingbashi to give us bread."

In the Turkish and Armenian homes women and children are sitting alone, crying and wringing their hands. For their husbands and fathers are gone, and who is to provide food for them. All is darkness and fear and misery. Now the time has come to go and see them, their hearts are wounded and perhaps they will listen. They are in need of consolation and sympathy, and now they must feel that we missionaries are their friends.

Every day we have telegrams from Constantinople but the message is always the same, Germans and Austrians are victorious, taking thousands of prisoners. One day it was 100,000 Russians and large quantities of guns and flags. To judge from these telegrams the Germans must soon be all over Europe. Never a victory to the English or French. How we are longing to hear the real truth. One day last week we learned that Denmark had also declared war on Germany. But now the Germans are denying it. They say the Danes are their friends and the telegrams say nothing in this respect. What is one to think?

The other day some officers turned up, sent by the government. They demanded our houses, the missionary dwellings, for use as officers' accommodation. Their demand was refused. Where should we go? But they did get Wheeler Hall, a large building that would accommodate several thousand. It was just across the street, but for how long we do not know.

A very serious trouble is the fact that we have no money and cannot have any sent out. The Americans, however, are not so badly off. They still have some left, enough for a few months. But the Danish Children's Home is facing the most difficult situation. They do not have a penny and are compelled to send the children away to friends and relatives until money arrives from Denmark.

On August 21st Karen-Marie came to Harpoot and stayed till Monday morning.

In the afternoon of the 21st there was a solar eclipse lasting from 2.30 to 5.00. Tea was served while we watched the sun and the moon through the large stereoscope and through smoked glass. It was also very interesting to see how all shadows became longish and took on the shape of a crescent.

On Monday August 24th I went to Emaus together with Karen-Marie. We tried to have the children sent away but we were not particularly successful.

On Sunday the 23rd a serious insurrection of Kurds came to our knowledge. It was in the vicinity of Malatia and several regiments were dispatched from our area.

We also learned that there had been a major fire in Diarbekir and 1,600 shops were burnt. Somebody started it deliberately, of course. It is above all the Armenian shops that are afflicted. There has been so much unrest since mobilisation began.

24 August. Today it is rumoured that the German Emperor and a large regiment have been surrounded and that the German Crown Prince has been wounded.

25 August. The Emperor launched a successful attack and is now free. The rumours about the Crown Prince are now said to be false.

29 August. Also today telegrams reported great victories to the Germans and the Austrians both in Belgium, France, and Poland.

I felt so strange today. I wonder if anything has happened at home? Towards evening I went to the Shuga to hear news but it was as usual, the Germans were advancing victoriously. Today it was said, however, that Sunday was a quiet day spent in the Garden.

On Monday September 7th we moved into town. Wednesday, September 9th. My rooms are now almost in order again. Doctor Ruth Parmelee and I are opening a clinic for women together. I am also taking up house calls again and my language studies.

Today it is said that the Germans have decided not to take Paris now, and are consequently on their way back to Lees. Also that the Russians are bombarding Königsberg, that 30,000 men have arrived at Marseilles from India, that 200 British and French warships are fishing up mines, and that there are plans for bombing all major German cities. It is reported that Britain and Russia have prohibited Norwegian and Swedish food exports to Germany. Whether all this is true we do not know yet.

It seems the soldiers have settled down here for a prolonged period. They have manoeuvres in the narrow street just outside our windows. In the evening they have music and dancing. The food is cooked in the street. Some soldiers are sent to the market-place every day and there they take what they need without paying for it. They hand over a piece of paper but no one ever expects to see the money. There is an Arab sitting in the street, crying. He has done so for five days now, for the government has taken his 30 camels but paid him nothing. Now and then he shouts, "Why did you not take me as well." A proof of the great lawlessness and misery in this country.

There are a number of Kurds among the soldiers, and the poor creatures, who do not understand Turkish, are having a very hard time. Commands are given in Turkish and those who do not understand the language make many mistakes. The officers have no mercy and hit them with sticks or kick them. It is terrible to look at. Oh, how we long to see Jesus Christ King in their hearts and in all of this unhappy country.

Friday, September 11th. Yesterday there was a telegram from Constantinople saying that the government could not accept any responsibility for the foreigners and their property. We are not sure what this means, only the future can show what the consequences will be. But one thing we realize, when such a telegram has been announced all over the country, every minute we can expect Turkish officers and Kurds to come and demand our houses and whatever else we have. There is no way of telling what cruelties these savage and ruthless people might think of. We are seeing again and again that we are living on the edge of a volcano that may erupt at any time and we never really know how many dangers we are exposed to. But one thing we learn every day and that is that there is a living God, and He is our Father, and He has said that no one can touch a hair of our head without His will and on that we can rely. He, our Saviour, has said that He will be with us until the end of the world, and if He is with us we have no need to fear what is to come. Also now during this difficult and grave time we are granted to feel the blessed peace which keeps our hearts and minds in Jesus Christ.

So we have reason to be happy and cheerful in spite of all the unrest and evil rumours and threats around us. All our times are in His hands. My request is that I may be preserved faithful in spite of everything until such time as I am going Home to Him who said that He would return to take His own Home to Himself.

All the Armenians are so frightened. Their view is that if our situation is like that, what will their situation be like? Many of them have hidden away their possessions in underground cellars, then covered them with earth to prevent strangers from finding them. Mr. Harry Riggs and Mr. Pierce have gone down to see the Vali and the other high officials on the occasion of the sultan's birthday. Now we are anxious to hear if they spoke to them and to hear news. The soldiers at Wheeler Hall are very lively at night. They are playing, singing, and dancing. They are wearing their clothes to pieces and there is no one to do the mending, so many of them are actually wearing rags. Every morning an old Turkish woman collects the laundry. Only those well off can afford a washerwoman. Most of them simply take off their shirt and wash it.

They dry the clothes just outside my windows where they spread them out on the street, sit down beside them, and spend the time catching and killing fleas and bedbugs. Many other dreadful things happen which cannot be related here.

September 12. I received a letter from Mr. C. Riggs, Constantinople. He wrote that there also everything was in a state of confusion, and drummers are still walking around the streets to announce the orders from the government. One day the message will be that everybody is to be registered in the course of the day or they will be killed, the next day another two weeks is granted and those paying their Baedael, 43 liras, will not be required for services this time. All shops are robbed by the government of items, from provisions to sewing thread and silk fabrics, even silk stockings. Where all this goes nobody knows. Only one thing is certain, these articles are not given to the soldiers as we are told. All types of machinery have been confiscated, and the other day there were orders to the effect that everyone who had more than one adult daughter was to send her to some government premises to sew clothes for the soldiers. All sheep and horses have been confiscated. In return for everything they take they give a piece of paper offering good intentions of payment "in the sweet by and by" but who believes that?

All this mobilisation can only mean war. Turkey is not actually threatened, but Enver Bey wants war with Greece to take back Gerne, and he has dreams of invading Bulgaria to take back all old possessions, but the top ministers are in disagreement. Something has happened to Enver Bey and he is kept inside his own four walls. It is said that he is suffering from blood poisoning, but the true story is probably the one that one day one of the princes turned up and demanded exemption from military service. Enver replied that only the Sultan himself could grant that, whereupon the prince became angry. When he was about to leave, Enver added that not even the Sultan could exempt him from military service. The prince now flew into a rage and shot at Enver Bey who was hit in one leg and now has to keep quiet. Also the missionaries are expecting the Turks to come into their homes every moment and take what they want. There was a telegram received today to the effect that 4-5 German ships have been sunk, but no British ships. The Russians have taken Königsberg, the French and the British have checked the German advance on Paris.

Sunday, 13 September, 1914. Very early this morning the street was crowded with people who had come to take final leave of the soldiers. The latter are to travel today, or rather walk, to Erzeroum, to meet the Russians there. The large military band from Mezreh came up and played two tunes, after which the many thousands of soldiers marched to the mosque in Harpoot for prayers. They then marched past us here in the street and over the mountains to reach Erzeroum on October 1st. It was a tragic sight. Several of the soldiers cried. Some of the old Turkish women had ventured amongst the many men to have a last glimpse of their sons who were leaving, bound for certain death, for many of them would die on the way, and the rest would certainly be killed if there was war. So these old women were sitting all alone, sobbing and moaning without hope of seeing their sons again. It was very difficult to watch those sad people, living without hope of anything better in a world that contained only sorrow and misery for them. How happy and rich we are, knowing in our hearts that the present suffering is nothing when we can count on the glory that will be revealed to us. Indeed eternity does not seem a long time to praise Him with song.

Yesterday I had a visit from a young girl from Keghi in the neighbourhood of Erzeroum who told me that there were so many soldiers in Erzeroum that there was not enough room for them in the town. They are living in the fields like sheep, cold, hungry, and worst of all, suffering from thirst. There is not enough water and they will have to go for several days with none to drink. Still they keep on sending thousands and thousands more soldiers. Poor country.

12 October. Eight days ago Thomas Effendi, the English consul's dragoman, came here from Diarbekir. He told us about the fire there about 15 days ago. Rumours had been circulating that there would either be a massacre or a fire. The consul sent a messenger to the Vali, told him about these rumours, and asked him to investigate the situation. He warned him to be on his guard. The Vali promised this. Two days later he awoke in the night to hear someone shouting, "Fire!" At once he sent a man to the market to find out if it was only a fire, or if there had been a massacre too. The man hurried back to say that there was only a fire, and they hoped to be able to extinguish it. A stream of men poured in to help put out the fire, but they were stopped by the soldiers, so it was only extinguished in four places. It might all have been put out, but they were not allowed to do it, and since nothing was done, it spread very quickly until all of the Armenian part of the market was destroyed— 1,600 shops. The Armenians lost all that they had. The men are taken as soldiers, and there is fear of great poverty and want for the coming winter. There is a rumour circulated by the Turks that the Russians will come and take possession of the country. Therefore they want to burn down everything first and leave them only a scorched land. We are living in difficult times. There is unrest surrounding us on all sides and one never knows what the next day can or will bring. There has also been an uprising among the Kurds in the neighbourhood of Malatia, and last week there was a heavy earthquake near Smyrna with 8,000 killed. The steady stream of rumours becomes worse as time passes, and the continued mobilisation for war makes everything worse. Mothers sit around with flocks of children and without food. Every day, a poverty-stricken woman comes with two small sick children. The elder child is a little five year old girl, covered with tubercular sores. I treat her daily.

She was a terrible sight when she first came, blue with cold and only a cotton dress covering her little sick body. She had neither shoes nor stockings on her little feet and legs. It was touching to see the joy of both mother and child when I came with some underwear and stockings. She sits for four hours in the sun in the middle of the day and Mrs. Riggs gives her a hot meal. I asked the mother the other day what they had to live on and she said, "We have a little meal that we boil with water to make soup, and when it is finished, I don't know what we will do, but God will probably show us a way." Poor mother, she is sick herself and has two small sick children. She has nothing to eat, no clothes, and there is no work to be had. Oh, how difficult it is not being able to help them.

The other day one of the students in the Minister's College, who had been sent to a village as a minister, was brought back here in chains and put into prison in Mezreh. They say he will be put to death because he has run away and not reported to join the army. It is not true. All ministers are exempted and therefore he should also be. Nevertheless they have now taken him. We hope to have him exempted and freed from prison, but we are in Turkey—no justice. Oh, how we long for peace on earth again and goodwill toward men. Oh, how I am longing to hear from home. It is now two months since I last heard, but they are in His hands and He will protect them against all.

17 October. Mr. Riggs and I left for a village four hours away from Harpoot. As all horses of any value have been taken by the government, I had to hire a horse from the market. It was so thin that you could count all its bones. It also had a very bad cough and we expected to see it fall down and die any moment. Had I been in Denmark, I would have been fined, but we are in Turkey, and here unfortunately there is no society for the prevention of cruelty to animals. We reached our destination at 5.00 p.m. and went to the minister's house. We were invited up, but it was absolutely impossible to find the stairs. However, the "Pompish" came to our assistance to climb up a steep and insecure "hen coop" ladder. Some of the brothers came to greet us that evening. There were not many of them left, as nearly all had been taken as soldiers, except for the boys and old men. Every family has had to contribute clothes, wheat, and meat to the government. No one asks if they can afford it. What does it matter that there is neither food nor clothes for the women and children.

We did not bring our bedding with us as we did not expect to be away over Sunday. We received our bed clothes from them but we had brought the insect powder. We lay on the floor which we had sprinkled with powder, but it was not enough. None of us had much sleep that night. Sunday morning we rose. Mr. Riggs was preaching in the church at 7 o'clock on the text, "Let Him who thirsts come and drink." At 10 o'clock I had a meeting for the women. About 40-50 came with many children. I spoke on Daniel, Chap. 3, V.16-18, "But if not...." After the meeting we visited some sick people and had prayers with them. Then we saw Anna from the Children's Home and at 2 o'clock another service. Mr. Riggs preached "Have faith in God." In the evening we had a visit from the brothers and sisters, and after a very bad night we got up again and left at 5.30 in a downpour of rain, arriving home in Harpoot at 11 o'clock soaked to the skin.

21 October. We received a letter from Van and Mardin in which they tell us how medicine is being taken from the Mission chemist in Van. As Dr. Ussher would not give them the last of different medicines which he could not be without, the officers said they would take it by force. They sent for 20 soldiers, and since Dr. Ussher still refused to give them the medicine, they said, "We have been given guns to shoot with." Dr. Ussher and Mr. Yarrow answered, "Shoot, if you will, but you must know that we cannot give in to something so unjust." The officers discussed between themselves and said, "We must take the things from here because if we do not, we cannot take them from the other houses." Dr. Ussher was not meant to hear this but it made him certain that he should hold firm to his decision. Several times they tried to take him away from the door by force. At last the Russian consul arrived. He sent all the officers away and he and Dr. Ussher went to the Vali and complained. He answered that the officers had made a mistake and had believed that Dr. Ussher was an Armenian. This was a big lie, but they always find a way out of these things.

From Mardin we have heard that one night a band of Kurdish robbers broke into the school and took everything away, and now the government demands 100 liras in tax from the missionaries. All this because of the abolition of the Capitulations. They live in fear of what the next day will bring and do not know the day they will be sent out of the country. So far we have not had this anxiety here, but we do not know what tomorrow will bring. We are thankful for every day we are allowed to live in peace. But it is difficult for the poor Armenians. Everything they had has been taken from them, and no work is to be had. There will be great poverty and want this winter.

Today five rich Turkish ladies visited me, and after some time together, I showed them the Girls' College. They were very surprised to see it all. These Turkish women are also suffering because of the war, as their husbands and sons have been taken as soldiers. This war has, and will continue to have, a very bad influence on the Mohammedans. They do not know the difference between true and so-called Christians, and it pleases them to see how the Christian countries fight. A Mohammedan said the other day, "Oh, how happy I am to see the Christians eat each other's flesh and drink each other's blood. This is what I have been longing for and I am delighted."

Many have asked me, "Does your Book allow you to fight?" It gives us the opportunity to tell them of Jesus' words, "Love your enemies," etc. If only this war would end. But we say, "Thy will be done O God," because He knows best. Is this the way in which God will, and can, wake the world from its death sleep? Then we will give thanks to Him.

1 November. The last days have been full of terrible rumours. What we have been dreading for so long now seems likely to come true. It is said that Turkey is already at war with Russia, and rumour says that all men between 17 and 65 are to be called up. There is terrible pressure and uncertainty about everything and everybody. We had hoped that the winter, at least, would pass without war. What is going to happen to this poor country? And the poor soldiers—what will they have to suffer and endure on their march to the coast and to the Russian border, without food, bedding, or clothes at this cold time with heavy rain? Most of them will die, or suffer for the rest of their lives. Already there is great poverty and with it comes sickness and misery. What will it be before the winter is over? It is said that the road to Samsoun is closed to travellers, as it is to be used for the drilling of soldiers. We heard from the missionaries in Constantinople that the two ships Göeben and Breslau, which were said to have been sold by Germany to Turkey, have been put into service. The crews are German and they are sailing on the Black Sea. They have met the Russians and there has been a battle, or encounter, in which one ship has been captured by the Russians. It is said that Italy, Albania, Greece, and Portugal will enter the war. Soon all of Europe will be involved.

6 November. My 32nd birthday. It felt very empty not to have greetings from my loved ones. I especially missed letters from home and from Miss Blædel. Karen-Marie came here in the morning and having finished treatment of my patients we started preparations for the party in the evening. We had invited all the missionaries to a buffet supper. We met together at 5.30. The Danish sandwiches tasted good and were all eaten. Everyone was happy and Karen-Marie and I were glad to do a little for those who have done so much for us. At 8 o'clock we had prayers and afterwards started to go home. It was a special pleasure to have little Annie here. When I have had parties on other occasions she has always become sick some days before.

9 November. Today we received a message that we are no longer allowed to send off letters. However, German, French, Turkish, and Arabic letters are allowed. Even our American consul had a big bundle of letters returned today. He tried to telegraph the American ambassador but without success. So now we are locked in and we do not know for how long. Today we heard that Italy and Greece are fighting over Albania. We still hear that the Germans are pushing the Russians back, but soldiers are still being sent away. Today all tailors and shoemakers are leaving in pouring rain. Poor people—how will they ever reach the border through rain, snow, and cold, without

clothes or food? Yesterday the French missionaries left. I wonder how long we will be allowed to stay here? We are pleased for every day and have no fear for the days to come. There is no future without Jesus.

14 November. Today I was brought to a little sick child. It was a very poor home. The husband has been ill for several months with dysentery. There is no work for him. There are three children in the family with a fourth expected in a couple of months. The youngest, a little two-year old girl, has been very ill with malaria. I found her in a very poor condition. She lay on the earth in a cold damp room, covered with damp rags. She was icy cold and it was obvious that she could not live long. The father told me that she was always happy and lively when she had enough to eat, but when she was hungry she cried very much, though she tried not to. I can not get that home out of my thoughts. The father said, "She is the flower of our home. It will be very hard to be without her, but God knows best." The little mother sat there beside her dying child, crocheting lace—her hands blue with cold—to earn some few coins for bread. Another little girl, five-years old, is covered with tubercular sores because of bad nourishment. The death of this little girl is due simply to hunger and cold. In spite of this we never hear a word of dissatisfaction or envy or about help. Only on the way to their home, when we passed a nice freshly-whitened house, the mother said, "When I pass by here I think to myself, Oh, I wish that house was ours."

There are many thousands of homes like this one, and there will be many more as the winter progresses with no work to be had. Added to this are the fears of a massacre and separation from their loved ones. There is misery on all sides—behind them and before. Oh, if only in these hard times they could learn to look upward. The way is always open from whence help and salvation come.

In the last days we have heard nothing about the war, except for a rumour that the Russians are in flight on the whole border from Trebizond to Persia. Last Friday, the 13th, I had invited six little Turkish girls to a party, but only two of them came. The other four found excuses for not coming. However, it was not the children's fault but the parents. These children came from the homes of the richest and most influential men. The two who did come had one of the best times in their lives. We made a doll's house and dressed two little dolls. They had the house to take home with them. One little girl returned next day to tell me how much her parents had admired the doll's house, and also the parents of the other little girl. So this action may have a good influence.

On Sunday evening, 15 November, 1914, at 7.15 p.m. Douglas Shepard Riggs was born—an adorable little boy. Dr. Parmelee and I were present, and I stayed on afterwards taking care of Mrs. Riggs until nearly Christmas.

During this time rumours were circulating about the war and the distress around us. One day the French Catholic missionaries in Mezreh and Harpoot were given 24 hours to leave their houses, but our American consul arranged with the Vali to give them another eight days. During this time they sold their things at the market and left the town. As soon as they were out of their houses some officers came and took possession, and now the Turkish flag flies over the former Christian schools and churches. We later heard that the missionaries had been prevented from leaving the country and are living in one place or another. It would never do to let them get to Europe where they could tell of the dreadful situation in this country. On Sunday, December 19th, Mr. Riggs and I left on a little trip to Sheikh Hadji, arriving there about 5 o'clock. They have no minister there, so we had to stay with one of the brothers. There was sorrow in the village. None of us were known there and when I came in to the house, a lot of women surrounded me and asked if we were Germans. I said "No" and asked "Why?" They answered, "If you had been Germans you would not have been welcome here." The poor German missionaries are hated by everybody, also their nation, as it is insisted that the terrible war is all their fault. People down here believe that even missionaries are here for political reasons. The man with whom we lived is an old man of 65. The day before our arrival two Turkish soldiers came, lance-corporals, and searched different houses. They found a soldier who had taken ill on the way and had been sent home to get better, but these two lance-corporals now started to abuse and whip the young man and his family. One man had his arm broken, and the old man, with whom we were staying, received a severe blow on the head. This is not a rare occurrence but happens daily. Furthermore, they take everything they can lay their hands on. People have to give them whatever they demand—corn, meat, food, and clothes. If they do not receive it, the people are whipped. The day before we arrived, two men had also come, a Turk and an Armenian, both from Malatia. They had deserted from the army on the way to Erzeroum and they begged for shelter. Nobody dared to take them in for fear of the severe punishment that would follow if they were discovered, so they had to return to the mountains. Their feet were frozen and gangrene had started to set in. Poor people, now walking in the mountains and lying down to die. The men in the village told us that they had seen many corpses in the mountains—soldiers who have deserted will die of hunger and cold.

Sunday was a wonderful day. Both Mr. Riggs and I felt so happy to be able to bring these sad and frightened people the message from Almighty God, telling them of His faithful love and care, and encouraging them to be faithful unto the end, even in the midst of suffering and persecution to show Christian love and loyalty. As we left, we told each other that it was a wonderful labour that not even angels are allowed to do.

On Monday morning we said goodbye. It was raining heavily and the road was very bad with deep mud that reached up over the horse's knees. On the road we met several groups of soldiers who were on their way to Erzeroum. They were not in uniform but were dressed in their village clothes, consisting of white cotton trousers and shirt, with a little waistcoat, and some with coats. They looked miserable—dirty, wet, and frozen. They get no food. If they reach a village in the evening they sleep in a church or mosque without bedding or heat. So they are never warm or dry. There are no railways, no horses, and donkeys cannot even get through the deep snow and mud, so our poor soldiers must go on foot for three weeks. It is hard for anyone to imagine—even for us who see it daily—how difficult it all is. By the road we saw many dead donkeys, for, besides all the other miseries, disease also rages amongst the animals, and cattle and donkeys die like flies.

On Thursday December 24th at 10 o'clock in the morning I left Harpoot to go to Emaus to spend Christmas with Karen-Marie and Sister Jenny. I was in a real Christmas spirit and looked forward very much to being with the two Danes on Christmas Eve.

On the outskirts of Harpoot I saw a crowd of people standing still. I wondered what it could be, but as I drew nearer, I saw they were sick soldiers who were being brought to town. They had no transport, not even donkeys to ride upon, as the government begrudges even these to the sick young men who are giving their lives for them. They looked as if they had only a few minutes left in this world. Three other soldiers had taken them under their arms and dragged them up the hill. I felt my throat tighten and I could hardly breath as I saw them. These young men were people, the same as ourselves, who had parents, brothers, and sisters, who were mourning—yes—perhaps mourning far more than we knew, as they had no hope of seeing them again. The only thing I could do was to send a sigh up to our Heavenly Father to show mercy to these many poor people.

I continued my ride and a little later noticed four men carrying a stretcher on which lay the body of a man. Running after them was a Turkish woman, crying and singing a dirge, maybe it was this woman's only son—her hope, her joy and happiness. And now they were on their way to the burial ground. How much I longed to take her hand and tell her that he was not dead but alive and would live forever. But not even this comfort could I give her, for I did not know where his soul was. It was as though all my surroundings became hopeless and dark. But then I raised my eyes Heavenwards and remembered that Jesus had come on this very day and He will overcome. So I tried again to be happy and to continue.

Some few minutes later I could see a crowd of people gather down on the road a little bit outside Mezreh. I thought it might be more sick soldiers—maybe someone had died on the way, but when I came closer, I saw something much worse. It was a company of soldiers who had been sent to Erzeroum, many Turks and a few Armenians. One of the latter I knew well. He was leading and came up to me looking very pale, took my hand, and said, "Goodbye. I am going to Erzeroum (as if he meant he was going to his death). Give my love to my family."

In Mezreh sat his young wife, weeping with her four young children. Nearby an old father clung around the necks of his sons, kissing them again and again, then weeping and wringing his hands, as if he did not expect to see them ever again. From time to time the group stood still, turned towards Mezreh, and sent forth a dirge-like sound, which cut through the air, to bring a last greeting from the departing men back to the town, where the mothers, wives, and children sat mourning and weeping. This was almost too much. I could not breath and had to cry out. I had to weep, otherwise I felt I would choke, and for a moment I was overcome. So very many women have told me in these last months, "We pray and cry to God, and He does not seem to hear." And I said, "Oh, God, don't You see all the want?" Oh, yes. He sees it, and even if our hearts seem to break, we can be sure that it pains His Father's heart, which is love itself. We must therefore be faithful, and go out into the streets and bye ways and urge everyone to return to God.

At first I thought it would be impossible to celebrate Christmas, but when I reached Emaus and saw Karen-Marie, who had not seen all this sorrow, I began to feel better. Then the great joy returned to be here in this difficult time, and to be allowed to go around to all the many people who are suffering, to bring them help and comfort. So I could again say, "Thanks be unto God for His unspeakable Gift" and give thanks for the great mercy that I had a part in this gift and could bring it to others.

We had a lovely Christmas Eve—Danish, with Christmas hymns and a Christmas sermon by P. Busch.

On Christmas morning I left for Harpoot and had a lovely Christmas morning with the Riggses. Saturday evening I attended a Christmas celebration for the soldiers in hospital—it was really lovely. There were 50 sick soldiers and none of them had ever seen a Christmas tree. Mr. Riggs preached about Jesus as the great Gift—the Saviour of the world. In spite of all, it was a blessed Christmas. On Tuesday afternoon Douglas invited all the missionaries to tea. On Wednesday afternoon I had a Christmas tree for some of the poorest and for some Turkish women and children. They came before lunch. Later I heard that these poor ones had not slept the night before, as they were looking forward so much to the celebration. Each received a bag containing roasted peas and a little sugar, some raisins, and nuts. I had collected some old clothes, as I had no money for new ones. There was great pleasure as they received the various things. I wished I could have provided a hot meal for them, but as I had no money, it was impossible.

1 January, 1915 (Friday). Mr. Riggs and I left for a longer trip. We intended to visit a village two days' journey from Harpoot, Aghen. We spent the first night in a khan. I had a little room with a big window to the stable, and as there were about 100 donkeys in there. I did not get much sleep that night.

We left early next morning and reached Aghen at 4 o'clock in the afternoon. We had accommodation under the church. That evening a lot of men and women came to greet us. Next day we began daily services, morning and evenings. It was lovely to see so many people coming, hear them sing, and notice how they listened and participated in the prayers.

On Monday morning I commenced house visits. Everyone was more than kind and full of thankfulness for our coming. Every evening the brothers met together with Mr. Riggs, while I had a meeting with all the sisters in another room. I talked to them about child care and upbringing, together with other subjects. Twice I conducted women's meetings and the church was almost filled. These were lovely days we spent there. Most families had sent one or more of their men to the war, but they understood that only God can help, protect, and bless them, and therefore from each heart go the prayers up to God's throne.

On Thursday morning we took our leave of the many good friends and started for Arapkir. It was a wonderful ride down in a cleft between the tall mountains. Down in the cleft there was a river which we had to cross seven times. The water was so deep that it reached our feet and filled our boots. It was raining heavily, so we were soaking wet, but we reached Arapkir at 4 o'clock and were received by the minister and his wife. The next morning we had a service and when we came back Mr. Riggs had a telegram from Harpoot asking him to return home. He left at once, whilst I stayed here alone.

I started the house visits the same day, visiting 11 different houses each day, over a period of eight days.

Last Saturday a message came that all men between 40-45 should make ready at once to leave for Erzeroum. Everywhere we went there was weeping, for many men were liable, always the heads of houses with many children. There is great poverty here. Every house has a hand loom, but even when a woman works from early morning until the evening without a break, she only earns about 20 ghouroush, and when she has four, five, or six children, it is impossible to save anything. As soon as the war started, all work stopped, so the people are sitting at home in their thousands, without work, without money or food. Many suffer want, going for days without anything to eat. If it is so bad now, what will it be in the days to come? Now sick and wounded soldiers are coming back from the front—thus putting an additional burden of unhappiness on the homes. The soldiers who have returned tell of conditions there, and how terrible they are. There is no bread for them—only a ration of roasted corn, and not nearly enough—so they are starving. They collect undigested whole grain from horse manure, wash it, and eat it, resulting in much sickness. They say 2,000 men die daily in Erzeroum alone, all these are our best men. They all have parents, brothers and sisters, cousins and children, who all suffer beyond words knowing they are away out there in want, poverty, cold, and danger.

Only a few months ago these men left, fresh and strong. Now they are back as invalids, so starved that they are only skeletons, and so verminous that if you lay a hand upon their bodies it comes away covered with lice. Yesterday when I went house-visiting I saw three soldiers like this—all Turkish. They came from Erzeroum two days ago. They had got permission to lie and rest in a house belonging to the government, but today they have been sent away again. They are from Malatia and are now on their way home, but they are so ill that they could scarcely walk. They were dressed in the remains of uniforms, full of holes and very dirty. The stench from them was so strong that I could scarcely bear to walk beside them, even in the open street. They stood, backs hunched, before the door of a house, where they knocked, hoping for someone to take pity on them and give them nothing more than a piece of dry bread, but there was no one to open to them. I had my bible bag half-full of almonds, which were given to me in a rich home. I walked over to the men and gave two handfuls of the nuts to each. There were so many. Oh, these poor men, their dull eyes shone and they exclaimed, "Oh, oh." They started to swallow the almonds, too hungry to eat them slowly. I talked with them a little, but they were so dull, they could hardly answer. Fortunately I had some money with me, so I gave each 5 piastres—about one shilling—and how happy they became, shouting, "May Allah take you up to Heaven." It was so little I could do. How I wished I could have taken them in, washed them, given them clean clothes, put them into a good bed, and nursed them, but there was nothing I could do. They went out into the road in heavy rain and I could not help wondering if they would ever reach their homes.

Yesterday an Armenian also returned here, ill and very weak. When he reached his home, they were carrying out the corpse of his mother.

People sit and cry all around. When you meet them in the street (I mean the women) you see their unhappy faces—full of worry and sorrow—and they say to me, "What will become of us? Have you any news from the front? My sons are also there. They will never return." It seems as if all the will to live has been taken away from these unhappy people. I wish in their hour of distress they could learn to search after God with whole hearts, that He might again turn the light of His countenance upon them.

Today is our last but one day here. Tomorrow, Sunday, I shall hold another women's meeting. May it be a blessed one. On Monday we are to set out for a neighbouring village—Shepig.

On Monday morning we took leave of our friends in Arapkir. As we were leaving the town we saw two Turkish women standing on the road crying and screaming. When I questioned them, they pointed up the road to two men and cried, "Soldiers, soldiers." That was enough, we knew the rest. They had parted from these men without hope of ever seeing them again. No wonder they cried. Further on we met the men, both middle aged, about 50-55. They did not look fit to endure for many days the rain, snow, and hunger they would encounter on the road ahead.

We rode on, surrounded by beautiful scenes of nature. On all sides were high, snow covered mountains. Down in the cleft the water ran in streams, and where the water was, there was greenery. Up the sides of the mountains grew cedar trees, and every little bush was surrounded by flocks of sheep and goats grazing busily. When the grass was eaten down to the roots, the animals stood on their hind legs to nibble the lower branches of the bushes, as high as they could reach. Then we heard the shepherds shout, "Hra, hra," which the sheep understand so well. After that we heard a shepherd play on his little pipe, of which he is a master. How peaceful and lovely everything looked, but in these mountain areas lay thousands of sick soldiers on their way home from the front, dying alone, far from home and friends, away from even the sound of a human voice, and with no one to help them. How many of them have learned to know Jesus, the Saviour of the world, who is the Way, the Truth, and the Life? Only a few of them can say with David, "The Lord is my shepherd" and "Yea—though I walk through the valley of the shadow of death, I will fear no evil, for thou art with me." My heart cries out when I think of all these people, but it is filled with longing, also, to go to them with the Glad Tidings.

While we rode there, surrounded by nature's beauty, we met a crowd of Dervishes (Muslim monks). They wore high brown felt hats and brown robes. Most were young men, between 18 and 20. Each had an old-fashioned sword fastened to his side. Some old white-haired men accompanied them. Their priest rode on a mule, with their holy book bound to his chest. Another man carried their holy flag, green with a half-moon. These men looked very proud, dreaming that whoever they met should fall to their swords. They told us they were going voluntarily to Aleppo, Damascus, and Egypt, to kill all the Christian enemies. Some minutes later we met a group of our Armenian brothers who had been taken as soldiers. They were all over 40—some even 50 years old. They enquired anxiously for news. Unfortunately we had nothing to tell them that they did not already know. We talked to them of serving not only as soldiers of this country, but as soldiers of Jesus, before parting and saying goodbye.

All the way we met homecoming soldiers, some wounded, and others suffering from all kinds of sickness. It was a picture of misery. Some could hardly drag themselves along, and it was obvious that if they tried to sit down to rest they would never be able to rise up again. Everyone was dirty, verminous, ragged beyond description, and starved down to skeletons. If people in Europe could see this misery, the whole Christian world would rise up as one and put an end to the terrible war, which has also come to this unhappy country.

We reached Sjæpik by noon, stopping in the house of one of the brothers. It was the Armenian Christmas Eve and a crowd of school boys were going from house to house with lighted candles singing "Avedis," the happy message for the people. We held a service that evening in the school, as there was no church here. All the people came, mostly women, as only a few men were left. Next morning we held another service, and at noon a women's meeting, also fully attended. This winter there has come a young man as a teacher, who also preaches on Sundays. Great blessing has followed. Everyone says his life is a continuous sermon. A great awakening has begun here and it was a joy to talk to these many hungry souls.

Just after the women's meeting we started out for Dsak which we reached in the evening. There are no Protestants in this village, but we have started a school this year. We were glad we had come here, because the people had not celebrated Christmas. There is a Gregorian church, but no priest, so the building is never open. The next morning Mr. Riggs preached to quite a big crowd, also mostly women, who listened from their own compartment at the back of the church, surrounded by a close grille, so that no man could see them.

An hour's journey from the village we visited some old graves built into the mountain. In each grave there was room for three. They were very beautifully made—dating from early Christian times. It was in a similar type of tomb that the body of our Saviour was laid. There were sixteen of these graves left, the others having been demolished by the Turks, who used the stones for their own mosques.

We left Dsak about 10 o'clock and reached the next village Enætzik at 4 o'clock in the afternoon. We stayed there with one of the brothers also. I visited some homes to talk to the women. There were signs there also of an awakening, and the church was full for our service next morning. Before we left they gave us something to eat. It was barley porridge, with ground pepper in it, so strong that it burned long after we had eaten it. They have no milk, so we had to eat the porridge without it, but it was well to be "warmed-up" as we had a long ride ahead of us—eight hours—and it was a cold day. When we had ridden for four hours we had to cross the Euphrates. The ferry was an old, leaky tub. The current was very strong, and we did not like the look of it. There was just room for our two horses and ourselves, but we made the crossing safely, even though the old tub had shipped a lot of water. We recommenced our ride through snow and mud until we reached Chemishgezek at 5.00 p.m. This was a lovely place, with beautiful mountains on all sides. A strong stream ran down the cleft. On the mountainside were many caves, former dwellings in the old times. Now they are almost out of reach, so much of the mountain has fallen away, little by little. We had to pass through the market to reach the part of the village where we were to stay. We passed a government building and shortly after a soldier came running after us, shouting, "Stop! Stop!" We stopped at his command and he wanted to know who we were, what we were doing, and where we had come from. We told him we had come to inspect the Protestant church, and Mr. Riggs said he would come and see the Kaimakam the next morning, so the soldier allowed us to proceed. Here, also, we stayed in a private house. They have not had a minister for several years, so the town has been spiritually dead, but now in their hour of distress, they have begun to awaken, especially some of the younger women, who are open for God's Kingdom. We stayed only three days—Friday, Saturday, and Sunday.

The first two days I went from house to house from morning till evening, and everyone was eager and happy to listen to me. I was very surprised when I came back on Saturday evening and Mr. Riggs told me that the police inspector had sent for him and told him that I should not walk alone in the town as he was afraid I would be taken and imprisoned. Some time ago the government had received a telegram saying that they should be on the lookout for a Russian woman going from house to house and putting people against the government. Now all the Turks thought I was the Russian woman. The Police Inspector said, "I know perfectly well who she is— Miss Jacobsen from Harpoot—but how can I convince other people in the town?" Mr. Riggs thanked him, telling him that I was finishing my visits that day, and he could not get a message to me as I was going around the town. On Sunday we only had a service and I would not be out alone, and we intended to leave on Monday. Little did I think I had turned the town upside down, and that people had been planning how to catch me. On that day I had called at Turkish homes too, but I had said nothing about the war.

On Sunday we had morning and evening services. The church was almost full. At midday I held a women's meeting in the church which was packed. Most of them were Gregorians and they were not used to sitting still and listening, so I had to speak as loudly as I could, so that everyone could hear. There were many children, as it is not possible to have a women's meeting in Turkey without children playing, talking, crying, and running about. Therefore the great thing was to try to get them to be quiet. In addition it had been raining for several days and as the roof was leaking, there was a constant drip, my bible and hymn book became soaked, and the rain dripped on to my face. All this contributed to the disturbance, and I was dead tired when the meeting ended. However, there was no time to feel tired, as on my return home I found a crowd of sick people waiting for me, and I was fully occupied every minute until it was time for the evening service. The church was again filled to capacity. Mr. Riggs preached on the text, "Lord to whom shall we go? Thou has the words of eternal life," and the people listened with great attention.

When we came home and had been sitting for a little while, we heard a terrible noise. A crowd of Gregorian men had come, even before the last women had left the church, and begun to hammer on the walls, trying to break it down. The women tried to prevent it but were overcome by the men. They were struck down and even had their clothes torn. All this lasted for two hours. Later in the evening we heard that these men had been sent by a Gregorian priest to knock down the church. So now we saw once again how Satan rages and foams, and the persecution begins, as soon as God's people waken and begin to work.

Later that night men and women came to us and we talked with them, advising them to do nothing in the coming days, not even to protect themselves, but to show the same disposition as Jesus in everything. Before parting we read together from 1st Corinthians, Chapter 13—the Chapter of Love. We prayed to God to help us to love in every situation, and to protect our faith until the end.

We said goodbye around 9 o'clock, packed our clothes, and the next morning, before daylight, left for home.

We reached Harpoot at 6 o'clock in the evening after a very exhausting journey over mountains and through rivers—I with a terrible headache. All we had to eat was dry bread and a little cheese, which was hard to swallow. I had to take a pill to help my headache, but my mouth was so dry that it stuck in my throat. Then we remembered that we had a little jelly in a glass. I put the pill in it and down it went. We could not find water until 4 o'clock in the afternoon when we reached a spring. We were afraid of using water from the river, or stream, as the country is full of typhus and typhoid. It was good to come home again and rest a little after the exhausting trip. But they had been great days, filled with labour. Again and again I had to say, "How wonderful it is to serve God. Wonderful for man and woman to cast their nets out— heathen souls to win."

3 February, 1915 (Wednesday). When we had our meeting last night, the Doctor told us that the government was not very friendly towards them, did not keep its promises, and had forbidden them to hold meetings for the sick soldiers. He said that the Turks at a meeting had said that even if they killed all the American missionaries, America would not enter the war. It would not be possible to force the Americans into war. We feel, again and again, that everything around us is insecure. We never know what they might do, and we cannot help wondering what the next step will be. I wonder if we will even be allowed to live much longer. But we know that they cannot touch a hair of our heads without the Father's will, and if He allows it, He will also give us the strength to bear it and to be faithful.

Yesterday all schools in Mezreh were closed because of typhus and typhoid, which are now spreading outside the town. Now it is a daily occurrence for Armenians to be thrown into prison because of something they have written. They imprison with any excuse, for example the two youths who were working...* ...They do not need me any longer and that is why I return to my soldiers.

---

*·This sentence is truncated as the relevant pages are missing in original diaries.—A.S.

24 February. Today I had a letter from Mrs. Lange. We had begun to fear we would receive no more mail, but the other day a letter came which had been stamped, "This language is not accepted by the Turkish government." Now and again one is passed through. We live in Turkey.

In the last three days we have been reading in Ajans that the English and French have bombarded the Dardanelles. Hundreds of shots were fired, but their aim was so bad that they had no effect. On the other hand the Turkish fire was so heavy, that their enemies fled without causing any damage.

We also read in Ajans that a German flag had been raised in Northern France, and had been used by the French and English as a target. One hundred and eighteen cannon shells were fired before they succeeded in shooting it down. As another example of what they are doing to keep up the morale of the poor people, we read in Ajans some time ago that camel caravans would bring bags of sand to fill in the Suez Canal, so that the English could not use it. Ignorant people accept all these things. If anyone should contradict them, they will be shot, or thrown into prison, or the most severe punishment at the moment, they will be sent to the front.

8 March, (Monday). Today I start my work among the sick soldiers. I am glad to be allowed to help some of these many poor men, but it is almost unbearable to see all the suffering. Here we have 120 soldiers. Every room is occupied, and as we do not have enough beds, 30 patients will have to lie on the floor, but it is far better than the bare ground. We still have 40 patients with typhus—a terrible illness. When I came into the big ward I saw a dreadful sight. Two lay in their death throes, and a third had vomited about half a pail of blood over himself, the bedclothes, and the floor. All around lay other sufferers, muttering in delirium. Again and again I realize this is the result of war, and what will follow?

I am in charge of the whole of the ground-floor, of eight wards, and a total of 80 patients. It is a wonder that any arrive here alive, and a greater wonder that some of them recover sufficiently to leave. Before the government doctors see them and send them here, a week can elapse, and sometimes two or three. The many poor people suffering from pneumonia, typhus, and dysentery are in a very low state when they arrive. They are not driven, or carried here, but have to come on foot and very often they fall down on the way and die before reaching us. Others die three or four hours after arrival. In one ward I have 18 patients suffering from gangrene in the legs. Most of them have had half of their foot amputated. Others have lost the whole foot, or the leg up to the knee, and it is a question whether or not they will survive. It is a dreadful sight. The poor people.

12 March, 1915 (Friday). Baron Toros who has been working in our dispensary for four years, a fine young man, and a dedicated Christian, was taken by the police on February 2nd and put into prison because of a letter which had been sent in his name from a young man in the village, some day's distance from here. The letter said

that the Russians would arrive here in 14 days, and their flag would fly over the government building. This was enough to make them seize these two young men, and another six, and now they are imprisoned as rebels. Today, I went with his mother to visit Baron Toros. They are held in a little room in the barracks, containing 60 other prisoners—Kurds, Turks, and Armenians. I know the prison warden. His brother was in our hospital, suffering from typhus, and has now recovered. We entered his office, and he sent for Baron Toros. It was a pitiful sight. The prison had set its mark upon him. He was ill, with a high fever, a bad cough, and had lost weight. I was afraid that his old sickness had returned. Four years ago he was suffering from tuberculosis. We walked home with heavy hearts. It was hard for us, who loved him, to see him in these terrible surroundings—a hell on earth. As we entered the gateway we passed through a long dark passage. To the right they had set iron bars and in this space were imprisoned 1,000 soldiers who had deserted, been captured, and brought back again. These men have nothing but the rags they are wearing. At night they sit on the bare ground without any covering. They receive a little dry bread, otherwise nothing. Those who survive this will be sent to Erzeroum, a journey of 14 days, over high mountains with deep snow, chained together two by two, and, furthermore, treated like animals. No, animals are treated much better. Never had I realised how terrible these prisons are. The guards are real devils—and we can see how Satan rages. When, oh, when, will all this end? When we returned I at once dispatched some medicine to Baron Toros. On Sunday he sent a message to say he had diarrhoea, and again I sent medicine for this. He sent another message on Monday morning to say that he felt very ill, and Miss Campbell and I left at once to visit him. He looked very ill indeed, and could scarcely breathe, with a high fever and a pulse very fast and weak. We sent him back to the room as he was too weak to sit up. We both agreed that if he was kept sitting in prison he would soon die. Something had to be done. Several times I had discussed this with the Doctor, who had always replied that he could do nothing, and it was not possible to get him out. Now there was nothing to do but make an attempt myself. It is absolutely unheard of here for a woman to apply directly to the government, but it was a matter of life and death, and Baron Toros is his mother's only son.

Miss Campbell and I, accompanied by a man who could speak Turkish, went to Hakki Pasha, the senior military representative, and told him about Toros, how ill he was and likely to die, and that we wanted to move him to our hospital. He promised to do what he could, and we then went to the army's chief medical officer and told him the same. He is a very bad man and said it was impossible. He is very much against the Christians and does them all the harm he can. It was evening by this time, but on the following morning, Tuesday, we left again for [blank], told our story there, and afterwards went to the Judges' Room. Here we were told to send in an application, so we set off again, this time to a lawyer who could write it for us. On our way back with this, we suddenly thought of the German consul and officer, who had arrived some days earlier. Maybe they, as friends of the Turks, could do something? So we went to them and received a promise that they would discuss the matter with the Vali that evening. Now we could only await results.

Wednesday morning we returned to the German consul to hear the result. He told us that the Turks were not kindly disposed towards Germans who supported the Armenian cause. The consul advised us that our application to the Vali would not help. Indeed it might anger him, since the life of one Armenian was of no value to him. There was, therefore, no help here.

We now took the application and went down to the prison, to obtain Baron Toros's signature. We were shocked when we saw him. He looked terribly ill, could scarcely walk, his face was blue, and he was hardly able to write his name. We sent him straight back to the room. We realised that if he was not released that day, he would die. The application was signed by both the prison guards and the director, and we then took it to the government building. Here sat eight prisoners who were being interrogated. Many of them looked as if they had only a short time left to live. Their faces were distorted with suffering and terror. I wondered what they had done—maybe nothing—as most of the imprisoned people are innocent men, whilst those who ought to be in prison are ruling over the innocent. But we are in Turkey.

They took our application, read it, wrote something on it, and returned it to us. We thanked them very much and left them, with a Turkish greeting. Afterwards we were shown to the Judges' Room. There were many men here also, but they were very polite to us, giving us chairs to sit on, and talking to us about America, as they considered us Americans. The application was read, something was written on it, and it was then sent to another room, and returned shortly. The paper was now almost covered with writing. It was sent back and forward and, at last, the Judge said, "Olmaz" ["It is not possible"]. We had no one to translate for us. Miss Campbell could not speak Turkish, so I had to do all the talking. I said, "Well, what must we do now? Something has to be done today, otherwise the young man will die." The Judge said, "There is only one thing left now, and that is if Hakki Pasha will approve it." I said, "Thank you," and we set off at once.

Fortunately Hakki Pasha was available, and the servant advised him of our arrival. We were admitted, and I reminded him of the very ill young man, now close to death, and stated that we wanted his permission to have him removed to the hospital at once. He was very friendly, and told us he had not forgotten what he had promised us. But he said he thought we were intelligent enough to understand the impossibility of moving a prisoner from jail to our hospital. However, he would give his permission for the young man to be moved into a room by himself in the prison hospital. I asked to be given permission to nurse him, and for his mother to visit him, and this was granted. He even said that in the course of a day or two he might permit the patient to be moved to our hospital. This, I knew very well, was only a

Turkish promise. He then sent for Tevfik Bey, the chief military doctor, told him what he had agreed, and asked for a single room to be made available with new bedding. We expressed our gratitude, made a deep "Salaam," and returned with the doctor to his office. This doctor is a real fox. In front of Hakki Pasha he did not dare to say more than, "Euch [sic] Effendi " (Yes, my master), but now he started scolding and fuming, because we had been told of Toros's illness, and the government had not. I explained to this "high and mighty" doctor that Toros had not said anything to me, but that I had found him ill, and even if he had sent a message to the government, he would not have received treatment, until he was on the brink of death. This is how all prisoners are treated here. However, he did write asking that Toros be given a single room, on the orders of Hakki Pasha. With this piece of paper we were sent to another building near the prison. It was now past 4 o'clock, and my heart was beating with fear that we should not manage to have anything done for him that day. We waited more than half an hour. There was a friendly Turkish officer, who had seen me before, and he asked me about the fearful illness—typhus. While we were talking, I saw Baron Toros being brought out of the prison. Two men accompanied him, but as he was so weak that he could hardly walk, they almost had to drag him, his head hanging down upon his breast. Behind them came a soldier with an outstretched spear, so that if this nearly dead boy should try to escape, he would at once have a spear driven through him. This was too much for me, and I asked permission to go to his aid. The officer said, "Yes." So I ran down the prison yard and helped him, instead of one of these crude men helping him. We took him into the doctor's surgery, where the two doctors were good friends of mine.

I said, "He is very ill and cannot stand," and they told me that I could take him down into the prison hospital. They told a soldier to get a new mattress. I was so afraid that Baron Toros would die of heart failure. He was so very weak, but at last we reached the hospital, and it was not long before I had removed seven beds from a room—all on the floor—made up a new bed, and put Toros into it. His temperature was over 40 degrees C, but at least he could rest and have fresh air. I got hold of an Armenian man who promised to look after him during the night. I stayed with him for almost an hour, and before I left him, he said to me, "Now I am happy—I am not afraid any more." I said good night—promising that I would return the following morning.

On my way home I could hardly help shedding tears of joy, because I had succeeded in getting him out from that terrible place and had permission to nurse him. Yes, God hears prayer, and He is almighty to help and bless all who put their trust in Him. For man it looked impossible, but God did it. He should have all the honour, thanks, and praise.

25 March, 1915 (Thursday). It has been a very strenuous week. Beside all the hard work in the hospital, which keeps one more than fully occupied from morning till evening, Baron Toros has been very sick. I spend two hours every morning and evening with him—four hours each day. It turned out to be very severe typhus. He has had a very high temperature—over 40 degrees C all the time, and only yesterday did it drop to 39 degrees C. This evening it was 38.6 degrees C, but he is very apathetic now. However, I believe that God will save his life. It has only been a pleasure for me to be allowed to nurse him. How I wish I could remove him from prison and return him to his mother. But God is the same as in the old days. He can deliver him.

29 March, 1915. Now Baron Toros's temperature is normal, and we are all very pleased. I still visit him twice daily, as he is still very weak, and it is an encouragement to him so, as long as he remains there, I have decided to go to him every day.

However, I saw a terrible sight down there last night when 1,000 prisoners were taken into the yard. Each had to appear before a doctor, who was to examine them and determine if they really were unfit for military service. They were a miserable flock. Lame, blind, ragged, and starving. They did not look as though they could endure a day's journey before dying of exhaustion. The doctor did not examine them, merely looking at them before crying, "Churuk" or "Tabur," the last word meaning that he was fit to go. Almost half of them were unable to walk and were exempted. The rest had to go to Erzeroum. When all had been examined all the sick had to go two by two through the gate. There were quite a lot of Turkish soldiers (something like our lance corporals) standing there. They wanted to show their self-importance, each with a stick in his hand, and as the sick passed to be counted they were struck as hard as possible on the back—these sick and half dead poor people. Once there were three men in a row, and instead of telling the third man to go back in the row, one of the lance corporals flew at him, striking him very heavily on the head, while yelling and shouting. The poor sick man did not understand what it was all about, but stood shivering in fear. At last the lance corporal got tired of beating and yelling, pushed him in among the others, and the poor man went on his way. It is terrible to see how these poor people are treated—and this is a daily occurrence.

30 March, 1915. Things get worse and worse all the time. Sometimes I think I can not bear to watch all the suffering around us. But in spite of this I cannot leave, as I do want to help a little. This morning, when I went down to the prison, the gate was closed. I could hear the rattle of iron, and I did not know what to do. I was afraid of knocking on the gate, and I had to get in, as I was bringing Toros some food. We returned to the officers' building, entered, and from there came into the prison yard, which was filled with men. It was the prisoners from yesterday who had been passed for military service in Erzeroum. I felt terribly sorry for them. When I came nearer I

saw they were linked together, and a closer view showed that the chains were attached to thick iron rings around their necks. I went to Toros and just outside his window the poor men were waiting to have the iron rings put around their necks. It was a dreadful sight. Ten by ten they were linked together. Many of them had nothing with which to protect their bare necks from the iron, which in a few hours would give them dreadful sores, the rings being very heavy and rough. I thought my heart would burst at the sight of these poor ones. Oh, if only the high and mighty gentlemen who are sitting in their palaces and demanding the continuation of the war could imagine these poor people's suffering, then I think we would soon have peace. Then the gate was opened and they were lined up. Some of them were stronger than others and could walk faster, thus dragging the weaker along by the chains and rings. These poor men have souls like us. They have all left their homes, where they have parents, wives and children, and have nothing before them but terrible suffering and death with no comfort—no light in the dark. No one—simply no one—can imagine the conditions in this country, and what frightful suffering there is. The roads are filled with human corpses, and millions of homes are filled with mourning women and children, without comfort or food, who will never see their dear ones again.

1 April, 1915 (Thursday). When I came down to the prison today, I could feel that there was something the matter. I did not know what. Even Dr. Michael, who is highly respected by the Turks, feared something, and when he came to see Baron Toros, he asked me if I had noticed anything. I said, "Yes." He then told me that he had been shouted after as he had come along, and he had met policemen going two by two in the streets. All Armenians had been disarmed. He said, "These are very serious days. We do not know what will come."

When I returned to the hospital the doctor was standing outside, white as a sheet, and he told me that our chemist had just been there and had said all Armenians were in fear of a massacre at any moment. We knew the situation was alarming. The government has demanded all our buildings in Harpoot in a very nasty way. The Consul had gone and set the American seal on the doors, telling them that if they broke them, it would be at their own risk. Two hours later they broke them and moved in. They took over six large buildings. We feel strongly that the government is very hostile to all Christians and missionaries. Yes, even the German missionaries have been treated very badly. In spite of this I continued my work among the sick. I could not help thinking, "Maybe, this is our last day." I have only one prayer, and it is, "Lord, keep me faithful unto Thee through all and until the end."

It was the Thursday before Easter. In the evening I went over to the German Children's Home. There was a meeting with communion, and I walked home afterwards, happy and strengthened. It is good to know that our Father on high lives, knows everything, sees everything, and rules everything, and that we have no future without Jesus. Yes—God be praised.

2 April, 1915 (Friday). Good Friday. I had not much time to be calm. Ten patients were discharged, and 10 new ones admitted. There were more deaths. I still felt, "Maybe this is your last day," but I thank my Lord and Master for every day he allows me to live. I collected the young girls around me and told them of Jesus' words—"Inasmuch as ye have done it unto one of the least of these my brethren, ye have done it unto me." We had a lovely time together.

3 April, 1915 (Sunday). Easter Day. The morning was a busy time amongst the patients. In the afternoon I attended church and communion. It was a lovely service, and I returned to the hospital. In the evening I held services in the wards where there are Armenians. It was really nice. We have been ordered not to hold services for the patients, but I cannot accept this. It would seem to me as though I were allowing them to die without knowledge of the Saviour's message. So I say with Peter, "We must obey God more than man," and therefore I have decided to begin.

6 April, 1915 (Thursday). It has been a full day. I have not had time to sit down from early morning until now, but it is only a pleasure to be allowed to help some of the many people. Today we discharged eleven patients and took in thirteen new ones. We have now 120 and every spot is filled.

This evening we held a service in the big room where there are about 30 patients, and we called all the walking patients in. One of the nurses, who speaks Turkish very well and is a real child of God, sang three hymns with me. Then she read the story of the rich man and Lazarus. They were very attentive and during the prayer said, "Amen." Afterwards I told them my heart was full, that I wished to talk to them, and promised to do so tomorrow evening. It is glorious work. We can only sow, but God must give the growth, for he loves souls much more than we humans can or do. *

* Following lines are originally written in English. "Disciplineship No 2/Have you and I today/ Stood silent as milk? Church?, apart from/say or fray/Of life to see by faith His face;/To look, if such a moment, at its grace,/And grow by brief companionship more live,/More nerved so lead, so dare to do,/For him at any cost? Have we today/Found time, in thought our hand to lay/In this and and thus compare/His will with ours and [?]/The impress of his work? Be sure/Such contact will endure/Throughout the day; will help us work each/Through storm and flood; defeat/Within the hidden life, sin's dress, its shame/Revive a thought of love for him again/Steady the steps that matter?, Keep us see/The footpath meant for you and me." —A.S.

1915.[*] 5,000 donkeys were taken and sent to Erzeroum. Only five hundred reached there, the others died on the road. Soldiers are still being sent to the villages, to find out those who have horses and donkeys, and then these are being sent with their animals and corn to Erzeroum. This is a very difficult and dangerous trip, especially in the winter. Therefore, to avoid being sent, the people in the villages are killing their animals. Soldiers sent to Erzeroum desert on the way there. Men from Bizmeshen who had escaped returned to their village. Soldiers who were sent after them went into their houses and destroyed everything they could lay their hands on, bound the men, and brought them to the prison. Turkish soldiers go to war without any equipment, uniform, or food. Russian soldiers get good food and have good uniforms. Turkish soldiers go to war with their white shalvars and shirts. On the way to Houlakegh we saw a company of new soldiers who had been collected in the villages. They were very lightly clad, and in no way were they fit to be soldiers. Many of them looked much too weak to travel further. I could not help thinking what these ignorant, skinny, weak men could do for their country. Many of them will die on the road. The majority of them have never before set foot outside their village. Soldiers returning from Erzeroum say that corn is being stored in the mosques, where it lies getting mouldy, and from this, bread is being baked for the soldiers. Kavoorma which was sent from Harpoot and other places was destroyed on the way, and it is said that people passing it on the road have to cross to the other side. Soldiers find it nearly impossible to eat the food that is given to them. Many die of cold, and many more of the terrible sickness, typhus. Our hospital in Mezreh, which is now a Red Cross Hospital, has places for about 120 patients. Dr. Atkinson is the doctor. Many die daily—six to ten—because they have been brought there too late. Very often they have been on the road several days and die within a few hours of admission. There are a lot of them with frozen feet—frostbite. It is a miserable sight to see them, so thin, dirty, and sick.

Two men were hanged in the market today. Another man, now in hospital, is to be hanged as soon as he is well enough to leave. He had refused to serve as a soldier and when two soldiers came after him, he shot at them. Typhus rages in Mezreh. In one of the military hospitals 20 die daily. It has been said that conditions are terrible. Patients suffering from all kinds of diseases are in the same wards, and the wards are so full that they are almost lying on top of each other on the floor. Lice and dirt are everywhere. They have to brush the lice from the floor to make a place for a patient to lie down.

---

[*] Second book of diaries starts here.—A.S.

Recaptured deserters are sent to Erzeroum in hand irons. They are then sent to the front, to serve in the first line. Turks as well as Armenians are escaping in thousands and are being treated terribly. Their families are being evicted from their homes, and their houses burned.

A man here in Harpoot was taken away, though he was very ill with asthma. The soldiers afterwards came and told his wife that her husband had deserted and they wanted her to tell them where he was. She said he could not have run away as he was so sick. Then the soldiers took her 14-year old son and put him in prison. It is possible that the sick man died on the road to Erzeroum.

Conversation between a Mohammedan and an Armenian from a village. They came from Sheikh Hadji to Harpoot—the Mohammedan riding a donkey, and the Armenian on foot. The conversation was about Mohammed and Christ. The Mohammedan said, "You say that Christ is the Son of God, that we cannot believe." "Who do you say he is?" asked the Armenian. "We believe He was a good man and born of the breath of God, but He was not God's Son." "Well" the Armenian said, "If He is not the Son of God, whose Son is He?" To that, the Mohammedan gave no reply. Then the Armenian asked again, "Is your prophet dead or alive?" "He is dead," said the Mohammedan. "Is Christ dead or alive?" asked the Armenian. "He is alive," answered the Mohammedan. "Who shall come and judge the world on the Day of Judgement" asked the Armenian. "Christ will come and judge" said the Mohammedan. "Well," the Armenian said, "I will keep to the living prophet, you can, if you wish, keep to the dead prophet."

7th February [sic]. Today a proclamation was read in the church, calling all men to register as soldiers. It also stated that men who ran away will be treated as outlaws, and their homes will be burned. It mentioned the glory of the nation, and the honour it was to serve it. It also said it was not a war of Christians against Mohammedans, but a war against those who did not fear God. Think of poor Turkey talking about England and France as nations who did not fear God. Armenians are very unhappy of having to help the Mohammedans against the Christians. More of the men who ran away were shot in Mezreh today. Three of them were Armenians and four Kurds.

Soldiers die every day in Wheeler Hall. Typhus is spreading. The ill-treatment of soldiers is terrible. A human life has no value in this country. When a soldier dies, his corpse is carried away and thrown into a hole, with no more thought afterwards than if he had been an animal.

A soldier here in Wheeler Hall daily receives two small pieces of bread and five spoonfuls of soup. It is a very common thing here to see Kurds being beaten with a whip or stick. The Kurds do not understand Turkish and therefore cannot understand what is being said to them. One reason for being given a beating is failure to salute an officer. These Kurds have always been their own masters and do not understand respect for others. They do not understand, therefore, why they should salute. While they were out on exercise, a Kurd put his left foot forward instead of the right. When he was shouted at he answered, "What difference does it make? They are both feet."

Out of a regiment of between 200-300 men, only six or eight have guns. Each soldier fires six shots before being sent to the front-line. Men up to 45 years have been taken.

Soldiers die in great numbers in Wheeler Hall. One day we counted 50 patients lying out in the sun with the earth for a bed, and a stone for a pillow. One day a doctor and a chemist went around between the soldiers in our college yard. The chemist had a big bottle of castor oil and the doctor looked at each man's tongue and ordered oil for everyone, which the chemist administered. That was the whole treatment, and everybody got the same.

Bedding and foodstuffs are being taken from the houses. It is said they are for the soldiers but they are not being given to them. They are being taken to the officers' houses. The officers are filling their pockets while the soldiers die of starvation, lack of hygiene, and illness.

Many die in our hospital. One day 24 new patients were admitted with typhus, and of these 10 died a few days later. Another day 35 came in, and 10 of them were dead in a short time. Soldiers must go on foot when they are not in a condition to crawl. I have seen soldiers walking, when it looked as if they should fall dead, if only a shot was fired. It is the same everywhere. Our Protestant Church is now being used as a hospital. It was taken on April 5th, 1915. Badveli Vartan goes there every day to see what he can do for the sick. He says their condition is pitiful. They have no bedding, no food. They say, "We are not sick—only starving." To send an army out to Erzeroum is madness, when not one amongst them is fit for one day's journey. They will either die on the way, or try to escape. When neighbours or friends come bringing food for soldiers, they are driven away by the officers, because this gives the government a bad name.

On April 1st the Consul's seal was broken off the doors by the Kaimakam and the soldiers moved in.

1 May, 1915. There is great unrest in Harpoot. Many shops and private houses are being searched and closed up. Three of our professors and a teacher were taken by soldiers and brought to the government building. Later they were brought back to their houses, which were searched in their presence. Every piece of paper on which there was writing was taken, and all the men were put in prison. The same happened in Mezreh and Husenik. Everybody is frightened and expects a massacre.

2 May. Still many more have been put in prison. Together with the house-searching and imprisonment here, they have also started in other towns and villages—Malatia, Bitlis, and Van. At the same time guards were set in the streets, to make sure that people were not going from house to house, passing messages, or bringing things out. The young minister in Houlakegh has also been imprisoned.

3 May. Last night houses were searched again and people are in fear and dread. Today Perchenj and other villages are being searched and the number of prisoners increases. The poor, poor people. It will take a long time before all the confiscated books are censored. When food is brought to the prisoners it is eaten by the soldiers, so the poor prisoners have to live on dry bread. Everyone believes it is the beginning of a massacre.

4 May. The people are in great dread. They all say this is the carrying-out of a well-laid plan, and they are certain that it is the beginning of a massacre. A respite of five days has been given, during which all weapons are to be handed over to the government, but everyone says they will not obey, as then the Turks would become furious and take revenge. A lot of Armenians have been sent away to repair the roads. In Hooiloo 600 young trees have been felled to lay blame on Armenians and enable them to say that they punish with justice.

5 May. Turks and Kurds threaten and speak very roughly to Armenians, telling them that a massacre is on the way. Turkish women are also full of hatred and say that the Christians are to blame for the war reaching them, and it is their fault that so many die. They also say that the Christian doctors give the soldiers poison.

Mr. Ehmann has today been to the Vali, asking him to calm the people. The Vali spoke very beautiful words and said, "As long as I am Vali, nothing is going to happen," but can he be trusted, when one hears and sees everything that is going on? For who speaks the truth in these times? Even their Koran allows them to lie under three circumstances: when they want to seduce a woman; when they are attempting to reconcile two brothers, and all other means have proved fruitless; and when there is a war or an uprising. Yes, under these circumstances they are allowed to swear falsely. This Allah allows.

Daily, new orders are coming, to give corn, fats, cheese, sheep, goats, and blankets. Money is also being demanded now. The officers go to the Armenian shops and take clothes worth a lot of money home with them, pretending that they are for the soldiers. One man had to give 5,000 liras' worth.

6 May. Miss Campbell has returned from Diarbekir. She tells us about the frightful conditions there, including that shots are fired in the streets, prisoners are tortured, fingers and limbs are broken, and vartabeds' beards torn out.

9 May (Sunday). Our dear Mrs. Barnum today went Home to God. She had suffered a long illness, but was beginning to recover, and we thought she would be allowed to remain with us a little longer. But the Lord knew better, knowing what was in wait for this country. He would spare her all this suffering, and took her Home to Glory. All missionaries were gathered in Mr. Riggs's living-room for our little service of song which we have every Sunday morning. Mrs. Barnum chose the hymn, "In Heavenly love abiding no change my heart shall fear." After they had sung it, she asked to be helped into the bedroom, and an hour later she was Home.

10 May. Mrs. Barnum was taken today from the school building to be buried. Many friends, both German and Armenian, were present to say their last goodbye to her, who for more than 50 years had been their true guide and friend.

11 May. Yesterday we were informed by Ajans that there is a revolution in Constantinople. A nephew of the Sultan is leading a party wanting to kill the Cabinet members and all the German officers.

13 May. There is still much illness in the town. Approximately 60 people die daily. They cannot, as they did in the beginning, carry them one by one on a stretcher, but have to pile them four or five on top of each other in a cart which is being driven continuously. They are taken to a house near the burial ground, as the grave-diggers cannot prepare graves for all who die that day. Now they have started digging graves in long rows, so that the bodies can be laid close together, and the work may be done more quickly.

It is said that the police have encircled Houlakegh (so closely that it looks as though the town is besieged) to search for weapons. After flogging and torturing they found some weapons. The inhabitants are horror striken.

After a few days ravaging, drinking, and feeding, the soldiers and the Kaimakam left Harpoot, saying they would return.

Death reaps a big harvest also among doctors in this country. Up to this date 40 have died—most of them from typhus.

Things are still very bad both here and in the villages. Today another 15 men were imprisoned. A young girl from a wealthy Protestant family was put into prison because an Armenian patriotic song book was found in her possession. It is very difficult for her to sit among these rough women in the prison without being allowed to see family or friends. In Arapkir they have also imprisoned women and girls.

A young man, fleeing from Diarbekir, came yesterday. He said there are no young men left, they have all been put in prison. Turks are raping women. The old people do not dare talk together for fear of being put in prison. No one will leave their house.

Also here they have flogged one of the rich women to make her tell where her husband had hidden weapons. The Turks are full of hate. Even a man, who came to the hospital bleeding and dirty, said, when he was put into a clean bed and was asked if he felt better, "I will hurry to get well, so that I can go out and kill and rape their women." The Armenians who were taking care of him were beside themselves with anger and said, "Is this how you talk—here among the Christians who are helping you?"

As fear and dread weigh down upon everyone the normally clear sky becomes covered with heavy dark clouds, and a great storm breaks, with heavy thunder and marvellous lightening, together with earthquakes of a violence never before experienced.

19 May. This morning four people, two Kurds and two Armenians, are being hanged in the Square. Up to now no Turks have been killed, and they can do what they want in the way of unjust and cruel acts without punishment. The Armenians believe that their extermination has been decided upon and, in their hopelessness, they say, "Whatever is to happen—let it happen soon. We suffer and die every day. It is better to see the end of it."

Many are bitter and say, "In Europe they fight—and we Armenians die because of it." Badveli Yeghoian says, "We must not pray alone for the Armenians' deliverance, because the whole earth is full of bloodshed, misery, and sorrow, but they die like human beings for their country, and we die as victims of slaughter, and our women are ravished."

Doctor Topalian, a clever Armenian doctor, and a strong and handsome man, who has served as an army doctor, has been imprisoned in Erzeroum, and is to be brought here in chains to be returned to his home village of Diarbekir. It is terrible to think of him falling into the hands of the cruel and dissolute Turks there.

23 May. Badveli Vartan preached in the Gregorian church and entreated the people to surrender weapons to him, so that he could give them to the government, who had promised that they would not demand names. But when he brought the weapons they did demand names, which he would not reveal because of the promise given, and therefore put himself and his family in a position of danger. It looked bad for some days, but it now seems as if the government has been persuaded.

They are still taking men from their shops in the streets—yes, even from their houses. Only poor and old men are free.

There are rumours of murder and terrible torture of prisoners in Chunkoush, Maden, and other places in this Vilayet.

27 May. Today we were shocked to hear that judgement has been passed on Baron Toros and the other young men. The day before yesterday they had appeared before the judge and it looked as though Baron Toros had been found innocent. We were all

hopeful, and then we hear that he, and the others, have been sentenced to 10 years' banishment. The young man who brought the letter has been given six years and the writer of the letter condemned to death. This last man was immediately fettered by the leg to prevent him walking. The others were brought to another prison and put in with other prisoners.

29 May. A telegram arrived from Diarbekir saying that Dr. Smith wished Mr. Riggs to come as there was work for him. So he got transport and left the same day.

30 May. Badveli Bedros has got a message that his brother-in-law Bedros in Chunkoush has been ill-treated and killed in the prison there. He was a splendid old man and very popular with his congregation. This is a great sorrow. There are a lot of men in prison there also.

From other places we hear of terrible ill-treatment. It is said that in one place 13 Armenians have been crucified, nails being driven through hands, feet, and chest. In Severek the old minister has been crucified.

Yesterday Dr. Atkinson became ill with erysipelas. It is bad enough, with a big hospital, but Dr. Michael has promised to look after the patients. There are now not so many typhus patients, but dysentery, erysipelas and frostbite especially are bad.

We do not hear so much about the war, only now and then that some Russians have been taken prisoner, and that some Italian cities have been bombarded. It is rumoured that Van has been captured by the Russians, who are now near Moush. Many think there has been a massacre in Van and that it has also been bad in Bitlis and Moush.

1 June. From Tadem news is coming that 100 zapties went there. Plundering and arrests have begun. The women and girls had to flee to the mountains to escape persecution from the zapties. It is so terrible everywhere, these zapties and soldiers coming in the night and going on at them, now that there are no men to defend them.

3 June. A message has come that the ministers from Peri, Arapkir, and other places have been imprisoned. Many people in Malatia are also in prison.

Our professors and other men are being frightfully ill-treated in prison. This happens in the night. When the Turks go home at night from the cafés they go into the prison. The prisoners are sent for, especially the well-known men, and made to run around on the wet floor until their feet become sodden. Then they have to lie on their backs, with men sitting on their chests, while others flog their sodden feet until they are swollen and bleeding. They rip out their fingernails and the hairs from their beards one by one. They put their hands and heads in a sort of pinching machine until bones crack and break. One evening the Kaimakam came with other officers from the café, stopped at the prison, and demanded our two professors Lulejian and Budjikanian. The Kaimakam ordered them to tell where the Americans were hiding weapons. They answered that they had already said that the Americans had no weapons, and they could tell nothing else. Then the Kaimakam told them, "Your wife is here. If you do not answer, she will be brought in and stripped before everyone's eyes." The professor answered, "I have told you everything. If I say anything else I will be lying, and I cannot lie. What you do is your responsibility." Then the Kaimakam said, "All of you who love your country and religion, flog these men!" He himself was the first to flog them. When they had had their pleasure from this work, they dragged these two poor, half-conscious men into the lavatory, where they lay until next day, unable to move.

Now young people of 18 are also being called-up and the young men from the Tadaeus School have been called-up as well. They have promised that they will be Jesus' witnesses wherever they are sent. Badveli Yeghoian said to them, "You must keep in mind that death, sickness, and torture lie ahead. Others have to go through this, and it may be God's will that you should also suffer, but God can give His children power to cherish hope until the end and not deny Him."

We hear many Armenians say, "We do not want revenge upon the Turks, even if they torture us. We pray for them that they may receive the Gospel of Salvation. We cannot expect anything else from people who have guidance from the Koran, but we cannot forget that all this has come because Christian powers have plunged into a war of covetousness. We cannot forget the German Emperor's words to the Sultan, "I shall be the defender of the Turkish faith and the Turkish kingdom." These are the words that have made the wrath of God overflow and allowed all this to happen. The world has not forgotten the visit of Wilhelm II to Constantinople in 1908, and his declaration that only the Sultan could bring his rebellious subjects to peace (referring to the Armenian massacre).

5 June. In the last few days many Turkish officials' families have come from Moush and Bitlis. They have fled before the Russian advance.

On April 25th I became ill with typhus and some days later lost consciousness. I myself do not remember very much from that time, only that when I was conscious again I felt so terribly tired that it was almost painful. I could not move my hands or lift my head from the pillow. The nurse had to turn and move me. Karen-Marie was extremely good to me, staying beside me early and late. She did everything she possibly could for me. It is strange to think that I was so close to death that when they took the flowers for Mrs. Barnum's funeral, they left half of them, because they thought they would be using them for my funeral the next day or very soon. But it was not my hour appointed by God, and in His mercy He gave me more time in which to serve Him. On May 5th and 6th I was still very weak but was allowed to see a few friends. That day Baron Samuel from Husenik came and said that he had burned all the sermons he had written over the last six years and all his other books, not because there was anything illegal in them, but because should they search his house and find these written papers they would put him in prison. Years might pass before they could examine all these papers, during which he would have to wait. He said all this with tears running down his cheeks. Poor people. He also said that the day before one of our professors, Nahigian, an old man who lives in Husenik, was returned from prison. He was so severely flogged that his whole body and head were blue and swollen. He was unconscious and did not know his wife and children. All these men are innocent, have done nothing at all, but in this country lawlessness and injustice rage, and the Christians have to pay.

The young Reverend Kevork, who is imprisoned in Kessrik, has sent a piece of paper to his friends, asking them to send a message to the prison every day to ask if he is alive. He knows very well that it is only a question of time before he is killed as well.

Today Mr. Riggs returned from Diarbekir and brought Mrs. Smith and little Arthur with him. Dr. Smith could not come as there has been a massacre in the surrounding villages and wounded Armenians have fled to Diarbekir. He has taken them in and treated them, so he has stayed alone. As Mrs. Smith and Mr. Riggs came outside the town, some soldiers came and searched their belongings. They found some letters with Mrs. Smith, which they took. Among these was a telegraph code, which the missionaries had agreed to use if any disturbance arose. If they discover what this is, it will probably have unpleasant consequences.

6 June. Yesterday the government found some buried bombs. It is thought that their whereabouts was disclosed by someone undergoing torture. A chemist, Eduard Effendi, has been arrested as the originator, and many others have also been arrested. It is thought that this will have very serious consequences for the Armenians in the district. It is sad that so many innocent must suffer on account of the thoughtlessness of the revolutionaries. Unfortunately there are quite a lot of the latter, especially among the young men. Today a proclamation from the Vali was read in the church, asking the Protestants to help to persuade people to disclose what they have of arms and ammunition.

All houses, without exception, will be searched. If weapons are found, whether or not they belong to the house-owner, the latter will be flogged and the house burned. The same will happen if refugees and revolutionaries are discovered hidden. The latter will be hanged without trial and their houses burned.

7 June. Early this morning, before the missionaries had arisen, the Garden was surrounded by soldiers and the houses searched. There were nine soldiers and a general. They searched everything, looking in the most incredible places. They took away letters and magazines. They were especially bad to Mrs. Smith because of the code that had been found in her possession. They cut the telephone wires, giving as the reason that it was unnecessary to talk so much together. Well—it was not very comfortable. Now the Armenians became very frightened. If they would do this to the American missionaries, they could expect anything, so in the hospital they got

busy burning books, magazines, and pictures, because if the soldiers came there and found written things, would the owners be put in prison? Miss Campbell and two young girls locked themselves into the operating theatre and burned papers the whole day.

Now they have surrounded Kessrik and Husenik and this time it is worse, because they are locking up the men in the church while they search the houses, torturing children and raping women. The conditions are intolerable. When we talk with our Armenian friends, we do not know if it will be the last time we shall see them.

They could be in prison before evening.

Now they are also taking young men in the streets and putting them in prison.

People come together to hold prayer-meetings, and many shout, "Lord, we have sinned. Punish us! Oh, but with moderation. Let us not be completely destroyed."

[8] June. Conditions are getting worse and worse, even though we had thought they could not get darker. The villages are surrounded, the men imprisoned, the women ill-treated. They expect that the soldiers will come and search again, and they are being watched by the police and the Kaimakam, who will not tolerate our having anything to do with Armenians. I was worried about my book, in which I have written not a little about conditions in Turkey, and therefore knew that it would be dangerous if it fell into Turkish hands. I was reluctant to burn it, as everything would be lost. I did not dare hide it, as they look in the most incredible places. Yes, they pull down walls and dig up floors. Then I asked the Consul if he would hide it for me. He promised that he would, so I sent it down to him.

9 June. Badveli Vartan and Professor Vorperian were taken to the prison and forced to watch the torture of prisoners, most of whom are their friends. They were told that if they did not tell where the bombs were hidden they would be treated in the same way. They were allowed to go home. The professor lost his senses and ran up and down the street dressed only in his nightshirt. We got him down to the hospital, where he stayed until he was sent out and killed on the way.

10 June. Today I was driven from Mezreh up to the missionary Garden. I was carried to the wagon by two men. I cannot walk yet. With two helping me I can take five or six steps, but I have no strength in my back or legs. Karen-Marie and Miss Campbell went up with me. We also had a soldier with us. It was rather uncomfortable to drive through the market. All the Armenian shops were closed, and we did not see one Christian. The town was surrounded by soldiers. The people sat hidden in their houses. No one dared to show themselves, certain now that a massacre would begin, and the women be raped. In the evening, about 9 o'clock, while we were preparing to retire for the night, we heard shouting in Turkish outside my windows. I had a light in my room and I was afraid that they had seen Lucia, my nurse, whom I had brought with me to take care of me. We soon discovered it was a crowd of armed

soldiers who now began hammering on the door, which I thought would break. They shouted as loudly as they could, "Armenians—come out." I was alone in the house with some young Armenian girls. I was not yet able to sit up in bed, or walk, so I was not much help. Miss Harley who also lived in the house was down in the Garden and when she came back and saw these men she went into the other house for the time being. Then our gardener came. He is Turkish, and he talked to them, but they grew noisier, and he began to shout with them. "Open the door." Lucia found courage to go to the window and ask what they wanted. They answered, "Two young Armenian men came running. You took them in. Open the door." She answered, "No young Armenian men have been here, and none have passed by. We will not open the door until you bring one of the men from the other house." In the meantime Mr. Riggs arrived. He started to talk to them and got them over to the other house, where they stayed until midnight. They threatened Mr. Riggs several times and said, "Don't you see our weapons? We can do what we want with you." Mr. Riggs answered, "I am not afraid of you, or your weapons. There is a God above us. I trust in Him." At midnight they said they would go back to town to hear from the government what they should do. They went and did not come back. The night had also been very bad in Harpoot. The soldiers smashed in doors and entered houses, mistreated the people, and took whatever they wanted. Everybody was horror-stricken. No one dared to go out. They sat in their houses, without eating or drinking. If anyone knocked on the door they trembled with fear in case it was the soldiers. What does the prophet say, "I wish my head was a spring of tears. Then I would cry over my people's slaughter—my people slain." I cannot find words to describe the gnawing pain it is to see this people suffer so. See their fear. Hear them tell these terrible things in all their cruel reality. It seems that the depths have been reached. With devilish cunning and torture, they torment their miserable victims.

11 June. The city today is surrounded by soldiers, who are breaking into houses, looking for weapons, taking the men, putting them in prison, and torturing and beating the poor people. They let them run in water until the soles of their feet are sodden, put them on their back, one sitting on their chest, another holding their legs, while a third beats the prisoner's feet with a thick stick, until they are swollen and bleeding. They put hands and feet vices and torture them. In Kessrik they heated iron until it was glowing and made prisoners sit upon it. Who can save this unhappy people from this hell-fire? Only the Almighty God. Oh Lord, have mercy upon this people.

Forgive our many sins and listen in your mercy to the many cries that ascend to you day and night. Without you we have no helper. We surrender to you, Lord. If you want us to go through this suffering and distress, then we ask you to give us strength to endure and be faithful until the end. Yes, even in suffering to praise You, and magnify Your name, Your will, oh God, will be done with us, in us, and by us. Your Name to honour—Amen.

Many Turks in Harpoot say, mockingly, to the Armenians, "You say that your Jesus is the Son of God. If he is the Son of God why does He not save you out of our hands, those who believe in Him? No—our religion is the best." This is nearly more difficult to bear than the torture, and many whose faith is not well-rooted waver, begin to doubt, and then the strength to keep on is gone. Time after time we hear people say, "This time 20 years ago we had a massacre. It seemed to be terrible, but it was nothing compared to this. Then they ravaged for three days, and it was over, but this time it has gone on for months, and we cannot see an end to it."

In the afternoon around 5 o'clock some soldiers came and ordered both the Riggs brothers to come to the government building. Only Mr. Harry Riggs was there and he had to accompany them. Of course we were in terrible fear of what might happen. The soldiers were very rough on the way to town, with bayonets at the ready as they treat all prisoners. On the way they met the younger Mr. Riggs who was on his way to the Garden. He said, "If you do not return soon, I will come and see what has happened to you," but Mr. Riggs answered, "No, stay out in the Garden and take care of the women." Mr. Pierce, who has only been here for a year and does not speak Turkish, was sent down to Mezreh. We had no horses out in the Garden so he had to walk. Several times on his way he saw Turks, but he hid behind bushes so that he would not be discovered. He reached Mezreh and told the Consul what had happened. Miss Harley was also there. At noon she had gone with Mrs. Tenekedjian to see Mr. Ehmann as rumours were circulating that her husband, the dear old professor, was to be hanged that night. The Consul now brought back Mr. Pierce and Miss Harley. They were accompanied by the Consul's kavases. Mr. Riggs returned and our joy was indescribable as he told us that he had only been sent for to be informed that the government would give us four soldiers. While he was away we had imagined all the possibilities of what might happen. Our hearts were full of thanks and praise.

In the morning Mr. Riggs had been with the Vali. He had said he would not telegraph Diarbekir regarding Dr. Smith. We are very afraid for him. We knew it was serious since the Vali would not telegraph. We ourselves had telegraphed several times (reply paid), but there was no answer, which indicated that he was being treated as a prisoner.

How terribly difficult it is to watch all these fearful tormented people. They are all completely changed. So failed—they look like people who are suffering from starvation, and the expression on their faces is so tormented. Many say, "We cannot pray any longer," but Jesus has promised that the Last Days will be shortened, and if now is not the time for His coming, He will give His strength to endure. He will not put upon them heavier burdens than He will give them the strength to carry. Soon help must come. It is as if all hope is gone and despair has reached the deepest depths, but God the Lord is the same, yesterday, today and forever, and He who pitied the multitude when He walked the earth, must also pity this multitude of suffering people. His thoughts are higher than our thoughts, and the ways of the Lord are higher than our ways. Is it His will that the cup of pain is to be drained, and still more suffer death? Then we will say, "Lord—Thy will be done."

13 June. Mr. Ehmann, a Turk, and Badveli Vartan spoke today in the Gregorian Church about giving up weapons. Badveli Vartan's talk to the people and his prayer will not be forgotten. He stood like Moses and confessed his people's sins, asking for mercy and forgiveness.

The same night the prisoners were taken to Mezreh, more of them so ill-treated that they were unable to sit upon a donkey. It was said that they were only being transferred to another building, so they brought nothing with them.

15 June (Tuesday). The prisoners were sent away. Among them were a lot of our friends—teachers and professors—whom we know are absolutely innocent. They were sent away under the pretence that they were being exiled, but they had nothing at all with them, and they were not allowed to see their families or friends. They were sent away in the night in order that no one should see them. It was a hard blow for all of us. How much we longed to set them free, but our hands were tied. We can only pray for them, that they will remain faithful till the end.

17 June. Rumours were circulating that the prisoners who had been sent away on the 15th were to be returned. A committee had been appointed to examine them. The guilty would then be punished and the innocent set free. We were happy to hear this news, and we began to hope again, but it turned out not to be true. Then we heard that all these men had been taken up to the mountains and killed. At the same time all the young Armenian men who were soldiers were imprisoned in a large building in Mezreh for several days. They were given neither bread nor water, and they cried and shouted to the passers-by to give them just a drop of water. They stretched out their handkerchiefs from the windows in order that merciful people could dip them in water and give them back to them, but not even that was allowed, as the police who were patrolling did not allow people near the building. This big crowd of young men were then sent away—many of them had obtained degrees at our College—and we do not know exactly what has happened to them, but we fear that they have also been killed when they reached the mountains.

Today we had a telegram from Dr. Smith, saying that he had been ordered to leave Diarbekir and asking his wife to come as soon as possible. How delighted we were when we received this telegram. Mrs. Smith started packing at once, and Mr. Riggs went to the Vali and asked his permission to accompany her. But he said, "Definitely no!" No missionaries were allowed to accompany or follow her, and our hearts were heavy as we sent her on her way, together with the Consul's Turkish kavas, Mahmed, but we had no alternative. We knew that the way was dangerous, but we trusted her to the hands of almighty God, and great was our pleasure when the kavas returned and told us that they had arrived safely. He had seen Dr. Smith, who had been kept a prisoner in his house. They had been allowed to take some clothes with them for the journey, and had set forth southwards accompanied by the government soldiers.

They are still arresting people—all the better-off men are now in prison. Each day brings something worse than the day before. Never will it be possible for people to imagine such evil as rages in this country in these times. It is as if Satan were let loose in the Turkish people, and it seems impossible that even the Devil could endure to watch all this suffering. How can any human being devise such horrible things? Never did I think I would witness such terrible anguish, weeping, dread and misery. A whole Christian people's extermination in the most horrifying and devilish way.

26 June. It was proclaimed from all mosques today that all Armenians are to be sent into exile. They are to be given four days in which to dispose of all their possessions, and be ready for the journey to an unknown destination for an indefinite period. It is said that they will be sent down to the desert south of Ourfa. If this is true, then it is obvious that the whole meaning behind this movement of the Armenian people is their extermination. The Consul went to the Vali and asked if one of the missionaries would be allowed to accompany the Armenians from Harpoot, but the Vali answered that it was impossible. The Consul asked what would become of the thousands of people on the journey with sick people to care for, also the thousands of children, the old, and the weak? The Vali answered, "Doctors will travel with them." The Consul also reminded the Vali of the great number of prisoners who had been sent away under the pretence of exile, but who had been killed as soon as they reached the mountains. The Vali answered that they had been attacked by Kurds, but promised that the people being sent away now would be well-guarded. There was nothing else for us to do but to tell all this to the people to comfort them, but how difficult it will be to send them off, helpless, in the charge of the Turks, when we have so much proof of how they will ill-treat them. Oh, if only we could go with them. It would be such a comfort to them, and better for us, even to suffer torment and death with them, than to remain here and let them go alone.

27 June (Sunday). We held a meeting where we discussed how we could help best. We bought a quantity of linen and set the young girls in the College to work at sewing a sort of head covering bonnet and rucksack, and these were distributed. Mr. Riggs himself went to our bakery and started with some of the men to bake a kind of bread, which could be dried and kept for a long time. Miss Harley, Mr. Pierce, and Miss Riggs were to receive kitchen utensils and foodstuffs, which the people might wish us to store or sell for them, and Mr. Riggs was to take in money that people might wish to send to America through us. All this was decided and on Monday June 28th, the different people began their work. A lot of things were brought to us the first morning, but the government could not bear to let us do even that for our friends. The Kaimakam sent soldiers here to stop everybody who came to us and set

guards at all our doors, so no Armenian could contact us. Mr. Riggs went to the Vali in the afternoon. He said we could receive money and kitchen utensils, so we started again next morning. We were stopped immediately by the soldiers sent by the Kaimakam. Now Mr. Riggs went to him and said, "We have got permission from the Vali." The Kaimakam answered that he had received no message, and therefore could not permit it. So the week was spent going back and forward between the Vali and the Kaimakam. The latter's answer was always the same, that he had received no message from the Vali, and could therefore not allow us to have anything to do with the Armenians.

It became obvious that it would be impossible to send 60,000 people away inside four days. They began in Mezreh and some days afterwards in Harpoot. The town was surrounded by soldiers. First they took the part of Harpoot that lay on the other side of the castle. We did not know so many people there.

29 June. Mr. Riggs and Mr. Ehmann went to the Vali, who promised them that old people and women without husbands would be allowed to remain. We were very pleased and thankful because this would mean that a good number would be able to stay. Then we tried, as best as we could, to help these many unhappy people. It was terrible to see them—so thin and pale, and trembling with fear, not able to think or work.

6 July (Sunday). Terrible things happened today in Harpoot. Soldiers surrounded the town trying to capture all men and boys over 13 years. Two hundred were taken and sent to Mezreh where they were joined by prisoners already there, and all were taken to Khankeoy. There were 800 in all and they were then killed by their guards. Among the prisoners was our chemist Melcon Effendi. He returned to relate the following:

They came to the dispensary and said to him that if he would become a Mohammedan he would be allowed to stay free, but he told them he could not deny his Saviour, so they took him to the prison and next day sent him to Mezreh, from where, with the 800 others, he was sent away early in the morning before the town was awake. They were all bound together. When they had reached the other side of Khankeoy they were led off the road and over the mountain to a valley. Here they were told to sit down and rest. As soon as they left the road, they all realized they were going to be killed. Just before evening an order was given to the soldiers to shoot—and this was followed by a hail of bullets. But they ran out of ammunition before everyone was killed, so they began slashing with the small axes they carry in their belts, and with bayonets. Suddenly Baron Melcon felt that the rope which bound him was loose, so he jumped up and ran with about 30 others. Most of them were overtaken and shot down. Baron Melcon ran on and on—he did not know where. In the middle of the night he saw some lights and ran in their direction. On the road he saw a Turkish man and asked him what the lights were. The man answered, "Don't you know? It is Mezreh." When he heard the word "Mezreh" he ran as hard as he could and reached our hospital after midnight—completely exhausted and with swollen and bleeding feet. He also appeared quite distracted, and no wonder, after all he had seen. He was hidden here by us, until he could be sent to a more safe place.

Now we have news of the first group of our friends who were sent away, without permission to say goodbye to relatives and friends. A woman from Kayloo met them on the way. They were chained together, four by four, the sick being bound to and dragged by the others. Some ox-carts came behind in which the most ill were seated. Think what this means. After having been ill-treated and tortured, some of them being hung head downwards, now to be sent off on such a journey. They shouted to passers-by, "Tell them at home to send money." The government had told them they were being sent into exile. What sorrow there was, all around in the many homes, when the news arrived. Then the dreaded question was asked, "Was my brother/ husband/father among them?" Long were they held in gnawing uncertainty, because when they went to the prison to ask if their dear ones were still there, these unhappy women and children were driven away by the soldiers with bayonets who shouted taunts after them. Relatives now started collecting money and clothes, as the government had promised that these would reach the right hands. But the government took it all and sent it no further. The prisoners were killed. Many were thrown down over the cliffs near Goljuk. Is this not the depths of evil and cruelty?

It is announced at the mosques that everyone is to open their shops—there is nothing wrong. In order not to raise suspicion, these poor people have to go down to the market and open their shops. Then the soldiers come, take them, and put them in prison. Our hearts are broken to see all this distress. To see the innocent being tortured to death without being able to do anything for them. Then a strange thing happened. The prisoners, who had not been sent away, and amongst whom were known revolutionaries and others one knew had been found carrying weapons, had their names read out and their wives and children were given permission to see them before they were to be sent away the next night. They also had permission to bring food, clothes, and money for them to the government.

The Doctor told us about a young man in the hospital who had a friend among the Turks and had been advised by him to take flight. He said, "In the course of 14 days your annihilation will be decided upon. Your best plan is to escape to the mountains to the Kurds. They will want money—a lot of it—and it will also be very dangerous, as the soldiers are everywhere and are always on watch, and it will not be easy to pass the open spaces. To go would give you a slight possibility of escape, but to stay would mean you are doomed." The situation is very serious. One Turkish party in Constantinople, which has supporters here, has thought out a big system for blackmail. Some men, who are still free to move about, have had orders to collect a large sum of money. It is to be done in the strictest secrecy, and anyone who betrays one single word to a Turk of the other party will be hanged. They are demanding large sums of money—100 liras from one of our doctors—500 from a single man, and 1,000 from a third person. Anyone who cannot pay gets ready to escape.

Our dear beloved Dr. Michael is now also imprisoned. It does seem to be the end, because he has always been a friend to everyone, being looked up to and respected by all—even the top officials. Now that he has been taken, I cannot believe there is hope for anyone. Together with Dr. Michael, 18 others were also imprisoned.

The Doctor came up with a message from the Consul to all the missionaries to come down to the protection of the Consulate, because in the last few days there have been strong rumours of a massacre. There are patrols in the streets, spying on everything.

The missionaries discussed the situation together, but we were all in agreement that we should remain at our posts. If we left, and went down to the Consulate, the Armenians would be out of their minds with fear. So we stay—in the faith that the Lord will preserve us—if it is His will. The soldiers are now going from house to house making note of the number of people, and telling them when they are to be ready to leave on exile, in about four or five days. Everybody must go, rich, young, and old, crippled and sick. No one believes they will reach safety, in spite of all the government's promises. Even if they do reach their destination, what do they have in front of them? A desert—no houses, no work, no place where they can buy even the necessities. When we talk with them they say, "We have only death, swords, fire, hunger, and thirst before us. Most of us will die on the road, our women will be abducted, our men killed." A telegram came saying all hospital workers would be free and not sent away. So that means our dear friend Baron Roupen would be free, because he has been our buyer for the last three years. We still hope that we shall receive a telegram saying that all in German and American service shall be free. We now begin to hope for more good news. As soon as we see one tiny little ray of light, we expect much more, but our experience has been that one piece of good news is followed by 10 pieces of bad.

Today news came that all men and boys over nine years old have been slaughtered in Itchme. On Saturday evening they were collected together in the mosque, and on Sunday morning they were brought out to the mountains by Kurds and gendarmes. When the latter returned they openly washed their blood-stained clothes in the big spring in Itchme.

From Maden came news that all the young men there, who had been sent away from the Red Konak to Aleppo on June 10th, had been killed. They had been set to work for two days—of course to let them think all was peaceful and there was no danger. After that they were all bound and killed. This was the good news the Vali had promised the poor weeping and unhappy mothers, when they came to him pleading for mercy for their dear sons, for whom they were in fear and dread. This is more than cruelty.

As you know, we had a telegram yesterday saying that the hospital workers would be free. Now, today, the Vali says he has received no such order, and he can only give permission to those men who are serving as soldiers to stay. Baron Roupen, who yesterday was full of thanks and praise because they could stay, will now have to leave early tomorrow morning.

Some gendarmes are going around fastening a little notice to the door of each house belonging to those who have permission to remain. The old, blind women (not men), widows who have only daughters, and pregnant women, if they have sent in a petition to the government, may remain. How many tears are shed, how much running backwards and forward, and how many days people must wait in front of the government building, only to be driven away by the gendarmes, before they succeed in getting this exemption, which is given only to the very few. Everyone else was told, "You must be finished tonight. If not, you will be bound and dragged away."

Mrs. Ehmann has gone to the Vali's wife to ask for a respite for some sick people, but her answer was, "Where Allah has decreed they are to go on Saturday, it cannot be changed." She also said, "Allah has decreed that this year blood shall flow instead of water, so there is nothing to be done." Still the questions come, "What shall we do? We have no shoes, and they cannot be bought." "We have no animals, and no money, either." "What shall we do with our sick and old?" Everywhere there were questions incapable of being answered. Everybody says, "We know we are going to meet death. Oh, if only they would kill us here in our houses. Is it a sin to take poison?" Time after time the Turks say, "It is not us. It is all being done on the orders of Kaiser Wilhelm." We do not think that the Germans have the slightest idea of how things really are or of these cruelties that are taking place. Surely the Turks have told lies about the rebellious Armenians, and the truth is that there is not a single one who has offered any resistance. Without a murmur they have done nothing against injustice, paid what was demanded, reduced themselves to poverty to meet the hair raising black-mailing, and now they go to meet death as lambs go to the slaughter.

8 July. All the old men who had been permitted to stay because of their age were taken and bound together. It was a cruel, sad sight to see these old and sick, crippled and blind men standing bound outside our windows until they were led to Mezreh at noon. When they came down to Dancarpu the soldiers said, "Give your money to us, so that we can take care of it, because when we reach Mezreh, it will be taken from you." So the plundering had already started, only five minutes away from the town. In the crowd was our dear old friend Hagob Agha Benneian, an old man of at least 80 years. He was so weak he could hardly walk, and when the soldiers came to

him, he said, "Effendi—I cannot walk, I cannot walk." As they beat him with a stick they cried, "Heyde, heyde." That is how they talk to a dog in this country. So this dear old man of God must also leave his home and dear ones and go out and suffer death at the hands of these cruel violent men. The daughters and his old wife were out of their minds with sorrow. They neither ate nor drank but sat crying and wailing in their great distress. They told how, night and day, he had prayed and cried to the Lord to spare him physical suffering and let him die at home. But he always ended by saying, "Oh Lord, keep me faithful to the end, whatever happens to me." In another house the soldiers entered lay another old man, very ill with a high fever, and they whipped him until he got up and walked with them—to be bound, also, and sent away.

There is now distress and poverty without limit. The Turks have openly declared that the remaining women and girls must become Mohammedans—that is intermarry with them. The boys shall also become Turks and be circumcised. A boy came to the hospital who had been operated on violently in this way by the Turks using a pocket knife. They left him lying in a cornfield after they had beaten him, from where he escaped and came to the hospital. He had very bad inflammation which was spreading down the thigh. And the poor young girls—what terrible fate awaits them in a harem. The Kurds also take whatever girls they want.

A crowd of exiles has arrived from Erzeroum. They had suffered indescribably on the way from torture, distress, and danger. Many of the men were killed. The women and girls were ravished by soldiers. Many of them are being taken to Turkish and Kurdish homes. They were told they would be going to Harpoot and when, after weeks and months of suffering and danger they reached here, the men and boys who had survived were taken from them and put into prison. This means they will be killed. The women are being kept here for some days and Turkish men come and choose the prettiest women and girls, who are taken home to their harems. The sick who cannot walk are being taken out to the cemetery and left lying there until they die. The rest are being sent on further.

Everybody says that although they had trouble and great danger on the way, the most terrible suffering started when they came to Mezreh vilayet. Now the soldiers are worse than animals. All the men they can lay their hands on are being literally slaughtered, the women ravished and beaten with thick sticks.

10 July. Today the town crier went around with the proclamation that everyone must leave. Not one single sparrow must be left. We are afraid that we also will not be allowed to stay, and when they have sent all the Armenians away, then our turn will come. There is a rumour that we shall be put into a house, and kept there like prisoners, because they do not want anyone to leave the country and tell of all the terrible things they have done. If this is true, we would much prefer to leave rather

than be held like prisoners in a house for months, or years, and not allowed to do any work. That would be very difficult. But we won't worry. We will only try to use the moment, and each day, in the best possible way.

Now we have heard that anyone becoming a Mohammedan will be allowed to remain here in peace, and they come one after the other, to ask for our advice. Of course, we cannot advise anyone to let their faith down. They say, "We will only change for a time, until the danger is over, then we will come back to our faith. The Lord knows our hearts, and will look and see that in them we have not denied Him," but we can only repeat to them Jesus' own words, "Those who deny me before men, I will also deny them before my Heavenly Father," and bring the picture of Judas before them, he who did not repent. But of course it is a great temptation when they can see the exiled walking around—ragged, sick, forsaken, and dying. They lie outside our houses and die. They can lie for several days in the streets after they die and before the government buries them. Several lay dead outside our houses, and we had to go ourselves, dig the grave, and bury them. We walk around the houses, talking to the people, encouraging them to be faithful to the Lord and not deny Him. It is suffering worse than ever to hear one and another deciding to send in a petition to become Mohammedan.

It has been a great pleasure to us that none of our Protestant congregation has been amongst those who have decided to embrace Mohammedanism.

14 July. One hundred and fifty families from Vari Tagh left Harpoot today. They have taken their donkeys and cows with them. It was terrible to see them leave, knowing that suffering, distress, and death awaits them. The Turks said the other day, "You had better go up to the mountains by yourselves, so that we don't have to carry your corpses away."

18 July. Early on Sunday morning, before it was light, soldiers went from house to house banging on the doors, driving the people out with the greatest brutality. Many did not even have time to take the few things they had collected for the journey out of their houses before the soldiers had locked the doors and put the keys in their pockets. There were old, sick men and women, who were unable to sit by themselves upon a donkey. The many hundreds of children, who did not know what it was all about, walked around and played, and ate leblebi with which the mothers had filled their small pockets. One mother had at the last minute gave away her little 12 year old girl to a Turk, who now dragged her away, screaming and crying. The sound was heart-rending. She shouted as loudly as she could, "Mayrig, mayrig" ["mummy, mummy"], while the man dragged her away so that she could not see her mother any more. People fainted from exhaustion and fear, but no mercy was to be found. The whip and profanities surrounded these poor people. In this crowd were all our good friends—all the Protestant congregation—and they gathered around us in fear, all with the same question, "What will become of us? Where are we going?" Never

before, I believe, had there been so much crying as on that day. We knew only too well what would happen. The soldiers, who had been set on guard at our doors, said time after time to us, "Why do you give money and food to these people? They are only going out to the mountains to be killed." We gave money to each person in a family, and at this time handed out about 700 liras. In the crowd were Anna and Zaroohi Benneian, their eldest sister, who has been very ill for a long time and was still so weak that she could scarcely sit upon a donkey, and their mother, who was also completely exhausted. The two young girls looked like skeletons. Think what it would mean to leave their beautiful home and go out on the road to suffer infamous cruelty at the hands of these crude Turks. A few of them tried to be strong under the sorrow and suffering—they said goodbye for the last time on this earth, knowing that in a short time they would be allowed to enter the Joy of Heaven. To make things harder, they [the authorities] always choose Sunday for their most cruel work, because they know that the Christians always keep this day especially quiet and holy. We all think that our turn will come soon, and we must be prepared to die at any time.

We heard today that one of our best friends, Baron Setrak Sulumian, is dead. He tried to escape to the Moush area, where it was said the Russians had reached. But he only got as far as Haboosi, six hours away from Mezreh, where he encountered some gendarmes who shot him down.

Everyone has now been sent away from Harpoot, except for those who have gone into hiding, or paid large sums of money, or become Mohammedans. Syrians and Greeks have not yet been sent away. As soon as the people had left the town, soldiers came and took everything out of the houses and then sealed the doors. Before leaving, the people could bring their domestic goods and foodstuffs to the market for auction, but they got scarcely any money for what they had. One rich family who brought furniture worth 300 liras to the auction received only 10 liras. If anybody said, "We cannot sell at that price considering what it cost us," then the Turks would answer, "It does not matter—we will take it for nothing." As soon as it was announced that the people had to leave, the Turks came and walked in and out of the houses, taking whatever they wanted—machines, organs and pianos, carpets and other valuable things, together with clothes. They began to enjoy these things immediately—not even waiting until their unhappy victims were gone. Dressing themselves in the Armenians' silk clothes, they sat and hammered on the organs and pianos, on which they had not the slightest idea how to play. How it pained us to see the Turks and their women walking around shamelessly in their stolen goods.

21 July. There is a rumour that the Kaimakam has lost his position. We hope so much that it is true, because it seems to us that it would be impossible to have anyone worse.

22 July. Except for those Armenians who had handed over their daughters to the Turks, and five families selected by the government to remain because of their trades—namely, a shoemaker, a plumber, a watchmaker, a silversmith, and a bookbinder—all the others still remaining, for one reason or another, were driven out of their houses and sat from morning till evening by the entrance to Harpoot, in the burning heat of the sun, waiting to be driven out on the road to die.

The Turks are busy today—moving into the Armenians' houses which are mostly better than the Turkish ones. It is a sad sight to come into town now. All the area where the College is situated was originally Armenian, and the street in which we live was especially Protestant. Now all these houses have been taken by officials and officers. They have a soldier outside each house as a guard. They walk in and out as though the houses had always been theirs. How the town is changed. We do not see one single Armenian, only Turks and soldiers. The streets, which used to be well-kept, now already look like dung hills. We cannot walk from the Garden to the town without being sickened by the stench. For six months we have had 1,500 soldiers in our building. They are all outdoor people, and even if we had built a dozen lavatories, they would still prefer to go out on the mountains. The air is contaminated. Out by the spring they have a slaughter-house and a baking kitchen. Ten sheep and some cows are slaughtered daily, and the waste is thrown down the mountain. All the ravens and dogs are being so well fed this year that they cannot clear it all. So it lies around rotting and poisoning the air.

Today I have taken in a little child, Beatrice Dingilian, 14 months old. Her father, who was our secretary, was taken and brought to the prison in Mezreh. He was a man of serious beliefs. Down there, they very soon discovered that he was one to be trusted, so they put a band around his arm, and put him in charge of receiving and distributing the prisoners' food. His wife, though weak, walked every day to Mezreh to bring him food. She is also a splendid, faithful human being. They are some of the few, from whom we never hear complaints. They show no bitterness, or any wish that their enemies be harmed. Always they say, "We must pray for them, that their eyes be opened, and they see their sin and repent." He was also taken away, but we were allowed to see how God can strengthen His children's hearts, when they are in danger and suffering. When Mr. Riggs saw him for the last time, he said, "I am not afraid. I am ready to die. I have surrendered myself into God's hands. They can do what they want with me. They cannot separate me from God." Then he went out with a group of prisoners and was killed. It is well that there are some Christians who even under suffering and torture are faithful to their God and do not turn against Him. Maybe there are many more than we know of. He was not a brave man. I shall never forget a Sunday last winter. They had collected soldiers together and he had been down in Mezreh many days to pay his ransom. That day he had succeeded and now he was free. He was not strong. He was imprisoned without any reason for 14 months when he was young, and his health had suffered since then. Now he was at home. I came into the room, and there he sat with his two little boys—seven and four years old—on his knees, and his little seven months old daughter in the cot beside him. His face was alight with joy, and with tears in his eyes he said, "I would give everything I have, with pleasure, if I could be allowed to stay with my children." If he had to go as a soldier, I thought, would he die after a short time? He could not endure all the hardship on the road. He was then allowed to stay a little while with his children. One day he put a handkerchief over his head, under his fez, because of the strong sun. They struck him in the face and said to him, "Now you are a soldier and not a master, so take that handkerchief from your head." They spat upon him, amongst other things, but he was like a Stephen and said, "They know not what they do." Now he is Home together with the great crowd of martyrs, who are dressed in white raiment and sing hymns of thanksgiving with all tears wiped away. That is our great comfort when we think of them.

There are some Armenians who are very bitter towards the Americans, saying that out of fear for their own lives, they have done nothing to save Armenians. This is a great untruth, because day and night, they have all thought of and tried everything, walked from the Vali to the Kaimakam daily, sent telegrams every day to Constantinople—but all in vain. Guards were posted at all doors—even at the end on the roofs—so that the Armenians there would not be able to come and talk with us. Yes, there were even days when the soldiers forbade the missionaries to go in or out of their own houses. One day Miss Riggs wished to come out and visit some Armenians, but the soldier who stood by the door said he would not allow her to go. She answered, "It is wrong, we have permission, we live here. They are our houses," and she went through the door, but the soldier took his gun and held it against her. He was ready to fire if she had moved. In the end we could not go in or out, except through the stables. It was impossible under such strict watch, surrounded by 1,500 soldiers, to take in Armenians. The Germans have been able to help more because they are their allies in the war and therefore they have respect for them, but they have not been able to help many. One can understand very well that in their great distress the Armenians think we could have done more for them.

Conditions now are completely different from what they were during the massacre of 20 years ago. What could be done then is impossible now. The Turks know very well about the war raging in Europe, and that the Christian nations are too busy to take care of Armenians, so they take advantage of the times to destroy their "enemies"—not understanding that they are their friends.

23 July. The Turks continue in their strong efforts to make the women marry them. They tell them, "If you are sent away, you will be attacked on the road by the Kurds, who will rob you of everything. You will lose your children, and you will be either captured or killed yourselves. For your children's sake—surrender here." With all this talk there is many a mother who cannot resist. The missionaries in Mezreh and we

here in Harpoot go from morning till evening from house to house to talk with those remaining, whom we have heard are thinking of becoming Mohammedans, to persuade them to remain faithful to Jesus.

A great number of women and children from the villages are being held prisoner in the Red House in Mezreh where the men were imprisoned earlier.

The Consul and Mr. Riggs again went to the Vali and asked permission to open a Children's Home but, as earlier, he answered that it was impossible to give permission. They would open a Children's Home themselves and take care of the orphans. In Mezreh they have opened several such homes, where many children have been taken in, but because of lack of care and food, the poor little souls die like flies.

Dr. Atkinson had a visit from [unclear], the Head Doctor at the Red Crescent who said that in the last two weeks 1½ million people have been killed. The Turks, when they talk about the Germans' victory over the Russians, boast of their own achievements and say, "What of it? We kill thousands daily without losing one."

24 July. The crier has shouted today from the mosques and around the streets that any Turk who hides an Armenian will be hanged and his house burned. All houses from the poorest to the richest—even the Vali's—are to be searched.

Yesterday Vartabedian's beautiful 12 year-old daughter Rebecca came to the hospital. She had been captured by a Turk, who came with her to demand back from the Doctor all that her father had given him. How terrible it is to think of the poor young girl with this crude man, who has killed her father, and whom she must accompany back and live with in her parents' beautiful building. Today we had a little hope that a pardon would come for the few remaining Armenians, because of Independence Day. However, up to this evening, we have heard nothing, so we think this will be another disappointment.

25 July (Sunday). Mr. Riggs preached at our Service from Rev. 2, "Be thou faithful unto death, and I will give thee a crown of life." Faithful in work, faithful in suffering, faithful to Jesus. We cannot help thinking about how long we will be allowed to live, but it is our prayer that to the last we will be faithful to Jesus, and that we must help our Christian brothers and sisters about us.

After the meeting we discussed whether we missionaries should send telegrams to the different Ambassadors to seek permission for the few remaining [Armenians] to stay, but we realized it would be hopeless.

28 July. Today the rest of the Armenians in Harpoot are to be sent away. We went into town and stayed there until noon, but nothing happened until late afternoon. They took everyone they could capture. Our buyer's wife had gone to the market to buy bread, because there was nothing in the house, and as she was an older woman and not pretty, we had thought there was not much danger. She had her little boy with her, but she was also taken by the soldiers and brought to the government

building, where there was a big crowd of Armenians collected. While she was there she heard and saw many things. A young woman stood with her dying child in her arms. An old Turkish man came to her and asked her to go with him and marry him. She answered, "How can you ask me? Don't you see my dying child?—and you are an old man," but he still continued. Our buyer's wife did not see the outcome because her little boy ran home and related that his mother had been taken and Mr. Riggs immediately went to the government building and got her freed after a long wait. The officials had not yet risen, though it was nearly noon. At last Mr. Riggs was called by one official, who received him sitting up in bed. After Mr. Riggs explained that the buyer's wife belonged to our Mission and had been taken by the soldiers, he got permission to take her home.

Today an answer came to a telegram that had been sent to the German Ambassador about permission for all the crippled and the blind to remain. It stated that the Ambassador could not do anything further, as, according to the law, these people should not be sent away. The telegram had been delayed here for 12 days, while the government hurried away as many as possible of these poor people. This shows that, in Constantinople, they do not know what is going on here. They probably think that it is not so bad to send people into exile, as they are normally safely accompanied and in comfort. They usually say, "Take what you want of carts, animals and clothes, we will send soldiers with you to protect you." It sounds good, but the truth is that the soldiers only go with them to kill the men and the old women, and rob and ravish the young women. Our vilayet is a slaughter house. If people from other parts of the country arrive here they are killed. Some escape and come here to us by a miracle of God.

29 July. Last night about 100 Armenians were sent away from Harpoot, but they reached no further than the spring, two hours walk from the town. Here the soldiers started shooting. A 16 year old boy escaped. He had seen his mother, father, and brother killed. He himself had seven bullet wounds and several bayonet wounds in the back and head. He came to the hospital, where we dressed his wounds and gave him clean clothes.

Today we had our meeting. Mrs. Atkinson told us about her visit to the prison, where she saw quite a lot of Armenians who were very depressed. Dr. Nishan said, "We can't pray any more. Could you not send a minister here to talk and pray with the many Armenians?" There are still about 100 prisoners there. A coil of rope lay in the passage. Dr. Nishan pointed to it and said, "That is what will happen to us."

30 July. It is said that all houses will be searched, including ours, and all Armenians sent away.

31 July. The Vali has left for Dersim. It is said to suppress an uprising among the Kurds, but nobody knows the real reason. Even if he is a very cruel man and is to blame for a lot of the horrible things which have happened here, everybody would

prefer that he remained here at his post, as no one knows or can guess what might happen when he is away. Our chemist's shop at the Shuga has been closed by the government and this will harm our hospital very much.

A village, which earlier was mostly Armenian, was set on fire this morning. Mr. Riggs came back from Mezreh last night. There he was told that some exiled Armenians had hidden themselves in the mountains and returned afterwards to hide in a house that had been sealed by the government. The government sent some soldiers after them, but the Armenians started shooting, killing one soldier and wounding two. These two came back to the hospital. As the soldiers saw it was dangerous to try to enter the house they set it on fire and the consequence was that half the village was completely burned together with all the people hiding there.

1 August. Today a telegram came from Mr. Knapp saying he had left Bitlis and asking our advice about what route he should take to leave the country. It was very difficult to advise him in these unsettled times, but after much discussion, it was decided to advise him to go southwards, and not come here, as this Vilayet is the most unsettled. We also heard that Miss Graffam from Sivas had left there, taking the children from the Children's Home into exile, and the missionaries had received a telegram from her from Kangal near Malatia. Since then they have heard nothing and we have not heard anything from her either. So we are very anxious.

4 August. Last night part of the prison in Mezreh burned down, and 32 men there were killed. A Turk has said the following about it, "Some soldiers came to the prison to bring the Armenian prisoners out, but these men closed the door and would not let the soldiers in. So they sent a message to the Commandant who ordered them to pour petroleum and set the place on fire. They did so, and when the Armenians inside the burning building discovered this, they opened the door and tried to escape, but the soldiers standing outside shot them down. Amongst those who were shot were Dr. Nishan and my dear boy Toros. It was a heavy blow for me when I heard he was among them. I had not seen him since I had been taken ill in April. At that time he was still not very strong after his severe illness of typhus. All the time I had hoped he would be saved one way or another. All the prison guards liked him very much. I think he is Home with Jesus, along with all the many other martyrs, but I am terribly sorry for his poor mother, who has been allowed to stay in the Doctor's house so far.

Today the Consul received a telegram from Ourfa asking how the missionaries were. We were also told of Miss Ely's death, and that Miss Shane is very ill. We do not know if there are any other missionaries left in Bitlis except Miss Shane. It is so difficult to know that this young woman is alone there and very ill, and not be able to help her. Today my little girl's mother was also sent away, without knowing anything about it in advance. She had to leave without clothes, without food, and with her old weak mother-in-law and two boys. The youngest—five years old and weak—she had to carry in her arms. This afternoon a group of soldiers came to the hospital and ordered all Armenians to be handed over to them. Dr. and Mrs. Atkinson spoke up on the Armenians' behalf as well as they could but the patients were taken—12 men in all. Badveli Drtad, who was also sick, was dragged away, but got no further than the passage when he fainted and lay like one who is dead. So he was left behind. Badveli Vartan and some others, who said they were in our service and were not to be touched, had their names taken down and were allowed to stay in the meantime. The soldiers then drove the twelve unlucky men away. Among them was a man of 55 years who had lived in America for 25 years. He had just returned before the outbreak of war. On their way to the government building they passed our Consulate and Consul Davis happened to be walking down the road. The poor man called out to him, "I am a citizen, save me, save me," but the soldiers flogged him severely. "For how long, for how long, oh God, will this go on, before you show mercy to this poor people?" This is what our hearts are saying. We still think it is impossible for the situation to become worse, but in spite of this, it still becomes more terrible daily. "Lord, bend down to us in Your mercy. Stop these persecutions if possible. But, if not, then give us grace and strength to endure to the end."

6 August. Satenig Varzhoohi's mother came today to persuade her to become Mohammedan, and thus save her family. Satenig Varzhoohi lived for a time with the Kaimakam. He took her in to save her because she had been a teacher to his little boy, but when she had been there for a while he started to persuade her to become a Mohammedan. At last he threatened her, saying that if she did not go to the government at once and ask to become a Mohammedan, she and her family would be sent away. As she could not deny her Saviour, she fled from the house and ran over the mountains until she at last reached us. Now came the mother—an old woman and begged her daughter to become a Mohammedan to save the family. It was a severe temptation, and therefore indescribably difficult for her when she had to say, "No" to her old mother, "I cannot do it," thus putting her whole family into great danger and distress. The old woman went sadly away, and our hearts were sore to see these two part. But we were happy that Satenig Varzhoohi stayed firm.

7 August. Last night we saw a big area of Chemishgezek burning. Several villages and large fields and gardens lay burnt. Never before in my life did I see such a fire. It was very alarming, even though we knew that it could not reach us because of the Euphrates river which lies between us, but we could not help thinking of the thousands of people living in these villages. It was in this area that Mr. Riggs and I spent a month last winter, where we had so many blessed memories. I wonder if many of our dear friends were among those who perished? We constantly implored the Lord to have mercy and give His strength to the end. We did not sleep very much that night, as we could still see the flames over the mountains. It continued almost the whole day. Now there are only columns of smoke to be seen.

9 August. I went today down to Mezreh for the first time since my long illness. In the evening, when I returned to Harpoot, I stopped at the hospital to get a man to accompany me. When I arrived there I found everyone in a state of great terror about what might happen in the coming days. In the afternoon they had seen a big crowd of women and children and a few men from Husenik pass. They had been left behind in Husenik and now they were also being taken away. They do not make such great efforts now. They just take them outside the town and kill them. It would be more merciful if they took them as far as the river to drown, instead of torturing and flogging them to death. Mrs. Atkinson had been to the Commandant, who had told her that even the hospital staff were not safe. At the same time they had had a letter from Erzeroum stating that all their people had been taken and sent away, so there was no hope of keeping our friends. When it was time for me to leave and say goodbye to our Armenian friends, it was as if we could not separate, as none of us knew if we would ever meet again on earth. Badveli Vartan said, "I am ready to die. I will go to Jesus." What I still tell everyone here is, "Be ready any moment as we must go to Jesus when they kill us." I had to take their hands several times before I could part from them, and as I rode home, accompanied by a Turk, I had a strange feeling in my heart of sorrow and joy. It is so hard to see our friends suffer and die, but when I see again how the Lord can fill their hearts with peace and strength during suffering, and the hope of soon being with the Saviour Himself, then am I jubilant in my heart and filled with great longing to meet them soon again at Home. All the cruelty and suffering fade beside the hope of the joy that will be revealed to us.

12 August. I heard today that Professor Lulejian with his son Baron Roupen and a young medical student have fled from the hospital. The Kurds had come after them for a large sum of money, which is generally paid in order to save a life. Now we are waiting in great anxiety to hear if they succeeded in crossing the river. This will be at night, and each must pay 10 liras. The crossing takes barely 10 minutes. How pleased I am that dear Baron Roupen has been safe so far, and it is our hope that he will be protected. He has become an old man, grey haired, thin, and bent. But he is the same dear father, with sparkling eyes, as in the old days.

14 August (Sunday). Today Mr. Riggs, Alice, and I went down to Mezreh where, with Karen-Marie and the Consul, we went to the burial ground where the government has put all the sick Armenians. From a long way off we were met by a terrible stench and we knew we were in the right direction. As we reached the outskirts of the town we found the place, an old Turkish burial ground, surrounded by a high wall so that no one could escape. As we came to the entrance we saw a horrifying sight. Some soldiers were standing in the gate with their guns on their shoulders, and bayonets in their hands. They wore scarves around their faces in order not to breathe the foul air, only their eyes were uncovered. At first they would not let us in, saying, "You cannot stand this," but we insisted and entered with the Consul and his Turkish kavas. It is impossible to describe what we saw. No human being can

imagine such ghastliness. The large area was filled with the sick, but these poor ones no longer looked human. Not even animals could be found in such a condition. People would have had mercy on them and killed them, but these were the hated Christians—now in the hands of their enemies—who intended to make it as difficult as possible for them. As soon as we entered the gate a crowd gathered around us. All who could move jostled each other to come close enough to beg for money—ten paras for bread. I had about 20 kroners with me in coins and they almost pulled me down in order to get a few gurush. They looked terrible. Almost naked. Only some rags were left of what had once been their good clothes. They were dirty, with unkempt hair, and as thin as the people who died of starvation in India. Besides this, they were ill and black with flies. Many were too ill to rise and follow us, but they tried to sit up and they cried for help. Others were even too weak to cry after us, only raising their heads to see what all the stir was about them. Half naked women lay around, and one could not tell if they were alive or dead. Two little girls nine or 10 years old, were dragging away the corpse of a six year old boy. On one side of the great place stood eight soldiers with nose and mouth covered, as protection against the terrible stench. A very large grave had been dug and it was these soldiers' work to bury the dead. It was work enough just to cover them with earth, so great was the number of people dying daily. Every time someone died they were laid on top of the others with a thin layer of earth on top, and so on. It was impossible to talk to these people about God while they cried, pulled and tore at us, and the soldiers shouted at them and struck them with their thick sticks.

Not even that seemed to make any impression on them. They had become so used to ill-treatment that there was little reaction to it. Poor, poor Armenians, what you have had to endure. On the way home, we discussed whether it would be considered a sin to give these people poison to end their suffering. If it had been wild animals we would not have had to think twice about it. To think that human beings have been the tools that have wrought such terrible misery, and it is the government that promised us time after time that nothing evil would befall our friends on the way, and that doctors would be sent with them. This is the way they do it.

In Hooiloo all women were gathered together and killed. The men had been killed earlier. The women were ordered to remove their best clothes, and they were laid on top of each other, two by two, and beheaded. The ones underneath were not all killed the first time and the soldiers shouted to them, "Those of you who are alive—get up. You shall be taken to Mezreh and dealt with there." All who obeyed were killed, but some who lay quite still, as if they were dead, succeeded in escaping later. One of them, a girl of 12 years, came to Mezreh. She had a long and very nasty gaping wound in the neck, which gradually became very infected. Sister Jenny took her in to the Children's Home and every day she is taken to the hospital for treatment.

Round about the streets and ditches these poor exiles lie dying, and several days pass before the government can manage to bury them. Several times they have sent a man to throw a thin layer of earth over the corpses and let them lie in the street until the air is so contaminated that people come and bury it themselves.

There are not a few Turks who are against what happens, and they say again and again, "We will leave this country as soon as we can, and when we do, we will no longer be Mohammedans." Oh, if only these years of distress would bear fruit, so that Mohammedans may realize that Jesus is the Son of God, and Saviour of the world, and turn to Him. It is good that we can trust that God knows what He does when He allows all these terrible things to happen and we can believe that He is Love. Even if we cannot understand it now, we will thank Him one day for it. We can do nothing else but believe that so many having died in the faith must impress the Mohammedans. A man who was present at the killing of a large number of Christians told a grocer, who is Syrian, that just before the soldiers were ordered to fire he heard a father say to his children, "Be brave. In a moment we will be with Jesus." Then the soldiers started firing and a little later the father and his children were Home in Heaven. This Turk understood some Armenian and it had made a strong impression on him.

A Turkish woman had a dream. She saw as many green birds as there are stars in the sky. They twittered happily and she asked them, "Where do you come from?" They answered, "We are all the Armenians whom you have killed. You have sent us to a good place." This shows that their conscience is not at ease. Yes, there are many among the Mohammedans who are absolutely shocked about all the terrible daily happenings, but they always say as an excuse, "It is not us, but the orders of the Emperor Wilhelm which are being executed." In the hospital there are 50 wounded soldiers who came from Mezreh. One of them, an Arab, said that on his way here he saw hundreds of men, women, and children lying dead with their throats cut. He had seen women and children locked up in a house, which was afterwards strewn with straw and set on fire. These poor people were slowly burned to death. He had seen hundreds of men being tied together, petroleum poured over them, and ignited. He says, "When I am well again I will leave this country," but he is not likely to recover as his heart is very weak. He is not the only one to say this. More people have said, "I do not want to be a Mohammedan any longer. I do not want to live here in this country." But by far the majority seem to enjoy the daily happenings, and the longer it continues, the more blood-thirsty they become.

At this time there is a Syrian Arabic speaking doctor at the hospital. The Mohammedans consider him a fanatic, but to us he says he is on the side of the Christians. He states that he has accompanied several groups that have been killed.

He says that when a group is taken away to be killed, they make them first dig their own graves. But not all who are killed are buried. They lie close together on the roads, where they are eaten by animals and birds.

Rumours are circulating that freedom has been given to Protestants, but so far we do not know anything definite. Even if it were so, it would of course be held back, as was the case with Catholics. In the meantime they will do all the evil they can.

15 August (Sunday). The Kaimakam has lost his position and we are pleased because a worse man than he can hardly be found. He is to blame for much torturing and death.

16 August (Monday) Badveli Drtad's daughter died today of typhoid fever. We can only be glad when someone dies a natural death in these terrible times.

18 August (Wednesday). Today sister Helene died and was buried at 5 o'clock. Unfortunately we have just now received the message so we could not be present, and I am very sorry about it. I did so much want to be there, as I always liked her so very much. She was a marvellous woman, a true servant of the Lord. Now she is Home, where there is no sorrow.

Today it was announced that all Protestants who still remain are given their freedom. What happy news. But we are so unused to happy information that we can scarcely believe it, and we are afraid that it is only a trap to bring people out from hiding places, so that they can be taken and sent away. Anyway, we will try to believe and be thankful. It is the first gleam of sun in long, long months, which have brought only sorrow, suffering, worry, and great fear. Thanks be to God for this news, which means a few will be saved. It is hard, however, to think of the many that are no more, but we do not know what is best. We only know that the blood of the martyrs has always been the seed of the church, and maybe it has been necessary that this terrible bloodshed should take place in order that the Kingdom of God should be brought to this country. If this will be the result then we know that all who have died would have gone willingly—yes, even gladly.

26 August. Today government representatives came to Mr. Ehmann to ask for the children's homes, Pniel and Elim, but Mr. Ehmann said it was impossible for him to give the houses. At the same time they have come to us and demanded the Girls' School. We also said that it was completely impossible. We cannot give them the last building we have, as our girls who live there would have nowhere to go. But they insisted that they should have them as otherwise they would force an entry. So it was decided that they should have the two topmost floors, and we should keep the two lowest.

27 August. Today Sister Bodil and Alma came from Moush. I went down to greet them. They were both thin and looked exhausted. They had with them six girls, two women, a man, and a boy. This was all that was left of the whole Armenian

population there. The Armenians had refused to leave the town, so the Turks mounted cannons and bombarded the town for three days until everyone was killed. These two sisters came with the Police Mudir who was very ill. They were in fear on the way, but nothing happened. They saw many bodies lying along the road.

28 August. The gendarmes are gathering all of the refugees who are moving about. So the law about freedom has not yet taken effect.

30 August. Doctor Atkinson has rented a house where he will send a lot of children who have up till now lived in the hospital. Badveli Drtad will be Father to them. He is now much better. For a long time he was very weak, and nothing that was done for him helped. However, when the news came about freedom for the Protestants, he immediately began to liven up, and has been much better ever since. This was the medicine he needed.

31 August. Men who have been hiding out in the mountains for a long time and have become ill are coming to the hospital in charshafs so as not to be recognised. It is a terrible way of life—living in constant fear—and it is only a question of how long they can hold out in hiding.

1 September. Today is the Sultan's birthday and we had hoped a free pardon would come for everyone, but it is now evening and we have not heard anything. The two Mr. Riggses and Mr. Pierce visited the Kaimakam to offer greetings on the Sultan's birthday. They were told that both Van and Bitlis had been destroyed, and there was not one straw or tree in the whole district. It is very sorrowful to think of, but we had suspected it. For a long time Turkish people had been leaving the district, and the Christians have either been killed or sent into exile. So the Turks have burned and destroyed everything, in order that nothing will be left for the Russians if they come. We have had a conversation with Mariam Bagdasarian who was, earlier, a nurse in the hospital, and has just come from Diarbekir, where she was forced to marry a Turkish doctor. She said that Mr. Knapp came to Diarbekir under strong guard. No one was allowed to see him. He took ill the day after he arrived, and died the next day. From what we can understand, he had been given poison, from which he had died. It was a hard blow, and convinced us still more of how dangerous our job is. We were so sorry for his wife and children in America. Mrs. Knapp should have come here last autumn, but was held back because of the war. The Consul has immediately inquired of the Vali. He says he knows nothing, but will inquire of the Vali in Diarbekir.

A Turk said to Mr. Ehmann, "If there is a revolution in 20 years, it will be your fault. You have concealed over 6,000 murderers." It still plagues them that there are a few hundred children left behind in the Home. Mr. Ehmann assured him that there would be no revolution—there was nobody left.

3 September. Today Karen-Marie, Sister Bodil, and Alma came up to visit me. They stayed until evening and I went down with them to Mezreh, taking my little girl, to spend some days with Karen-Marie.

6 [September] (Monday). Tonight we had a big happy surprise. Karen-Marie and I, who were sleeping out on the roof, were awakened about 2.00 a.m. by one of the older girls, who came with a lamp and called Karen-Marie. A couple of minutes later I saw a woman with a charshaf sitting on the bed, and Karen-Marie was hugging her and kissing her again and again. Then another woman came and I recognized immediately my little girl's mother. I came quickly out of the bed and went and hugged her. They then told us there were many (17 in all) who had been brought here by some Kurds. They had taken them as far as the Turkish school which lies about 20 minutes' journey outside Mezreh, and they had come on alone from there. They had divided themselves up into little groups and proceeded very cautiously, almost afraid to walk on the road—frightened that someone would hear them. But they did not meet a soul, which was a miracle. They knocked on our door for a long time before anyone had the courage to come and see who they were. At last Baron Khatchador came, but he would not open the door, as he was afraid it was Turks making some pretence to gain admission. However, as they continued, he at last became convinced that they were the people whom they said they were, and the joy was great, both for them and for us. We went in and found the large number of our friends whom we had thought were dead. What a great joy it was to have them. Never before in my life have I been so happy as I was this night, but it was strange to see these formerly rich and happy people now having to lie on the bare floor; and what had they not undergone from fear and persecution! Their husbands were taken from them and killed, and they themselves had lost everything, so that they could only come back half naked, and had been pursued by Turks and Kurds who wanted to marry them. When they had succeeded in getting the Kurds to bring them here, it was necessary to give them everything they had. Again, we must say, God is the same and He still works miracles as in earlier times. Our refugees were full of holy joy and thanks and praise to Him who had brought us together again.

Several of them had very bad eyes. I treated them, but became infected myself with ophthalmia of a severe type and suffered very badly for a week, but it cleared up and I do not think it has left any permanent damage, for which thanks be to God.

20 September. Today six men were hanged as a warning to the soldiers.

21 September. Today the rest of the survivors from the cemetery were sent away into exile.

25 September. On account of the many refugees, people are again being sent away. When the soldiers see some Armenians in the streets or roads, they take them and send them to the government, from where they are sent away. But they take less trouble with them. They take them outside the town and kill them.

Today some soldiers came from the government and demanded that all Armenians from the hospital should come with them to the government. So with Dr. and Mrs. Atkinson and Miss Campbell in front, the large group of about 50 walked down to the government, where all their names and occupations were written down. All were frightened and in dread of what might come. Mrs. Atkinson, who is not afraid to say what she thinks and means, said to the soldiers who accompanied them, when she saw how roughly they treated the Armenians on the way to the government building, "Before you became soldiers were you Khaterdjis (muleteers)?" "Why, Khannum Effendi?" they asked. "Yes" she said, "You treat the Armenians as if you were well trained for that job." They laughed, but understood what she meant by the question. God be praised. They all got permission to return with the Doctor. It is the second time they have been to the hospital. It was said that they would also search the German Children's Home, but Mr. Ehmann stopped it in time. Well, they did not come to Emaus where they would have found not a few.

The Commandant comes daily to the hospital for electrical treatment. Some days ago he said to the Doctor, "I must have you turn Mohammedan or else you must turn me to be a Christian." He is not so afraid of the Doctor, but he does not like to come in contact with Mrs. Atkinson, for she "goes on" at him.

26 September. Today another crowd of people rounded up in the streets have been sent away. Just afterwards it was shouted in the streets that there was freedom for everyone, and that people should not be afraid, as everything was over. But the few remaining are afraid and still do not dare to show themselves.

27 September. Today a zaptie came to us in the Garden and brought a sick woman. She was one of the many exiles from Trebizond and had reached as far as Houlakegh. She had been left there with many others, too ill to go further. She knew there were missionaries in Harpoot and she begged permission from the soldiers to be allowed to come to us. At last she promised them money, and they gave her permission, but she could not walk and had to get a man to bring her. She looked terrible—a complete skeleton, unable to walk, and has to crawl along the ground. She was from Trebizond, where she had taken an examination at our College, and later had qualified as a kindergarten teacher. She had taught there for several years. Poor, poor soul. We got her in and gave her hot tea and bread. Oh, how she enjoyed it, after not having tasted anything hot for months. She said that there were many sick people out in the fields near Houlakegh. The village, which was once Armenian, is now completely empty, as all have been driven away and killed. These poor sick ones are not even allowed to go into the empty houses, but have to lie out in the fields, without clothes and food in the now cold nights. The heart feels constricted and it is nearly unbearable to hear this and to think about these poor souls. Oh, if only we could help them. I feel like a criminal when I go to my good, warm bed, and I think of these thousands who must suffer so indescribably. He got her into town where she

found her sister-in-law who was a minister's wife from the same place and was now, with her three children, in a miserable condition. There was great joy at their meeting. Yes, God is good and His mercy lasts forever.

We are now busy helping the many poor, who are left without anything. They are all in the same state, even those who were once very rich. We are buying wool, making bed-clothes, buying footwear, and every family or person gets only the necessities to keep them alive this winter. We cannot give more, because the distress is so great, and there are so many to be helped.

28 September. Forty men, who were captured in the forest outside Erzingan and Erzeroum and imprisoned here, are being sent away today. Everyone is being encouraged to become Mohammedan. They tell them the most terrible things to make them afraid and then say, "Become a Mohammedan and you will be free from all this suffering." This is a big temptation for those still remaining, after what they have seen and gone through so much. Some fall for the temptation, but thank God, many remain strong and say, "I have thought it over so much, but have come to the conclusion that I would rather die than become a Mohammedan. This life is short, but my soul will live forever. The Lord will help me to be steadfast to the end."

29 September. Today six Kurds are being hanged here in the market and 14 down in Mezreh to frighten the soldiers here, who are being sent to Erzeroum in two days, and to prevent them from trying to run away.

1 October. Today Heripseme died, a poor old mother, and Anna Varzhoohi must also take her two children, who are now orphans. She was ill-treated by a Turk, who broke into her house, and she died after eight days of great suffering as a result.

Today we also had a telegram from Constantinople, inquiring if we could send for the two women missionaries remaining in Bitlis.

2 October. The Consul went to Kezin Khan and said that the corpses of Armenians are lying so thick on the main road that there are too many for the animals to eat. How frightful it must be for those now being sent away, to see their brothers and sisters lying dead on the road.

A big crowd of Kurds has come to the town today and people again are full of fear about what will happen. The Kurds say they have been brought by the Turks to put an end to the rest of the Armenians. The Vali has sent a group to Goljuk with cannons, to shell the little island out in the lake where it is said a group of Armenians have hidden themselves.

3 October. Mr. Riggs and Mr. Pierce went to Hoghe to see to the survivors from the village. There are four men in the whole village and three are blind. There are, in all, 100 women and children, who were hidden by friendly Turks for high payment. Mr. Riggs met with them and came home the same day. In two hours walking he saw 40 dead bodies.

4 October. Today we had a meeting where it was decided that Mr. Ernest Riggs and family should travel to America and, on the way, make a stop in Ourfa to help Mr. Leslie with relief work.

4 [sic] October. Today all the soldiers left and our buildings were handed back, but in very bad condition, full of dirt, fleas and lice. You cannot go into a room without getting hundreds of them on you, so now we must have a cleaning which will give work to many of the poor. We have also got back our lovely little church, but they have taken the church bell, of course, to use in making bullets.

5 October. Today Dr. Atkinson went to Houlakegh to bring back some of the exiles, for which he had permission from the Vali. He took with him the Consul's Turkish kavas and the chaoush from the hospital. We sent all our horses and donkeys away. He was also allowed to take Mr. Ehmann's cart with him. He returned in the evening with about half naked, starving, poor people. He selected those whom he thought had some chance of survival. They were delighted and full of thanks, saying, "You have saved us from the dogs." They looked miserable, ragged, stinking with dirt, and full of lice, bigger than we had ever seen before. Now we have them placed here in Harpoot. We have, little by little, collected a big crowd of widows and orphans, which we now must support. These are human beings from all parts of the country to the north of us, who by one means or another have been left behind by the crowds. We put them into the deserted Armenian houses around us. It is better, at least, than lying out in an open field. All the best houses have been taken by the Turks, and the rest plundered. The windows and doors have been taken, so they are completely open to the wind and rain. It will be really terrible when the cold weather begins. We must give them all that is needed, because they have nothing, and we must buy back at a high price, bedding and kitchen utensils from the Turks, who have stolen them from the Armenians. Everything is now terribly expensive—four or five times higher than before. It costs 35 piastres, 650 grush to have a pair of shoes re-soled, and they only last a couple of weeks. A little box of matches costs 20 grush. Many things are impossible to get any more. What shall we do if there is no change very soon? Already we use 200 liras a month for help and maintenance of the exiles, who have come to us here, and we cannot help the many villages and bigger towns where there are also people remaining. Mr. Riggs does a great job handing out money to the many who get help from their relatives in America. In the last six months 11,500 liras have come through him. The other day 2,000 liras came, with a list of people for whom the money was intended. There were 250 people on the list—of these only 10 have received their money. The rest have been killed, or sent away, and we do not know where they are. How sad.

7 October. Today we had a meeting in Mezreh chaired by Dr. Atkinson. He asked us to talk about some of the bright things we have seen in this long, heavy time. Many gave testimonies of our friends who had suffered and were going to their death with faith in their Saviour.

We were told how they prayed day and night, and when they were taken, to be led away and be killed, they said, "If only they see Jesus in us as we die, then we will be happy to go." It was a nice time, giving us courage and strength to go on.

8 October. Today I went into town and gave my little girl back to her mother, who would have preferred that I should keep her. But it seemed to me right, that I should give her back, as her mother is alive, though it was hard to do so. I have come to love her and will miss her very much.

10 [October] (Sunday). After church service today we held a station meeting at which it was decided that Miss Riggs should stay in Harpoot.

11 October. This morning we had another station meeting at which Ernest Riggs requested that I should go with them to Ourfa, but the whole station voted against it, so I am staying. I moved today into town. It is 10 months since I have lived in my apartment, and it was very good to be back.

12 October. So many sick people came in the morning, just when I had to go over and eat lunch at the College. A card was brought from Dr. Thom in Mardin, written in Diarbekir on the 8th, where he said, "We are coming through your town on Monday evening." This was Tuesday lunchtime and we had heard nothing of their arrival. We realized there was something wrong. Maybe they will come later today. Dr. Atkinson should have a message about it. There was no one who could leave, so I hurried with my meal, took a horse, and rode as quickly as possible. Mr. Riggs, who was there, and the Atkinsons, were very worried, and we went down immediately to the Consul, who was also worried, thinking that they might have been sent out of the country. He said that he would go to the Vali at once to inquire, and would send a man out on the road to watch. They would send a message to all the khans to see if they were, or had been, there. So I returned, glad that I had brought the card down and set people in motion.

13 October. Mr. Riggs went down to Mezreh early this morning, and when he came back, he was able to say that the missionaries had arrived. There was Dr. Andrus, 74 years; Dr. Thom, 71 years; and Miss Fenenga, and they were heavily guarded.

After the Consul had been to the Vali, he went with the Doctor to the main road to meet them. After they had been out about a quarter of an hour, they met a cart in which were the missionaries. They began to talk together, but the gendarmes said they must not speak in English, only Turkish. They thought this would be impossible, but when they heard them speak in Turkish, they said, "You must not talk with one another." They were now close to the town and the Doctor had just enough time to say, "If we do not see each other again, we will send food for you." It was now rumoured that American missionaries had been brought in as prisoners and people flocked here. At first they were brought to the Gendarmes' House, but that was wrong, and they had to leave again in a completely different direction. Now people had crowded around—at least 1,000—and followed them through the town. The Consul, who had also followed, asked the government for permission to take the missionaries home for food and accommodation. After a lot of trouble he got permission and a soldier accompanied them as a guard. While they were eating, another soldier came and said they could not stay overnight in the Consulate, so they had to return with the soldiers. After a lot of effort they were allowed to eat lunch at the hospital, guarded all the time by a soldier. There was talk that they would be sent away on the same day. Therefore, Dr. Parmelee, Miss Harley, and I left at once, as they had permission to have supper at the hospital also, and we had a very good talk with them. They did not know why they were being sent away. They told us that one evening some soldiers came to them in Mardin and said, "We will give you 10 minutes for all to go over to the building." They quickly collected their bed clothes and went over. There was a guard posted outside. The next morning some soldiers came again and said that before evening all the missionaries had to leave the town. But shortly afterwards they returned to say that only the three were to leave. However, they were given a respite of 24 hours. They were told they could choose between Diarbekir and Harpoot, and of course they chose Diarbekir, because it was closer. They then left Mardin with 12 gendarmes, reached Diarbekir, hoping and waiting to be questioned there. But no, one day the soldiers said, "Be ready to go to Sivas." They then had to hire carts. They succeeded after much trouble and had to pay 35 liras for a cart for this distance which normally costs 7 liras, but the two old men could not travel any other way. They said, "If we had not had Miss Fenenga with us, it would not have been possible for us to endure such a journey, but she cooked and cared for us." They were not allowed to bring a servant with them. They said, jocularly, "We are guests of the government, but we have to pay our own expenses. It will be an expensive affair as it will cost a lot of money to pay zapties, besides khans, carts, and everything else." Some time before they were sent away, some officials had come and had emptied their cash-box of 1,000 liras, although Mr. Andrus had said that it was their own money. It was very difficult for these two old men to be sent away like this. Dr. Andrus has been in this country for 44 years, and has always been a man very respected by government officials. Dr. Thom has been here for 41 years and has in all these years treated Turks as well as Christians. When he was sent away, he had his hospital and boys' school filled with soldiers whom he had treated. But the Turks have lost their minds in their excessive fanaticism, and we must earnestly beg and pray, "Father forgive them, for they know not what they do." Dr. Thom's wife had died a month ago, and Mrs. Andrus is a very weak old woman who has not been outside the house for 10 years. She can only get from one room to another with the aid of her husband and two sticks. How difficult it must be for these two old people to part like this.

This morning a representative came from the government to question them. First, he asked where they were born, and afterwards, why they were leaving. Dr. Andrus answered, "Hykamet bilir" (the government knows). Then he asked again, "Where are you going?" Again Dr. Andrus replied, "Allah bilir" (only God knows). The man looked very surprised, but said nothing. He wrote down the answers in a book and went to the government with it. The Commandant said, they had to leave next morning, even though their cart had rolled down the mountain on the way here, and has to be repaired, and the work cannot be done in one day.

The missionaries also said that in Mardin the Christians had been sent away. They are not Armenians, but Arabic-speaking Syrians and Assyrians. First the men were taken and sent away, and afterwards all the rich women and children. They were allowed to hire wagons and bring horses and donkeys with them. But they did not reach farther than a six hour journey, when everything was taken from them, and the women were killed. All their belongings were brought back to Mardin and sold by auction at the market. Afterwards the poor people were sent away, so it seems that it is not only the Armenians alone who must suffer, but that all Christians are persecuted. The holy war has begun.

The missionaries had met the Syrian doctor who has been at the Hospital for a long time. He told them that he had found some Turks who knew what had happened to Mr. Knapp. They had shown him his grave. The body had not been covered properly and bones were visible. This is something that the Turks do not consider bad.

15 October. Today Karen-Marie came here to spend a couple of days.

17 October. This morning our friends left. The Consul could not get permission for them to stay longer, although he has been working all the time. So far no telegram has arrived from the Ambassador, although the Consul has sent several every day. This shows that something is wrong. The Vali told them they had to leave today. "If a telegram should arrive giving them permission to stay, I shall send my own wagon after them to bring them back." It sounds very kindly, but we have a feeling that it is he who has held back the Consul's telegrams. This affair has contributed to our few Armenian friends' anxiety that we shall also be sent away, and what will become of them when they are completely abandoned to Turkish hands? This is now the fourth place we know of, where they have sent missionaries away, and we do not know for how long we will be allowed to stay here. Our thoughts and our prayers go with these three friends on their way, that they may be protected and led in safety to their destination, wherever it may be.

In the afternoon we had a church service in the Girls' School, when Mr. Riggs preached on the text, "Thus far has the Lord helped." There were quite a few women, about 90, but only four men. It was the first service for several months, and it was good to gather our Armenian friends around us and hear the word of God. Mr. Riggs spoke very earnestly to them to rely on God. He has helped us thus far, and He will also help us in the days to come.

All are in fear of another massacre. It is said that people will be sent away after Kurban Bairam, but we know nothing definite. It is a great delight to the Turks to see the Christians in fear and dread, so they do all they can to frighten them.

18 October. Today I went house-visiting and came in to the Kazandjians. It was hard to see them in their poor home, which was once so rich. They had collected some bits and pieces together, which they had washed to make mattresses, but they were thankful to be alive. How good it is to hear people's gratitude for the little that is left to them. We had a really grand time together when we talked of the Home up there that waits for us. Afterwards I visited two young widows exiled from Erzeroum, who are stranded here, and also my little Bessie's mother and Flora.

19 October. Today I visited Heripsime Khanum, a bible woman from Ordoo. She is also one of the many exiles who remained behind because of illness and then fled to us. She is a marvellous woman. Peace and happiness shine from her eyes, and she is full of praise and thanks, although she has lost everything, and now sits here in a little room in a strange place. She has nothing except for the two loaves we can give her, and no assurance that she can stay here. She is the living proof of how the Lord can support His children during their sufferings. How pleased she was when we brought her a pair of spectacles and a bible. During the months she had been on the road she had had no bible, and she had become so weakened that she could recall nothing from memory. Now she could read again and find food for her soul.

Afterwards I went to a sick woman and found her in a terrible condition. She was very weak and looked as though she could not live much longer. She lay on some rags upon the floor, and beside her lay her nine year old son. He had a very bad throat, and could neither swallow nor speak. As I asked him to sit up and let me examine his throat, his little two year old sister awoke. I had not noticed her before, as she lay with her little face buried in the dirty rags. There was no one to nurse them. It was really a cavern of misery. Oh, if I could just open a home for these many poor little souls, and one for the many sick. But we have no resources and how difficult it is to say "No" and "No" again. They do not understand that we are unable to help, as they think our sources are unlimited. Oh, if we could just send a message home, telling of all the boundless want, then I think that many would be happy to help. But, unfortunately, it is impossible now.

Some women, whose husbands were taken away to be killed and who married Turks in order to save their children and themselves, have now heard that their husbands had escaped and fled up amongst the Kurds and are alive. These women are now suffering in a double sense.

18 October. Rumours are spreading that the Russians have destroyed the whole Turkish army in Erzeroum and the Turks are in flight. The rich families here are now anxious and are also preparing to flee. Many have left for Constantinople.

19 October. Today the Vali has left for Erzeroum to attend a conference with the Vali there and the one from Sivas on how they will provide for the soldiers in the coming winter.

I spent the morning on sick-visits.

20 October. Today is Kurban Bairam and everywhere in the streets the Turks slaughter their sacrificial lambs. The two Riggs brothers and Mr. Pierce pay visits to all the high-ranking officials.

21 October. The two Mrs. Riggses, Miss Harley, Dr. Parmelee, and I paid six visits today to Turkish homes. Every place we came there was much surprise that we had not already left. They asked us who would be living in the missionaries' empty houses, and who would take care of our belongings. The Turks say to each other that they will now have to be very kind and friendly towards us for a little while, in order that we will forget all the evil things they have done, and then we will be sent out of the country. They had already heard that some of us were leaving and were very surprised that we were not all going. This evening we received a telegram from the Ambassador advising all missionaries, very urgently, to leave, and that ships would be ready for them. A second telegram asked us to collect the two women missionaries from Bitlis. A third asked for the names of the Mardin missionaries who had been sent away and their whereabouts. These telegrams created quite a lot of agitation. It was very clear that he had special reasons for asking us to leave. We all know that the situation is very uncertain and insecure, but how can we go and leave behind the few surviving Armenians? It would be impossible to abandon them. They would be even more ill-treated than before and utterly destroyed. We had a long meeting. It was voted that the young Riggses, with their two children, and the Pierces with their two children, and Miss Riggs, should leave. Dr. Parmelee and her old, weak mother, should make preparations, so that if it became necessary, they could also leave quickly.

22 October. This morning the men went down to the Consul to discuss our travel plans. Early tomorrow morning we will all have another meeting at which we will discuss whether or not to leave.

All the Armenian children who had been collected together in Turkish children's homes have been taken away in ox-carts and thrown into the river.

23 October. This morning we gathered again to make a decision about leaving. The Consul sent a message that he had heard from Ourfa. A card had come from Mr. Kuenzler saying that all Armenians had been ordered out of the town. They refused to leave, and the Turks set up cannons and bombarded the Armenian part of the town. Mr. Kuenzler did not know if Mr. Leslie, our American missionary who lived there and whom the Armenians depended upon, had managed to escape or lay buried under the ruins of the missionaries' houses. This was another sorrowful message. We discussed back and forward during the meeting, but we arrived at the same conclusion, that the two families with little children should leave as soon as possible, as we do not know what the next day will bring. If we should be sent away by the government it will be impossible to care for the little children. The rest of us will remain for as long as we can. May God allow us to become a help and blessing to the many needy.

24 [October] (Sunday). At 6 o'clock this morning Mr. Riggs, Mr. Pierce, and I left to visit the village Haboosi five hours ride from Harpoot. It was a lovely morning. Everything around us looked so peaceful. The beautiful blue mountains, the clear blue sky, the vineyards with the wonderful golden life. We rode quickly, as we wanted to return the same day, and we wanted to spend as much time as possible in the village. An hour before we reached our destination we had to cross a river and when we were in the middle of it my horse lay down and I was soaked. When we reached the other side, I had to wring my clothes and go on, as I had nothing with me to change into. It was lucky that the sun shone, so it helped a little, but I did not become completely dry before we reached home in the evening. The village, that was once wholly Armenian, was completely changed, and now swarmed with Kurds, Circassians, and Turks, who had fled from Bitlis and the Van areas. Yes, there were even some who had come all the way from Russia. These Circassians are of a race that we have never had here. Tall upright men dressed in long fitted coats and high fur hats, and every man and boy has a dagger in his belt. The women are dressed like Kurdish women, hung all over with jewelry. Around about in the village were ox-carts and carts such as are used in Russia. When we arrived we asked the way to the head person's house, and several men went in front to show us. We came into a room where two clerks sat with their ledgers. They were very polite and greeted us in a very friendly manner. We sat down cross-legged on the floor, and it was not long before the room was filled with all kinds of men. I was the only woman and was therefore much more interesting to look at.

One of the men who had been in America and had seen how men honoured women said, "Bring a chair for Khanum Effendi." The answer was that there was no chair in the whole village. But he ordered that one should be found, and some time later a man came in with a large armchair. In front of the window was a platform where the most honoured person sits, and the armchair was placed upon it with two cushions, and I was invited to take the seat. I assured them that I was sitting very comfortably and thanked them for the offer. I said it was impossible for me to accept such a great honour as sitting on the platform. However, they insisted, and at last I had to take the chair, where they looked at me with great satisfaction, as though to say, "We can also honour women." Then coffee was brought in. The cups had not been washed since they had last been used, but we had to get it down, so down it went, in a great gulp, the sign by which enjoyment is indicated. Then a ragged dirty Kurdish woman was brought in, and I became uneasy in my mind thinking that maybe we were in a courtroom. I was sorry for the poor woman being interrogated in the midst of a crowd of men. But nothing so bad was revealed. Instead of our being in a courtroom, as I had first thought, it was a Relief Office. They questioned the woman—what was her name, where had she come from, how many children did she have, how old was she, and finally, what did she possess? Her answer to this was, "Nothing but the clothes we are wearing"—these were not many. So they wrote down what she should have—bed, clothes, cooking pots, a cow, a house. After that several others came. A man, who looked very intelligent, came in and sat down and they questioned him about himself. "Have you a wife?" "Yes" he answered. "How old is she?" The man did not answer. The men said among themselves, "Of course 45 years," and wrote it down. "Have you children?" "Yes." "What are their names?" He gave a boy's name. "Have you any more?" "No," he answered. "Have you no girl?" "Yes," he said. "What is her name?" "She has no name." They said, "You must give a name." So the man turned to another who had come with him and asked what the girl was called and so on. This shows the position of women in this country—they are not even worthy of a name. All these refugees are getting what the government has taken from the Armenians. Many of the men must give an undertaking that they will become farmers. Then they are given oxen and ploughs.

After I had sat for an hour, the chieftain came in and asked me to follow him over to his harem, which I did. He had two daughters whom I saw and to whom I gave medicine. His wife also came in, wearing a small fortune in gold coins around her neck. Some time afterwards some Armenian women came in whom the chieftain had hidden and protected. He was very proud of all the good he had done and praised himself in a loud voice. After we "had sat" with the head person for an hour I had permission to go with the Armenian women to their house and hold a meeting with them there. All the women and children who were left were about 50, with 35 women. We had a very good meeting together. I talked to them about the text from Matthew 10, "Whosoever therefore shall confess me before men, him will I confess also before my Father who is in Heaven." The great danger now is that the Armenians remaining are being pressed to become Moslems. Several of the women did not even know that it was Sunday. There were six men remaining in the village who had also been hidden by the Chieftain. One of these had become Turkish, had changed his name, and bound a white turban around his head. There was another man who was a living picture of what these poor people have undergone of dread and fear. He was so thin and pale and his face wore such an expression of suffering. He had earlier been one of our children in the Children's Home. As we were leaving, he followed us to the outskirts of the village and said, "They will try to make us Moslems, but I have taken my stand. I cannot do it. I would rather be killed." God help him to hold out to the end. The women told me that all their husbands were taken a little way out from the village where they were killed. The soldiers brought their clothes back and washed them at the spring. Afterwards the women were taken away. Many were killed, the rest were sent off.

25 October. Early this morning Dr. Parmelee and I were called down to a patient, an exile from Erzeroum. She had given birth to a baby. I arrived before Dr. Parmelee and found the baby lying in rags of dirty sacking, completely blue, and not breathing. I started immediately to work with it and after an hour it had enough life to begin crying weakly. It was a tiny little girl weighing scarcely 2 lbs. It was impossible for the mother to take care of her, so I took the baby home to nurse as well as I could, but she died this evening, after a life of only 12 hours. The mother was very weak, and I am afraid there is not much hope for her. There is a little brother, nine years old, the only one left in the family, and if she dies, he will be all alone in the world

The Consul and Dr. Atkinson went out to a village, one day's journey from Harpoot. They said on their return that they had seen between 5,000 and 6,000 bodies. They are not even being buried. Conditions are terrible. It is a wonder we have not had cholera and pestilence raging here. It is well that the sun is so strong and can kill many germs.

Mr. Riggs paid a visit today to the Kaimakam, who said that there will not be another massacre, but it is being said that the remaining Armenians and all Syrians must join the army. Bedros's father, a Kurdish chief, came to visit Mr. Riggs. He advised them not to travel yet, as the road was not safe. Mr. Riggs told him what the Kaimakam had said, and he answered, "You cannot depend on what they say. There will still be a massacre." They have talked like this all the time and our experience has shown that not one single word, or their good promises, can be depended upon.

27 October. Today I went down to Mezreh and visited Sister Bodil, together with Karen-Marie and some Turkish sisters. There we saw an account of the great Turkish blood-bath of the Armenians in a Norwegian newspaper from September 30th. We were glad to see this. If they know about this in Norway, they must also know in Denmark and can follow us better in thought and prayer. This we need in these distressing times, that the friends at home share in our suffering and carry us forward to the Mercy Seat. When I went home the Consul handed me a telegram he had received from the Ambassador. It read, "Wait a short while. Meantime bring Miss Shane and Miss McLaren to Harpoot."

28 October. We had a meeting again today when we discussed the Ambassador's telegram. It was voted that the Riggs and Pierce families and Miss Riggs should leave on Tuesday, and that Miss Campbell should be invited to accompany them.

31 October. Today we had a meeting in the Girls' College, where Miss Riggs spoke on the text, "God is mighty." Afterwards Mr. Pierce gave a talk on his impression of the Armenian people. Then Mr. Ernest Riggs spoke about being faithful until the end. We finished with Badveli Vartan asking those missionaries who were leaving to take their thanks with them to the American Board and all American friends, asking them to pray for the few remaining Armenians. It was a very moving meeting, and I believe that we all felt, more than ever before, the seriousness of the times. Then we parted after singing softly, "God be with you till we meet again." We had another meeting at 4 o'clock where it was decided that the two families and Miss Riggs and Miss Campbell should go as soon as they can and obtain permission from the Vali, and that the Consul should send his Turkish kavas early tomorrow morning to Moush to collect Miss Shane and Miss McLaren. In the evening all missionaries were together at the Pierces' for a service of song.

2 November. Last night we were all invited over to the Girls' School for dinner as a farewell party for the home-going missionaries. We were served meat and pilaf, aubergine, rice pudding, pakhlava, and grapes. After dinner the missionaries went up to Miss Daniel's room, together with the teachers and the senior pupils. We had music on gramophone records, and devotions.

3 November. I went down to Mezreh yesterday to do some shopping for the Trade School, which I am beginning today for the poor Armenian exiles. While I was down there with Karen-Marie, our Professor's wife came, Digin Floritza, beaming with joy, and told us that the Turkish officer who is engaged to her daughter had said that he gave them permission to take her away. He had nothing against her going to school in Harpoot, and they have decided to come here in a few days. Oh, how wonderful it would be if this splendid young girl could be released from the Turks. The mother told us yesterday how difficult it was for the father when he discovered that this officer wanted to take Maritza. The mother was willing that the daughter should go in order to save her husband and little son, but the Professor said, "No, I will not give her away. Let us all rather be drowned in the Euphrates." When they reached Malatia the Professor was taken away and killed. The mother gave her daughter and thus saved her 15 year old son. This Turk tried very hard to persuade them to become Moslems, saying that it brought shame upon him that not one of them had become Moslem. That is probably the reason why he is willing to let them go to Harpoot.

4 November. This afternoon, when we had our weekly meeting, Garabed Yeghpair came and told us that the hospital had been surrounded by soldiers. He and his son, Karekin, had been out at the cemetery to bury a woman, when his little son came running to say, "Don't come back. The hospital is surrounded by soldiers." They left

the corpse and ran to tell us about it. The Doctor left at once. Everything was still quiet here. At 5 o'clock Professor Khachadoorian and Baron Sarkis came and told us that tomorrow there would be a massacre. A Police Mudir had told Baron Sarkis to come to us. This was a hard blow. It had been reasonably quiet for the last couple of weeks and the people who had been saved had begun again to have hope. As soon as we heard about it Miss Harley and I went over to Badveli Vartan's to help get them over to us, and this we succeeded in doing, together with the bible woman. Afterwards we had Aghavni Varzhoohi, her mother-in-law and three children brought in, as well as Sara Varzhoohi and her four children. Dr. Parmelee got her girl in and I mine. Now a few had discovered that there was danger about, and they came to the gate and begged to be allowed in. It was terribly difficult to have to say "No." There was a mother with a little boy on her back, and she begged us to take him, then she would not mind facing death herself, if only her little boy could be saved. But we also had to say "No" to her pleading. As Mr. Riggs accompanied her to her house at the other side of the street, he met a band of soldiers, walking up and down. Then we knew that we could now do nothing more. We went to our rest with heavy hearts, as dark clouds were hanging over us, and we did not know what the next moment would bring.

5 November. Last night I did not get much rest. As soon as I had fallen asleep I was awakened by the sound of talking down in the street. As the sky lightened I went to the window and saw two soldiers with guns and swords, one on each side of our door, and I knew that soon something would happen. A little later I heard the shrieks of women. I now dressed quickly and went again to the window from which I saw that soldiers now stood outside Mr. Dingilian's house, and I could hear the children screaming. I ran as fast as I could to the Riggses' and asked if they thought it would be possible for me to go down and try to save the little girl and boy, also Digin Nazenig, who was in a state of advanced pregnancy. They said "Yes." Then I called Miss Harley and Dr. Parmelee, and the three of us went down as fast as we could and just reached the house as they were driving the old woman and Anna Varzhoohi out of it. In the street the nine little children were standing—the eldest nine years old. Only three of these are Anna Varzhoohi's own children. The other six belong to her two sisters who have recently died. The fathers were killed. The poor little souls were standing shivering and crying in terror. They had been thrown out of their beds and had not even had time to dress. There were three little girls of 18 months. Two of them cannot walk. My little Bessie lay in the street wet and dirty, rolled in a blanket. There were four soldiers and they pulled the women by the hair, beat them with their guns, flogged them, all the time shouting and swearing. The old woman of 70 cried aloud, moaned, and called to God for help. Anna Varzhoohi, who has been very ill for the last three weeks with inflammation of the kidneys, was very weak and could scarcely stand on her feet. She looked as if she would collapse and die. When they saw me they shouted, "Oh, save us! Oh, save us." I beseeched the soldiers to let them

stay, as they were ill. At last I was allowed to take the little girl, as I had had her in my care earlier, and I was allowed to take care of Digin Nazenig. I took the two into one of the rooms, while the others were driven out of the house, and the soldiers then shut us in. I could watch their progress for a little way down the street, and how it cut to my heart to see these crude soldiers beating these poor women with their guns, pushing and kicking them because they could not walk fast enough. Digin Nazenig had been so beaten that she could hardly move and it seemed as if she had lost her mind. I put her to bed, and little by little she became quieter. Little Bessie clung to me as if she also understood the danger that surrounded us. While I was sitting there, locked in, I saw one crowd after another being led away. It was heartbreaking to hear these miserable women's and children's cries and screams. The soldiers flogged, pushed, and kicked them. They dragged a woman by her hair along the street. When they got tired of this they pointed their guns, as though to shoot her, but she got to her feet and went on, subject to their pushes and kicks. One crowd after another passed like this. When I had been there for almost an hour, Dr. Parmelee came and stayed with Digin Nazenig, while I carried little Bessie home. I had expected that the soldiers would forbid my taking her in, but they did not. So I was happy and thankful. While I was eating, Mr. Riggs came with Digin Nazenig, but they had to carry her the last few yards, and when we got her up, she was very weak. After we got her to a safe place where she could rest, she began to feel better. This took up all morning, the driving-out of these people and taking them to the government building where they were put into some cells. At 1.30 five soldiers came and ordered us to hand over the men and boys whom we had. Mr. Riggs called them together and they went off to the government building where they were held for a couple of hours, and then returned. A little later the women also started coming back. I hurried there to help Anna Varzhoohi. The old mother had been so badly beaten that she could hardly move her right arm. Her eyes were swollen, black and blue, from the severe blows. Anna Varzhoohi was exhausted and miserable and on the point of fainting. All the little children screamed with hunger. They had had nothing to eat since the previous day. The older children were so glad to be home again, and they ran about to see if anything was missing. Unfortunately quite a lot had been stolen. A little six year old girl stood with shining eyes before me and said, "God looked upon our faces and therefore we were saved." There was gladness and thankfulness in our hearts. I was busy, lighting fires and cooking food for them, and a young girl from the senior class came over and cleaned and made beds. When I went home it was a happy crowd I left behind. We cannot understand why this suffering continues for so long, but there is a lot that we do not understand, and we must wait until we arrive in our Father's Home, where we shall see Him with uncovered eyes. Our prayers are still the same, "Lord, keep us faithful until the end, so that we may inherit a crown of life."

This is the Turkish Sunday, and there is no school. All boys and young men were out to enjoy watching the suffering of the poor Armenians. I saw a terrible sight when I came with little Bessie. Two gendarmes were dragging a very old woman down a very steep street. When they reached the bottom she looked on the point of fainting. Behind them came 10 or 12 older Turkish boys who were laughing and amusing themselves at this sad sight. How difficult it must have been for her dear ones, who were there and unable to help her. What cruelty. What cruelty, and committed by human beings created in the image of God. "Oh God, how long will you hesitate before helping these poor tortured people. Have mercy upon them and come to their aid."

November. This morning I was called to a house where different exiled families live. We had given them bedding, clothes, food and the necessary household utensils. While they were in prison yesterday everything had been stolen. An Armenian family had given their daughter to a Turkish gendarme, and when the arrests began, he had helped to hide the wife and the children, and then emptied five different houses. This was a great sorrow but I played the part of the police and he gave most of the things back.

The commandant came up at noon. He was not satisfied with the work that the new Kaimakam and the police commissioner had done. Baron Antreas and Professor Khachadoorian were put in prison because on the day before they had hidden themselves in a Turkish home. In the afternoon rumours started that people would be picked up again, and there was panic among the unhappy women and children. Towards evening Miss Harley, Mrs. Riggs, and I went down to some of the streets where Armenians live. They were afraid to remain indoors and gathered around us in the street. We comforted them as well as we could and got them back to their houses, but how difficult it is to see them in such fear and so hard to be unable to save them. How often I have wished I could gather them all in and fold my wings over them, keeping all danger away from them. Karen-Marie came up for a couple of hours to greet me. She could not remain long because of the situation. In the evening, after supper, all the missionaries came to my room, and we had a devotional hour together. It was so good to have dear little Bessie again. I was busy sewing clothes for her as she has nothing. We do not know the moment they will come and send us away, so I have collected necessities together, so that, if needed, I could be ready to leave at once.

7 November. We had thought that there would be another massacre today. As soon as it was light this morning we went to the windows to see if there were any soldiers at our doors, but there were none, and we were very relieved. It is doubly distressing to have these terrible things happen on a Sunday. Thank God—the day has been quiet. At 9.00 a.m. Mr. Riggs took six men who are here with us down to Mezreh to show them to the Commandant who was in Harpoot yesterday and had said he

would come and inspect our buildings because we were hiding refugees. When he saw them today he said, "You can go again. I thought you had the houses filled with young men." They returned more light-hearted than when they left. They had thought they were going to their death and were as white as a sheet as they said goodbye. There was great joy over their return.

This afternoon we had a meeting. Badveli Vartan preached on the text Psalm 84-6-7, "Who passing through the valley of Ba-ca make it a well, the rain also filleth the pools. They go from strength to strength." We are passing through the valley. Let us go with song, helping each other. An officer at the hospital had told him, "When I was out with one of the crowd of Christians who were to be killed, there were some who stood with uplifted hands. Their faces turned to the sky, as if nothing was going to happen to them. It was terrible to shoot them, but we had to. The government had sent us." A Gregorian priest who was with a crowd said, when the soldiers began shooting, "Wait a moment, there is something we must do first." Then he shouted to the big crowd, "Be strong and cheerful. In a moment we will be with Jesus." Then the shooting began and soon everyone had left this vale of tears. Never before have we understood the books of the Prophets and the Ecclesiastes as now. It is as if, time after time, we must say, "Ezekiel, is it today you have written it? From where comes your knowledge of our situation so exactly." Never before has John, Chapter 14—the words of Jesus—"Let not your heart be troubled" been understood as they are now. For now we know what fear is, and this whole blessed chapter, how precious it is. Anything else we read now does not sink in, but these blessed words of Jesus sink into the heart, because it is these words that we need.

As darkness fell a young Armenian man came to my room. I had stitched a wound in his head last Tuesday. He was wearing a charshaf and veil and was as white as a sheet with fear. He told me that he and Baron Levon must leave in an hour with some Kurds for Dersim. A Turkish friend of theirs had sent a message that he should leave as soon as possible because a massacre would begin again tomorrow and not even the Protestants would be safe. So now, again, everyone is in fear and dread. But God is mighty to turn away the evil, so it will not happen. He will do it in His mercy. We say with Setrak, Misak, and Apetnakov—our God is mighty to save us, and He will save us. But if He does not, then we will love and follow Him anyway.

8 November. The day has passed quietly. There was no massacre, and everyone has breathed easier. I was visiting some of the sick. How hard it is to see them lying on rags, shivering in cold rooms without windows and without anyone to nurse them. Many took ill last Friday when they were driven off to the government building. They have seen so much, and endured such hardship, that they have become sick from fear. I wonder how they do not die of it.

Baron Antreas and Professor Khachadoorian have been imprisoned. We feel very sorry for Baron Antreas because he is an honest and serious Christian man. Professor Khachadoorian, as far as we know, has not been completely true and honest under these heavy persecutions, so maybe the punishment is coming now.

Today a crowd of 35 men and 400 women—Armenians who have been collected together from those remaining villages—has been sent away. Several of the men had become Moslems, but it did not help them. It is terrible to think of these poor people out on the road, without food or clothes, now that the rain has begun, but maybe they will not be taken very far before being killed. The Commandant, who at this time is acting in place of the Vali, has again promised that they will be safely guarded. But what happened to their earlier promises? We simply cannot believe a word they say.

[9] November. Today I have been in four different houses, all full of sick people, everyone with high fever around 40 degrees C. A mother lay in a room with her four sick children beside her, the one more ill than the other. Another room held another sick mother and her little daughter. In a corner of a living room lay two small children, a boy of three years and a girl of one year. The mother had died the other day. Now both children are sick. The wind swept through the rooms, and outside the rain poured down. When the Armenians were sent away, the Turks plundered the houses, removing everything, including the doors and windows. Now these refugees must live in these open rooms. We cannot get windows. Glass can no longer be found, and we have no money to have frames made for paper to be stuck over them. The only hope we have for them is that the winter will be mild, so that they will not freeze to death. I held devotions in different places.

10 November (Wednesday). I have visited more sick people today. I was over with Anna Varzhoohi to tell her that Karen-Marie is not allowed to take children in now. It was hard to see her so ill and unable to work with the eight small children around her. She has become very much worse since the last massacre, and the old mother, a fine lovable old woman, sits and cannot move. She was so badly beaten. One eye is still badly discoloured from the heavy blow a soldier gave her with his gun, but we never hear her complain, even under such a heavy burden. Oh, if only I could help her.

11 November. I have again been around on sick-visits, and found some of the patients a little better. I also visited the Kazandjians and how different it was from my last visit. Then they sorrowed and wept over their husbands and sons who had been killed. But now they said, "Blessed is your will oh God. Thank you, that you took them, so that they should not live to see all this misery. We die every day, if only we could die quickly and reach Home."

I also went up to Baron Antreas's home to visit his mother and his wife. I found only his mother, as his wife had left earlier for Mezreh to beseech the high ranking government officials to release her husband. I was so glad to see and talk with the mother. She said, "He is all I have left, all my other children have been killed. I can only pray to God the whole day. He is the only one I have faith in. There is no one on earth. Whether I get my son back or not, blessed is His will. I only long to be permitted to go Home." Then she said, "Oh, I would be glad if cholera would come, and we would all take ill and die. That is how I would like to go, for I am afraid of death coming in another way, afraid that I should deny my Saviour." But now, if it is His will that she should lose her life, he will also give her the strength to endure. A woman came at noon and told me that one of my patients was dead, a 10 year old boy from Erzingan. When Mr. Riggs went down at 2.00 p.m. to bury him, he heard a sound as soon as he entered the room. There was no one with the body, which was rolled up in a cloth, and when Mr. Riggs lifted it from the face, he saw that the boy was still breathing. He returned and told me, and I went straight there, but there was nothing I could do. Anyway it was better for the boy to die as he was completely alone in the world, his parents having been killed on the way here. As I was coming away again, I met Mr. Riggs bringing Baron Antreas and Professor Khachadoorian home. The Kaimakam had given him permission to take them from the prison. Great was our joy. God indeed hears prayer.

At our meeting in the afternoon it was decided that we should open a hospital for the many sick, if we can obtain government permission.

15 November. It now became a matter of seriousness that our friends should leave here. At 7 o'clock this morning three arabadjis came with two wagons as it was impossible to find proper travelling carriages, although one must pay twice as much as before. One of the arabadjis was a real devil. He looked capable of anything bad, and it was not a comfortable feeling for us to see our friends in the company of such a man. After we had had devotions together and commended each one to the Almighty's hands, they set off. Mr. H. Riggs, Dr. Parmelee and I went down to Mezreh, where a cart should have been waiting with Miss Campbell, but when we came we found that it was in pieces, and we had to wait until they put it together, set new wheels on, and a lot of other things. They left at 11 o'clock and it was a large party. There were four carts with two zapties. Three officers from the hospital followed on the road, also the Consul, Mr. Picciotto, the kavas, Mr. H. Riggs, Dr. Atkinson, and I. We went a short distance past the nearest village of Kessrik. On the road we saw three skeletons lying on the edge of a ditch. They had been covered with a thin layer of earth, but the heavy rain of the last few days had washed it away, so we saw them quite clearly.

It is very dismal now to come to the Shuga. There is not a single Armenian to be seen. Only dirty, ragged, wild and crude Kurds and Turks. Also high ranking officers who walk around so proud and bold, as if the whole world belonged to them. For all that, they are not secure but afraid. They see the soldiers walking around the streets with loaded guns and bayonets. No wonder that they have no peace in their hearts.

16 November. This morning, when I went around my patients, I met a little boy at one of the houses. He was only five years old and told me that there was no one in the house. All had fled the previous evening in fear of a massacre. The boy's mother had died a week ago, so he and his little two year old sister had been alone all night in the house. But what was worse was that, as the two little ones lay together, the little sister died in the night, and the boy lay with her till the morning. This cuts me to the heart. Oh, how I long to be able to take children like this into a home and care for them, but the government will not give permission. People are again in great fear of a massacre. The Vali has returned from his trip to Erzeroum and there are rumours that he has brought back with him 200 young Armenian men who had been sent to Erzeroum to work. They are being put into the Red Konak, where everyone had been held before they were taken away and killed, so this is obviously what will happen to them. Oh, how long can this go on? Lord, come quickly and take your own Home in whatever way is your will. Oh, but come quickly.

18 November. Mr. Riggs went down to Mezreh to find out the truth about the young men that the Vali is said to have brought back. It is true that they were brought here and are now imprisoned. No one is allowed to see them. How dreadful it is to think about these poor souls now we know what lies before them, and to be so completely tied that we can do nothing to help them. We cannot even come and try to comfort them. Mr. Ehmann has promised to go to the Vali to see if he can have permission to do anything. Today we received a letter from Miss Riggs and Miss Campbell. It was written in Kezin Khan, a day's journey from Mezreh, but it took two days to arrive. Everything has gone well so far. The weather has been glorious, but they have not been able to enjoy the scenery. So many corpses lie along the way, many only a day old. Poor, unfortunate Armenians, what must you suffer and experience.

This morning I went down to help at the funeral of one of my patients who died last night. She was an 11 year old girl, but there was only gladness that the Lord had taken her Home, away from this vale of tears. Some weeks ago there were some Turks who wanted to have her, as she was a beautiful and charming little girl, but she was hidden down in a dark cellar, and there she sat and prayed to the Lord to save her from the hands of the Turks. She became ill some days later, and now she is Home with Him, whom she loved. A lot of women had gathered to comfort the mother. One of them, with her 12 year old daughter, had been sent away during the last deportations two weeks ago. When they were near a little village, three hours journey away, she met a soldier whom she knew, and he helped her to escape, but she went through a great deal before arriving here this morning. She explained how the soldiers had said to them, "If you have money with you, give it to us, you will not need it any more. You are going to die." They took their clothes from them first, so that they would not become bloodstained. But they did not see so many corpses on this side of Keghvank. This was because the Turkish Beg in Keghvank had heard that an American Consul would be coming, so he had got busy, getting men to go out and clear the roads. Everybody said, "Oh if only we had been among the first to go. We are going the same way, but we die every day, and this fear is worse than death." Never before have I understood the words of Jesus so well as I do now, when he said that if the time was not shortened, not even the believers could endure it. So we cry to Him, "Oh Lord have mercy upon us. Stop these cruelties, but if it is not your will, give us strength to endure."

19 November. Amongst the sick I visited today was a young girl of 20, named Tsavalits, which means "child of pain." Her parents had given her this name because she was born at the time of the massacre, 20 years ago. She came here last night from Hoghe, her feet badly swollen, and trembling from weakness and nervousness. It was no wonder, poor child. Her history is as follows:

Together with other Armenian women and children she had been kept in a Turkish Beg's house in Hoghe. Some soldiers came to the village two weeks ago and took these women and children, but said to them, "You must not be afraid, you are only going to Mezreh to show your papers. Protestants, Syrians, and Catholics will then be allowed to go." So they went, happy in that belief. They were put into a walled graveyard, and shortly afterwards a man came and asked for their identification papers which they gave him. Now they were all sure they would be free, but a few minutes later the Police Mudir came in and said, "Make ready quickly, there were deportations a short time ago, and you must join the others and go with them." There was weeping and lamentation. One of the soldiers said to Tsavalits, "Go over into that corner. I will save you." So she did as she was told, and he sent five others who had given him money. After the big crowd had left, he took them off. It was now dark, but the moon was shining. When they had walked a little way they met an armed Kurd, one of those hired by the government to patrol the roads and the mountains and shoot down any refugees they met. This man said, "Where are you going? I will kill you." The soldier tried to persuade him not to, but the Kurd said, "No, I have orders to kill everyone. Nobody shall escape me." The soldier realized that he could make no impression on the Kurd, so he started to plead for Tsavalits, saying, "I want to take her away for myself." Then the Kurd said, "Go into the side," so she did, and the soldier said to her, "Run, I can't save you." She started running and the Kurd fired three shots after her, but he missed her in the darkness. She ran until she came to a cleft in the mountain. There she sat and rested. After she had collected her strength, she went back to see what had happened to the other five she had left on the road. When she got there she found them all lying on the ground. Two elderly women had been shot in the head, and had died immediately. A young girl was still warm. A young woman, also shot, but not yet dead, shouted, "Kill me, kill me. Don't let me lie here like this." A little 12 year old girl had been shot at such close range that her clothes had caught fire and she was burning. But Tsavalits could not stay put. She ran as hard as she could to the village to see if she could get any help. It was night and there was no one there but Turks who would not come to help. When morning came the 20 year old girl, Tsavalits, felt warmth as she lay on the ground. She had recovered consciousness and said now she saw the little 12 year old girl's body burning, and the young woman who had crawled towards it to warm herself at the flames. But she was so weak she fell down on the girl's body and burned herself. She could not bear it any longer, so she struggled up and tried to walk to the village, which she reached in the morning. This girl and Tsavalits have been brought here by the Turkish Beg in the village, the first girl with a bad gunshot wound in the back.

20 November. We received 400 liras for our relief work, and are now able to buy more bedding and clothes for these poor ones. The few who remain are afraid of staying in the villages, so they come here to us without anything. The rumour got around that we had something more available and this morning there was a crowd assembled outside our doors. One was a woman who had been reunited with her two children after having long given up hope of finding them alive. They had been living with some Kurds but had now arrived here. The little girl of five years said, when her mother spoke to her in Armenian, "Mother, you must speak Turkish, otherwise the soldiers will come and kill us." It was impossible to persuade or make her speak Armenian.

Three little orphan boys came and said, "Mayrig, can we have a vest today?" As Mrs. Riggs said, "Yes, come and see if we have some to fit you," the little boys said, "Mayrig, the other day you told us there were none, and that you had no money, and that we should ask God to send you money. We asked God every day—did the money come?" Mrs. Riggs said, "Yes, children, the money came," and with shining faces they went in, and a vest was found for each. How wonderful it is to be able to help these poor, poor people. Many of them used to be rich, now they have nothing more than the dry bread we give them. Nevertheless they are full of thanks and praise for it.

22 November. Today we had a visit from Karen-Marie and Sister Jenny. We also had a telegram from our friends who have left. They reached Diarbekir on Friday. The journey took twice as long as normal, because of the evil arabadji. We hope they have succeeded in changing them and will be able to make quicker progress.

This afternoon we had a visit from Baron Antreas. He told us that a Turkish friend had arrived from Diarbekir having seen the last large group of exiles who had left here. He had met them at Mardin, and they numbered about 2,000, with 50 soldiers and one officer. Baron Antreas asked his friend how the soldiers were treating them, and he answered, "What can they do? They drive the crowd in front of them, and if any are too weak to keep pace with the rest, they knock them down or shoot them and throw them down the mountain side. All along the road one could hear the cries of these half-dead people." How terrible it is to think of our friends going out on such a journey, certain to meet death. It would be much more merciful if they killed them at once, instead of taking them on journeys of several days in this cold and rain, without food or clothes, all that they had of these and money being taken from them shortly after setting out. They lie out at night. Just imagine what that means at this time of the year, when it rains day and night, added to what they already undergo of taunts, blows, and shameful treatment. The poor women now understand quite clearly that the Turkish objective is simply to exterminate the Armenian nation with as much suffering as possible. We can only pray to the Lord to strengthen them in their suffering and keep them faithful till the end, so that they may inherit eternal life. "Oh, think, when the saved communion from all the generations of the earth will meet in Heaven's glory. Oh, think, when the Lord's army of witnesses, the millions of His servants on earth, will meet Him who heard their prayers." Yes, what a reunion it will be, when we meet in Heaven's glory.

27 November. Today we assembled at Dr. Atkinson's to celebrate Thanksgiving Day. We had a lovely quiet day. First there was a Thanksgiving Service at 11 o'clock, during which each of us stated what we were thankful for. What permeated everything was the knowledge that we are alive, that we are still here, and that we still have a few friends left to work for. I stayed overnight with Karen-Marie. In the morning I returned from Mezreh in pouring rain. Both little Bessie and I were soaked, but I had to come back, as this afternoon I had a group of the poor women coming to whom I am teaching handiwork.

28 November. This afternoon a large crowd of Armenian women and children gathered in our school for church service. The very few men who are left also joined us. It was a lovely occasion and it gives one strength to hold out when we can meet in this way. A united "Amen" was heard when Badveli Vartan gave thanks to God for the peaceful days we enjoy just now, and his sermon went straight to our hearts. He preached on the text, "My son do not regard lightly the discipline of the Lord, nor lose courage when you are punished by Him,"[*] showing us that it is true that God loves us, and He punishes because He loves us. It was exactly what we needed. So

---

[*]·The words, beginning, "My son" must be from the New English translation of the bible. The old words are, "My Son, despise not thou the chastening of the Lord, nor faint when thou art rebuked of him." Hebrews 12. V.5.—K.V.

many say to us, "Can God love us, when He allows these terrible things to happen?" Yes, in fact there are not few who say, "If there is a God, why doesn't He help us?" All these questions were answered, and we hope and pray that this sermon will bear fruit a hundredfold.

29 November. Today I opened a soup-kitchen, and soup was sent out to 20 sick people. The pleasure and gratitude were great. Some poor souls who were standing outside our doors in the beggar's alley were brought in and I gave them each a helping of hot soup. How pleased I would be if I could give all the many poor ones a hot meal every day, or at least the little children. It is terribly difficult now in the severe cold not to have any hot food, only dry bread, but it would cost a lot of money to give food to about 300 people. I am very pleased and thankful for what I can do, and this is only possible because of the goodness of friends at home.

1 December. When we got up this morning we found winter surrounding us. Everywhere snow lay like a white carpet, and when I went out on my rounds it was difficult to keep one's feet in the streets, as many of them are very steep. How very hard it is to go around and see the many poor people lying in ice-cold rooms, without windows or doors. Their bedding consists only of some useless rags. In several places the snow had drifted a couple of feet into the rooms and the sick lay there shivering with fever. Nevertheless, most of them are so thankful for what they have. Everywhere I went they asked, "What news do you bring? Is there any cause for fear?" How often have we experienced what fear really is in these last months.

There has been great apprehension again today. It was being said this morning that there would be another massacre today but nothing has happened so far. It gives the Turks great pleasure to forecast terrible happenings in order to keep the poor Armenians in a state of terror. The Turks also say that just as Jesus is not saving or helping the Armenians now, neither will He help nor save them on the Day of Judgement. They will be shut out, but Mohammed will be standing under a large tree, where all the Moslems will gather from the four corners of the earth and, with Mohammed leading, will go straight into Heaven. They say that, after the war, all the Germans will come here and become Moslems.

20 December. Three weeks have passed since I last wrote and so much has happened since then that it will be impossible for me to remember everything. The days have been so filled with all sorts of work that it has not been possible to find the time to write.

Although there are still rumours that there will be a massacre and great fear among the few poor women and children who remain, no one from here has been sent away. We thank God for every day He allows us to keep our friends. But still multitudes of young Armenian men, who during the year had been sent away as soldiers, are now being sent here. After an overnight stay, without being allowed to see anyone, they are sent southward the next day. They reach no further than the mountains, where they are killed.

The other day two young men came who had escaped from one of these crowds. They said that when the journey started there were 2,000 of them, now only 300 were left. They die of hunger and cold. They get nothing to eat except what is given on the way through the villages, but as there are no Armenians left there, nobody gives them anything. These two young men clearly revealed the extent of the Armenian affliction. Only a few rags covered their bodies. They were bare-footed, starved out of any resemblance to human beings, and looked completely cowed. At this time of the year they cannot even find grass to eat. Last week a group of 300 young men were sent southward, accompanied by 15 policemen. When they reached Keghvank, four hours away from Mezreh, where the road goes up into the mountains, they knew they could expect nothing but death, and in their despair they killed the 15 policemen and fled. A couple of them arrived at the hospital and asked for admission, but we could not do this. If it was discovered later it would bring disaster upon the other Armenians here. This incident aroused the fury of the Turks, and now it is said that everyone will be sent away next Wednesday. If this happens it will be terrible. Just imagine what it means, to turn out women and children into such cold winter weather, without clothes or food, and without shelter. We know very well that they are not taken far, but it means that their suffering and their last hours will be more bitter and hard.

On Sunday the 12th, Miss Harley, Dr. Atkinson and I went to Keghvank to meet Miss McLaren and Miss Shane, who were arriving from Bitlis. We reached Keghvank after a three hour ride. On the way we saw the corpses and skeletons of at least 100 people. It was dreadful to see how the bones were spread over the road and in the ditches and fields. In several places ploughing was in progress and bones and skeletons were scattered over the field. The corpse of a man lay on the road. It could only have been a couple of days old. It was naked and the dogs had torn away the hands and feet. When we returned in the afternoon, half of the body had disappeared. These are the remains of human beings, who had brothers and sisters and parents who loved them. How must these families feel, thinking of their loved ones meeting death in such a terrible way, with their poor bodies left strewn upon the earth to be eaten by dogs and wolves. I think how it would be if it were my father or mother or little sister. The road was filled with Turks and Kurds on their way to Mezreh. A lot of them came from a village, Kurdemlik, from where thousands of Armenian men, women, and children were taken away and killed. This village lies on the way to Goljuk. Never before had I seen these people look so rough and wild. Even young boys consider themselves powerful lords. They shouted after us, "Gavur! You Christian dog."

The two missionaries arrived at 2.00 p.m., but unfortunately alone. We had hoped to bring the few young Armenian girls who stayed with them at Bitlis, but the government would not permit it. They would not even allow them to bring one as a servant. It had become late, their horses were in a bad condition and one was dying. We realized that it was impossible for them to reach Mezreh that evening, so Miss Harley and I left them near Vartetil and rode as fast as our horses allowed to get home to Harpoot before evening.

The Dr. and Mahmed kavas gave their horses to the two women, and they walked the rest of the way leaving the cart in the village. They arrived in Mezreh next day. The two women had arrived at 8 o'clock in the evening, dead tired after the strain of the harrowing journey. On Monday evening they came to Harpoot. How difficult it must have been for the two of them to be in Bitlis alone after Mr. Knapp had been taken away. Some days after his departure the German sister Martha died of typhus. Miss McLaren had to perform the funeral service as there was no minister or other man in the place. All the Armenians have been sent away except for some school girls, who will be taken by the Turks now that the two missionaries have left. They wanted to take the girls away on different occasions but had been prevented by the missionaries. A lot of Armenians from the town itself had been killed on the outskirts. They now told us the reason why Mr. Knapp had been sent away. When the government began sending people into exile, the missionaries had taken in about 300 women and children. They sent a list of them to the government, asking for permission to keep them. Some time later some soldiers came to examine their house and as they were leaving a man sprang up in one of the windows and fired a shot after them, wounding one of the soldiers. When they broke into the room from where the shot had been fired they found a man dead. He had shot himself afterwards. This man had come in disguised as a woman together with the 300 some days before and had hidden in a big container which was used for storing corn. None of the missionaries knew that he was in the house, but now the government insisted that it had been planned by Mr. Knapp, and a delegation came ordering them all to leave that day. It was of no help for Miss Shane and Miss McLaren to tell how often Mr. Knapp had entreated the Armenians to give up their weapons. Miss Shane was ill and had had a very high temperature for a long time. She had so far not been out of bed but got up and went down as the delegation came. She said, "It is impossible. I cannot leave." They listened to her, and said that they could all wait until she was strong enough to travel. They could then leave together, taking their school children with them. But all this was only a made-up story. They returned on Sunday and said that Mr. Knapp had to leave at once. He was sent away at 2 o'clock in the morning accompanied by 16 policemen.

They saw the same as we did here, how the Armenians' houses were plundered and burned. The whole way they had travelled was a field of corpses, and there were places where they had to drive over them. How dreadful.

They have both decided to stay for the winter. Miss Shane will help in the school and Miss McLaren in the hospital.

Dr. Atkinson and the Consul left some weeks ago for Goljuk. They rode around the lake, a journey of a couple of hours, and saw about 10,000 corpses lying unburied. They were naked and so dreadfully tortured that it cannot be described here.

Almost every day new refugees arrive here and their histories are terrible but true. Even if later, if an account of them makes dreadful reading, I feel it is necessary to write them down in order that our friends at home may learn what these, our poor brothers and sisters, have gone through.

One of my patients, Zartar Antonian, from the village Itchme, six hours journey on foot, told me the other day how she had been saved. All the Armenians from that village were taken up into the mountains nearby. The men had already been taken. In the mountains they were divided into groups and moved apart from each other. There were 17 in her group, including herself and her five children, and they began to kill them with knives. She saw four of her children killed, from her baby of six months to her eldest of 12 years, and she was unable to cry, her tongue cleaving to the roof of her mouth. All around were people lying in their own blood. She laid her head down on the body of her three year old child begging them to kill her also, but her only remaining child, an eight year old boy, clung to her, sobbing and crying. Whether the soldiers were touched by the sight, or whatever the reason was, the two of them were left alive. When the soldiers left, the mother and child fled here. The poor mother cried as if her heart would break when she told me this, and I cried with her. We have God's permission to weep with those who weep. She ended her story with these words, "Now I know why I was saved this time. If I had been killed I would have been lost, but now I am ready to die." Now she lies very ill with erysipelas. Maybe she will be allowed to go Home now. Everyone has a wish to die a natural death and when they become sick they are thankful, but it is surprising how often they recover.

We now have 40 patients with typhus or scarlet fever lying in the houses. We can do so little for them. We have made great efforts to reopen our hospital, but cannot get government permission. They say it is not necessary, and from their point of view this is true, as they want all the Armenians to die. Why, then, should we be allowed to help them when they are ill and likely to die? The Turks are also furious because we help the many poor people now. They do everything they can to kill them, and we oppose them by trying to help. The other day an old woman met a Turkish boy. She had a bread ticket in her hand which we had given her. He snatched it from her and tore it to pieces, and she came crying to us.

Another little mother told me her story. She comes from Hooiloo. As in all the other towns and villages, the men here had also been sent away, and afterwards all the rich women and children. One day some weeks ago soldiers came and collected the remaining Armenians. There were about 300 women, each with four or five children. So it was a large crowd that they took up into the mountains to Lake Goljuk. When they reached the Kurdish village of Kurdemlik, the Kurds reinforced the soldiers, and together they drove these poor women and children along passes so narrow that they had to go in single file. So they set guards on the sides of the mountain, who could shoot down anyone trying to flee. Then terrible things started. Women and children were killed one by one with knives and stones. This woman was beaten and fell down. Just beside her they tortured another woman and she saw that they continued with this as long as the woman moved or made a sound. The blood from the poor tortured woman stained her. They started beating her again. She must have fainted and they gave her up for dead.

The Kurds came and removed the heads from the corpses. When this woman recovered consciousness in the evening she found herself naked. They had rolled her down the mountain. All the Kurds and soldiers had left when she got up, and there was only a field full of naked corpses. After searching up and down she found her little six year old daughter sitting and crying on a rock. She told her mother that the soldiers asked her if she had any money and said, "Then give it to us, and we won't kill you." The little girl had one mejidie, about four kroners, which the mother had given her when they left home, and she gave it to the soldiers, so they left her in peace. But the Kurds had taken all her clothes, and this child had sat there, naked and alone, surrounded by tortured corpses. Just think about what this little child has seen and gone through of terror. You mothers at home—think if it had been one of your children, whom you protect so tenderly from all sorrow, suffering, and all the distress of the world. This mother had lost three children but she counted herself fortunate to have kept this one. The two of them now began on their way in the dark. They came shortly to a village, where they begged for a few clothes, but the people there would not take them in. So they had to go on and have now landed up here with us.

In the same room as this woman, there is another from the same village. For some time she was kept by a Turk, but she ran away a few weeks ago and came to us. She cries unceasingly and says, "Oh, my children. Oh, my children, what a horrible death. Oh, if only I had stayed in America, I would have been spared this terrible suffering." She had earlier lived in America for some years but had come back.

In the same house in another room lies a woman suffering from typhus. She has 14 large knife wounds in her body. She had also lost consciousness, and they had believed her dead and left her lying.

In a third room are 18 orphan children from Erzeroum, Erzingan, and other places. A young girl of 19 from Erzingan acts as a mother to them. Think what each one of these children has lived through, of terror and suffering, in their short life. They look wretched, starving, and frightened. Oh, if we could only take them into a home, to guard them, care for them, and take the fear away from their hearts, but we are not allowed, and can only help them in this way, sending them around into different houses. For the dry bread alone that we give to our poor people we pay 1,200 kronera month. This is only in Harpoot. Down in Mezreh we pay another 300 kroner. We give them bread tickets, and afterwards we pay the bakers. Apart from this we must give them clothes and all the other necessities. All this is made possible by the goodness of our friends at home. Without this help all these remaining people would die of starvation, as none of them has any money, and there is no work to be had.

17 December. Eight days ago our dear little Annie B. Riggs became ill with something that looked like a very heavy cold. As she had no fever we had taken the illness quite calmly, until a couple of days ago, when her eyes and throat began to swell. Yesterday, Thursday, she became worse and was very weak. Dr. Atkinson came up to see her and said it was very serious, but none of us could or would accept the thought that we might lose her. She has so often before been very seriously ill, but always recovered. It would seem impossible to live in Harpoot without this lovable little girl, so pure, so obedient, so devoted to God, so wise and loving. She has been a missionary in the true sense, bringing Heaven nearer to all who knew her. So today came the hard time when we must let her go. I was with her the whole day, when we worked to the end to help her. She was conscious to the last, and time after time called on her mother, always saying, "Oh, mother dear," but whatever else she tried to say we could not understand. When Dr. Atkinson had told her parents that there was no hope, Mrs. Riggs said to her, "Little Annie, Jesus will soon come and call you Home to Himself, would you like to go?" Little Annie said, "Yes, mother." Shortly after she was borne Home to Jesus. It was hard to look upon the dear parents in their sorrow. The light, joy, and love of their lives was taken from them. They sat for a little while by the bed, then they arose and said, "It is all right. God did it in love." So they went out and Dr. Parmelee and I went in and set everything in order.

She was laid to rest on Sunday morning, the 19th. We had collected all the greenery and flowers that could be found, and the beautiful white coffin was completely covered with them. Early in the morning I went out to the Garden and decked the grave with greenery. First, all the missionaries gathered in the living room for a little service. Mr. Riggs himself read different passages from the bible. First, "He shall lead His sheep like a shepherd. The lambs shall He carry in His arms" and "Suffer the little children to come unto me, and forbid them not." Also a part of Revelation, Chapt. 21 and 22, verses 1-5. Afterwards the coffin was carried up to the Girls' School where we had a Children's Service in the Varzharan Hall. Badveli Vartan talked about Jairus' daughter, "She is not dead, but sleeping" especially for the children. The small children sang some of their own hymns. After the service we followed the coffin out to the Garden where she was to be buried. There was a freezing fog, when we had hoped for sunshine, but though it did not shine, the beautiful trees in the Garden were dressed in shimmering white, and glittered with purity. So we returned home. It was nearly impossible to believe that we would never again hear her call and run when she came to see us, or never again see her sitting with her mother. She was a lovable child, of whom we all said, "She was not made for this world." When her grandmother died some months ago, her mother said to her, "What shall I read to you, little Annie?" She loved her mother to read aloud to her, so she said, "Please read to me from the bible. There is nothing so comforting as that." Her prayer that evening was, "I thank you, dear Lord, for Grandma, and now Thou hast taken her to Thyself I pray Thee to fill the empty place in our hearts." So often when we had our daily prayer-meeting, she said, "Mama, may I pray?" and she would pray like a grown-up person who had lived in close communion with her Saviour many years. How she loved God's glorious nature—first flowers, then animals, and the many little Armenian children. No matter how poor and wretched they looked, she saw something lovable in them. The day before she took ill, she stood with me at the window. A poor little boy came running down the street, ragged and bare-legged, and an ordinary person would not have noticed him, but she called, "Oh, mother dear, come quick, come quick" and when her mother came she said, "Oh, mother, is he not dear. Oh, isn't he clever."

She was a real little mother. How lovely it was to see her sitting with her dolls. She had 19 and had never broken one. All were equally cherished, each of them had its special place in her little motherly heart. Every Sunday she had a little Sunday School for them. Every one had a verse to say. One of the big ones had to play the organ when they prayed, and they all had to kneel down. Each in turn was brought down with her to the dining room table where she set down a little plate with food for them.

There is much more I could say about our dear little girl, but all I will say is that I thank God for every day she was allowed to be with us. My life has been much richer for knowing her and for being one of those for whom she cared.

20 December (Monday). Today there has been a great flock of the poor outside our house, and Mrs. Riggs has found it necessary to give them every minute of her time. She could not help them very much during the days of Annie's illness.

Dr. Atkinson is now ill and we are a little afraid that it is typhus. If it is, it will certainly be very bad, as he is a very strong man, and the stronger people always have it much more severely. He himself and the other doctors do not think that it is typhus. I have been around many different houses today to see to patients. There are so many with typhus and scarlet fever. In one of the houses I saw a man as sick as he could possibly be. A year ago he was so strong and healthy that he could rightly have been described as of giant form, but now he is only a stooping skeleton. He used to be rich, and one of our most learned men, now he is without even rags enough to cover his body. His face is distorted and disfigured from the great suffering he has undergone. He was originally from one of the best Protestant families in Erzeroum and was taken by the government to work on the roads with other Armenian men. He had worked like this for a year without any pay. Now that the government has no further use for them, they are being sent off southwards in droves. They reach as far as here, but no further. From here they are sent away in batches, which means they will be killed. This man and two others escaped when they were in the neighbourhood of Mezreh, but they dare not show themselves outside, otherwise they will be taken and sent off again and their torture will certainly be worse than before. I went with him to see his two fellow sufferers. We passed through several dark rooms until we came to a hole in the ground. There was a little hole in the wall, through which a faint ray of light came in, and it was cold and very dismal. The three men had a ragged mattress between them and a little stone jar for water, which a little girl fills for them once a day. These are all their earthly belongings. These three are the picture of wretchedness and suffering, and their condition is the same as the few men who are still alive. Oh, how hard it was to look upon them in their pitiful state—ill, starved, and in dreadful fear and uncertainty. Oh, if only we could help them, and shield them from their enemies, but we can do so little. But one thing we can do—talk and pray with them, encourage them to be faithful until the end, that they may inherit a crown of life. Oh, how many times we have said that it was easier for the first groups of people who were taken away. They knew nothing of the suffering and death that awaited them, and these were soon over, but those who still remain live in constant terror, so that they say, "We die every day."

I went home and told of what I had seen, and Mrs. Riggs said she would look out for some clothes for them. I sent some charcoal down, so that they could have a little fire to warm themselves, and I also sent some medicine. But I cannot go down very often in case the Turks should see and become suspicious.

Mr. Riggs has received a letter from the government, requesting him to supply a list of the money and possessions the Armenians have left with us. This has again awakened great fear among the Armenians. The same evening that Mr. Riggs learned that such a letter was on the way, he gave some large sums of money to some of the remaining Armenians to whom it belonged. If they come to take what we have belonging to the Armenians, they will not find much, for Mr. Riggs immediately sent all money to America, and what we had of kitchen utensils and other articles we had bought, we have already given to the many poor.

The other day the Kaimakam and the Police Commissioner were called down to the Vali, who said all Armenians in Harpoot were to be sent away. At this time there are some men here who were sent from Constantinople to examine the circumstances of the Armenians, and it is said that these men will order the extermination of them all and obtain their money in the process. The reason for this is that the government has not had nearly as much money as they had expected from the Armenians. It has gone into the pockets of the local civil servants, who have now gone off and will live well for the rest of their lives on their plunder. Our Police Commissioner is a very kind and good man who has done much to help the Armenians. He has given many a fatherly talk to the Kaimakam, and the latter's answer to the Vali's order to exterminate the Armenians was, "I am not in a good state of health, and cannot do this work. If you want it done you must dismiss me, and do it afterwards." The Police Commissioner answered, when he was given the same order, "I cannot do it. If you commend it, you must dismiss me first, and then do it."

An old sheikh in Harpoot went down some time ago to the Vali, cast himself on his face at the Vali's feet, begging and praying him to stop the persecution of the Armenians. "It is enough now. Let the innocent go free. Our Koran does not allow all this cruelty." The Vali solemnly declared to him that this was the truth and that the persecution must stop, but this evil man cannot live without seeing the innocent people suffer.

Another good Turkish man in Harpoot had an Armenian man hidden in his house. When the government ordered the Armenian to be handed over to them, the Turk answered, "I have known him since he was a boy and I love him like a son. I know he is innocent, and I will not hand him over. If you want him, then you must first take and kill me." It is so good to meet such people, who really suffer with the Armenians, but unfortunately there are very few. The others are many times worse than before, and the seven Armenian men, who were permitted to stay in Harpoot because they were craftsmen, are treated far from well. One of these is Sukias Agha, an old man, who is one of the leading figures in our Protestant Church. He was the only watchmaker and was therefore allowed to stay. He is not a strong man and these last terrible months have taken their toll of him. Though he is sick, he must go to his shop early in the morning and remain there the whole day. There are times when he has so much work that it is impossible to take more. When he says so, the Turks answer, "What do you think we keep you for? You must do it." He receives no payment for his work, all must be done free, so his life is not to be envied.

21 December (Tuesday). I asked Mr. Riggs to tell the Doctor's family that if they wished me to come down and help to nurse Dr. Atkinson I would be glad to do so. Mr. Riggs returned in the evening and said they were very happy with my offer. If it was typhus they would like me to come, but they still believed it was recurrent fever and therefore it was not necessary. We were all happy to hear that it was not typhus.

22 December (Wednesday). Dr. Parmelee came back from Mezreh yesterday evening and brought us the distressing message that Dr. Atkinson has typhus, and that they wished me to come as quickly as possible. This morning I was busy packing a few clothes and giving instructions about my work, which I must hand over to the others.

23 December (Thursday). I came down to Mezreh at 11 o'clock and gave Bessie into the care of Karen-Marie. After I had eaten lunch, I went to the hospital and found the Doctor very ill. He was conscious, knew me, and tried to say, "It is good that Maria has come," but he was scarcely able to speak. His heart was weak. Towards evening we gave him a saline infusion and when I left at 9 o'clock, I thought he was a little better. However, when I returned at 7 o'clock next morning I found him still weaker, and I was uneasy about him all day. We could scarcely feel his pulse, but had to listen to his heart, which was very weak. Constantly we gave him injections of strychnine, caffeine, and camphor oil, with a saline infusion every three hours, but it did not appear to have any effect. He seemed to be conscious all the time, and when his children came in he smiled at them and tried to move his hand out to caress them. The whole day he lay and smiled, but could not speak. When I left in the evening I thought his heart was a little stronger, and I began to have a little more hope.

I had just gone to bed and fallen asleep when one of the children came and called me. A naephar had come to collect me as the Doctor was very ill. I dressed in a flash and ran there. I found him lying in a daze, and it looked as though death were near. His temperature was very high, 41.4 degrees C. He lay in this state until 2.30 a.m., when he died. Two young men from the hospital and I washed and dressed him, and I left at 4 o'clock. It was Christmas morning. It was wonderful to see how Mrs. Atkinson accepted this, and to hear her talk to the children about their father, who was now in Heaven, and tell them how glorious it was.

26 [December] (Sunday). Just a week after our little Annie's funeral, we went the same sad way to follow our friend and brother to his last resting place. All the missionaries gathered in their home at 9.30 a.m. where a short service was held. First we sang the hymn, "Asleep in Jesus," and then Mr. Ehmann read different passages from the bible, followed by a prayer from Mr. Riggs. Before the coffin was carried out, Mrs. Atkinson and her three children knelt down beside it and thanked God for every day they had been allowed to have him. The coffin was brought over to the hospital and set in a large corridor which has been converted into a hall. Outside a regiment of soldiers was drawn-up, who had come to attend the funeral. Also attending were a number of officers, the Commandant, a number of Turkish doctors, all the German missionaries, the Consul, a number of Armenians, and all the young men and women who work in the hospital. After we had sung an Armenian hymn, Badveli Vartan read the first part of the 12th chapter of Hebrews and spoke briefly about his impression of Dr. Atkinson. Afterwards Mr. Riggs spoke from John 11, "He is not dead," and we then sang a Turkish hymn. Mr. Riggs closed with prayer and the blessing. Zia Beg arose and gave thanks on behalf of all the Turkish officials for what Dr. Atkinson had done for them. "We will remember him, therefore he is not dead, but alive." Finally, Mrs. Atkinson spoke, and said that love

was the greatest power in the world. As a little boy Dr. Atkinson had understood God's love towards him and all mankind, and it was this that had driven him here to show God's love to this people.

The soldiers formed up into two lines, between which the coffin was carried out, young men from the hospital and soldiers acting as bearers the whole way to the Garden. Officers rode at the front and rear of the coffin, and we missionaries led the way. When we arrived at the Garden the soldiers formed a circle around the grave, while the missionaries stood beside it, and we sang the beautiful hymn, "The City Foursquare." Mr. Riggs then read Cor. 15, V. 54-57, and the coffin was lowered, and the grave filled in, while Mr. Riggs said in a loud, clear voice, "Glory be to our God the Father of our Lord Jesus Christ, who comforts us with all comfort, that we may be able to comfort those who are afflicted likewise as us" and ended with the blessing. Then we made our way home. The Riggses had invited all soldiers and officers to come in and drink tea. Karen-Marie and I went down to Mezreh again where I thought I would stay for a couple of days and rest a little.

It is so strange, yes, nearly impossible, to believe that we shall not see the Doctor again on this earth. But he was glad to go Home, where there is no fear, no sorrow, only joy, and we know that he has received a warm welcome there from the many friends who have gone before. All the many Turks who took part in the funeral service were very quiet and one of the officers wept. We hope that they may have caught a little glimpse of the glorious hope we Christians have.

31 December. It is with a strange feeling that I say farewell to the year 1915, in which so much has happened. It has been the most distressing and most grave I have experienced, and not only for myself, but for thousands, yes, millions of people. It is good that we cannot know what the future will bring, but only live one day at a time, knowing that as our day is, so shall our strength be. This we have been allowed to learn in a strange and wonderful way in this very difficult year. If we had known last year what lay in wait for us, I am afraid we would have given way under the burden, for there has been unimaginable fear and suffering. But God was the same faithful and mighty Father who gave His children strength to hold on during the inhuman suffering, which has to be endured, before coming Home to Him, where there is no death, no pain, and no fear.

"Before God's face they sing and pray, their voices blend with angels lay, and all conspire a joyous choir to laud Him night and day."

Oh, thank God for this Home, and thank God for each and everyone who reached there. Now that we shall begin the new year, 1916, there is a feeling of uncertainty, not knowing what lies ahead, of suffering, danger, sorrow, and distress. But there is also a blessed feeling of security because the Lord is the same yesterday, today, and for forever. He, who in the difficult days that are past, gave us all the strength we needed and special grace every single time, will also give us all we need day by day in the future. So shall I put my hand in His and pray that He will guide and lead me, keeping me close to Him, until I am allowed to stand before His face, in the company of the many friends who have gone before us.

1 January, 1916. Mr. Riggs's prayer this morning, as we assembled for breakfast, expressed perfectly the feeling in my heart. "Oh Lord, we thank Thee for this new day of this new year, and even if the clouds are thick around about us, we can always enjoy the sunshine of Thy presence with us." Now it is the evening of the first day. Mrs. Atkinson came up here with the three children, so that we could have a little Christmas celebration for the children's sake. We had not celebrated Christmas this year. As you know, Dr. Atkinson died on Christmas morning. They came so that we could have dinner together, and Karen-Marie joined us. After dinner we played for an hour with the children, then we had cocoa and gave the children a few presents. They returned to Mezreh at 4 o'clock.

Dr. Parmelee is ill. She began to feel ill yesterday, just one week after Dr. Atkinson's death. I am afraid it is typhus, but I hope it will not be severe.

4 January. It has now been confirmed that Ruth (Parmelee) has typhus. I have found the rash upon her. Her temperature has risen, but her pulse is steady, and there are no complications so far. I hope the disease will run a normal course, and that she will soon recover. I have almost more work than I can manage to do, so many people are sick. There are 25 typhus patients who are very ill, and I must tend them daily. Every day there are new patients, and I have the supervision and care of Ruth besides all my other duties. There are no doctors in Harpoot, and only Dr. Michael is left of our Armenian doctors. All the others have been killed. Dr. Michael also has a lot to do, as he has been in charge of the hospital since Dr. Atkinson's death, so he cannot come every day.

Yesterday the town crier rode around the town accompanied by two soldiers. He proclaimed that there will be no further massacre of Armenians, and that they should come out of hiding. Those working for the Turks should demand their pay. If anyone mentioned the word massacre he would be put to death. It is almost ludicrous to think that the Turks now have such concern for the Armenians that they would kill anyone who would frighten them. Now the Armenians are again in great fear. If nothing had been said about massacre, it would have been easier to believe them, but in view of all the previous proclamations encouraging people to come out of hiding and to demand payment of their money, we feel this present announcement clearly indicates their intention is to set a trap for the Armenians. Each time such promises have been made so far, something terrible has resulted, so how can we believe in anything good now?

Today the Kaimakam left. He has been transferred to Arapkir. He was not a man after the Vali's heart. We can only think that the reason for his transfer was his objection to carrying out the Vali's order to exterminate the remaining Armenians on the grounds of his own ill-health. Now he is sent away 14 days later. What can this mean? The Turks insist, of course, that this is not the reason, but we cannot believe them.

6 January (Thursday). Yesterday evening Mr. and Mrs. Riggs went to see the Police Commissioner. He was not at home, but he came today to pay a visit. Mr. Riggs queried him regarding the proclamation of the town crier, and his answer was not especially reassuring, merely, "Ishallah bir shey yoktir" (God forbid that anything wicked will happen). The Commandant has sent a message that he will come again tomorrow and inspect the school. This has frightened all the pupils and teachers. Why should he want to inspect the school? Of course, because he wants to see how many young girls there are.

Ruth is now well covered with the rash, but her heart is good, for which I am very glad, as I am alone with her. We have no doctor here. Dr. Michael is in Mezreh and has not been here since Monday. Every day I visit the sick. At present there are 26 typhus patients, and it is so difficult to see them in their poor homes and be unable to help them very much. Much snow fell yesterday and overnight, and today it is beginning of thaw, with water dripping through the roofs. In one place I visited, where there were four typhus patients, there was not a dry place in the whole room. Water was dripping down on the beds and the bed-clothes were wet. I found another empty room in the house, though without windows or door, and with the help of some women, I moved the sick there. One woman was dying, lying in the same bed as her little 10 year old girl. There was no one to nurse them, but after much searching, I found an older woman who is always willing to help. She is on her own and has recently been sick. She took her bedding, and what other things she had, and came to help. This is only one place, but all around they are lying about suffering in the same terrible conditions. Mothers with their little children are lying dirty and sick in the same bed-clothes. I cannot get around more than once every day, and even if I get someone to help them, I cannot depend on them, as even relatives are afraid of becoming infected and do not want to be near them. What a blessing it would be if we could open our little hospital, but the government will not give permission.

[No date]. It is a long time since I have written down something of what has been happening around us in the last two months.

On January 9th I became ill with a high temperature. At the beginning I hoped it was only some passing thing and I said nothing about it until the missionaries found out themselves that I was not feeling well. I had then had a high temperature for several days. I found it impossible to go to bed. So many of the sick were depending upon me. Dr. Parmelee had not reached the crisis of her illness. She had been sick for 12 days, and besides her, I had 36 typhus patients and a few with scarlet fever whom I attended daily, giving them medicine at midday. I also had the soup-kitchen and the milk and food delivery to attend to, as well as the supervision of the needlework and other little things. In between, time had to be found to comfort a sorrowing sister, listen to a poor mother's story, smile and nod to one or the other, and attended to the many little orphan children who have seen so much of want and misery, suffering and loss. We must show our love and sympathy to these poor ones. How could I possibly go to bed? Never before had I felt so happy in my work. All the other missionaries had also more work than they could manage, but the Lord saw that they could do without me, and when my temperature went over 39 degrees C., I had to go to bed hoping it would only be for a couple of days. However it turned out to be typhoid fever and it is now eight weeks. I have come here to Mezreh to spend some time and gather strength here in "Emaus" before starting my work again. I will try to write down what I can remember of the past two months. Around January 8th we received a letter from Dr. Merrill telling of Dr. Shepard's death. It was a hard blow, another of our missionaries had left us. What a loss this will be. This faithful servant of the Lord, friend and helper to all—Christian, Turk, Kurd and Arab—honoured, respected, and loved by everyone in Turkey. To think that he should die at a time like this. They had sent the Armenians away from Aintab and only a few of the missionaries could attend the funeral along with the few Armenians who had special permission from the government. Soldiers were also sent to keep watch at the grave. Never will I forget the Shepard's home in Aintab in 1908, when I saw him at his daily work. As soon as we came down in the morning for prayer and breakfast we found a flock of people waiting outside the house to speak to him before he would reach the street, because he literally "galloped" to the hospital, where hundreds of patients awaited him every day, of all races and religions. He said two things that I will never forget. One was, "We cannot help everyone, but everyone who comes must feel that we have sympathy for them," and all knew that he had. The other thing he said during the Medical Missionaries' Conference in Aintab in 1908, when he made a speech about the necessity of reading medical literature. He said that at the beginning of his service in Aintab he had a visit from his brother and the two of them set out on a walking tour. On the way his brother became ill, and Dr. Shepard diagnosed appendicitis. The brother died, and Dr. Shepard found that his diagnosis had been wrong. He said, with tears running down his cheeks, "I have never recovered from this. Maybe because it was my brother. But," he said, "if it had not been my brother, it would have been someone else's brother." I think there was not a dry eye when he told us this. It was this spirit that inspired him. He was not only a doctor but also served as chairman of the Church Council, and as a member of many other Committees. His day was filled, from early morning until late at night. Mealtimes were all he could spend at home, when he was always full of life. He could tell stories like no one else I have known, and he always had an amusing anecdote to relate, keeping his listeners in continual laughter. Missionaries have their own anecdotes which are told again and again, but no one knew as many as Dr. Shepard, and no one could tell them like him.

Some months ago he went on a trip to Constantinople and when he returned he went to Ourfa, where Mr. Leslie, our only missionary, had died in such sorrowful circumstances. He had found all the Armenians gone, and the missionary buildings in ruins. When he came back from that trip, he had said often, he felt tired and was longing to go Home. Then the Lord called him Home on December 18th, after 13 days of illness. How our ranks have been thinned out. In this part of Turkey 13 missionaries have died. The gate of Heaven is wide open and there are many who enter. We know that for them there is only happiness and glory. How often have the words, "Well done, good and faithful servant" fallen from our Saviour's lips, to the many who have come, after having been faithful to the last. I have in the last year thought almost daily of the lovely hymn of Brorson, "The great white flock we see." It is so suitable for the Armenian people, so many of whom are in the multitude of martyrs. What a joyous reunion for the Armenians who are already Home to meet their missionary friends from whom they had previously parted in sorrow and weeping. Whilst I have been ill the dear Baron Roupen has returned from Dersim. I have not seen him myself, but others have said that he looks pale and thin. It has not been an easy time up there. He existed solely on dry bread and onions, and did not really feel safe. Every time soldiers came, if there were many, he had to hide in stables or in the woods. He has also described how the many poor Armenian refugees go around in the mountains, starving and without clothes. Many become sick and die. We knew very well that our friends were suffering up there, but we have not been able to send any help, as we cannot entrust money to the Kurds who go to and fro. One of us would have to go and that is impossible. The government would never allow it. Around January 23rd a little group of Armenian young men arrived, all together 43, from Diarbekir. Some of them had been working for Dr. Smith and had been imprisoned since he had been sent away. They had been tortured to force them to say that Dr. Smith was the leader of the revolutionaries in Bitlis. One of them, a splendid, faithful young man, confessed this under great suffering. They have now been brought here to face an Army Court Martial, which seems ridiculous, after the government has been responsible for killing so many Armenians without trial or examination. They probably use these single instances to show that justice is done in all cases. Mrs. Atkinson has visited them and says they look very miserable in their suffering. What must it have been like for them to have spent a year in such a hell, where one would think a single day would destroy them. Several times recently great fear has arisen about a massacre, but it has still not been carried out. Again the Turks rejoice to see the fear of the poor Armenians. What physical suffering there is in this land of our Christian brothers and sisters, also sorrow, loneliness, poverty, and want. Added to these, the continuous fear, that a horrible death may await them. No one at home can even imagine what it is like, not even we who see so many frightful things daily and meet our suffering sisters. It must be experienced personally. Not even we are safe, or know what the next moment will bring. I don't believe there is one of us left who has not thought at some time—yes, even been prepared for—the day that it will be demanded of us that we give our own lives. Never before has the longing for Heaven been so strong in my heart as in the last year. What would it not mean to leave this vale of pain and reach Home where we can forever serve Him whom we love, be together with our friends, without suffering and without fear and sin. Oh, thank God we are on our way Home.

11 February. Now we have the same story as last year. The town crier proclaims daily in the streets that everyone must join the army, from boys of 14 years to men of 55, also the Christians—Syrians and Armenians. The poor people know better than they did last year what this means. Of course the Christians will not be given any weapons. They will perhaps be employed on some work for a while, and after they have no further use for them, they will be killed. No wonder there is renewed fear and sorrow among our few friends. Everyone who can is thinking of fleeing to Dersim. We have a little group of men and boys, some teachers, some theology students, and a few of our past pupils, who have now decided to leave. They have said nothing to us about where or when they will go, so we can say with a clear conscience, when the government comes after them, that they just left one day.

Around the 14th some of our men prepared to go away. Some Kurds came around in the evening and those leaving divided themselves into small groups. The first of these waited until dark and then came out on the road next to our garden. They saw two soldiers riding and they became very frightened. Baron Kaspar, who was riding on a Kurd's horse, took the saddle on his shoulders and let the horse go. He ran, and the others ran in the opposite direction. When the next two groups came out through the gate, they saw soldiers on guard outside the wall, so they went back immediately. Some hours later everyone from the first group, except three, returned. It was now midnight, but the news got around that they had returned and everyone felt uneasy. Those poor people who should have left were quite distracted and now have no more courage to try to escape. We were very worried about the three who failed to return, but next morning we heard that Baron Kaspar, after several hours of walking in the mountains, had reached Mezreh. We have heard nothing about the other two, a young woman and a sixteen year old boy.

21 [February]. Two officers appeared this morning in the street outside our buildings. One said to the other, "We have received news by telegram that Erzeroum has fallen, but, of course, we are not spreading the news around." However, we have heard this, and others must surely have heard it also, because down in Mezreh and Harpoot there was a terrible panic amongst the Turks. They have feared the Russians for a long time, and especially here in Harpoot, Turks have gone to the few Armenians and asked if they would take them in and defend them if the Russians should come.

Many have even busied themselves making crosses, intending to hang them on their front doors in the hope that the Russians will not open fire on their houses. All the rich Turks are making preparations for flight, and many families are leaving daily. They are also selling their possessions for next to nothing, almost like the Armenians last year. There are now rumours that there are Armenians in the Russian army, and that they are out for revenge. Many Turks are openly confessing that this is coming as a punishment for their sins. "Why did we kill the women and children? They were innocent." But with others the talk still goes on that they must exterminate the rest of the Armenians before leaving the town. They actually discuss how they will do it, burn the town when the Russians approach and then flee, but not one Armenian will be allowed to stay alive. There is not one of us who doubts their evil intention. However, we hope and believe that they will be so scared for themselves and so busy saving their own lives that they will not have the time, or that they will simply forget, to do all the evil things that they have planned. But the poor persecuted Armenians, who have seen and endured so much, are again full of fear of what might happen. People come to us every day asking to be taken into our houses, but we have to refuse, because, so far, there is no danger. If it comes, we will take in as many as possible. Some come and ask us for an American flag, to display if the Russians come. Turks also come, asking us to take them in, or keep things for them, but our answer to the latter is always, "No." It is only important to save life, not goods. If it should happen that the Russians come, we will take in as many women and children as we can make room for, both Christian and Moslem. Up to now we have not really believed that the Russians would come, but now it looks as if they might. We in Harpoot have always said that if it were possible we would remain while there was still one Christian left, and, if necessary, stay on if every one was gone. So, should the Russians come and the Turkish government demands that we leave with them, we have all decided to say "No," and remain at our posts. There will be a lot of work to do. But if the Russians come, and afterwards withdraw, as they have done in other places, then we will have to go with them. What would it be like to have to travel to the Russian border, and what could we bring with us? Nothing. The missionaries from Van reached Tiflis in a very poor condition, without money or clothes. We are glad that the days are passing and bringing us nearer to spring. It would be terrible to go now, at this time of year, when the mountains are full of snow and it can be very cold with storms and frost. Up to now the Lord has helped and on Him we depend. We have wonderful experience of how He gives us strength, peace, and cheerfulness from time to time.

22 February. The government announced today that the Turks have recaptured Erzeroum, but no one believes this, thinking it is only being said to keep the Turks here calm and to avoid a panic flight from the town. The Turkish women cry and lament, and they will not eat or drink. Up till now they have been living extravagantly on the goods they stole from the Armenians, and now that this life is

disturbed, they vent their anger on the Armenians again and say, "Don't be happy too soon. Not one of you will remain alive. You will all be killed before the Russians come and not even a chicken belonging to you will remain." It is a strange feeling for us missionaries in Harpoot.

Last year everyone thought that the safest place to be was with the Germans in Mezreh. Now everyone feels it is safer to be with the Americans.

26 February. I came down here today to Karen-Marie and little Bessie to gather some strength. I should have come last Monday after they had paid me a visit of some days, but I was not strong enough. This last illness has taken a good deal of my energy, and my legs and back are still weak since I was ill with typhus. Because of this, it is now taking me longer to recover and it is a little difficult to walk. It is lovely to be with the dear little girl again. She is always alight with happiness, a real little sunbeam. She has changed very much in the two months she has been away from me and is now beginning to walk and talk. On Thursday the 24th the soldiers returned to occupy our buildings and soon everything was changed in Harpoot, which is now noisy and filthy beyond description. We had been so glad that the winter rain and snow had washed away all the dirt and mess the soldiers had left last summer, but now it is all back again. It is certainly not good for our Armenian refugees, all women and children, who live in the surrounding houses. Many are without locks or even doors, so anyone can go in and out of their dwellings. It has been said that some of our buildings will be used as a hospital, as 3,000 wounded soldiers are expected and are said to be on their way. Only a few hundred have arrived so far, and none are badly wounded. It may be that the more seriously wounded have died on the way. It is said that a large number die of tetanus, which is not surprising when one sees all the dirt and filth in which the poor soldiers must live. The few who have come are in a pitiful condition. They are so weak because of improper care that they cannot tolerate the cold and arrive with frozen feet and hands. One soldier with a minor bullet wound in the arm had it bandaged in the neighbourhood of Erzeroum and was sent on here. The bandage was so tightly fastened and left like this during the whole journey, that the arm was dead by the time he arrived, and the poor soldier must suffer amputation. He is not alone but only one of thousands who must suffer because others have failed to do their duty.

In the last few days the Turks have been praying in a field a short distance away from the Danish Children's Home, and it looks as if the situation is not as well as the government does all in its power to have the people believe. They are saying that the Turks have recaptured Bitlis, Van, Moush, and Erzeroum, but who believes it? How often we wish we could have a newspaper that tells the truth, so that we could know the true situation.

Today we had a visit from Mariam Khatoon Manigian. She is a lovable woman, one of those who has not broken down going through the furnace but has emerged whole. She is one—or rather used to be one—of the richest women in Harpoot. All her brothers, her husband, and her son—a promising young man—have been killed. She alone remains, and it is often very difficult for her. I said to her when we talked of the many friends who have gone before us, "Think how many of your friends have reached Home, and when we arrive there one day, then there will be no more parting," and she answered, "And who is our King there? Our Lord Jesus." He is Alpha and Omega and the mightiest for her. She talked a lot about what the Turks are saying at this time. One day she went to the house of a Turk, who had, in the past, been well-known to her. They had taken in an Armenian girl, and like all the others, had given her a Turkish name. When Digin Mariam had come, she had to speak in Turkish to the girl and address her by her Turkish name. However, when she called again the other day, they said, "No, Mariam, talk in Armenian, as we do." So do all the Turks now, because they are afraid of the Russians, and hope that it will make them more friendly towards them to know that they have taken in an Armenian, even though they have whipped and tortured them during the whole of their time with them. An old Turk said one day, "We go everyday to our Mosque, say our prayers, wash ourselves, and after all, things go badly for us. Curse us, but do not pray for us. When you pray for us things always go badly, but when you curse us things go well." The Turks show clearly that they do not enjoy the peace that Jesus talks about. Their conscience torments them, and still they will not yield to it. But maybe never before have there been so many prayers for them as now from those who have suffered so much, and we know that these prayers are heard, and they will sooner or later bear fruit.

Today a group of mounted soldiers arrived from Moush. They were a wretched sight. The horses were completely bald, and covered with scabies, as were the soldiers themselves. Great crowds of Turkish refugees are still coming from the Erzeroum district, Bitlis, Moush and Keghi. They also look terrible. They are as black as negroes, clad in dirty rags, and with unkempt hair. Many of their number died on the road. It must have been dreadful for them. Think what they must have suffered. It took them two months to make the journey, which is normally done in 10 days, over the high mountains in deep snow and freezing cold. No wonder the Turks say to the Armenians who remain here, "Your massacre was in the summer, but ours is in the winter." Yes, they suffer, but it is not in the same way as the poor Armenians. They have their animals with them, oxen, cows, mules and donkeys, who carry their bedding, cooking utensils, and food. They have no soldiers to flog and ill-treat them on the way, or even kill them—yes, actually slaughter them. So they have come here and filled the empty houses left by the Armenians. The soldiers are now beginning to go around and drive out the few Armenians who are still left. When the latter question the soldiers, "If we leave the house, where shall we go?" the reply is, "You can go to Malatia." We had hoped that these few remaining Armenians would be allowed to live fairly peacefully, but it does not seem likely now. They must go out on roads and die to make room for the Turkish refugees.

How different everything has become in the last year, and it appears now that all our work has been completely destroyed. Instead of the clean, intelligent, and enlightened Armenian people, there has now come an ignorant and completely uncivilized people. It would have been impossible for us to have imagined such a change. It is terribly hard to go down to the Shuga now. We never see an Armenian, only a few Syrians. Many of our friends' shops are still locked with the government seal. Some have been opened by Turks, and it feels strange to go into them. They hold so many memories, and it is like a frightening dream that becomes more real every day. The soldiers have not much enthusiasm, and only long to be sent home. The other day Mr. Riggs went past a regiment exercising outside the hospital. It had been raining and the ground was wet. The soldier who was in command ordered them to lie down, but they did not obey and supported themselves with their hands on the ground. Then the soldier in command said, "Lie down! When the Russians come you will have to lie down," but the soldiers shouted, "No, we will run." This shows the spirit that inspires them, and these are the soldiers who are to save the country. When the enemy comes they will run.

1 March. Today a little group of Armenian craftsmen were brought to the prison here. They had been living in Erzingan since last summer.

2 March. The Armenian men who arrived yesterday are being sent away. No one knows where, but obviously the same way as the thousands of others.

8 March. An officer who had travelled with Sister Bodil from Moush has said that the Turkish government had sent her away when the Russians advanced. She was allowed to take her little Armenian flock with her, but when she came to Bitlis, they were all taken away from her, and the government told her to leave town. She refused to go without the Armenians and said she would stay and see the Vali and telegraphed Constantinople. The Police Mudir said there was no Vali and asked her to leave, or he would come himself and see that she did so. The next morning, therefore, she left alone, leaving her friends in the hands of their enemies. The officer said she was inconsolable and cried constantly. When she reached Diarbekir she telegraphed Mr. Ehmann, but he could not do anything. Now she is on her way to Marash. Yesterday Sister Hansine and Schw. Clara left. It was strange to see them go, and strange to remain here. But no, I could not go and leave our friends behind.

9 March. We heard today that there has been an uprising of the Kurds in Dersim, and they have attacked Khozat. It is said that they have burned Chemishgezek and that there has been an uprising in the neighbourhood of Malatia. This has disturbed everyone who knows the Kurds. They say if they have risen, it must mean that there are sufficient numbers of them, and the Turks can do nothing about it. Seven years

ago they had an uprising. The government sent soldiers and there was a war, but the Turks did not succeed. It is up amongst these Kurds that our Armenian friends are living, and the Turks say there are 3,000 of them, armed alongside the Kurds against them. The Armenians here say in answer to this, "Where did 3,000 come from? You have killed them all," and the Turks reply, "It does not matter how many we kill, we cannot destroy these people."

Some people think that the Russians have reached Keghi. If this is so, then the Kurds will probably join them. The Russians can then walk through Dersim and arrive here any day. But what do we really know? Nothing, only wild rumours flying around, and one is contradicted by another at least several times a day. We can only pick out from it all what we believe is true, and it is not easy. It is also not easy for the poor German missionaries who have many children in children's homes and cannot leave them. They dread the coming of their country's enemies, the Russians, but can—or will not—leave their posts without taking the children with them, and as the government will not allow a single Armenian to leave, what can they do?

10 March. Today we visited the Consul. In the course of conversation he mentioned that two men had been killed between Mezreh and Bizmeshen, which is one hour's journey from Mezreh. These two men had been in the Consulate for a long time and had therefore been safe. One went out to the village the other day, but did not return. His donkey was found and it looked as though something had happened to him. His brother went to the government here and told them what had occurred, and they sent him with two gendarmes to the village to look for his brother. Just outside the town the two gendarmes opened fire on him, but he was a strong young man, and he ran from them and reached the village. The gendarmes followed him there, and searched until they found him, saying they had orders to bring him back. They took him with them, but they returned alone to Mezreh. So these two brothers are also killed. The second young man went openly to the government about his brother, because he had become a Moslem, but even that did not help, and it has been the same in several cases. The Consul said that it was obvious that the government intended to kill all the men. This would not be difficult, as there are only a few left. The question of money is a problem at the moment. All the many sums of money that have been sent to us over the last few months are being paid to us in paper. There is no gold in circulation, and we have now reached the point where no one will accept paper money. We have nothing else and it is nearly impossible to get foodstuffs and other necessities. How will it all end? We cannot even leave the country, so we must sit and wait. Up till now we have not actually suffered want. So we are not fearful for the future.

11 March. Baron Khachadoor saw a crowd of Armenian men being led through the town today. Everyone wondered where they were going. A Syrian in the army told him that the soldiers were carrying ropes to bind the men together outside the town.

So now we know where they are going—up to the mountains to die. My thoughts have been with them all day. I can only pray, "Lord, keep them faithful until the end. Prepare them to meet You."

It is said today that Pertag has fallen to the Kurds. If this is true, it is not far away from us. The town lies only three hours' journey from Harpoot.

12 March. Today it is said that the war with the Kurds is bad. Fresh troops are being sent away constantly. A rich landowner from Mezreh, who was taken in a troop of soldiers to Dersim, has returned as a refugee. He says that all of his troops were killed, also the Kaimakam in Chemishgezek. He also says that half of Pertag has been burned. Turkish families are still moving out. Now the Vali's harem is going and also the Police Inspector's, so it looks as though those in authority, who know best how things are, do not feel secure.

Contact with the outside world is also very bad. It has not been good for me, either, since the war began. Apart from a few cards at Christmas I have heard almost nothing. It has also been a great loss to have had no newspapers for the last six months. They came earlier, and were a great comfort to me. I am not suffering alone, as the other missionaries do not get as many letters and magazines as formerly. Not even the Consul can send sealed letters to the Embassy in Constantinople, and a good many of his telegrams are not getting through either. The other day he received a telegram from the Embassy, asking him to send different telegrams that had not been received. The Consul telegraphed a reply, "Demand them from the authorities who have stolen them." The Consul has also sent 1,100 dollars to his wife in America, and this was stolen as well. He said, for fun, "They must open a relief fund in America to help Consuls' wives." Last summer he worked very hard to get all of us missionaries out of the country. He also wanted to go himself. Now he says the same as us—that he won't leave, even if the Turks order us. But if the Turks actually bombard and burn the town, as they have threatened to do, it will not be any joke to be here. However, we have all decided to stay, even if the Turks leave, and the Russians come. Should the latter withdraw again, we would have to go with them, and what would that entail, going all the way to the Russian border as refugees? Yes, we are sitting very well in this country. Everywhere is closed around us. Only one way is open—upward, and thank God, no one can close that. In this thought lies all our strength and cheerfulness.

16 March. I took little Bessie up with me to the hospital to spend a couple of days with Mrs. Atkinson and stayed until noon on Saturday. We both enjoyed the little visit. Bessie played with the children whom she loves. Mrs. Atkinson and I spent most of the time talking about the past and the future. It is so strange to be in their home without Dr. Atkinson. There is a big empty place there. The children miss him terribly. Miss Harley came on Saturday morning to collect us and we reached home in time for dinner. It was lovely to be home again among dear friends.

For the first time in three months I attended church service on Sunday. How wonderful it was to join again with our Armenian friends, to sing hymns and hear the preaching of the Lord, even if we are not allowed to assemble in our own nice little church, which lies only two minutes away from here. It has been taken by the government for the use of soldiers, along with five of our other large buildings.

A large crowd of women and young girls came to me on Monday for handiwork. Unfortunately I did not have work for all, because I do not have enough material. Among them was a 13 year old girl who arrived here last Friday from Mazgird alongside other refugees. She said that the town was attacked by Kurds, who killed the Kaimakam and his wife, and every one else they could lay hands on. They burned the town. This little Armenian girl, who had been looking after the Kaimakam's children, took them and ran away. The Kurds recognized her as an Armenian and asked her who the children were. She answered, "My sisters and brothers," and the Kurds let them go. There had been rumours for some time that this town had been burned by Kurds, but we never know what to believe. In the afternoon an old Kurdish man, the Mufti from Peri, came here to greet Mr. Riggs. We have also heard rumours about that town, but we did not know what was true. Now he has said it all. He said, when the Kurds came and started to burn the town, he took his two horses and escaped before the Kurds reached his area. Mr. Riggs asked him, "What has become of the soldiers who were sent up there by the government? Did they not arrive in time?" He answered, "The whole Tabur regiment is surrounded by Kurds at Khozat. Some have escaped, and they came here last night, completely exhausted with hunger and cold." He also said that there were a few soldiers in Peri, who were sent in small groups to the mountain tops around the town, but the Kurds came and killed them all, and then began their attack on the town. The old man was completely demoralized. He said, "If you wanted to go to Peri now, you could not do so, because the road is so full of refugees."

Among the many soldiers we have in our buildings there are 400 Kurdish volunteers from the Malatia district. They are of a different race from those in Dersim and are not friendly towards them. These Kurds are in Wheeler Hall, on the other side of the street, just in front of our building. They look and behave like wild animals, and their way of life is as different from ours as it could possibly be. Their greatest pleasure and occasion for celebration is when there is a massacre, and it is these Kurds who have been used to kill our many friends. They arrived here eight days ago, and the government has its hands full, as they don't know what to do with them. They are afraid that if they are given weapons they will run away and create another uprising. They would prefer to keep them here in the hope that they will be of help should the Kurds from Dersim come. So the government treats them in a very friendly way, giving them their food and a place to live (or rather we do that). They have freedom to come and go as they please, and do what they want. The only thing they do is tear down houses. There are certainly many empty houses since our friends left us. These they tear down, taking the timber for firewood. They chop firewood all night long. Oh, how hard it is to see one after another of our friends' houses being torn down by these men. How different the town has become—yes, the whole country—in the last year.

Whilst I was preparing Bessie for bed I heard a yelling and squealing as if all the women in the town were in the greatest distress. I thought immediately that it was the massacre that has been threatened for so long. My heart thumped, my legs trembled, for what could it mean, other than death for these poor women and children, to be moved out in a dark, cold night, in pouring rain. In a flash I had Bessie in bed, and ran as fast as my legs would carry me up to the Riggses' to hear if they knew anything more. How great was my joy when I heard them say, "It is our friends, the Kurds, holding a religious service." My ears have not been very well so well since my illness, and I could not tell from which direction the sound came. The screaming was so terrible that the government sent a man to find out what was going on. When he heard it was a service, he went calmly home, but our poor Armenian women, who live around here, were out of their senses with fear, and they began to stream to us. We had to send them home again, reassuring them that there was nothing to fear. It was all over at 10 o'clock, and things became reasonably quiet. All this took place in the dark. They danced, groaned like dogs, and squealed terribly.

21 March. The air is thick with rumours today. They are saying that the Kurds have certainly attacked the town of Pertag. This has been said before but was not true. This time we dare not believe before we have evidence, but the Turks are not happy. The Kaimakam has been out inspecting the district and has decided on several places to build forts. But if the Kurds have really begun to attack Pertag, there will not be time to build anything, as that town is only three hours' journey from here, and we can see it clearly from our Garden. Today the town crier has been calling out in the streets, ordering everyone who possesses a spade or shovel to hand it over to the government immediately. Suddenly at 7 o'clock we heard a terrible noise, like a number of wagons driving at full speed. When we went to the windows we saw the Kurds running out of Wheeler Hall, each with his little bag and few belongings. Our first thought was that they had set fire to the house and were running from it. About a third of them ran as hard as they could down the street. An officer suddenly came from one of the other buildings and ordered them back. The running Kurds stopped when they found that the rest were not following and started to return. So they did not succeed to get away this time. It is with a strange feeling that we go to rest, expecting anything to happen. We do not know what will happen in the night, surrounded as we are by enemies on all sides. But I say like David Ps. 3, 5, "I laid me down and slept, I awakened, for the Lord sustained me." Never before have I experienced so fully how rich and happy it is to be a child of God. He preserves us in perfect peace, and gives strength for every moment and day.

22 March. Today we learned the reason for the panic among the Kurds last night. Mr. Riggs had a visit from the officer who is in charge of them and who said he had seen the new military hospital in Mezreh on fire. He watched it for some time and saw that the fire was spreading. He knew there were many wounded soldiers there who might need help, so he called one of his subordinates and ordered him to go with about 10 Kurds and offer help. This man, instead of informing only the 10 Kurds needed, he let all the others hear also, and they immediately began speculating amongst themselves about the fire. In the end they concluded that the Russians must have arrived and set fire to the hospital, and all they could do was flee. They all ran out to the street in one body, shouting and screaming enough to frighten away a whole army in Europe, before they were stopped.

The fire at the hospital turned out to be in a brazier in a field outside the building. These Kurds are volunteer soldiers, said to have come to help the Turks, but the latter must have some doubts about their usefulness after last night's performance. It is said that they have really come to get weapons from the government, after which they will rise up against them. Mr. Riggs complained to this same officer that the houses were falling down in this wet season. He answered, "Yes, that is how God always punishes. First He takes away the understanding, and then He lets the powers of nature loose. Then it is over." This is a common opinion among the Turks, that God is punishing them for what they have done to the Armenians, and many of the higher officers complain very much that the country is allied with Germany. Mr. and Mrs. Riggs went down to Mezreh this afternoon. On their return journey they met a caravan on the road from Pertag. It was a high ranking officer, Mr. Riggs thought the Mufti. They talked and the officer said that the Kurds had begun to attack the town. Mr. Riggs asked if there were sufficient soldiers to defend it. He answered, "I telegraphed the Vali that 300 soldiers must remain until I got myself and my possessions away. The Vali gave permission." So it is true this time about Pertag, and all the Turks are terrified. Many come and ask us to take them in but, up till now, we have not taken any. If we start, there will be complete panic in the town. People will think that we have special information if we do this. We do not have room for many people, as the government has possession of five of our biggest buildings, so we must wait until it becomes necessary.

23 March. Mr. Riggs, Miss Harley, and I rode out this afternoon to the Garden in order to see from the mountains if there was any sign of smoke or fire in Pertag, but there was nothing to see. Everything looks peaceful—the magnificent mountains dressed with snow, and the lawn like a green carpet. The sun was shining so beautifully that for a moment we forgot all the misery and sorrow around us and could only feel delight and pleasure in God's magnificent nature.

Some refugees arrived today from Pertag and they all said that the Kurds have reached there.

24 March. Our local Kurds, for the third time, broke into our church today and began tearing it down. How it hurts to see the little church, which we had built six years ago, suffer such sacrilege. Mr. Riggs went to the government, who sent immediately for some of the men, and said they would be put in prison, but whether or not they were serious about this, we do not know. There were wild rumours going around today that the Russians are advancing in three places, at Erzingan, Bitlis, and Tchabaghchur, and that the Kurds are also advancing. It is again said that the Vali's wife is leaving, and also the wife of the Police Inspector, who is busy packing all her belongings to send to us.

A Turk told Mr. Riggs today that the Vali had a dream. A giant, with a long white beard and great eyes, stood before him. The Vali trembled, but the giant said, "Don't be afraid. You are a good man and no harm shall come to you. But if a hair is touched on the head of a single Christian, you and yours will come to grief." This is a good story to have going around from Turk to Turk right now, when they do all that they can to convince Armenians that not one of them will survive this time round. It does not matter if the Vali really had this dream or not.

27 March. Yesterday, Sunday, our local Kurds were imprisoned, and a guard stood outside the door the whole day. Some of them had run away, and the rest were therefore being punished. But they are not easy to control, as they love freedom and sunshine, and it is difficult to keep them in. There were many fights to get out, as only a few respected the guard. Some crawled through a hole in the ceiling and enjoyed their freedom up on the roof sunning themselves. They took all their clothes off, even their shirts, and removed the vermin from them.

About midday a crowd of men were brought here. They looked wretched and could scarcely drag themselves along. One man looked about 90, very much stooped, with a long white beard, like a real Father Christmas. He supported himself on a stick. Another had very bad eyes and could scarcely see. A third had a great sore on his breast that looked cancerous. This was clearly visible, as all the men's clothes were open down to the waist and their chests were bare. There were some boys, who looked about 10 years old, but who were now also soldiers. This was apparent from the white linen bags they carried on their backs. How it hurt to see these old men, sick men, and boys, who have been torn away from their homes and sent out in utter destitution and misery. Where they had come from, I do not know, but it was clear that they were so tired that they could scarcely walk. Meanwhile, they stood waiting in the street. The office where they have to register is across the way from my window. Some small boys came with bread, and the men fell upon them, tearing like wolves to have it. It was plain to see that they were starving.

At 8 o'clock a regiment of soldiers came to spend the night here. It was pitiful to hear them cough. It sounded as if they all had pneumonia, and still they must march on their way, in the storm and rain, without proper clothing.

Around midnight we were awakened by terrible shouting in the street. It appeared to be a number of soldiers, who were bringing bread from Mezreh for the new arrivals.

Today rumours are still flying around us. We feel as though we are on top of a volcano, which is ready to erupt at any moment. Every time we meet each other, maybe five or six times in the day, our first question is always, "Anything new?"

A lot of people came to us again today, asking for permission to bring their belongings here. We have said yes to a few and would like very much to say yes to more, but we know so well that if we do, there will be panic among everyone. Therefore we still say "No" and hope that we shall have time to accept things and help them all when the danger is really here.

Mr. Riggs said that he had had a visit from one of the leading Turks from Tadem, a village here on the plain, a few hours journey away. He said that there are 300 acres of land belonging to the village and there are a number of Turkish mohadjirs there. The government has given them enough corn to sow the 300 acres, but they have eaten most of it and only sown 30 acres here and there. They now hope it will grow. This is only one place, but it is the same in all the other villages now that the Armenians have been sent away. There is no hope for this country. Famine will surely come. This Turk said that he had also enjoyed the Armenians' misery for a time. He had not taken anything from them as long as they were there, but when they had gone he had enjoyed their garden and vineyards. "But," he adds, "I have not had peace since. First my mother became ill, then my wife. I have only had sorrow since." He meant that God was punishing him.

A Kurd also came today on a visit. He said that when the Kurds had conflict with the Turks, they said to them, "You are Kaspar, you are Hovhannes" and so on, giving them Armenian names, and afterwards killing them. They did this so that the Turks should understand that they were being punished for what they did to the Armenians.

1 April. At last things have become serious enough for the Vali's wife to go. She went away today and this has created complete panic in Mezreh.

Today a young German engineer came to install a wireless telegraph. The Turks consider it important to show that the Germans are their friends.

9 April. In recent days the wireless telegraph has been set up, only five minutes away from our buildings. Three Germans have come, but only one has stayed. One was sent to Erzingan and the other to Diarbekir to operate the wireless telegraph there. Harpoot and Mezreh are to be a military centre and new troops are arriving daily in the most wretched condition. Sick, starving, nearly naked, and dirty beyond description. In the last three days troops have come from Gallipoli. They are better dressed but look miserable. Many have died on the way, and it is a question how many of the rest will survive the coming summer.

Cholera is beginning to appear again. There have been three cases. The first patient recovered, but the other two died. If this illness breaks out among the soldiers, it will be very bad. They live under such insanitary conditions that any epidemic would carry off thousands. There are almost no doctors remaining here. A few Turkish ones, who do not know much, our dear Dr. Michael, who is still alive, and a couple of Armenian doctors, who have become Moslems. What are these among thousands of people? Here in Harpoot the Gregorian School is being used as a hospital, and every day a flock of about 50 men are sent there from our buildings. They can hardly drag themselves there, but with four or five lance corporals striking them with the sticks they carry, they gather a little strength together and drag themselves off. Oh, how much we would like to do something for them, help them, talk to them, so that they might come to know that in Christianity they will find joy, peace, strength, and love. Oh, how we would like to lift our dear Saviour up before them, so they might see Him as He is. But we must do nothing, for this is a holy war, and the government will not allow us to do anything for them. Just opposite our windows there are 1,000 soldiers in one of our buildings that was used earlier for our church services, and we can see clearly how they live. Every morning and evening they get a piece of bread, the size of a penny loaf. Then they are called out, 100 at a time, and they sit down in circles of 10, and a container that formerly held petroleum is then brought to them. It contains soup, made from oxen, the colour of dirty water, but down it goes. Every man brings his own spoon and when the meal is over he puts it down his stocking— if he has any—otherwise into the clothing on his chest. As there is always fear that the soldiers will run away, there are always guards on the doors, and because there is no water in the house, they suffer from thirst. When it rains they stay out on the verandah and hold their cups to catch the rainwater running down from the roof. It is dirty—but down it goes. We would like to give them drinking water, but the government will not even allow that.

The other day I was down in Mezreh. On the way home I met a Turkish woman, and we walked together for a while. She told me, in her naive way, that the Germans had come here and built such a wonderful telegraph. In the wires there are some enormous strong iron men, and when the enemy comes, these iron men will come out and kill them. When the Kurds hear of this they will say, "Yes, we will do no more harm." This woman actually believes this, and many others do so with her.

We have not heard much news in the last few days. We long for something definite. The continuing uncertainty saps our strength. Not that we go in fear of what is to come, for we are in the Lord's hands, and He has preserved us through countless dangers. If He wills that we shall live, He will also preserve us in the future, but the uncertainty makes people feel hopeless and work becomes much more difficult. Armenian refugees are still coming in. They have, until now, been in Turkish villages. Now that they can no longer stay there, they come to us for help, to stay out of the hands of the Turks. But we cannot help more because at the moment we are giving bread to the value of 3,700 kroner a month to people here in Harpoot and Mezreh, besides the help we are giving in the villages.

No money has come to us recently, and what we give is in the hope that help will come. But it is difficult to say "No," especially when there is such distress, and to also know that our refusal may mean that they will have to spend the rest of their lives as slaves and victims of the Turks. These things drain away one's strength. We often ask, what will the future bring? But we know that our Heavenly Father has all things in His hands. As our day is, so shall our strength be. So we can sing, "Trusting and happy in Jesus' name, He is our King, and all must serve with honour, to benefit the least of His brethren, because our Father in Heaven He Lives.

14 April. On Sunday the [American] Consul and Mr. Picciotto went to Pertag. A little cannon was mounted on this side [of the river] and a few soldiers could be seen here and there. They crossed the river and rode up to the town. There were also some soldiers there, but far from enough to defend the town. Some houses had been burned, but they did not find as much as they had imagined. Following the boat crossing to the other side, after two hours they had to get on it [again] in order to return before evening. On Tuesday we heard that the Kurds have begun to plunder and burn down Agn, Arapkir, and Aghen, and that they have again attacked Pertag. Refugees are coming from different places, and more and more Armenians, freed by the flight of the Turks, are coming to us. On Wednesday Mr. Riggs received a number of magazines from America. This was the first we had heard from the outside world, and how happy it made us all feel, when Mr. Riggs told us that it was said that the beginning of the end had started, and that maybe we would have peace again by the autumn. Oh, if only it would become a reality. Up to now it has seemed an impossibility that we should ever see peace again on this earth. If peace comes and this country comes under a Christian government then we will again see our Armenian friends come out into the open and be allowed to live. Oh, if only that day would come soon.

[18 April] Thursday. While we were having our meeting soldiers came and drove our Armenian sisters and children out into the street, carried out all their belongings, and took over their houses. What will they do now? For some months the soldiers have been tearing houses down and taking the timber to burn. The few remaining houses are so full of people that the occupants have scarcely enough air to breathe. Now there are about 100 women and children standing in the street without a place to go. All their houses are for the use of soldiers and officers. It is obviously only a question of how long we will be allowed to remain in our houses. Great fear has arisen again among Armenians and there is renewed talk of a massacre. The evil spirit in Harpoot, Deli Hadji, has returned from Constantinople, and he cannot bear to see the few poor women and children who remain. He says, "There are too many

Armenians here, there must be another massacre." It seems to me darker now than ever before. War, murder, and fire surround us. The few Armenians we have been able to keep alive, with the help of our friends' gifts from home, are now set out in the street, with no place to go, surrounded by enemies, and we are unable to help them or take them in, because all our houses have also been taken. It is well that summer is coming when it will make things easier. Our hearts are bleeding also for the poor Turkish soldiers. How we would like to help them. They only have a piece of dry bread, not nearly enough to satisfy hunger, some few spoonsful of soup, which is unfit to be eaten by civilized people. This is their food from morning till evening, accompanied by beatings and abuse. New crowds of men, who have been collected here and there, are arriving daily. The old, crippled, and sick are being driven away until they fall down dead. Yesterday I passed such a crowd. A man had fallen and died. The Onbashi stood and shook him, ordering him to rise. I said to him, "Can't you see that man is dead?" Then they walked on again. The dead man lay outside our houses, until they got him carried away. This is how they are being treated. Whipped till they fall. Poor souls. There is no pity, mercy, or love. Oh, how they need to have our Lord Jesus come into their lives and change them, so that they might have His disposition. For us it seems impossible, but for God all things are possible.

19 April. Today a Tabur (company) of soldiers left here for Malatia. Other companies have already left for Dersim. The Turks say they have been sent to destroy the Kurds, in the same way as they put an end to the Armenians, by plundering, ill-treating, murdering, and burning. But this time the job will be more difficult, because the Kurds are very brave and cleverer at fighting than the Turks. Soldiers are leaving here daily, and all of them are going to Malatia. The officers say the reason is that they cannot get enough food for the soldiers here, but the general opinion is that it is because the Russians are coming nearer, and they cannot defend the towns here because of their position. This is probably true. The government must have known what food supplies were available before they ordered all the soldiers here. We are glad because it was nearly impossible to walk in the streets, which were always full of soldiers. The air is completely foul with dirt everywhere, as well as noise and brawls day and night. Added to these, there is all the misery to look at. It was nearly unbearable. Many of the new soldiers are only boys of 14, 15, and 16 years. Yesterday morning we heard one cry very pitifully outside our windows. We thought that it was a little Armenian boy whom the soldiers had seized. When we looked out we saw a young soldier, a boy of about 14, being placed on an ox-cart, bound with rope on his chest and legs. The poor little one was sick. He lay in a convulsion with nothing under him in the cart and only a few rags on his body, which exposed his bare chest and legs to the down-pouring rain. It would take at least a couple of hours before he reached Mezreh, and it would be evening, at least, before he would be seen by a doctor and admitted to the hospital. No wonder that the number of dead is so great.

In this part of the country, 350,000 soldiers died of typhus alone last winter. And now another sickness rages amongst the soldiers here. We have a suspicion that it is cholera. Great crowds of people are coming here every day to be sent on to other places, and they can scarcely drag themselves along. I was called to a woman the other day who had suddenly taken ill. She had cholera, and we immediately informed the government. They sent a doctor and two officers, who said it was nothing of consequence and went away again. This was what we expected them to say, because here in Mezreh there have been three cases that Dr. Michael treated, which the government doctor refused to confirm as cholera. They will not admit that there is such an illness here, in case the people become more afraid, and it is bad enough as it is. If the war does not end soon, we do not know what we shall do. It is nearly impossible to obtain the most necessary items for money. We never see gold, and the shopkeepers will not take paper money, with the result that the available food is being hoarded, and nobody can get it even if they can pay for it. Maybe the Russians are nearer than we think. Some say that they have captured Tchabaghchur, but that they will not come forward quicker than they can prepare the way. If they knew what conditions are like here, and the pitiful state of the soldiers, they would probably come today.

23 April—Easter Sunday. It was a blessed and long awaited day. There have been many prayers that we might be allowed to celebrate Easter, and the Lord heard them and gave us a blessed day. We had a service at 9.00 a.m. when Mr. Riggs preached on the text from Colossians, Ch. 3. V. 1, "If ye then be risen with Christ, seek those things which are above." After the service there was a meeting for church members who wished to come to communion. At 2 o'clock in the afternoon there was a service of baptism, when 20 children were baptised. Amongst them was my little girl, who was named Beatrice Arshaluis Dingilian. After the baptism service, 12 young women were received as members of the church, and this was followed by communion. It was a very solemn and peaceful service. It was full of joy and thanksgiving, because we were permitted to meet together around the Lord's table, but most of all because our Saviour lives, and we shall therefore live also. We had brought our pot-plants up to the Hall, much was also beautifully decorated with flowering almond tree branches, and it looked both festive and peaceful.

28 April. On Monday morning I went down to Mezreh with Karen-Marie. She had come up on Saturday to be with us on Easter day. I stayed with her until Thursday morning. On Monday afternoon we went out on a three hour drive, which we all enjoyed, including Bessie. Everything was so beautiful, the green fields, and the fruit trees in bloom, but all the way the misery that is around us was clearly visible. There were great droves of Turkish mohadjirs, coming from Van, Bitlis, and Moush areas, dirty and ragged to the last degree. It was pitiful to see the old men and women so poorly that they could hardly drag themselves along, and also the many, many small

children. More and more refugees are coming constantly, and with them also Armenian women. On Tuesday and Wednesday we spent peaceful afternoons in the Germans' garden.

We heard, a couple of days ago, that Trebizond has fallen. There is also a rumour that Constantinople has fallen, but this we cannot believe. But one thing is certain, the Turks are in very bad spirits, and they are saying again and again, "It is over with us."

All the soldiers are now leaving Harpoot and our buildings have been given back to us, but for how long we do not know. It is said that 5,000 sick soldiers are coming, and all our houses are to be used as hospitals. But one thing is said today, and something else tomorrow, and we never know what is going to happen the next moment.

9 May. It is so strange to think a year back at this time. It is just one year since our dear Mrs. Barnum died and I also lay very ill. How many terrible things happened at that time. Then the troubles had only just begun. Some of the leading Armenians had been imprisoned. It is well that no one then knew the terrible things that were about to happen. It is well that we only live one moment at a time.

There is much moving around these days. It is rumoured that Enver Pasha is coming here on his way from Sivas in an automobile. The Germans and some Turks are very happy at the thought of his visit. The Armenians are afraid. They say he is responsible for their extermination. A good many Turks hate him, saying he is to blame for their suffering. He is said to be so afraid for his own life that he always comes unexpectedly.

11 May. This morning a group of khodjas went off to Mezreh to meet Enver Pasha. There was great activity around us, with a special cleaning of all official buildings and the streets.

The Police Inspector left some days before to have the road cleared of skeletons. The day before yesterday an order came from the Commandant that all hospital beds were to be made up with white sheets, all patients should be dressed alike, and all nursing orderlies should wear white overalls. All this was impossible because white linen has not been available for a year. Enver Pasha came, and the people were very curious, many as interested in seeing the automobile as the man himself. He came to see our hospital at 6.00 p.m. He walked around with Dr. Michael, Mrs. Atkinson, Miss McLaren, and Mr. Riggs and talked to all the soldiers, asking if they were well cared for. He told them to get well quickly, so that they could go out and have their revenge. After seeing the hospital, he went over to Mrs. Atkinson's, saying that he was very touched by the great work Dr. Atkinson had done. He asked if they had a son and Henry was called in. Enver Pasha took from his own coat a war medal and gave it to Henry. It was a half moon and star of silver with red enamel. This pleased Mrs. Atkinson very much. He was altogether very friendly and everyone was happy that he came. Tonight the Vali is giving a dinner and early tomorrow Enver Pasha is leaving for Diarbekir. We hope that his visit will not have an ill-effect on the remaining Armenians. He is, unfortunately, no friend of the Christians.

17 May, 1916.[*] I had hoped things would be looking brighter by the time I would be starting this book. When spring came with sunshine and warmth, and new life sprang up, there was reasonable peace around us. We began to breathe more freely again and thought we had seen the end of the atrocities that have occurred in the last year. But everything can change in a moment, and it is with a heavy heart that I sit here and write tonight. The situation looks alarming. The storm rages outside, and the sky to the south looks like a sea of fire lit by lightning. People who have been out on the mountain with their cattle and sheep are hurrying home. Children are crying, dogs are howling like wild hyenas, and in a little while the rain will pour down and more houses will collapse. So many hundreds of houses have fallen down during the winter. The Armenian area where we live is in ruins with only a few houses left. The poor Armenians are not even allowed to live in these. In a house nearby there was a woman ill with typhus. The roof had collapsed in several places, so she had to be moved to an open shed. But the other day the Turks came and moved her out into the street. They then tore the house down to remove the timber. This morning we heard that a group of Kurdish women and children had arrived here and were immediately sent away to Keghvank. They were accompanied by some soldiers and it was obvious that they would be killed in the same way as the Armenians. This afternoon we saw a crowd of women and small children. One of the soldiers said to our Baron Asador, "They are going the same way as you." It is impossible to describe how painful it is to see a crowd of people being taken away to be put to death in the most cruel way. Then immediately comes the thought, "Oh, may no evil come to our Armenian friends at least." They are again, of course, in fear—and no wonder. Sister Mina has arrived here from Marash. She has told us that just before she left there were several massacres there. We have also heard that the Armenians have been sent away from Aleppo. These places were not so bad last summer. The news has come to us through Ajans that there is great tension between Germany and America and that there is fear of war. If there is war, then all the American missionaries will be sent away at a few hours' notice, and what will happen to the poor Armenians. They will be exterminated after being ill-treated in the most terrible way. When we think back to this time last year, when the troubles first began, and think of the months that followed, one becomes almost sick. There has been so much of tears and suffering, fear and death. The fact that some have survived all these is a wonder. We have also, in a wonderful way, experienced that the Lord can preserve in perfect peace those who put their trust in Him, and He gives strength in the same measure as it is needed. Therefore we will not fear what is to happen in the days to come. If we

[*] Third book of diaries starts here.—A.S.

should go through deep waters, He will be with us. Yes, even through the valley of the shadow of death, He will not forsake us. His rod and staff will comfort us. Blessed certainty. There is a Sabbath-rest remaining for God's people. A Home where God himself is, where we shall see Him as He is. Where there is only joy and peace. No tears, no fear, no suffering, no death, but only hymns of thanksgiving through all eternity.

Oh, mercy that He found me
Oh, mercy that He won me
Oh, mercy that He carried me Home to Himself
Oh Lord preserve us in Your mercy, faithful to the end.

19 May. We heard today that amongst the Kurds sent away yesterday to be massacred were the mother of one of our children in the Children's Home and a young Armenian man who was in prison. Last year, during the deportations, this young man escaped to the mountains. He returned eight days ago with some Kurdish Aghas to see Enver Pasha. He was arrested immediately and now he is gone.

22 May. Kurds have still been sent away during the last few days. Today, about noon, a crowd of about 800 passed our windows. They looked tired and miserable. It was terrible to see the soldiers whipping them. In the early afternoon, as we were looking along the road, we saw a woman lying a short distance away. We could see that she could still move, and I went in and spoke to Mr. Riggs about her. It was agreed that he would go to the government and I should take a donkey and one of our men and go down the road to pick her up. I was soon on my way. All the Turks on the road looked at us and talked to one another. We came down and found an old woman lying prostrate. There was not much life left in her as she had been badly battered. A Turkish khodja was passing, and he came and helped us to lift her onto a donkey. Another Turkish man also helped us. They seemed to be terrified about what is going on. They shook their heads and said a prayer. Maybe they really were sad at what is happening. On the way back we passed another Kurdish woman, who also lay on the road, with three children. They looked terrible, but we managed to raise them, although they were so weak they could hardly walk. The baby girl, who was about one year old, lay dead beside the mother. One of the men carried the dead baby. I led the donkey, and the other man walked alongside and supported the old dying woman. The other woman and children followed. The eldest little girl, about 10 years old, was wearing only a shirt that reached to the hips. We had to pass some streets to reach home, and many Turks watched us. Arriving home, we were surrounded by Armenian women who had seen what had happened, and who now saw these Kurdish women and children in the same pitiable state as they themselves had been in. Tears ran down their cheeks and they shouted, "Oh Lord, if you did not hear our prayers, listen to these calling to you." When we got the old woman down from the donkey and I gave her some water, she opened her eyes and looked at me with a grateful expression.

A little later we heard that an Armenian girl, who had been taken by a Kurd and married to him last year, was deported. Yesterday she gave birth to a child on the road to Mezreh. She could not walk further and was lying there. We had her brought here with her little child. Then two small children were brought. They had been left behind by their mothers, lying on the street while they were passing through the town. One was a little girl, only a few weeks old, and the other a little boy of a couple of months. We now got busy to find mothers for them, but it did not take long. Two women came immediately and received them with great pleasure. One of the Kurdish women said that they had been about six or seven days on the road and that there were many Armenians amongst them. Last night many people were killed up in the mountains behind Harpoot. Oh, how cruel it is to think these terrible things are starting again. It seems impossible that we should live through such a time again. Maybe we will see even more cruelty than in the past. We can only call upon the Lord to have mercy on these poor souls, put an end to all this misery, and preserve us, and all His own, faithful to the end.

23 May. A woman was brought to us today. She had been left out in the mountains in a pitiful condition. She has no hope of survival. The old woman we brought in yesterday died last night. We found another woman lying dead outside one of the neighbouring houses. When I went out visiting the sick this morning, I found a 16 year old boy lying outside one of our back doors. He was very skinny and weak, and had crawled in here during the night. We took him also into Wheeler Hall and gave him some hot soup, but he was too weak to enjoy it. I am afraid there is not much hope for him either. More people have been brought to us during the day.

This afternoon Mrs. Riggs, Miss Harley, and I went out for a ride in the mountains, to see if there were any poor people lying in the clefts. We did not find any but, of course, it was not easy to search very carefully. We hope that if some are lying here and there, they will be seen by people passing to and fro to their gardens. We saw several places that looked like graves—that is, corpses covered with earth. We also saw clothes lying here and there and many birds of prey flying around. How I wished to shout out aloud, "Are there any wounded?" to see if there was any movement, towards which I could hurry with help. It was impossible, and our work of saving people must be done in secret. Soldiers and police were out on the mountains, and they saw us riding from one cleft to another. Maybe they guessed our purpose, but they said nothing to us. We were happy for the ones we were permitted to take in the last hours of their lives. Today we have buried three of them.

Mr. Riggs paid a visit to the Police Inspector, who was very sad that all these cruelties have started again. He said he believed that terrible things will come to their nation as punishment for their many sins. He also said that there were 3,000 Kurds waiting at the river to be brought over. The Kurds say they have been tricked into leaving. They were told they were going to Harpoot to live in the Armenians' houses. They did not know that it was a deportation.

Mr. Riggs returned from Mezreh and said that he had seen the Kurds being led away from there on their way over the mountains again. They have been told that they are going back to their villages. Can we believe that, or are they only leading them up to the mountains to kill them?

24 May. This morning a little 14 year old girl and a baby boy of 10 months were brought to us. They had also been found on the mountains. The girl was very weak and could not swallow when I tried to give her some stimulating medicine. The baby boy was only skin and bones. I gave him some warm milk and laid him out in the sun to get some heat into his body until we could find a mother for him. He must have felt better because he fell asleep. Shortly afterwards a little 10 year old Armenian girl was brought. She was found in a Turkish cemetery, where she had been lying for several days. She was also in a pitiful state. After I had given her some warm milk she begged me for a mattress to lie on, but as we had none, I could only give her a blanket, and I laid her in the sun until we could find a place for her. In the course of the day more came whom the others dealt with, but just after we had eaten our evening meal, a girl came running to me and said, "Khodja Ariz is bringing a little girl she has found." When I went out I saw a woman coming with a little naked baby girl by the hand. She was only about one year old and had been a healthy and strong child. Her little body was somewhat thin, burned by sun and wind, and her little feet were swollen and blue. She shivered with cold. A policeman had found her lying completely naked and alone out on the mountain, and he had brought her in to us. This is a wonder, for he is one of the men who has ill-treated and killed thousands. Can some of you at home understand what I felt when I saw this sweet little innocent child being brought to us in such a state? I felt a constriction of the heart and could not hold back the tears. I took her up in my arms and hugged her, and she could feel my love for her, because she cuddled close. I gave her some warm milk, bathed her, and dressed her in clean clothes. I lifted her into my arms again, and she cuddled close to me and fell asleep. How I would have loved to have kept her with me, cared for her, and loved her. Oh, if only I had the means to take all these little children in and give them a home, where they could be shielded from harm and given love. What can we say about suffering when there are mothers who can endure no more and leave their babies behind on the mountains and roads to die a slow death. It is too painful to think about. No wonder that these mothers, if they survive such adversity, can never be comforted. Oh Lord God have mercy on these unhappy people. If it is possible, put an end to this adversity. Save the few who remain, but help us to say in our hearts, "Thy will be done."

Today there are rumours of deportations again. We have heard it from different sides, but we can not be certain of anything. Everyone is full of fear again. We hope it is only a rumour that will not come true. Today Mr. Riggs has been in Mezreh, where he heard that the Kurdish Aghas, who came here to greet Enver Pasha and were decorated by him, have sent a letter to the Vali saying that, if the exile of Kurds did not stop immediately, they could not hold Khozat and that district. When the Vali heard this, he gave an immediate order that all the Kurds who have arrived here should be sent back. Mr. Riggs saw them being led back over the mountains. It is said that there is heavy fighting at Tchabaghchur. There are even rumours that it has fallen. The Turks are very depressed. With the enemy's approach there is no place to which they can flee. Cholera has broken out in Malatia and 100 die daily of typhus. Dysentery rages also. The army there will soon be wiped out without a war.

25 May. Today many more Kurds have arrived. This morning two women were brought to us by a friendly-disposed man. He found them on the road. A man was attempting to strangle one of them, but this man came to her aid and saved her. They were both in a pitiful condition and were starving and sick. The same man told us that there were others on the road in danger of being killed by the Turks, so I set off at once with a man. On the road we found two women and three children, the youngest of which was three days old. I also took them home with me. A little later in the day an Armenian woman came who told us that she and her family had arrived with the Kurds. Earlier they had lived in Palou, but last year, when the massacre started, they had fled to the mountains to the Kurds. They had now been sent away with them. Their men had been killed and now the Kurds expected to be killed at any moment. When they reached the Euphrates, her daughter gave birth to a baby, and they threw it into the river immediately. They thought it was an easier death that what the child might suffer at the hands of the Turks. These women had been left in the mountains because one of them was very ill. Now they have come here. The poor mother had been so badly beaten that her whole body was black and blue. More small children have also been brought to us today, having been found on the road. An Armenian soldier, who has become a Turk, was sent with the Kurdish exiles. He accompanied them to the river. He returned today and told Baron Asador that 500 died on the road. Many were killed and the others died of starvation and sickness. Now there are 200. It is a three hour journey from here to the river, so how many will be able to reach their villages? The few who do arrive, what will they have to live on? Their houses are burned, and their belongings have been taken by the Turks, so their chances of survival is small. They will starve to death if help does not come soon.

27 May. We had the great pleasure of receiving a telegram from Mr. Peet, saying that we can use 600 liras for relief work this month. We have now decided to start a kind of industry to give work to the women, and we have begun preparations. We have

thought of weaving linen, making blankets, and knitting stockings. We also have our needlework school. We have also given some women the job of fixing the road out to the Garden, which had been nearly washed away.

29 May. Mr. Riggs went down to Mezreh this afternoon and when he reached the hospital he found that all our Armenian young men, who had been working there, had been taken away. Mr. Riggs went immediately to the Commandant, who said that because they had not registered for the army they were considered deserters and would be treated accordingly. This means that they will be sent to the frontline. These young men are to be sent to Malatia the day after tomorrow. We thought that they had all been registered, when men in their age group had been called up, and Nedjie Bey, the chief medical officer, had taken their names and promised that he would get permission for them to work in our hospital. So we thought everything was in order. They are now in prison where they are to remain until their Tabor leaves. We can well imagine their forboding. None of us know what will happen. Maybe they will not be long on the road before they are killed. We had been so glad that these young men had been spared, and now, suddenly, they are taken, and Mr. Riggs does not think there is much hope of freeing them. Oh, how hard it is to see the few survivors being taken away one after another. It is said that the war rages in Tchabaghchur. Some of the soldiers who were sent to Dersim are being taken away from there and sent against the Russians. Oh, how we long to see them come—how we long for peace. Sometimes we are almost afraid that we will have a stroke, should a message of peace reach us. Because we know nothing in advance, it will come so suddenly, and the joy will be too great and overwhelming.

30 May. Early this morning we heard that some of the young men who were taken from the hospital yesterday and imprisoned have escaped. One of them broke a leg jumping from a window but managed to get away. He is lying hidden in a house in Mezreh. How he escaped we do not know yet. Five others ran away and five more are still in prison. We are sad about this escape, as it may have bad consequences, but we do not dwell on it. They must have been beside themselves with fear, knowing how all the other Armenians have been treated. They surely thought that staying meant certain death, whereas trying to escape gave hope of survival. Only little hope, but human beings will cling to that to the end. Mr. and Mrs. Riggs have been down in Mezreh this afternoon. We thought that the government would have begun a search for the runaways immediately, but officers in charge of the prison are said to be afraid to admit to the escape and are keeping it secret. One of the Turkish doctors at the hospital has promised to work for the release of two of those remaining in prison so that they can return to help in our hospital. Another one of them will perhaps be allowed to pay ransom, so only two will remain. Maybe, one way or another, they can also be free again.

25 June. I have not written for a long time, but not because there has been nothing to write about. The days have been full of evil rumours, of forboding, and now and then of hope and expectation of brighter times, but we still live in uncertainty. The young men who escaped from prison are now certainly up in the mountains. Three of those who remained in prison have been freed and are working again in our hospital. The Lord heard our prayers about this and gave more than we dared to ask for. Since I last wrote, Izzat Pasha has come here with some high-ranking German officers. The latter have now left for Tchabaghchur. It is said that there has been a big battle there, at which the Turks have lost 8,000 men, together with all the cannons they brought so laboriously last month. We are not certain about all this.

This day has been a blessed Lord's Day. We had a service at 9 o'clock this morning with Communion. First a young girl was baptised. She stood up and professed her faith in the Trinity. After that 12 young women were received as members of the church, and they too professed their faith in the Trinity and their intention to try to live solely for God. This was followed by Communion. Mr. Riggs preached on the text, "The New Covenant," and spoke very earnestly about renewing the covenant with God if it has been broken. He showed us how the Lord was longing for this and was ready. I think there was many a soul that surrendered itself completely to the Lord and promised to live a new life with His support. When we stood up to sing the last hymn, it was as if our thoughts and feelings were really expressed by the words, "When I come and kneel at Thy cross, the sun and the world fade before my eyes. What is the world's glory? You and your pain are enough for me. Let me live under your cross. Here I see my sins, and here I seek no more honour but to live for Thee."

The afternoon service was just as solemn. It is the last Sunday before the holidays, when there is always a special talk for the young who are taking their diplomas and leaving school. The Badveli, the priest, spoke very earnestly to us on the text from Isaiah, "Whom shall I send, who will go?" It was the anniversary of the great expulsion from Harpoot. He painted three pictures of the surviving Armenians who need help. First, the great flock of children, who go around the streets of the different towns without parents, without friends, starving, ragged, and begging, learning evil by experience. Who will go and gather them together, take them in, protect them, love them, and bring them up to become men and women who love God? Second, the great number of young women who have been taken by Turks and Kurds, and who sit and sigh with longing to be free. Most of them never hear one word of God's but are given over to sin and uncleanliness. Who will go to them, and whisper in their ears that there is a living God, who has not forgotten them, who remembers them, sees them, and loves them? And lastly, the great crowds of old and suffering. Who will go to them, love them, and help them? If we, who have been spared will say, "Lord, here I am, send me," we will go with the Lord's blessing.

30 June. In a card from Mrs. Getchel from Constantinople we have heard that all missionaries from Marsovan and Sivas have been sent there by the government. All those with children are being taken on to America. The rest hope to be allowed to return to their stations and resume their work for the many suffering. We also heard a few days ago that missionaries from Caesarea and Talas have been sent away. Now we often wonder how long we will be allowed to remain. We often hear from comments by Turks that our work for the suffering Armenians is a thorn in their eye. Often we hear them say, "What do you get from it? What praise have you for it?" We say, "Nothing. It is Christianity. It shows the difference between your faith and ours." On Monday, the 27th, dear old Mrs. Parmelee died. I was with her during her last nights. She had been very weak for a long time and had a great longing to go Home. She was buried out in the Garden on Tuesday afternoon. In the last year our little churchyard has received four of our small flock.

1 July, 1916. I have come down to Mezreh today with Bessie to spend a little time in Emaus with Karen-Marie.

13 July. Today I went over to the hospital to spend a week with Mrs. Atkinson, who is alone at present, as Miss McLaren is in Harpoot. Ajans informs us about the terrible fighting in France in recent days and says that the Germans have withdrawn from several places. This encourages the hope for peace in the near future, but we know nothing for certain. We have no magazines and almost no letters. Nothing that tells us what is going on around us. We hear that there is cholera in the country, in Malatia, Ourfa, Diarbekir, Aleppo and Marash, and we can certainly expect that this terrible illness will also come to us. The other day a company of soldiers arrived from Malatia, and among them were nine suffering from cholera.

On July 11th we went to the Garden where we celebrated Miss Harley's birthday. We had our weekly meeting in the afternoon, and had our evening meal out under the trees, eating chocolate cake and ice cream for dessert.

14 July. I was out today with all the Harpoot missionaries on a tour of "buzlük" ice cave. Most of the company spent an hour in the cave, creeping on all fours, sliding on their stomachs down the great stone, and came out safely covered in mud from head to foot. We then ate our evening meal out of doors, with a beautiful view of the mountain plain and river Euphrates. We rode home in the lovely moonlight and for a moment could forget the endless suffering surrounding us on all sides.

24 July. Today it is just one year since little Bessie came to me. At that time she was a little weak child. Now she is a strong healthy little girl, who spreads happiness and sunshine around her.

There are still rumours that the Russians are coming nearer, and people are fleeing. Today I heard at the Shuga that people were saying that we missionaries in Harpoot will be sent away. I comforted them, saying we knew nothing about this. They also said that the Germans will flee from here. The other day we were invited up to the Germans' garden by Lieutenant-Colonel Herselberger for chocolate. It was rather nice. We enjoyed the good chocolate and the good tea. He said we should stay calm as the Russians will not come here, but we are not really worried about that. Of course they would not do us any harm. What we are afraid of is panic amongst the Turks, causing them to put an end to the few remaining Armenians.

In the last few days Turks are again beginning to leave the town. Even those who had left in the spring, had endured so much, and afterwards had returned. There are rumours that Erzingan is about to fall. It is also said that Keghi and Baibourt have fallen. There is no doubt that Keghi has fallen. Before the Turks left the town, they burned it.

30 July (Sunday). The town is full of wild rumours that the Russians are near. The Turks will send all the Christians away. Some Turkish officers paid a friendly visit to Mr. Riggs, and because of this, the frightened women believed that we had been told to leave town in four days, after which there would be a massacre of all the Christians. All this for no reason, except to express their forboding in words.

31 July (Monday). Today is Bairam. There is not the same celebration as in other years, but they do their best to forget their sorrows. It was said today that Erzingan has not fallen, that they have taken back Bitlis and Moush, and that they are making preparations to regain Van. Everyone who wants to believe that can do so. However, it does seem to be true that they have regained Erzingan. We hear that the Turks have collected all the Christians, as well as those who became Moslems last year, saying they would lead them away, but killed them just outside town. This is not difficult to believe after all we have seen in the last year. Now everyone is in great fear, and those who can scrape a little money together are fleeing to the Kurds up in the mountains, from where they hope they can join the Russians in the hope of finding safety. On Sunday evening we saw a big crowd of Armenians being led back from the river by three armed soldiers. They had left Harpoot on Friday evening and were caught at the river, when the Kurd who led them there went to a village to see if everything was in order. It made our hearts heavy to see them being led past our houses, and we feared that the consequences would be bad. However, our good Police Commissioner released the women and children the same night. The men are still in prison because they are in the age group that should be in the army. We thought this would stop people from going to Dersim but we were wrong. The other day a crowd of 50 people left and as far as we know succeeded in getting away. In the last few days many letters have come from Armenians in the mountains containing farewell messages. They hope they can manage to go over to the Russians.

Today 4,000 mounted soldiers came armed with long lances. They went down to the river to go out against the Russians. They were accompanied by a German major, who accidently met Mr. Ehmann, and told him that 40,000 soldiers would be coming from Constantinople under a German general. This has given the scared Turks more courage, and also Mr. Ehmann, who has lately been thinking of leaving.

The fact that the Russians are so near has had a bad effect on our money, which in the last year has become paper of nearly no value. A bank note of 100 piastres is now worth only 35 piastres. People have stopped accepting them in the last few days.

3 August. Last night we heard the sound of many pistol shots and our thoughts turned immediately to the Russians. Then it suddenly stopped, and everything was quiet again. Last night many refugees came from Khozat and Mazgird. They said they fled when the enemy came.

4 August. Every evening we go for a walk on the mountain with our binoculars to see if any fire or smoke is visible. Last night we saw the Pertag road full of people, but we could not see if they were soldiers or refugees. Today we heard they were the 4,000 soldiers who had left the other day and were now returning. No one knows the reason for this.

5 August. Today the 4,000 soldiers went in the direction of Agn. There are now rumours that Sivas is empty, or has been emptied. We do not know if this is true.

Badveli Vartan is our guest out here in the Garden, and the female teachers have come out on a visit. Badveli Vartan has been here for two weeks. He is giving us lessons in Kurdish, which is very interesting. Maybe we will have a use for this language sooner or later.

7 August. Yesterday we heard that there are riots in Constantinople and that Talaat Bey and Enver Pasha have been killed. A son of Abdul Hamid has taken over Enver Pasha's position. This new party that has taken over power is said to be on the side of the British and will not harm the Christians. We did not believe this yesterday, but the Turks are still talking about it in secret today, so we are beginning to think that there might be some truth in it. We do not know if any good will come from such a change, but conditions now are so sad, that we look with hope on every change for something better. It seems impossible that it could be worse.

Today we had a visit from a Protestant Sister from Haini, who has just come from Diarbekir. She says that Siirt has been taken by the Russians. On the way she heard soldiers saying that the Russians were nine hours' away from this side of Tchabaghchur which means only 15 hours from Harpoot.

The Turks are very anxious. A Yuzbashi's wife paid a visit to Mrs. Riggs this afternoon. She sat and said how highly her husband thought of Mr. Riggs, and how much she thought of Mrs. Riggs. She also said that the Turks have packed up all their belongings in readiness for flight and were only waiting to see what will happen. People are constantly leaving for Dersim and farewell letters are still coming from Armenians there, who are waiting to join the Russians.

22 August. At the beginning of the month Ajans reported that the Turks had regained Bitlis and Moush and are now on their way to Erzeroum and Van. We do not know whether this is true or not, but it has calmed the people and the exodus is not so great. We have also heard that Erzingan has fallen, and that all the Armenians who were in Dersim have been taken over by the Russians. This is a great joy and comfort to us, that a few have been rescued. We only hope that they will have something to live on and not suffer hunger and distress, but we know that whatever happens to them, it can only be an improvement on their life here, where they existed in continuous peril and fear. In the last few days we have seen crowds of Turkish mohadjirs coming from the Khozat area. Whether this means that the Russians really are there, or that the flight is in fear of their coming, we do not know, for no one tells the complete truth. It is also said that Khozat is burned and only ruins remain.

On Sunday the government collected all the donkeys together and sent them to Khozat and the river to help the Turkish mohadjirs. If a man was seen in the street with a donkey, it was taken away from him. It is said that several hundred families are coming here in flight, but where will they live, for there are no houses? We are afraid that the Turks will drive the Armenians out of their wretched dwellings and give them to the mohadjirs. There is also the big question of food. Everything is so frightfully dear, with nearly nothing to be had even for money, and money is not coming to us. We write and telegraph but receive no answer, and our stock is almost gone. What will the 2,000 people do when the day comes that we can no longer help them? Yesterday I was out in the town for the lace work. This is a day that saps one's strength, not so much because of the work, but because one sees so many people endlessly in need of help. They beg and plead for work, and I have to say, "No, I cannot. I have no material and no yarn" and then watch them go away crying. It takes the strength out of one's life.

A flock of new Armenian refugees have come to us for help, but we cannot help any more and must say "no." They say they will go back and throw themselves into the river. Some Armenian women have come with their children from Palou, and we have had to refuse them as well. They say when they go back they will throw their children into the river, as they can no longer bear seeing and hearing them cry and plead for bread while they are unable to give them any. It will be a terrible day, if it should come, that we must stop our work. How much more misery and sin would there be, that up to now we have been able to avoid. But our hope is in God. The Lord has helped thus far, and our expectation is in Him. Only from Him does our help come.

An officer who has returned from Tchabaghchur has told Mr. Riggs that it was not true that Bitlis and Moush had been regained. The Turkish position at Tchabaghchur is very bad. He also said that the Russians have taken a great many Turkish soldiers prisoner at Keghi. We had already had our doubts about the truth of what we had previously heard. Maybe the Russians are nearer than we think. It is not pleasant to live under these conditions. Several times we have begun to pack necessities together, in case we might suddenly be forced to flee. Then comes the thought of how impossible it would be to go and leave our friends behind with their enemies, without protection, without help, and without the means to live. We cannot dwell on all this, but resign it all to our Father's hands, and go the way he reveals to us. We can be certain that He will give us just what strength is necessary day by day.

23 August. Again our hearts are filled with anxiety about what the future will bring. Some days ago we received a card from a former woman teacher who last year was sent into exile. After several months walking she reached Der Zor, where she has remained since. This is the place to which the Turks said all Armenians should be sent. Some reached there, but only a few of the 2½ million who were sent away from their homes. She wrote in the card that she, with all the Christians, was to be sent away again, and if we did not hear anything more from her in four days we could be sure that she was gone. It is now more than four days since we heard from her so we now know that all these poor people, after all their suffering on the road last year, and their hope that when they reached their destination they might be liberated, sooner or later, are again sent away. What must it be like for them, knowing well what this means. She wrote that we would see each other one day, but before she saw us, she would see Mrs. Barnum and Annie. This shows she was sure they would be killed, and there seems to be no doubt that this was the intention. Why should they move them again from this place? They cannot say now that it is because there are revolutionaries amongst them, as there are only women and children left.

Mr. Riggs was down in Mezreh yesterday and returned with a heavy heart. He said that the Consul has received a letter from Consul Jackson in Aleppo stating that all the Christians in that town had been sent into exile about 10 days ago and no one remained. The investigation beforehand had been more thorough than ever before. He also said that Enver Pasha was expected in Mezreh today, and that raises the anxious thought, "What will his visit bring?" Last time he was here, in the spring, he arranged the Kurdish massacre. Now that so many Turkish refugees are arriving for whom there is no accommodation, and there are fears of a famine, the simplest answer may be to send all the Armenians away. It is evident that they will do all that they can to destroy the remaining women and children. It is impossible for us to obtain money. We write and telegraph, but receive no answer, which would seem to indicate that all letters and telegrams are being held back. If we receive no money, we will not be able to help the thousands who get bread from us, and they will starve to death. If this is what is to happen, it would be more merciful to take them away and kill them. In several places conditions have been made so unbearable that even missionaries have had to leave. This has happened in Marsovan, Sivas, and Caesarea. Yesterday we received a card from Mrs. Getchel in Marsovan saying that some of them had returned. The Getchels only had one room in their own house, and the women missionaries also had one room in the school. All the rest of the houses were occupied by sick soldiers. It looks as if the government may force us out in the same way, but we are not anxious for our own sakes, only for all our Armenian friends. We cannot understand why help does not come, but we try to wait quietly upon the Lord, and continue to look to Him with expectation. Our daily prayer is, "Oh Lord, be gracious unto us, we have waited for Thee, be Thou their arm every morning, our salvation also in the time of trouble." Es. 33-2.

This morning we saw two regiments on the way to Dersim. They passed here, and they had a flock of sheep with them, so that they should not be without food. We are glad for every single Armenian who has reached Dersim so far and hope they have now joined the Russians. We only wish that many more had left. Now it is probably too late, as a lot of soldiers have been sent there, and the Kurds have not been going there recently. It is difficult to know how to advise people because up there they are starving and sickness rages amongst them. We do not really know if they are safe there.

25 August. It seems as though more dark clouds are gathering again. We say to one another that it is like living on top of a volcano, waiting every moment for it to erupt. The Vali and the Police Commissioner have sent their families away, likewise all the government officials. We had a card from home saying that the Russians are getting closer, and they are wondering how long we can stay here. Mr. Ehmann had a telegram from Germany saying that they must remember to leave in time. Mr. Ehmann wants to send his wife and children away, but she does not want to leave yet. We also had a card from Mr. Maynard, who was earlier a missionary in Bitlis. He wrote from Stockholm that he, Dr. Reynold, and Mr. Yarrow from Van, are on their way to us through Russia, bringing money with them from the American Red Cross. This gave us great pleasure and encouragement. Maybe they can help those of our friends who went to Dersim and from there reached the Russian side. They are probably in need of help. This is probably why the missionaries are returning, to seek the lost sheep. Many women and children are thinking of leaving, but no trustworthy Kurds are coming, so it is a bit difficult. The other evening a crowd was preparing to leave with some men amongst them. The Kurds had taken all their clothes and tied them on donkeys. Then they had collected one lira from each person and sent off the donkeys in advance. When the people were supposed to leave, the Kurds said there were too many of them and the women should wait until next day.

However, the Kurds failed to turn up next day, and now these people have lost both clothes and money—a great loss to them as there is no prospect of getting them back again.

The Russians have taken Kara Hissar and there is heavy fighting at Keghi. The other day we saw several taburs of soldiers pass on their way to Pertag, a village four hours away from here. Ammunition supplies are still being sent. Sometimes we hear people say that they hear gunfire, but we do not believe this can be true, as we have heard nothing ourselves.

27 August. Tonight there was a severe earthquake, the heaviest I have felt here. Last night, when we were out in the mountains, we saw a lot of wagons returning from Dersim. We could not see what they contained, but thought that it might be wounded soldiers. Today we heard it was ammunition. The soldiers are returning, and it is said that things are now quiet up there. There is supposed to be peace between the Turks and the Kurds.

28 August. The Kurds who were to have accompanied the Armenians have returned, and a large crowd is supposed to leave tonight.

29 August. Last night, as darkness began to fall, we saw more small groups of Armenians round about in the mountains, waiting for their Kurdish guides. When it became dark, and we were preparing for bed, we suddenly heard a shot, very close to our house, followed by another, and then many shots. One after the other came whistling past. We knew at once that they were after the Armenians and thought that the soldiers had been sent by the government to capture them. Three young men came running down the mountain to our door, but we had to say to them, "Hurry away. You cannot stay here." Then we heard shouting and screaming. We were sure they had been captured, and we suffered terrible feelings. We were all very anxious about the poor souls who were out there. We knew that if they were captured, the young men especially would never leave prison alive. We were also very afraid that the young men had been seen running from our house. If they found anyone hiding with us we would be surely sent away. There are many Turks who cannot bear the sight of us, because we help the Armenians, whom they only long to see dead. They are only looking for a good excuse to send us away. We know all this, and this is why we are anxious. Around 10.30 p.m. one of the young girls from the crowd, attempting to get away, came to our windows and called us. We let her in and put her to bed with the other young Armenian girls who stay with us. Around 11 o'clock everything was quiet again and we went to bed, but we expected the soldiers to come back during the night to search our house. However, they did not come, and next morning, when it started to get light, they returned in small groups. We did not sleep that night and next day we were all very tired. We then heard that two of the young girls had been captured by the men who had shot after them. These men were our Turkish neighbours who said that they thought the girls were thieves, but we do not

believe this. They had seen at once that they were Armenians and fired upon them to frighten them into giving up their money. The Police Commissioner sent for Mr. Riggs to discuss various things with him, including what had happened last night. This Police Commissioner is friendly towards the Armenians and Mr. Riggs said he tried to enquire as little as possible.

30 August. I was in town today. Everybody there was very anxious. An officer came to a house where Armenians are living to search for two Armenian men who were in prison last year. They had paid the Prison Inspector 500 liras to be set free and since then he has considered the two as his servants. About eight days ago they heard that orders had come that they were to be hanged, so they ran away and were amongst the crowd trying to leave the other night. One of them was shot, but they both got away, and we do not know where they are now. One of the women in this house is from the same town as the young men and she was taken to the prison. Several soldiers went around the houses this morning, whipped the women, and took more to the prison. The two young girls, who were captured and taken home by the men who had shot at them, were given some money and allowed to go, but they are now being sought by the government. The Police Inspector said to Mr. Riggs, "All the Turks say that you help in these escapes, but I say, 'No,' though I cannot make them believe it." So we feel that many Turks look at us with eyes of hatred, but as long as the leading officials are our friends, and remain here, it will be difficult for the others to get rid of us. If these officials should be transferred and others come, I do not know what will happen to us. It is not pleasant to think about it. All boys over four years old in Arapkir have been rounded up and put in prison, along with all who were working for Turks. The purpose is, of course, to kill them, and this has created great fear of what will happen here.

How good it is that we can bring all our sorrows, worries, and forbodings to our Heavenly Father, and be sure that He understands and is mighty to help. How often have we experienced that when we cry, "He hears us." How wonderful it is to feel how He gives strength and power to endure. Praised be His name. How often we say, "Praise the Lord for He is good."

31 August. We heard today that Romania has entered the war against Germany, and we again hope that this may eventually bring peace nearer.

1 September. We heard today that the town of Chemishgezek is being attacked, some say by the Russians, others say by the Kurds. This town is only 12 hours away, and I have travelled to it on horseback in one day. So now they are really closer than before. There are no towns between us and Chemishgezek, only little unimportant villages, so if they want, they can be here in one day.

However, we have seen that the Russians do not hurry themselves, and it is said that they do not proceed quicker than they can prepare the way. This is very necessary as the roadways around the country are only narrow lanes.

23 September, 1916. I went down to Mezreh on the 5th [of September] to help our hospital, as Miss McLaren has not been able to look after it. She had a fall from a horse one day on her way to Harpoot and sprained her knee. Mrs. Atkinson did not feel very well either and needed to get away for a little while. The day after my arrival we saw several hundred Russian prisoners being taken to Harpoot. They looked very miserable and could hardly drag themselves along. They were the first prisoners we have seen during these two years, though the Turks often say they have taken thousands. It is said that they kill their prisoners at once, and this is why we never see them. This we can well believe, having seen so much of their cruelty. Until a short time ago we had 100 soldiers in our hospital, the rest of the places being used for private patients, mostly Armenians who needed care badly. While I was down there, the Government ordered 50 beds for the daily arrival of hundreds of wounded, all in miserable condition, dirty, starving, and so weak that they can hardly drag themselves along. The other evening, after 9 o'clock, we admitted 36 new soldiers, who had come from Sheitan Dagh (Devil's Mountain), three hours on the other side of Keghi, which is four days journey from here.

They had been travelling for 16-19 days, walking here without having their dressings changed and without any proper food. The road goes over high mountains, where the snow has already fallen, and it is very cold. Eight days ago we had a severe storm, lasting for three days, during which 200 horses froze to death. They did not say how many people. The consequence is that they are so miserable when they arrive here that many of them die before anything can be done for them. Their wounds are terrible, all very inflamed. Among the last arrivals there were several whose wounds had become putrid and full of maggots. One man's arm was dead—absolutely black and cold. Besides, they are suffering so badly from malaria that they quickly waste away with high fever. We have no quinine in the country and dysentery rages amongst them. The food is so bad that even healthy people can hardly eat it, much less sick people. It consists of whole-grain boiled in water, like pilaff, and a couple of mouthfuls of boiled meat, twice a day, and occasionally a sort of soup—the smell of which would drive people away—made from water boiled with a thickening of black meal with a piece of bread. That is their full diet. For fever and dysentery patients we prescribe milk and cornflour, but they never send what we prescribe. One third milk and two thirds water in a cup, per meal, is all they get. How can these poor men gain strength?

We have now 1,500 wounded in this town, with more coming daily. All the larger buildings are being used as hospitals—also our school buildings—so we are once again surrounded by sick soldiers. It is said that the Turks will withdraw from Tchabaghchur to Palou, and that the military centre will be here. Recently we have had quite a lot of German officers, and the other day two German doctors arrived. Wednesday evening two German junior officers came to Mezreh. They knocked on the door of Sister Katherina's Children's Home and said that they had been told it was a German inn where they could buy food. They had come to prepare a flying ground, as in the near future more German fliers would arrive here from Diarbekir. It is said that Enver Pasha is on his way here again. Yesterday he was supposed to have been in a village near Palou. Everyone is again filled with fear of his arrival. The rich Turkish families are still leaving, and it is said that after Kurban Bairam all Turks will leave. Government representatives have been going around during the last few weeks taking down the names of all Armenians. We do not know the reason.

While I was down in Mezreh I was asked urgently to come down and take over the supervision of the big Mezreh Military Hospital where all soldiers are first admitted, and where all operations are performed. The missionaries agreed, and I accepted the invitation. If all goes well, I am to commence on October 1st.

One day I went up to see the hospital and did the rounds with them. All wards and passages were overfilled with patients, more than enough for the staff to cope with, and they do not have a single trained nurse. There are only four doctors for several thousand patients, so there will be plenty for me to do. I look forward to beginning my work there, but unfortunately I cannot give all my time, as there is so much work in Harpoot to be done for our poor Armenians, whom we must not neglect. I will go down to Mezreh every morning and stay until noon. In the afternoon I will attend to the handiwork industry, the soup kitchen, and the eye clinic.

Today I came back to the Garden with my little girl to spend another Sunday in the lovely fresh air. We hope to go down to town on Friday and also hope that the rain will come soon, as the streets are badly in need of washing. The air is contaminated in there. How wonderful it is to be well enough to work, and thank God for His grace in allowing us to remain here so far, as there is so much work to be done. My heart fills with joy, thanks for His unspeakable grace, that I may stay here and work for Him and His. How wonderful it is to serve God.

1 October, 1916. We are now in town again. We moved in last Thursday and are pleased to be here again, where we are closer to the many who need our help. It is not without anxiety that we face the coming winter. The many thousands who actually do not have a mouthful of bread, except for what we give them, will have a hard time. Already we are not able to give them as much dry bread as they can eat, only enough to keep them alive. If we do not receive more money, we cannot even give them this. We write and telegraph for money, but without result. We never hear from Constantinople. Fortunately, no one can close the way upwards. We bring our need and the need of all the many poor souls before our Heavenly Father, and we can truly say with the Psalmist that God is to us a God of continual deliverance when we are in greatest need, but we are in great want. If we are informed by the bank that money has arrived then the pleasure is great, not only for us, but for the thousands of poor who go in fear of losing the little bread they have. Last time we had money there were rumours that five donkeys loaded with gold had come to Mr. Riggs, and the

result was that the next day he was surrounded by crowds of people. All our buildings are full of wounded soldiers. The lightly wounded are sent up here. We have 1,500 and are completely surrounded by them, but new ones are coming every day. They look miserable, complete skeletons, worn out, apathetic, and demoralised. It is quite clear that the Turks cannot win with these kinds of soldiers. They are nearly naked, and now that the cold has started, in another month they will break down, as they have no powers of resistance. The Turks are still continuing to flee from here. Every day 10-15 families leave, going to the Marash-Aintab area. It is the rich who are going. The government officials are sending their families now, to be ready to flee themselves when the danger is near. Everyone thinks the Russians will be here this winter. At the moment it is said that there are peace negotiations at the front at Palou. We do not know if this is true or not. Last Monday Enver Pasha came, but he left again after a couple of hours. There are many rumours about the reason for his departure. Some say there was a major Turkish defeat at Palou and that he had to go there immediately.

29 October. It is about four weeks since I last wrote, partly because things have continued as before and nothing special has happened, and partly because my time is very occupied and it is not easy to spare time to sit down and write. I have now for three weeks gone daily to Mezreh to the Military Hospital. I go in the morning and stay until about 1.00 or 2.00 p.m. There are operations three times a week. The other days we dress wounds. Unfortunately many of the operations are performed too late and the patients die after a few days. All soldiers coming from the front come directly to us and every one has bad wounds. They remain here for a while before being moved to other hospitals. We have a German and a Greek doctor, but there are 350 patients, and new ones are still coming. So it is impossible to manage all the work.

Yesterday, Saturday, thirteen young Armenians were hanged in the Market at Mezreh, and among them was young Baron Muggerditch who had been in prison since last year. He had hoped to be freed. He had come here from Aintab 2½ years ago to study for the ministry. He was a real faithful man and his life down in the prison has surely not been in vain. He had one wish to the end—to be free to serve his Lord. Now he is Home with the Saviour whom he loved. How I would have liked to have seen him before he died. It is a long time since I last saw him. This has filled everyone with sorrow and fear for the few who are still left. We tremble to think of the coming winter because, if the Russians come, the population will of course be sent away and there is no doubt that the Turks will put an end to the Christians. Should any escape the hands of the Turks, they will surely die on the road from hunger and cold. The poor people. There is always fear and horror around us, and it is the innocent who suffer, and it is the government that creates the lawlessness. "Oh Lord! Oh Lord! How long will you hesitate?" This we cry time after time. Recently many Armenians have left for Dersim. Naturally, as many as possible want to get away, but it is not easy, because the Kurds demand a high price. Besides that, they can expect to be robbed of the little they bring with them. Then there is the danger of being caught on the road, which is what they fear most of all.

Yesterday the government ordered that all men up to 45 are to join the army. Also those who have paid Bedel, which will now be refunded. But who believes that? Nobody. When has the government ever kept a promise? It is just something they say to make the injustices look better. This shows that they are very short of soldiers—something we all know.

Thousands of sick and wounded soldiers are continuously coming and most of them die. This cannot go on for years without seriously reducing the ranks. The Turks themselves curse their own country and government. All officers and government officials live off the produce of the land, while the soldiers and their families suffer hunger and cold, and moreover, are slaves to the officers.

Digin Vershin, a very beautiful young Armenian woman, who had lived in England for 12 years, came here on a visit with her husband just before the outbreak of war, and then she could not leave the country. Last year they were sent away in exile. They left in the company of a number of French Sisters and had papers from the government, authorising them to travel in safety. When they were only two hours away from Mezreh they were attacked by Kurds, who killed all the men and several of the women. Digin Vershin was taken by a Kurdish chief and brought back to his house in Mezreh, where she has been ever since and has undergone a terrible year. We have often thought about getting her to run away, but she and everyone around is afraid of the man, and she has still not tried to do so. Karen-Marie and I visited her and it was wonderful to see how calm she was under all her suffering. Her faith in God had not wavered. He was her trust, and help, and refuge in all her adversity. She had an English hymn book and bible with her, which gave her great comfort. Six weeks ago the Kurd began to talk about sending her away, saying he regretted that he had not killed her. This made her anxious, and she was in constant fear that he would kill her. When Karen-Marie visited her one day, she thought she was a little strange, and we were afraid she might lose her mind. So Karen-Marie went to the Kurd and asked him to allow Digin Vershin to come here and pay her a short visit. After much talking back and forth he gave his consent and she came the same day. She has been with us since and is much better, and what looked impossible to us a month ago, God has accomplished in answer to prayer. She is free. There has been a rift in the Kurd's family. His brother, his wife, and her father were all against him, because he had taken Digin Vershin to live with him without being married, and this may be the reason he has given her her freedom. We are in great joy to have her away from his house. He could easily have killed her.

Yes, we know that God hears prayer,
Yes, we believe that God hears prayer,
Yes, we have seen that God hears prayer,
Glory to God.

"Have faith in God" echoes continually in my heart, when everything seems impossible. If we have faith, we shall see God's glory. God be praised that we are His children and know Him as our Father. We must leave all in His hands, let Him rule us, lead and guide us, and we will just follow. If our road goes through deep water and dark ways, He will not forsake us, so we put our hand in His, and say from the heart, "Yes, Lord Jesus, I will follow Thee all the way."

6 November, 1916. The Armenians were not allowed an unrestricted departure to Dersim for long. Last Saturday and Sunday nights many were seized, and on Monday the town was encircled by soldiers, who went to and fro to prevent people from going out of the town. They are still going around, so it is impossible for anyone to leave. Snow is beginning to fall in the mountains, so in a short time it will be impossible to get through. Fifty Kurdish Aghas were here last week to get one of their Aghas out of the prison. He was seized six weeks ago for leading Armenians away. A great number of Armenians were to have gone back with them, but it is impossible with the strong guard around the town, and even people going about during the day are being taken away. If we knew that it was safe here, we would prevent them from leaving, for there are many dangers on the way—robbery, rape, and murder. But we know nothing of what will happen here, so it is difficult to say what they should do. The other day an Armenian man came to visit Badveli Vartan. He has been an army officer since the beginning of the war. He told him that a short time ago 31 Christian soldiers were taken out of the regiment at Palou, bound, and taken away towards Diarbekir, certainly to be killed in the same way as thousands of other men last year. Afterwards eight officers were taken out and sent away, and this man was amongst them. They were very badly mistreated by the Turkish officers taking them, and one of the Armenians said, "I cannot endure it. I will kill them one way or another." He managed to free his hands, grabbed a pistol, and shot one of the Turks. He fell from his horse, and the others fled. All the Armenians ran also. This man just returned to the front, went to Izzat Pasha, and told him he had been in war service from the beginning, had done his duty loyally, and was willing to die on his feet, and he told him how he had been treated. Izzat Pasha told him not to be afraid, "Stay with me and serve me." So he has been sent here on an errand as Izzat Pasha's servant. But what does it all mean? The same as last year, that the Christian soldiers are being separated from the others and sent away. The Turks are always saying, "Don't be afraid, there is no expulsion," but who can believe this, seeing all that is going on around us. Oh, how we long for something to happen that will end all this tension. The few remaining Armenians suffer terribly under the strain and the frightful uncertainty and fear of what might happen. How many women during the

last year have been driven to lie and live immorally because they were forced to have something to live on? We must remember that all strong Christians, who chose to suffer and die rather than commit sin, have long ago been taken from the world's suffering, and the majority who are left are those who, when the troubles were at their worst, tried to save their lives in one way or another, even if it meant denying their Saviour. But they are not all this type. There are individual people whom the Lord has preserved throughout the great adversity, confident that they will help the many fallen. Oh, how we need people who will sacrifice, love, and suffer with the many poor in spite of everything. At the moment it looks impossible, but we know that for Him nothing is impossible, and we must not judge. "There is a wideness in God's mercy like the wideness of the sea." Oh God, be praised for it. We will only be faithful and work and leave the result to Him.

It is a year ago today since the terrible massacre when I saved my little Bessie who lay out in the street, wrapped in a blanket. At that time she was a poor little weak one, whom we all thought would never be strong. How different she is now—a big, strong girl, full of life and energy, and a joy to us all.

26 November. Since I last wrote we have had a visit from Izzat Pasha, who came from the front. He stayed for a week and had conferences with the Valis of Diarbekir and Mezreh. Some Germans have arrived, among them three pilots with their aeroplanes. Last Sunday one of them flew to the front to drop explosives on the enemy. When they arrived they found that they would have to go 400 metres higher to reach the enemy, and the machine was not able to do this, so they had to return here in the afternoon without doing anything. They have been making alterations to the machines during the last week and doing a lot of flying around here. They soon expect to make a more lucky trip to the front. This place looks more and more like a military centre. One hardly sees any civilians, only soldiers and officers. The streets are full of horses and mules bringing supplies and ammunition. We still see crowds of sick soldiers, dressed in rags, stumbling along the roads, and all day long we have the unpleasant sight of the wagon driving from one hospital to another to collect the dead and bring them down to Merkes from where they are taken to be buried. About 50 die every day. Now the terrible typhus is raging again, and not many survive this. The cold weather will soon begin, and there will be many suffering from gangrene this year, because they will be less able to stand the cold due to exhaustion and hunger.

If the war continues much longer, we do not know what conditions will be like. There are many things that are now unobtainable, and what is available is almost impossible to buy. Large crowds gather outside the bakers' shops from morning till evening, shouting, screaming, and fighting to obtain bread that is almost inedible, and many times more expensive than before. It is also nearly impossible to go around in the Shuga to find some clothes. All the shops are nearly empty. Nothing is being imported, and there are no Armenian shops left. They were the ones who were leading trade. We are making hats from dresses this year, and shoes from hats. Who knows what else we must do before we are finished. It is also nearly impossible to obtain fuel, as very little is being brought here, and what comes must be paid for in gold. This is also four or five times more expensive than formerly. This year I have bought cow dung for fuel. This, too, is expensive, and burns quickly, and I cannot get as much as I need. Out on the mountains you can see Armenian women and girls gathering weeds and roots to burn, so that they can boil a little water now and then. It is all they can boil, as their only food consists of two small loaves a day. Recently the soldiers have clipped the manes and tails of the horses, throwing away the hair in the fields. This is also being collected by the women to make bedding. Nothing goes to waste. Many of these women were formerly well to do people. No one who has not seen them can imagine their circumstances now.

28 November. Today when I came down to the hospital I found that the Mudir had whipped six of the Armenian women who work there because one of them had gone away from the hospital without asking his permission. He had also spat on them and derided Jesus and the cross. I was terribly sorry for them. I decided to go and speak to him about this and to say that I did not allow him to beat these women. If he did it again, I would have nothing more to do with the hospital. Unfortunately I could not find him today but I told the doctor and will tell the Mudir as soon as I can get hold of him.

A German doctor, Dr. Asbech, has arrived here to work in the hospital. He is so nice, friendly, and very clever. It is a pleasure to work with him. It is so good to have someone who is kind to the patients and does his best for them, taking a real interest in each one. He has told me several times that he had been shocked to see the misery at the Dardanelles, but it was nothing to what he sees here. It is indescribable, and the reason is that nothing is being done for the patients. If they live, they live. If they die, they die, and then they are out of the world. Poor, poor people. At 9 o'clock this morning I heard a terrible sound of shooting. It sounded as if the house was falling down. I had not noticed it before, but just outside the hospital is the military prison, and there, beyond our window, were soldiers drawn up in two ranks. One soldier was bound between two upright posts and the ranks opened fire upon him. Of course, he was killed immediately. It was a soldier who had tried to run away, but he is not the only one. Thousands flee, and we do not know why this one was shot. Several of the patients had tears in their eyes and sighed. It was a terrible moment and I felt as if my heart would break. My throat constricted. Oh Lord, have mercy on these many, many thousands who suffer so indescribably. No one understands like you what suffering, sorrow, and need is borne by each one in these terrible times. Sometimes it seems impossible to bear, to see all the suffering around us, without being damaged in some way ourselves. The only thing that keeps all of us going is the thought that we must try, as well as we can, to relieve the misery of the many poor souls.

The Armenians are still trying to flee. They do not dare to stay because there is still talk of massacre. Soldiers are still in wait to catch anyone trying to leave. On Saturday evening a group of 20 women and children were caught and put in prison where they still remain. We are afraid that they will carry out their threat to send them away in exile. Our dear Baron Roupen, who up till now has been hidden by the Consul, also took flight and was imprisoned, but fortunately he was set free by giving the soldiers 15 liras and 2 gold watches. We are naturally very happy about this.

7 January, 1917. Another Christmas has gone. It was brighter and happier than the previous one, when little Annie died five days before and Dr. Atkinson himself died on Christmas Eve. Naturally it was not the same Christmas as in earlier years, but we were together with Mrs. Atkinson for dinner and the Christmas tree afterwards. It was a real children's party. The children sang and played their Christmas carols and recited their poems so nicely. Bessie could also take part this year and was delighted with everything. She received a lot of presents from her many, many friends. Bessie and I spent Christmas Eve in Emaus with Karen-Marie. On the Wednesday after Christmas, Bessie had invited 18 small children to a Christmas tree. They ranged from three months to three years, and each received a little jumper and cap, a small toy, and a bag of sweets. They were so few, when we think of the many hundreds of little children who are out there in cold and misery without any joy, but we could not have them all and had to be content with those in whom Bessie has a special interest. Now winter has arrived with its cold. For two weeks we had thick fog, followed by several days of a heavy snow storm, and now a hard frost. The streets are full of deep snow up to the roofs of the houses, and it is nearly impossible to get through them. In the middle of the day, when the sun is out, it melts the surface, but by 3 o'clock in the afternoon it is like a sea of ice. Those of us who have clothes and shoes can manage well enough, but it cuts us to the heart, more than we can say, to see the many, many poor souls, who come to us daily in the hope of getting help. They are clad only in rags, insufficient to cover their bodies, and with bare legs. So many come, standing from early morning till evening outside our doors. The distress is so much greater this year than last, when we were in a position to give them enough bread, bedding, and clothes. But this year it is impossible. There is a steady stream of new arrivals who up to now have been living in either Turkish or Kurdish villages or Turkish homes. Now that living costs are so high, they are being sent away without anything, so they come to us. In earlier times we fed and clothed over 5,000 here in Harpoot and Mezreh, besides sending help to Malatia, Arapkir, and Diarbekir. Now we can only give a half portion of bread to each, and it is impossible to get clothes for them, as there are none to be found in the market. We have begun weaving, but we cannot get enough cotton, so there is only one set of bed linen to each, and bedclothes are unobtainable. Money is losing so much value that when we receive one lira, which used to be worth 108 piastres, it is now only worth 34, and the value is becoming less all the time. Everything is becoming dearer, and soon we will not be

able to buy anything even if we have money. We have only enough corn to last until March, and it is not to be had now. We do not know what we will do when we are no longer able to give the 5,000 the little bread they have. We dare not dwell upon it. Think of all these people, after all the suffering they have gone through, starving to death at the end. We cannot contemplate it. It would be impossible to endure this sight and be unable to help. We cannot worry about the future, but only take one day at a time. The Lord has helped us thus far and we put our trust and all our hopes in Him. What would the friends at home say, if they could only come and sit in our living room, from where we can see the many people who come to us. Everyone is in the same situation. The former rich people, who always lived in abundance, now come to us in the same condition as the most poverty stricken of earlier times, half-naked and without dry bread. What would our Danish mothers say if they could see the many little children who stand shivering and crying outside our house, waiting in the hope of receiving a piece of clothing. They wear ragged shirts, no stockings or shoes, and nothing on their arms or head, all unkempt and dirty. They cry and lament saying, "Oh, mother, my feet! Oh, mother, my hands!" for the ground under their feet has changed to snow and ice, and their little feet are red and blue with cold. But there is no mother to pity them, for both father and mother have been killed long ago. I suppose every single mother at home would say, "I will take one, I will take one." If only we could come home and tell you of the immeasurable distress around us, so you could have a share in the blessed work of helping these poor souls, before it becomes too late, because if help does not come soon, one way or another, most of these people will die.

A great many people in the last week have been suffering from frostbite. One little boy of six years was brought to us with frostbite in both legs up to his hips. Poor little child, what he must suffer before he goes Home to his Father's house, where there is no affliction or pain, no father or mother at home could bear to look upon. And this little boy has no mother to care for him in his suffering, to comfort him, and love him. He is one of the many hundreds of poor little ones who live in a cold dark room, without windows, without heat, and without even enough dry bread to satisfy hunger. Many die daily. The other day we found a little child lying dead in an abandoned stable. The little legs had been dead for a longer time, and this is one of God's little treasures here on earth. What we do to one of these, we also do to Jesus.

Fuel cannot be found. Before the snow came we constantly saw women going out on the mountains, plucking the little weeds that are found there to make a small fire. But there was only enough to heat a little water once or twice.

When we meet the women on the roads now, they no longer look the way they used to—in attractive and well kept clothes. One could always recognize an Armenian in former times, because they were always dressed in lovely and clean clothes. Now we recognize them because they are dressed in terrible rags, but they all try, more than at any time, to cover their heads and hide their faces. For this purpose they use blankets, table cloths, yes, even sacking. Most of them are bare-legged, and the fact that they have not all had pneumonia and most of them have not died is unbelievable. The prices of different things are: 1 yard woollen fabric, 180 piastres; 1 kilo wheat 624 piastres; 1 kilo fat, 42 piastres; 1 egg, 60; 1 sugar, 95 piastres; 1 box matches, 5 piastres; 1 soap, 100 piastres; tea, 300 piastres; 1 bread, 9 piastres; 1 wheat, 12 piastres; 1 yard cotton material (very thin), 13 piastres. Next year it will be impossible to have meat because everyone is killing their animals now due to the high cost of animal feed, which is also nearly impossible to obtain.

11 January. Today I have been down in Mezreh with the Commander of the Military Hospital. Dr. Asbech and the Greek doctor, Dr. Loffaelitti, were present. During the last three weeks the government has not given me any feedstuff for my horse. Yesterday they said that they had no more and therefore could not give me any, and this is what I came to discuss. If I cannot have this I can no longer come down to the hospital. However, they continued to say they could not give it to me and that all doctors and officers had to pay for the feeding of their own horses. This is impossible for me, as it costs 5 liras a month to do this, so I had to bid them goodbye. I was very sorry to have to do this as I would much rather stay and try to help some of the poor soldiers. A new Ser Tabib arrived eight days ago, and it is he who will not give me fodder for my horse. We think it is because he does not want me to see the frightful conditions in this so-called hospital.

23 January. I am now up here in Harpoot full time to look after the sick, and there is more than enough for me to do. There is so much sickness—typhus, smallpox, and an acute stomach sickness that looks like cholera, as well as frost bite and pneumonia. It is no wonder that sickness rages. The few houses that still have roofs are so crammed full of Armenians that they must sleep lying close together and infection passes from one to the other. Most of them lie on rags, so poor and dirty, that, if one of them was lying in a street in Denmark, everyone would go a long way around to avoid it. I don't think it would be possible to find anything at home to compare with the bedding and clothes that these poor ones lie on and wear. They have no cooking pot, no plates or cups, and though they have no use for them now in their normal daily life, they need something in which to collect the milk and soup I give them when they are sick. They have no money to buy a bowl, so they find a broken one, or a tin can, or a lid of one kind or another, and collect the milk or soup in these containers. When they have to have a bath, we give them soap and something to make a fire, as they have neither. We also supply charcoal and oil for lighting to those who are very sick. Though we would like to be able to give to all, we cannot do so. There are people who have been here for months, going around in the most miserable rags, with bare legs, and lying on the bare earth, because we can find

neither clothes nor bedding any more. It is impossible to get these items for them all. Now that money has so little value and all the prices are so high, we must be glad just to be able, if we can, to keep them alive, until better times come.

There are only four bakers here in the town and a big crowd of people stand outside every day from early morning until evening, shouting and pushing each other to get near. One can hear them from a long distance away. Many have to go away every day without getting any bread. What will it be like in a few months?—or next year?—since nothing, or almost nothing, has been sown. The government gave corn to the Kurdish refugees for sowing in the different villages, but the Kurds ate the corn and have now been sent away to another part of the country. Now the government is without corn or workers. Earlier, it was the Armenians who produced everything. Now they are dead and there are no craftsmen nor farmers. The country is completely changed in the last two years, and there is nothing but want, misery, immeasurable ignorance, and uncleanliness beyond description. So many people die and houses collapse. Nothing is being built or kept in order. All trees are being felled and used for burning, so there will not be any timber for building. There will only be a little fruit, because all gardens and vineyards are trodden down. Everything is in a most terrible state, and there are no words strong enough to describe it.

20 January. The government has again asked for one of our buildings, so we have promised to empty one of our schools on Monday. Now we have only the Girls' College left and we will be very glad and thankful if we may keep it.

25 January. At the same time as the government demanded a building from us, they also demanded two from the German missionaries in Mezreh—Sister Jenny's and Sister Katrine's Children's Homes—two large, beautiful, and very well kept buildings. Mr. Ehmann would not hand them over before he had a message from Constantinople, but the Turks continued to demand them, so Mr. Ehmann went to the Commandant on Tuesday and said he could not give more houses as he had already given enough. He said there were many large empty houses that could be taken into use first. The Commandant became very angry, asked Mr. Ehmann who had appointed him as "Inspector of Houses," and left the room without taking leave of him. On Wednesday morning a party of soldiers came and surrounded Sister Katrine's Children's Home. They would not allow anyone to enter or leave and ordered Sister Katherina to move out. But she answered, "I am staying here. You must kill me first, and afterwards you can do what you want with my children." The Turks wanted Sister Katherina to go with all the small children, and they wanted to keep all the older girls to work for the soldiers. When Mr. Ehmann heard this he came down at once, but the soldiers would not let him enter, saying his work had finished there. He went off to the Commandant again, promised to give Sister Jenny's and our Danish Children's Home, and came down and told Karen-Marie to move. She began to do so immediately, but before long, the man who was to have the

houses came and said that she need not move. He did not want her house as it was too small but wanted the two German houses. Mr. Ehmann did all that he could to prevent them taking Sister Katrine's house. It is their largest building and all the corn for the Children's Homes and the poor is hidden there. If the government sees this they will take it all. We are terribly sorry for the German missionaries. We had a similar experience two years ago of being treated in the same way. Then the Turks were friendly towards the Germans, now it looks as if all is changed and they are very friendly with us. We ourselves think the reason is that if the Russians come here, many of the Turks who are unable to get away in time will seek refuge with us. But we know nothing of what the next day or even the next moment will bring. Every time we hear a shout in the street, or a knock on the door, we expect something bad. We live in frightful uncertainty. How often have we thought about gathering a few necessities together, in case it should become necessary to flee. Every now and then we talk of what it would be like to come home, to live where there is security, and where we are not surrounded by endless misery and the gnawing fear that we all have. But we can bear it. At the moment the time seems so long—so long. The last three years have taken more of our strength than 10-15 normal years would have done. "But God is our refuge and our strength, a very present help in trouble." Oh yes, God be praised that this is true. If it were not true, it would be completely impossible for us. It is this alone that upholds us, and when everything looks darkest around us, then He is very near. He supports us. He gives us strength to endure, and He gives us joy and peace in our hearts under all conditions. "Therefore we will not fear, if the earth be removed, and though the mountains be carried into the midst of the sea, though the waters roar and be troubled, though the mountains shake with the swelling thereof, the Lord of Hosts is with us. The God of Jacob is our refuge."

We heard this evening that the three German doctors have had a telegram instructing them to leave Mezreh and go to Aleppo to await further orders. We do not know if this means that the Russians are approaching here, or if there is a greater need for them in Aleppo. We cannot believe the latter, since it is not a military centre. Now many more of the poor soldiers here will die, because the German doctors worked hard to save them. The Turkish doctors did literally nothing for the sick because, firstly, they have little knowledge, and secondly, a human being counts as nothing with them. If he lives, he lives. If he dies, he dies. The doctors are quite happy either way. Poor people.

29 January. My days are now fully occupied going around to see the sick in their houses. There is a tremendous amount of sickness. The people are crammed together in small dark rooms. It is terribly cold with snow frozen into ice. The poor people never see a fire and never have a hot meal. They have so few clothes on their bodies, and many have no bedclothes, that they feel the cold dreadfully. The few clothes that they have are hardly ever washed and become infested with lice, which carry the fearful sickness, typhus, from one person to another. Scabies and black small-pox

also rage, and in the last two weeks, pneumonia. It is a miracle that so many recover. During the day, when a little sunshine thaws the frozen roofs, and the water drips down into the rooms, it is impossible to find a dry place. It is dreadful to see that all this misery, poverty, and want are driving many a mother and child to lie in order to obtain an extra piece of bread a day.

One of my patients at the moment is a mother who is very ill with typhus. She has three children, the eldest seven years old. This little girl nurses her mother and little sister, who is also very sick. They lie in a dark and terribly cold room, with water constantly dripping from the ceiling. The floor is a layer of mud. All four share a little mattress and a padded quilt. We can only give one set of bed clothes to each family. There are several places where eight children are in one bed. A bed now costs one and a half lira in gold (about 24 shillings). When a lira reaches us in paper money it is only worth about six kroners.

I found a little 10 year old girl lying in a stable, on some stones, and covered with a piece of sacking. She was a weak little skeleton, her feet swollen with frost, and there she lay, alone, surrounded with dirt. We had her taken at once to be cared for by a woman, but it was too late. She is now dead. I could continue telling of similar cases.

A lot of children are suffering from diarrhoea, and it is impossible to stop it, because we cannot give them the right food, and they slowly waste away and look like skeletons. If this misery does not end soon, the people will come to look like famine victims.

Rumours that the Russians are coming nearer are beginning to go around again. It is said that they are building a bridge over the Euphrates near Palou, which may mean that the rumours are true. It is also said that the Russians have attacked Sivas, that the Arabs are attacking down by Baghdad, and they have taken Mecca and Medina. It is said that the Turks and the Arabs are fighting over Mohammed's mantle. One thing which is true is that the Turks are very depressed and say that they are destroyed.

30 January. Today when I went out to visit my patients I found a little six year old girl sitting in the snow, clad only in a shirt. Her crying could be heard a long way off, and she was freezing cold. I went over and spoke to her and she told me that they had just arrived here. They had been in a Turkish house overnight, but had now been driven out. The mother had gone to find a place where they could lie down. This will not be easy, as there are no empty rooms, and all the houses are more than overfilled. I took the child home with me to get her warmed up a little. She said her name was Yerchanig ("Joy") and that she used to have a little brother, but the Kurds with whom they had been living since the massacre had strangled him. She said, "They would have strangled me also and taken my mother, but she took me and ran away. There was a man who helped us. If it had not been for him they would have

killed me." Think what such a little child has seen, and heard, and gone through in her short life. And there are many like this. Yes, all who are alive have gone through these terrible things.

7 February, 1917. The four German doctors have been up to dinner with us today. Mr. and Mrs. Ehmann were also here. The doctors are to leave on Monday. After dinner we gathered in the Riggses living room to enjoy some music and afterwards we all went for a walk to see the beautiful Dersim mountains now clad in white. It is a magnificent view when one stands up on the mountain behind Harpoot and looks over the plains and the high snow-covered mountains around us, with the soft blue gleam which rests over them around evening. After our walk we returned to my living room where I served tea. I showed the doctors the Armenians' handiwork and sold them some. They left around 5.30 and it was a really special and pleasant day.

This evening when Mr. Riggs received Ajans (the Turkish news) he was dumbfounded when he read that America had broken off relations with Germany and each country had recalled its Ambassadors from the other. Because we receive no newspapers, we do not know what is happening around the world, only what we hear through Ajans and what the Germans tell us. The doctors told us this afternoon that the British had said they would arm all ships with cannons and the blockade would be worse because the Germans would attack all ships. What it all means, and what it will lead to, no one knows, but when Mr. Riggs told us this we were all as white as sheets. It was exactly this that we had talked about and feared would happen some months ago, and now it has become a reality. If this state of affairs between America and Germany should extend to America and Turkey, we cannot tell what the result will be. We imagine ourselves being sent one place or another in this country, where we will be unable to help any Christians. It would be too good to be true that they would send us out of the country. We feel our hearts constrict when we think about it, not for ourselves—we are only a few—but for the many poor Armenian women and children who will then stand without protection or help. They will die of hunger, if they are not killed, and they will be ill-treated by the Turkish men. Now that this has happened we can only pray and hope that the war will have a quicker end.

8 February. The news about America has left a great impression on everyone, especially on the few remaining Armenians, who are now afraid that the American missionaries will be sent away and leave them unprotected. Dr. Asbech said this morning that he thought it would also mean war with Turkey, and that all Americans would be sent away. We must consider the possibility, however reluctantly, and make plans accordingly. It is necessary to do so, because if the time comes, we will not be able to plan then. How terrible it would be if we have to leave our dear young girls in the College, who up to now have been kept pure, and who are almost ready to help in the work with the poor, as soon as conditions allowed it. Also most women are like

small helpless children. It seems impossible that it should come to this. Our faith, confidence, and expectation are all in our Almighty God and Father, who has helped us so wonderfully up to now, when it looked so dark. He is mighty. For Him nothing is impossible. He will be our help, and when distress is at its greatest, then He is nearest. Oh thank God for that.

9 February. Yesterday was Karen-Marie's birthday and all the Germans and Americans were invited to afternoon coffee. It was very cosy and the atmosphere was pretty good, for which we were very grateful.

Today we heard that whilst we were down in Mezreh yesterday, a big crowd of Turkish women came to our buildings to buy our belongings. They had heard of the break between Germany and America and thought we would be leaving immediately. They were scolded and sent home again. It is said about our good friend, Sabria Khanum, a Turkish Major's wife, that she has cried her eyes out since she heard about America. Other Turks have said, "If Germany wants war with America, well, let them have it themselves. We will not help them." So it seems that the mood here is not against America, even if there should be a war with Germany. Perhaps we will be allowed to stay and continue our work. The soldiers are being withdrawn from Tchabaghchur and sent to Baghdad where it is said the war is bad with the British and the Arabs. Even the cannons have been sent down there, but as they have no horses to transport them, they are using Kurds—40 to draw each cannon. They will not be able to reach Baghdad before the summer, and then there will be no British there.

The German doctors have succeeded in getting 50 horses for their baggage and are to leave on Monday. Since they received the horses two days ago, 10 of them have died. Perhaps by Monday all horses will be dead. This shows the pitiful condition of the animals.

25 February. During the last two days soldiers and officers have been coming constantly to take possession of the Girl's College. We have kept this news secret until today. They came again this morning and demanded the building immediately. Mr. Riggs said that today was Sunday and we could not move out, but they carried on. This afternoon Mr. Riggs went down to Mezreh to talk to the Commandant and the Vali. They said that the command had not come from them but from the doctors. While Mr. Riggs was down in Mezreh, 12 doctors and officers came here and demanded the building. Mrs. Riggs invited them in and entertained them until Mr. Riggs returned. Then he took them around the College and said to them, "We have given up 11 buildings in which there is room for several thousand patients. You have only 200 patients in occupation. We have only one building left and now you demand it. If you mean to persecute us, then go ahead, but if you don't, then I can show you a better way." They said they were certainly not trying to persecute us, and that we need not move out today but could wait until tomorrow. Nadjeb Bey would

talk to the Commandant and send us word later. If this building is taken from us, it will be a very hard blow, as we will have no place to meet for service. And where shall we send the 60 young girls and their teachers who have no place to go? They are all pretty, well-educated, young girls, whom the Turks are still trying to get into their hands. Before the church service we had a period of silent prayer, that God would preserve us from this evil, and allow us to keep this place, where we can gather around Him. Our evening meeting in the school was a blessed one. First, we spent a time in prayer to God, that we might keep the school if possible and many prayers ascended of thanks for what we have received up till now, for home, for protection, and for the future. If it is God's will that they must also go out and meet adversity, then they must hold firm to their faith and resign themselves to God's care. Badveli Vartan spoke about worshipping God also in adversity. We all went home feeling strengthened.

It is a strange feeling to be surrounded by soldiers who demand our houses—yes, anything they want. Nothing we say will change them. We are a little flock of six missionaries, to whom 5,000 helpless, needy, persecuted women and children look and from whom expect all their daily needs. And we are surrounded by a crowd—yes, a whole country full of enemies, who try in every way to prevent us from doing our work. Every time we hear voices in the street we think it is soldiers coming for one thing or another, and we are still prepared to be sent away to some terrible place. We live in constant uncertainty and long fervently for peace to come. No one who has not experienced this could ever imagine what it is like to live under these conditions, when we do not know what the next moment will bring. We often wonder if we will ever see our friends at home again. And not the least difficult part is the thought that tortures us—if we are sent away what will happen to the women and children. So we say with the Psalmist, "Why art Thou cast down oh my soul? And why art Thou disquieted in me? Hope Thou in God, for I shall yet praise Him for the help of His countenance" (Psalm 42, V. 5). We have daily experienced that He is our Saviour, and when it looks darkest He is our light. He supports us when we are sinking, and gives us everything we need from time to time.

26 February. Again today soldiers have been here several times, ordering us to begin moving out, so we have made a start but still hope that we will be allowed to stay. However, we still have not had a final answer from Mezreh. All this has filled the Armenians with great fear that we will be sent away, and they will either be killed or will starve to death. Recently some of them have set out for Dersim, but it is very difficult, as the Kurds demand several liras for each person, and nobody has money. We help as much as we can because if they stay here we must feed and clothe them whereas, if they get to Dersim, they may perhaps find work or have help from the missionaries there who can get money from outside more easily than we can. On Saturday evening a group of about 60 left. When they reached the river they found that a Kurd from a neighbouring village had taken charge of the ferry and asked a

little boy in the crowd, "Where do you come from?" The boy said Harpoot and the Kurd then went off to the village and returned with some other men who demanded money or else they would send word to the government. They gave them the money they had and the men then plundered the few clothes that they had. Two days later they returned here without anything. Many of them had frozen hands and feet because there was a biting frost. Poor people, they are in danger wherever they go. Fortunately things do not go so badly for everyone. Many are getting over and finding work.

New crowds of Armenians are still arriving here, having been driven out from other places by the Kurds and Turks. They bring nothing with them, not a penny, nor clothes enough to cover them, no bedding, no food, no household utensils. So, if some leave here, twice as many arrive from elsewhere. We receive only 2,000 liras a month, and because banknotes have so little value, it is extremely difficult to manage.

27 February. Praise the Lord! We have received a message that instead of the Girls' College they will temporarily take the Junior School where we have children up to 14 years old. We are jubilant over this. Yes—if God be for us, who can be against us? Again we have experienced that God hears our prayers and nothing is impossible for Him. They have said that when the other buildings are full, then they will take over the Girls' College also, but we will not worry about tomorrow. We will only be happy and thank God for His help today, and for the promise of His help in the days to come.

11 March (Sunday). It is now two weeks since I last wrote, and much has happened since then. The days have been full of evil rumours of war between America and Germany. It seems that the situation is becoming more and more critical and an end must soon be near. Then a few more quiet days follow, when we begin to hope once more that we will be allowed to continue our work here. The government is taking over all the houses around us, saying they are to be used for the sick, but we think this is only a pretext to get us and the Armenians driven away, because the eleven large buildings we have given them are still standing empty. People say that preparations are being made to send us away. They are sending the Armenians off beforehand, so that when we go, we will not be able to hand any of our belongings over to the Christians. The Turks also say that our departure will be arranged properly, with each of us being given 100 liras. This will of course be taken from our own funds. Somebody else says we may be allowed to stay, but not allowed to work for the Christians, and that soldiers will be posted on guard around our houses. We are prepared for the worst, knowing that we can expect nothing good from the Turks. We are ready at a couple of hours notice to pack the few things we shall need to take with us. It has not been easy, having been cut-off from the outside world for years, and not knowing anything other than what Ajans—the local Turkish newspaper—

tells us. It is a quarter sheet of letter paper in size, and printed on only one side, always about the defeat of the enemies. The German missionaries receive their own newspapers, but these also only describe victories over their enemies and stories about the enemies' misdeeds. If only we could have, once in a while, a neutral newspaper and learn the real truth.

The Armenians are again more fearful, now that it looks as if America will enter the war, and all who possibly can are trying to get to Dersim. Recently several groups of them have been captured and imprisoned here in Harpoot and in Mezreh. There has been a fight between the Kurds and the gendarmes who are keeping watch on the river.

The present Vali, who is a Kurd, has been dismissed and is now going to Constantinople, and everyone is anxious to get away before he leaves, as they are afraid that the new Vali will be more severe. This Vali, up to now, has done nothing worse to the women and children than keep them in prison for a while. Some have been whipped, but sooner or later they are set free. We are waiting anxiously to see if the latest groups to be imprisoned will also be given their freedom.

Three days ago the gendarmes seized a young man in the street, flung him down, and stoned him to death.

It is now nearly impossible to find bread or any kind of food. Even if you have money there is nothing to be had. Is it any wonder that these poor souls try to run away when there is a little hope of reaching somewhere better.

Izzat Pasha is expected here in the near future. He is to live in Mezreh and have quarters here. It is said that the Military Headquarters will be here, which will mean that all food will be much more expensive and maybe impossible to find in a short time. The soldiers look like skeletons, and a sabid who has just returned from the front says that the soldiers there are in a pitiful condition. Many die of starvation and cold. They kill dogs and cats for food and have sent telegrams many times to Mezreh asking for immediate help because they are starving. They received a telegram in reply saying, "Sons, be of good courage and have a little patience, then you will be helped." The conditions are indescribable.

In the last week two of our helpers have died from typhus. They were men who had been allowed to remain, one because he was a tailor and the other because he was a plumber. This is a great loss, as they were both earnest, faithful men, who did great work among the refugees. We have only about 10 men left here in Harpoot, and several are very old, while others are unable to work, so it was doubly hard to lose these two. One was called "Hayrik" (Father) by everyone, and he was a real father to all—rich and poor, young and old. We can ill afford to lose the few friends and helpers whom we have, but God knows what He is doing and we are happy and joyful that these two are now Home to glory. They have not had an easy time in the last year since the deportations. The Turks tried to force them to become Moslems, but they refused, and remained firm to the last. Now they are Home and have heard the blessed words, "Well done, good and faithful servant. Enter thou into the joy of thy Lord."

They have come back again demanding our Girls' College, saying that they must have it in a couple of days, so we do not know now how long we will be able to keep it. But we will only take one day and one moment at a time and be glad for every day we are allowed to keep it.

There is so much sickness. Typhus, black smallpox, dysentery, pneumonia, measles, and much else. Many are dying. It is so very hard to see so many poor people lying on the bare ground, shaking with cold and fever, without being able to help them. New crowds are coming constantly. They are people who have lived among Kurds and Turks and know nothing of Christianity. They are like wild people, many cannot even explain their own name. Many amongst the Kurdish refugees also die daily. They have no help and if one becomes sick they just lie down in the dirt and filth until they die. What a country, what a people, what misery! Oh Lord, come soon to save Thine own, and to reveal Thyself to the many, many who dwell in darkness, that they may see the light, and come to love the light more than the dark.

18 March, 1917 (Sunday). They have not taken the College this time, and the Commandant has said that it will not be taken before the other buildings are full. If they are not filled then we will surely be allowed to keep it. Last Sunday a crowd of Armenians were caught on the way to Dersim. Two of them are from the College and we are very sorry for them. We can do nothing to get them released because any attempt would harm both them and us if the government gets the idea we are involved in these flights.

Up to now all the women and children who have been captured were set free after a short stay in jail, so we hope these others will also be freed. A 10 year old boy, who was also captured, has given Bessie's mother's name as one who had helped them to get away. We heard this on Sunday evening, so on Monday morning I sent her down to our Children's Home in Mezreh, knowing that Karen-Marie would take her in. It has been a refuge before for people in danger and many have been saved because of it. It was well Bessie's mother left Mezreh, because the police came at noon to search for her in her home. When they did not find her there, they thought she was with us, but we could all say "No" to that. Later in the afternoon they came and took her old mother to the government for questioning, but she was freed again in the evening. Since then they have been after her a couple of times, but we have not heard of anything in the last two days. It is said that they will search in Mezreh, but I don't think they will find her.

There have been no Kurds here in the last week though messages have been sent to them. We don't know if they are now afraid to come. Soldiers are going around in the mountains to catch anyone trying to escape. The fight between the Kurds and Turks at the river was quite bad with eight Kurds and 17 Turks killed. Maybe this is the reason the government is so severe.

The Vali left last Sunday and all the Christians are afraid. The road to Dersim will be completely closed now that Izzat Pasha is coming. He should have arrived yesterday, but it is said that he is going to Tchabaghchur instead of coming here. Is that really true? This may mean that the fighting has started again. The Turks have been very depressed and worried since a speech by Enver Pasha's was printed in Ajans saying that the enemy was preparing on all fronts, that the Turks were also preparing, and that he hoped the result would be to the advantage of the Turks. Enver Pasha and the other high officials in Constantinople can hope, but everyone here who sees the real conditions does not have much hope left and fears the worst.

Two German officers have been in Mezreh some days in the last week. They told us of the conditions at the front. They said that the Russians have laid good roads all the way that they have come, and it was therefore not difficult for them to get supplies of everything they needed. On the other hand, the Turkish soldiers are starving, and the officers have telegraphed here about this. The answer they received was that they should take foodstuffs from the people around them, but there was nothing to be found. So they sent another telegram informing them of this and were told that they should withdraw. Although it was very late and the snow very deep, they obeyed the order and withdrew through the deep snow. Each cannon cost the lives of 200 men. They had no resistance and their hands and feet froze. There are no animals left to help pull the cannons. The men die in droves, and the few who are left are miserable and weak. These officers said that if the Russians wanted they could walk in here without any resistance. It is also said that the British have taken Baghdad. We don't know if this is true or not, but it is no wonder that the Turks are depressed. Their future does not look very bright. The law passed by the government a short time ago about the price of foodstuffs and other things has been rescinded because everything disappeared from the shops and became impossible to find. If we went down through the market we would see one shop after another, where a man or a boy sat on a chair, selling Turkish cups or other things that they were certain no one would buy in these times. But all the necessities of life had disappeared. The government could do nothing other than recognise the situation and rescind the law so that the shopkeepers would bring out the hidden goods. There is no question about how terrible it is to go through the market now and see the great flocks of people standing outside the few bakeries that open now and then, shouting and screaming like wild animals and fighting to get near. A woman was killed the other day, and yesterday another had an arm broken in the fight to get in. If something does not happen soon to change the conditions, the day will soon arrive when there will be no bread.

New crowds of people still arrive, all in the most terrible condition. They do not look like human beings. Crowds of children lie nearly naked in the streets, rooting in the dirt with the dogs, trying to find something with which to fill their empty stomachs. It is so hard to go from house to house and see the many sick. Many die daily, but new ones come in their place. It is impossible to talk with them about spiritual things because their only thought is for bread, clothes, and a bed. To every question I ask I get only one answer, "Mayrig, I am naked, and lying on the ground. Give me a note for a bed, some clothes, abour (soup), and milk." It is not just one person who says this. In a single room there are very often more than 20 people, and they all fall upon me like ravenous wolves. It is as if their brain can only hold the one thought. These are all the new arrivals, who have lived among Kurds all their lives, and know nothing of Christianity. It is so refreshing and glorious to come to one place or another where they want to hear. The other day a young girl died. She had typhus followed by dysentery. A week ago I told her that I thought she would not recover and asked her about her relationship with God. She said, with beaming eyes, "Oh, is it true? Do you think I will die? Oh, my Jesus, how I am longing to come Home. Oh, take me, take me." Now she has gone Home to glory, where there is no want, no fear, and no danger. There are rumours again about our being sent away. Yes, it was even being said the other day that the government has given us three days to make preparations. This has put all the Armenians in anxiety and fright, and they come running to us to hear if it is true. The other day an elderly woman came running to me in the street trembling with fear, white as a sheet, with her heart thumping. She asked me if the rumour was true. I asked her, "Is what true?" She said, "That there is a massacre." I said, "No," trying to calm her as well as I could. Such are the conditions under which these poor people live—hunger, cold, nakedness, and sorrow, added to the fear, day and night, of deportation, infamy, torture, and death.

It seems impossible to think of another winter under these conditions. If a change does not come it will not be possible to find the means for survival. The people will just die of hunger. Indeed, it has already begun now. It is mostly children who die. The poor little ones cannot live on a little piece of bread a day. How hard it must be for a mother to watch her child sinking daily, to hear it cry and beg for bread, and have none to give. Never could we have dreamt of such misery. We call and pray to God daily to shorten this time of suffering for these many poor people. We dare not look to the future, but only live a day at a time. Our Father will give us, hour by hour, the strength and special grace we need and want. Oh Lord, keep us in Thee, and help us in life and in death, even through suffering, to glorify Thee.

5 April. Again, it has been a long time since I have written and many things have happened. The last crowd of Armenians that went away to Dersim, including two young girls from our school, were captured on the way and brought to the prison, where they were held for over two weeks. Thank God they are now free again and have once more tried to leave. Yesterday the Kurds came again and a crowd of about 30 people set off in the evening. We hope and pray that they may get away in safety. Among them is Digin Vershin, who was in Emaus for several months, after we had got her away from a Kurd. It has been said that they will kill anyone trying to escape, but not even this can hold people back. Everyone who can scrape together the means is leaving because it is impossible to live here. It is getting worse every day, and the hope of anything better is slight. New crowds of Kurdish refugees are still arriving and among them are many Armenians. When they arrive, the Armenians are being separated from them, and the Kurds sent on from here. The Armenians must stay, though they have begged the government to let them travel with the Kurds. This the government will not allow. We can only view this with alarm. What does it mean? The Christians are coming here, where there is no food, but the punishment is death for any of them who are found attempting to leave. They get nothing from the government, neither housing or food. Up to now we have been able to support 5,000 people, but we received a letter from Mr. Peet two weeks ago, saying that we could only expect money for the month of April. If this is the last money we receive, what will these many thousands of people do? They will starve to death if the government does not send them away to meet the same fate as the many thousands two years ago. All the new arrivals look like famine victims, and we must say "No" continuously. None of us could ever have imagined such misery.

Every day this week, from early morning until late evening, a crowd of about 700-800 have been standing outside our doors. They shout and scream, cry and whimper, so loudly that it is nearly impossible for us to hear when we speak to each other. They come to get their bread tickets renewed, but it has taken longer this time, because we have to investigate each one. There has been a lot of cheating, and the bread that is available must be distributed fairly. We must send back those who come from villages, because they can find grass there, if nothing else, and even this cannot be found in Harpoot. However, it is hard to send them away, when we know that they are not safe in their villages amongst the Turks who are so immoral. They cry and beg us not to send them—just to give them one single loaf. How we wish we could take them all in and give them everything they need, but we have not the means and we cannot take them. Mothers are sitting with their little children, looking like skeletons, dirty, naked, full of sores and vermin. The children cry and shout, "I am hungry, I am hungry," but the mothers sit like stone—they do not listen any more. What is the use when there is nothing to give them. You see children and grown ups searching around in the gutters for refuse which they eat. Things that a dog would turn away from. Is it any wonder that there is so much sickness?

Izzat Pasha has arrived and is to live in Mezreh. Also the head of the German Army has come to take up quarters here. He was formerly in Diarbekir, but it is said that the Russians have taken Siirt which lies between Bitlis and Diarbekir, so it sounds as if they have really begun to awaken and are maybe thinking of coming here. It has also been said that the British have taken Baghdad, that the enemy is moving forward to Jerusalem, and that the Arabs are near Aleppo. Whether all this is true or not, we do not know, but there must be some truth in it when the Turks themselves are saying it. Last Sunday Izzat Pasha came up here to inspect the hospital and all the buildings we have given them. He also visited Mr. Riggs and stayed for quite a long time. He listened to the gramophone, and it was altogether a very pleasant visit. He seems to be a very nice man. It is said that a massacre of the Christians was planned, but that Izzat Pasha said it will not happen as long as he is here. Yesterday evening Mr. Riggs came up from Mezreh and told us what we had been fearing for so long and had hoped would not be a reality—that America is at war with Germany. We were all very sad to hear this. We hope and pray that it may mean that the end of this cruel war will come more quickly. He also said that the Consul has received letters from the Ambassador and Mr. Peet urging all female missionaries and children to leave their stations and prepare to come home. This of course made us all worried because this is not an easy step to take. We must be certain of what is the right thing to do.

Today we had our Station meeting, when we discussed the present situation. We came to no final decision because after all our thinking and talking it was still not clear what would be the best thing to do. One thing was decided immediately—that the Riggses, Miss Harley, Dr. Parmelee, and I should stay. Then there was a discussion about Mrs. Atkinson, with her three children, Miss McLaren from Van, and Miss Shane from Bitlis, who came here one and a half years ago. It is not certain that they can leave the country, and it would be much worse for them to go to a place where they have no friends to help them. The roads are very difficult now and full of danger. Maybe they will not even find transport or food, as contagious illness rages everywhere, and they have no man to accompany them. On the other hand, it is also very unsafe to remain here. Sickness rages as never before. Everything is so expensive and the time may soon come when we will be unable to find a means of living. Sooner or later this place where we are living could be the battle front itself. We must also remember that if America and Turkey are at war, the sending of money will be stopped, and where would the missionaries find anything to live on?

There are no other consulates and the missionaries can expect nothing but being sent away to one terrible place or another, where they will be unable to get in touch with anyone. All these things we must take into consideration and we can not be certain of making a right decision. It was decided that the Consul should make enquiries to see if some of the female missionaries would be allowed to leave if they wished. We will all give it some days' thought and ask the Lord to lead us in the right way, because if we are where He wants us to be, we have no need to fear.

10 April. Once again clouds begin to gather, dark and threatening. The last crowd that left were captured at the river and some of them were led back after a three days' walk in the mountains. They are now in prison in Mezreh. Several of the party did not return, among them Digin Vershin, her little girl, and Pompish Arusiag's daughter. It is said they have been killed, others say that Digin Vershin has been taken by a Kurd. We do not know which is true, and we are terribly sorry for the poor people. It is said that this time the punishment will be severe. If poor Digin Vershin has once again fallen into the hands of a Kurd, it will be dreadful for her to go through all this again.

On Saturday afternoon I received a message that Karen-Marie had taken ill on Friday with a headache and a high temperature. My immediate hope was only that it would not be typhus. It is as though we cannot endure more. I went down to her on Sunday morning, Easter Day, and found her in the same condition, with fever and a headache, but otherwise without pain. I am fairly certain that she has this frightful illness, but just hope that she will not have it so severely that she will be robbed of her strength for months. If it is only a mild attack, then she can move around afterwards, without fear. I returned home about lunch time, but I could not rest all day. I did not have much sleep that night, as I was thinking about Karen-Marie, and I was determined to go down again next day. Monday is my busiest day in the whole week. I went around to my patients and handed over the most sick to Dr. Parmelee. In the afternoon I had my lace work, but as soon as I was finished, I took Bessie and we came down here to Emaus, where we have remained for the last five days. The spots are beginning to come, but Karen-Marie is still remarkably well and has no pain. She has some headache, and some nausea now and then, but otherwise she says, "I feel fine." Dr. Asbech, who is treating her, keeps telling her it is not typhus, which she does not like, because she knows that it is. He has also forbidden her strongly to have her hair cut, which also annoys her, because it is still falling out, and she can rest so much better without it. Otherwise he is a really fine and clever doctor and we know he will do his best. Up to now Dirouhi has been with her in the night and will continue with this. If there is anything wrong she can call me. In the last two days women going out into the fields to collect some green plants have been taken and put in prison. Mardiros Effendi, our chemist, has also been taken and put in prison, along with others—they say 15 Armenian men. Mrs. Atkinson and Miss McLaren went down with him and afterwards spoke to the Commandant. He said he could not do anything as he had orders to imprison him for some days. Some policemen came and searched his house, taking all papers and cards away. His wife was also searched. Today three policemen came to Badveli Drtad's house to search there. Miss McLaren had come down there just before, which was good for Pompish, as they were very rude, searching through everything. They found a box of clothes and said to Pompish, "You are certainly rich," but Miss McLaren answered that they were ours. They asked what we used them for and who she was. Miss McLaren said she was an American and that we gave the clothes to the poor, which was nothing new to them, as we have been feeding and clothing about 5,000 people daily for two years. They wrote down Miss McLaren's name and took her card-index of the poor and all the papers they could find. They also took the deceased Badveli's written sermons. Some rough Turkish women were brought in to search Pompish, after which they all left. They returned in a couple of hours and took Pompish to the prison. Mrs. Atkinson and Miss McLaren went down with her, and I still do not know the result.

A couple of days ago a big crowd of Armenian children were brought here. Some say from Damascus and Aleppo, others say they are Christians from Palou. They are being held in the Red Konak, where all the young Armenian men were confined two years ago. Even the name of this place makes us shudder, there are so many terrible memories of it, and we wonder with fear and trembling, what this now means. It is exactly the way they started two years ago, searching people and their houses and putting people in prison. This time there are no men and they are now taking the women. How terrible is this state of affairs! How long will it be before all this cruelty comes to an end? Does the Lord want all these women, young girls and innocent children, to go through more torture? How can we bear to see the suffering of these poor people and be unable to help them. Oh Lord, you, who have been our help in the last dark days, be near us, hour by hour, and give us strength to bear what is to come. Help us not to lose the vision of Thee.

11 April. Poor Pompish, who was put in prison yesterday, is pregnant and her time is due in two weeks. While they were waiting in the Police Station, she started to have pains. Mrs. Atkinson, of course, was very anxious, and tried to get permission to take her to the hospital. But nothing she said was any use. All the senior officials were out to meet the new Vali who arrived yesterday afternoon. After a wait of two hours they were led down to the men's prison, where they had to wait again to see the Prison Inspector. Mrs. Atkinson tried also to get permission to take her away. Strict orders were then given to take her to the women's prison. Poor woman, she then had to go through the market again, but with the help of Mrs. Atkinson and Miss McLaren, she reached the prison. After much talking and pleading one of them got permission to come into prison with her. There was a room and a yard where all the prisoners were. The room was dark, damp, and had a stone floor. Two small holes in the wall admit light and ventilation. Poor Pompish must remain there in these terrible surroundings and in her condition. It is good that there are so many Armenian women there—all those who were captured on the road and in the mountains—and

they will help her. She was in good spirits, not thinking of herself, but only of others and the children. The last thing she said was, "Don't be worried. Keep the children's spirits up." She has a family of six, the youngest three years old.

Mr. Riggs worked also at trying to get her freed, but it was impossible. He went from one to another without result. They all talked about America starting war with Germany. They were not as friendly as before. We can see that it won't help to work from our side to get Pompish out because of the unfriendliness of the Turks, so we have asked Mr. Ehmann to work for her and the others. He has promised to do what he can.

Yesterday Miss McLaren received a card from Miss Foremann in Aintab. She said that the previous day had been terrible, and she felt as if she had been pressed through a keyhole. Their workers were being taken away to work elsewhere. By this we understand that something has happened there. Maybe the Christians have been killed. Poor, poor people. Now they are living in fear again and dread a massacre. We are also afraid that something will happen. This morning, it was said that Izzat Pasha has sent a man around the town to tell people not to be afraid, as nothing is going to happen. They only want to prevent the people leaving for Dersim. But even this does not calm people. We are so used to good promises from the government, which have up till now nearly always meant something bad.

We heard that Austria has declared war on America and everyone here thinks Turkey will do the same, not of their own free will, but because of pressure from Germany. Now it is a question of what the government will do with the missionaries. It is clear that the remaining Armenians will soon die out. The government will not give them food, clothes, or houses, and no help can come to them from outside, as the government will not allow letters to or from America. The Consul himself has had an order from the Turkish government never to write anything about the Armenians and his letters are heavily censored. In the last few days the Consul has received two letters from the Ambassador and Mr. Peet, both strongly advising the women missionaries to leave the country. We have thought that Mrs. Atkinson with her three children, and Miss McLaren should go, if permission can be obtained. The Consul has inquired of the Commandant who said that if anyone wished to travel he would telegraph Constantinople and ask if they could have permission. But now that Austria has declared war, it is impossible for them to go to America, or to any neutral country, so I think that the result will be that they will stay. The rest of us feel that it is our duty to remain, for how could we go and look for something easier and more comfortable and leave these many poor souls to their fate amongst their enemies. I have sent a telegram home to Miss Blædel today telling her that Karen-Marie is ill with typhus. She is exceptionally tranquil, has no pain, except a little headache, and is only sick occasionally. However, her temperature is high today, up as high as 40.4 degrees C.

15 April (Sunday). I received a letter from Miss Blædel on Friday, saying that the Committee wished me to move down to Emaus immediately. In the last few days there has been a great deal of talk that Turkey will declare war on America, and if this happens, the Turks will send the Americans away so that they can have their great riches (by which they mean what we have up here). This was a hard blow for me, as I did not believe the Americans would be sent away. I will be very reluctant to part from them, and from the work I love, work which is so necessary. There is no one who can take it over, everyone has already more than they can cope with. Since January I have seen 913 patients in their homes, all suffering from severe illness, such as typhus, recurrent fever, black small-pox, pneumonia and dysentery. Every morning I have held a clinic for about 50 patients. I have looked after the soup-kitchen and the handiwork, and led the women's weekly meeting. Now that I must give it all up, it is almost more than I can bear. I would have liked so much to have waited and seen if it was necessary to leave. Down here I am not needed so much because there are not so many Armenians as in Harpoot. But I must abide by the wishes of the Committee. If only I could just write home and explain everything so that they could understand that we are doing the right and best thing. We had already decided to take this step as soon as it became necessary. It is impossible for the friends at home to understand the conditions here, as well as us, who live out here, especially now when we can write so little home.

Yesterday, when Karen-Marie was fairly well and I had set her in order, I went up to Harpoot to pack my things and send them down. I had to hurry as I could not be away from Karen-Marie too long. I was not up more than half an hour before everyone knew that Miss Jacobsen had come up to pack and move down to Mezreh, and it aroused a great deal of panic. This showed me another reason why I am necessary here. One after the other came crying to me, asking me why I was going. I told them all about the telegram and the letter, but they did not believe that this was the real reason. I came home again at 4.30. I had not packed everything, only the most important things. Karen-Marie knew nothing about it, as we cannot allow anything to upset her. I brought four young girls from the College down with me, and they will stay here in the meantime. In case of anything happening, the first thing the Turks will do will be to try and take the young girls in the College, and this is something we cannot bear to think about. Miss Harley and Mr. Riggs came down here on Friday to discuss this with the German missionaries, and Mr. Ehmann said that he believed the best thing to do would be to send the young girls, who had absolutely no other place to go, down to Emaus. Kevork Agha will give us three rooms so that I can supervise them, and so it was arranged. We still do not know when they are coming. Of course the Americans will give us money for their maintenance. Maybe it will not be necessary, but it is good to have a plan arranged.

If something should happen, we will not be given much time, maybe only a few hours. There is still talk here about a separate peace between Germany and Russia. I wonder if it is really true and what the result will be.

To our great joy, our chemist, Mardiros Effendi, came out of prison yesterday. It is also said that Pompish will soon be free, as no forbidden papers were found with them. This has calmed people a little bit, as no one thought they would be released.

16 April (Monday). I have just received a letter from the Consul, saying he has received a telegram from the Danish Ambassador concerning us three Danes here, and he asks me to come over and see him sometime today.

Yesterday Digin Sara's three children were released from prison and are now here in the Children's Home again. A soldier said to them yesterday, "You can go home. Your mother will come tomorrow," and all the children were sent away. Today we heard that Digin Vershin and a boy from the Children's Home have been imprisoned. They were brought here yesterday.

23 April. The last eight days have been very busy. My things arrived in good order. It was rather difficult because I could not tell Karen-Marie anything, and we had to be careful not to make any noise that would arouse her suspicion. I had to steal away for short intervals whilst she was asleep, so it was not easy getting things moved up and down. It took time. I did most of it in the evening after I had got her settled for the night and she thought I was in bed.

At the beginning of the week 16 young girls from the College came down here temporarily. They have been given into my care, so I have to find a place and arrange a special establishment for them.

I went to the Consul with Jenny. He had received a telegram from the envoy in Constantinople who asked if we had considered travelling home. Because this is impossible at the moment we agreed that a telegram should be sent back saying "No."

Dr. Parmelee came down on Wednesday and told me Mrs. Riggs was ill with what looked like typhus. She asked me to speak to Dr. Asbech when I saw him in the evening. He promised to go up next day. He wanted me with him because if it was typhus he wanted me to stay up there and nurse her.

Karen-Marie is beginning to recover. The crisis is over, but she is still very weak and I would have liked to have stayed with her longer. However, Miss McLaren will come and stay with her. So I packed a few things together and rode up with the doctor at 11 o'clock. I found Mrs. Riggs a little better. Her temperature had gone down, so we began to hope that it was not typhus. I returned to Mezreh in the afternoon, happy to be back with Karen-Marie until she was completely well. Next morning I heard that Mrs. Riggs's temperature had gone up again and stayed high all day. On Saturday I went back up again and saw that it was really typhus. This was what we had feared and hoped would not happen because she is not young any more. She is weak and very tired and that is not good. In the afternoon I saw the doctor and he promised to come up the next day and if necessary live here until the crisis is over. Things are still not too bad. Her heart and lungs are good. Her temperature is high and she is covered with spots. She is very nervous, her whole body shaking so violently that the bed also shakes.

We had begun to hope that the situation between America and Turkey would remain good, but yesterday morning at 11 o'clock the Consul telephoned, asking me to come down as quickly as possible. I had to leave Mrs. Riggs, change in a hurry, and ride down in a gallop all the way. The Consul told me immediately that the break between the two countries had come, and he was waiting for a message to leave at any moment. There were a lot of things he would ask me to do. He handed over a list of Armenians who are American citizens and gave me 200 liras in gold with which to help them. He gave me a lot of other money as well, for different people, and some of his papers and books. Then there was a little 12 year old girl who, with her family, had tried to reach the mountains last year. All the family had been killed, but the girl had managed to make her way to the Consul, with whom she has been ever since. She has a brother in Europe and one in Erzingan. So we hope we can look after her until she can go to one of her brothers. After being authorized by the Consul to continue this work I returned home. Mr. Riggs went down in the afternoon, by which time the Consul had received a telegram informing him of the break. Then a policeman was sent by the Vali with the same message and a request that the American flag be taken down. Up to now the government has been exceptionally polite to us. Izzat Pasha and the Consul are friends, but orders must be followed. When the Consul receives a message about travelling he will ask Izzat Pasha for permission to take some of the missionaries with him. It has still not been decided who should go, but Dr. Parmelee will remain behind to help with Mrs. Riggs. We will try to send some of the little girls away today, before they come and take our house, so none of them will fall into their hands.

26 April. Several days have elapsed since we learned that diplomatic relations between America and Turkey were severed. On Tuesday the Vali sent a policeman over to the Consul who thought immediately that he had a message about his departure. But the policeman sat down, nodded and smiled, and said that the Vali had sent him to say that although the two countries had broken off relations with each other, it did not mean that their friendship was over, and the Vali wished to know if there was any way in which he could serve the Consul. This was extraordinarily friendly. Yesterday the Consul received orders from Constantinople to prepare to travel as soon as possible, and that he should take as many Americans with him as he could. He should pay rent on the Consulate for six months in advance, and set seals on the doors before leaving. It has been decided as well as can be decided, that Mrs. Atkinson and Miss Harley should go with the Consul if

permission can be obtained from the Turkish government. We are now waiting for final information about how they can travel and what they can take with them. They can easily be ready, as it is certain that they cannot take much baggage with them and must leave everything behind. The Turks will take and enjoy it all, as they have long had their eyes on our house and possessions.

It is impossible for Mr. and Mrs. Riggs to leave as Mrs. Riggs is very seriously ill with typhus, and it is a fight between life and death. It is terribly difficult to have so much happening under these circumstances. First Karen-Marie was sick and now Mrs. Riggs, and neither of them know anything of the events of the last week. Yesterday some policemen came to Pompish Yughaper and confiscated all the clothes we had for the poor, together with all the corn and money, so this puts an end to our help there. We are waiting for them to come up here at any moment, but they still have not arrived.

We very much fear that something will happen to the Armenians. Dr. Asbech told us the other day that an order had come that the Armenians were to be sent away, but Izzat Pasha was supposed to have said that nothing would happen whilst he is here. However, we can never believe their word, and Izzat Pasha might leave for a couple of days, when the others could commit any atrocity. It will not be difficult now, with no men, only women and children, weak and ill. We only live for the moment as we do not know what the next day will bring. In the evening we go to bed, thinking that tomorrow we might find our house surrounded. I keep my passport with me to show that I am Danish should anything happen. In the last few days there have been rumours that Denmark is at war with Germany. We hope it is only a rumour, but if it is true, then our turn will soon come.

22 May, 1917. Almost a month has passed since I last wrote. It has been a terribly difficult time. What we had feared for the last two years and hoped and prayed would not happen has happened now. They have been indescribably difficult days, but even through such a hard time, I have been permitted to experience that the words of the Lord are the same when He says, "When you go through the water and the fire, then I will be with you." It is only through His strength that I have come through these dark days.

On April 26th, when I last wrote, Mrs. Riggs's condition suddenly worsened in the afternoon. Her temperature was very high and it was only the 10th day. About 2 o'clock her heart began to weaken, and her pulse was rapid and very weak. She became very blue and could hardly breathe. I was all alone with her as Dr. Asbech and Dr. Parmelee were both down in Mezreh, as was Mr. Riggs. Her condition deteriorated so rapidly that I became very afraid she would die before I could get a message down to them asking to come up. All the injections I gave her had no effect. When they came at 5 o'clock she was very ill, and I was relieved not to be alone with all the responsibility. We gave injections of caffeine, camphor-oil brandy, but nothing helped. Sometimes it looked as if she had only a few minutes left, but suddenly the pulse became a little stronger and we began to hope again. I stayed with her till 10 o'clock, and as her pulse remained steady, we all hoped that a recovery had begun. I was persuaded to go to bed, and I slept a little. At 4 o'clock in the morning I was called up again. Mrs. Riggs had become weaker. It was a very hard day. Sometimes the pulse would steady, and our hopes would begin to rise, but it was only for a moment, and our hopes sank again. She was conscious all the time, but too weak to speak, and at 2.30 she died. It was terrible to see poor Mr. Riggs in his great sorrow. How difficult it was that there was no other man here to come and talk to him and share his grief. I set everything in order and laid her in the coffin. The women missionaries also had to arrange the funeral, which was to take place next day, Saturday, at 2 o'clock. First we had a very short service in the home, and afterwards another in the school, at which Mr. Ehmann and the Badveli spoke. A number of officers attended the funeral, one soldier brought a very large wreath of flowers and laid it on the coffin. The government asked permission to show their respect for Mrs. Riggs by allowing soldiers to carry the coffin to the Garden. Mr. Riggs agreed to this. It was a sad journey. How difficult it will be to work here without Mrs. Riggs, no one can begin to realize. How she resembled our Saviour in love, patience, and compassion. She had time to see and speak to everyone, even when she was tired and ill. Even when the doctor had told her to go to bed and rest, she would spend the whole day from morning till evening in her office, receiving one after the other, and there was always a crowd of several hundred outside her door. At the beginning of every month she distributed bread tickets to several thousand. 5,000 received bread and clothes through her. She never spoke to them angrily but always with love and compassion. We are happy for her sake that she is there, where her heart was, Home with her Saviour, where all her friends, her parents, and her little girl are. She gave her life for her friends and the poor ones. No one possesses greater love than those who give their lives for their friends. We held a memorial service on Sunday afternoon, when the Badveli, one of the teachers, and Professor Khachador spoke. It was a beautiful service. The Great Hall was packed, and there was not a dry eye in the whole crowd. Mr. Riggs stood up last and said that many good things had been said about Mrs. Riggs and they were all true, but he just wanted to add that the reason for all these good things was that she had given herself over completely to her Saviour. In her prayers, morning and evening, her only sorrow was that so many poor souls were in earthly need and she had so little time to work for their souls. Often when she came up, dead tired in the evening, she would say, "I am so sad because I have not been as patient as I should have been." That was her own idea—no one else ever saw impatience in her. Many of us prayed to the Lord to make us the kind of worker she was.

The home, the whole station, the whole town, and Mezreh, felt the same loss now that she has gone. The last words she said to me before she took ill were on the day I went up to have my belongings moved down to Emaus. In the evening, when I went to say goodbye to her—and it was very difficult for me to do so—she said, "What shall we do without you, Maria? But we must not look at it that way. It will soon be summer and when we move out to the Garden, you and Miss Petersen will come and see us. We must look on the bright side."

How hard it was for me to leave them that time. How little did I think that she, so dear, would be taken from our midst so soon, that the other friends would be going away, and I would be the only one left. Truly nothing is permanent here. In the last year so many friends have gone Home, where there is no sorrow, suffering, fear or death, and we also long to go to that Home. The evening of the day Mrs. Riggs died it was decided that all the American missionaries should leave. It was thought better to go now, and not wait for the government to send them away. We also hope that, if they can leave the country, they may find a way to send money to us, who are staying and will continue the work. If they were to remain, they could expect to be sent off at any time to one village or another, or be confined in some way to prevent their being of any help to the suffering Armenians here. All this had to be taken into consideration. On Monday May 30th we started making preparations. There was much to do, collecting everything in one place. All the missionaries' personal furniture and belongings were brought up to the attic in Triple House. I spent 10 days up there setting things in place, as well as seeing to things in Mr. Riggs's house, because his time was fully occupied in paying out money that people had left with him. They were very difficult days. People were coming to see and talk to those who were leaving, so they could not find time to arrange their own things. It was especially hard for Mr. Riggs. His great sorrow was enough to drain his strength, but he also had to see hundreds of people and to sit up in the last nights to arrange the accounts. When he left he looked like an old man who could be blown over by a puff of wind.

On top of everything, we had to suffer the pain of ceasing to give out bread to the 5,000 poor people because it was impossible to find wheat. So from morning till evening we had to send people away to the villages. We gave them paper money but could only give a little, which really has no value since it is impossible to find bread. All day long, big crowds of several hundred people, sat crying aloud outside our houses and begging for bread. There were mothers with their small children who cried and said, "Bread, bread. I am hungry. I am hungry." Mothers who have nothing to give them, and who are dead tired and hopeless, would even hit the small children to make them stop crying. Mothers were walking around with dying children, like small skeletons, in their arms. Some had a cup with water in it, which they would give now and then to their child. Other mothers would take the children on their knees and let them gnaw on a dry bone, without any meat or juice left in it, in the hope of making the child forget for a moment the terrible hunger. In the streets mothers and children were searching in the gutters for the refuse thrown out of the Turkish houses. Onion skins, perhaps potatoes—there is no time to consider whether it is dirty or if they should take it to a spring and wash it—down it goes to try to ease the terrible hunger. Mothers go out where there is still a little green grass to collect and bring home, spreading it out for the children to eat. They cannot cook as there is no fuel here, and they have no salt, so they must eat it as it is. They will not even be able to find this much longer, now that the rain is over and the sun is burning, withering everything green here. The Turks will not allow them to go further afield. Poor people. We had hoped to be able to give them at least a couple of mouthfuls of bread a day, but this hope is now gone because it is impossible to find the wheat.

Our young girls from the College, whom we have shielded from harm, have been sent down to Emaus, where Kevork Agha gave us two rooms and a corridor, and I can look after them. We were very happy to have succeeded in getting them out. The Police Commissioner, a terrible man who was here during the massacre in 1915, sent daily messages that nothing must be taken away from our buildings, but the Commandant, who has always been well disposed towards us, again gave us permission and we used the time to get the young girls out. Some terrible days followed when the Turks came into the houses to buy the furniture and other things. They sat around and smoked, opened up everything for examination, and paid nothing. Everything was sold for a very low price. At the end I had to act as a policeman, as none of our departing friends could do it. I set a guard on all the doors to stop people getting in. But still people got in, in spite of this, and I had to ask them to leave. If I had not done this, all the friends would have been ill before going away. We offered our house to the Kaimakam and he was very glad for this. Mr. Riggs let some furniture stay in different rooms for their use, and we also left the curtains hanging. The part of the house where Mr. Pierce lived was divided from the rest by a partition-wall. Here some German Sisters were to live and to continue the work that I could no longer do, I having had orders to live in Mezreh. On the day appointed for the arrival of the German Sisters, a letter came from Mr. Ehmann, saying they were unable to come. He gave several reasons, none of them very weighty, but he proposed—to my great joy—that I should take over the work. I thought that the Committee at home would consider it all right, since Mr. Ehmann had suggested it, and so it was arranged that I should live up here and undertake the work. As I have also a lot of work in Mezreh, I must still spend a couple of days a week there. It will not be easy since all my things are now down in Emaus.

12 July. It is now over two months since I wrote last. Though I would like to, I cannot find the time to write down all that has happened around me, and it is impossible for me to remember everything. Not a day passes without an experience worth describing and which I want to remember so that I can share it sometime with

the friends at home. When I last wrote I had begun to say that before the missionaries left, we had a telegram from the American Ambassador stating all the American citizens should go to Constantinople, but the government here would not give permission. Telegrams passed back and forth for over a week. On May 17th all the missionaries set off on their journey. I accompanied them as far as Mezreh and it was very hard to take leave of them. When they were out of sight I went home. I had to get back to Harpoot quickly because we expected the Turks to come and break into the houses. When I came up I found the Kaimakam's wife and some other Turkish women walking around in the houses. They left before evening and did not come into my house. Next morning they returned and I saw them take the curtains down. I thought perhaps they were having them washed, but at noon a woman came running and said they were taking the furniture away. I went there immediately and found several soldiers in the act of taking Mr. Riggs's large desk away. I asked them to put it back. Then I saw the wife herself and said that the furniture must not be taken away, as it had been left to be used whilst they were living in the house. I found that most of it had been removed and only the very heavy things were left. She said that the Kaimakam had sent her to see the house, and if she did not like it, she could bring the things home. She now let the soldiers bring the desk back and went home. The Kaimakam himself came to see me in the afternoon. He told me that he will not be coming here but would leave the house in the same condition as it had been when he had accepted it. I could not say anything to him but I told Mr. Ehmann about it. He said he would not take the key and that the government should have it. A few days later the hospital's Mudir and Ser Tabib moved in.

I was living up here the first time the Christians were in great fear of a massacre. Elmas Kuir and her two daughters, who had lived in Mr. Riggs's house for 18 years, moved in to live with me. Several times, every day, Turks came who wanted her to live in their houses. They were in great fear that the Turks would come and take them by force, but I said a decided "No" to everyone who came, and they have now become tired. Elmas Kuir is now happy and settled. Now came a very busy time for taking over everything. Relief work had to be started from the beginning again, and every person had to be interviewed. It was not an easy job, as most of those who are left do not know their own names, and it takes a long time to find these out. Also where they are from, and how many children they have. One must cross-examine them, because they cheat and tell lies to obtain help. As we cannot give complete help to the many, many people, though we do what we can, we have to choose those in greatest need. A lot of people come to see me every day to encourage each other. All that happens in the town that in any way concerns the Christians, equally in regard to buildings, street cleaning, lavatories, the sick and the poor, find their way to me. So much of it is new to me that it is not so easy to make arrangements, but I do my best.

We collected together 440 small children who were living in the streets like puppies, digging in the refuse thrown out from the shops and going around begging. They were in a terrible condition, looking like skeletons and indescribably dirty. Most of them had a scalp condition we call "Kael," which is not found in Europe and resembles a type of leprosy. They looked more like a herd of frightened animals than children. We had no clothes for them, but I rented 11 different houses from the government who had taken them from Armenians, and in each I put 40 children with two mothers. I selected the best women, and several of our best young girls from the College offered themselves for the work, although we could only give a loaf of bread a day. It is a pleasure now to go around the different homes and see the change in these children. They are all clean with their hair cut and dressed in white suits. As it is impossible to find clothes on the Shuga. We have made ourselves some very coarse linen which we use for our children and the poor. Their faces are so different. They smile now, yes, even laugh heartily once in a while. Now one or another little boy or girl amongst them will suddenly stand up and begin to sing and dance in the Kurdish manner. These little ones, who did not even know their own names six weeks ago, and could not speak Armenian, can now sing several hymns. Many of them wish to die so that they can come up into Heaven to Jesus. But there are still many among them like little skeletons, who suddenly become ill, and as they have no powers of resistance, they die in the course of a couple of days. About three children die every day. These children can only have one little piece of bread a day, not as big as a penny loaf.

We view the future with anxiety, as there is still no money coming in. I have received several telegrams saying, "There is no money. When it comes we will certainly let you know." We have as much money as will give these children we have taken in one little loaf a day this month. After that it is all finished, what shall we do then? It is terrible to think of turning these little ones out into the streets again, after they have been sheltered and cared for for so short a time. We still live in the belief that God will send help one way or another. These many little ones are His.

As well as the many children in Harpoot, I have three little newborn babies in Mezreh. The first, only eight days old, was left outside my door. The mother had had her bread supply stopped, and in her despair, she had to go to a village to find work. The Turks will not take them in if they have small children, so she had to relinquish her baby in desperation. I took the little one down to Mezreh, where one of my young girls is taking care of her under my supervision. Two days later, some women brought a four day old baby which they had found in the mountains lying beside a spring. It was a lovely little child, but in a pitiful condition. I took her home with me also. One week later I got the third little one, two weeks old. The mother had died in great wretchedness.

Some days after the missionaries left, some soldiers opened the sealed door up in the Girls' College. I went up with Baron Antreas, one of our men who has survived and works in the hospital laboratory here. We found the door open and some things removed. We sent a message to the senior officer, who promised to have the things returned and the door closed. We heard about two weeks ago that the door had been opened again, and we then sent a message to the Commandant. He wrote a letter to the senior officer in Harpoot, giving strict orders that everything taken away should be brought back and the door sealed, and that nothing belonging to the Americans must be touched. Again I went around with Baron Antreas and the Mudir and found tables and chairs in the officers' rooms, and a lot of school tables and benches set up in the hall being used by the soldiers. When I went into the room that had been opened, I found it nearly empty. Tables, chairs, and stoves had been taken away, and it is said they have been sold. So many things were missing that it was impossible to get them back, so I demanded a list of them all. I closed the door and sealed it. They promised very earnestly that it would not be opened again. While I was there they hammered planks of wood across the door which were to be whitened like the walls. The Mudir said the soldiers would not know it was a door and there would be no risk of its being opened. They put all the blame on the poor soldiers who were whipped before our eyes and accused of opening the doors. There the poor cowed soldiers stood, accepting the blows and cruel curses without saying a word. We knew, as well as the soldiers, that they were not responsible, but the officers who were beating them. This is a little picture that shows the injustice and oppression that rules this country. While the Mudir whipped one of the men, I said to him, "If the soldiers have opened the door and taken the things without your permission, how can it be that the tables and chairs are in your, as well as the soldiers', rooms? If it was against your orders then you should have had them returned at once and sent us a message." When I said this, he started to blame Baron Antreas, who is, of course, an Armenian, but the high ranking officers were very embarrassed that I should come with such strict orders from the Commandant, which they had to obey immediately in my presence.

Then came the terrible day, July 1st, when we had to stop the bread distribution, followed by some dreadfully painful days, when I sat from morning until evening, telling the unfortunate poor people that we could no longer help them, as we had no money. Some turned away very quietly and departed in tears. Oh, it was hard to see their patient sorrow and suffering, knowing how great was their need, and how small were their chances of survival—and still have to refuse them. How difficult for such mothers, many of whom were rich before the time of the terrible deportations, and now weak and in extreme poverty. Up to now we have been able to give them only a little bread to take home to perhaps a crowd of children, or, maybe, only one or two little ones—all that is left of a large family—the others having died of hunger, want, and suffering. The ones that are still left cry and beg for a little bread. They cannot understand that there is none, and it cuts the poor mothers to the heart to see their children's hunger, hear their cries, and still have to say, "No, I have none." How many mothers have come with their little child in their arms and begged and beseeched me to have mercy on their child and to give just a piece of bread a day. "Don't give me any" they say, "Only my child, or she will die, and she is all I have left." When I say "No," they cry still more bitterly. The mother clasps the child still closer, pets it, and loves it as only she can do. Can you understand how hard it is to see this and say "No"? Those who have children whom they love can understand. Then there are others who will not accept "No." They stand talking back, begging and pleading. They kiss my hands and feet. They cannot understand or believe that it is really the truth that there is no money and think I am just being unfair. At long last they go out, disappointed and crying hopelessly, but resolved to come again every day until I give them bread. It is impossible for them, suffering such hunger pangs, to believe and understand, that there is no bread. Others come, and as soon as they hear what I have to say, they begin shouting, screaming, and crying. They stand with upraised arms, cursing me and wishing I may find myself in the same circumstances as they. There are women who have stood outside my window from half an hour to one hour, shouting and shrieking like mad people, wishing all harm to come to me. It is misery and endless affliction that has brought these unfortunate people to this point. There are many who have cried so much that they have almost lost their sight. I say to them, "You must not cry. You will become blind." But they say, "We cannot stop it. All is dark—only dark—and there is no hope or ray of light. If only I were alone, but there is this poor little starving one." This is what the Turks have longed for and are so glad to see. The Americans, who up to now have sheltered and helped the many poor souls, have now gone, and there is no help coming. Oh, if only help would come from home.

I have just written a letter home, with the following scriptural texts, which describe the conditions around us:

"Genesis Ch. 47, V. 13. There are many in Numbers Ch. 21, V. 5 and there are many who wish they had died two years ago, and now are afraid will be found in 1st Samuel. Ch. 28, V. 20. They can be found in Lamentations B. 2.19, and Satan works eagerly as is written in Revelations Ch. 6, V. 8. I am afraid that we will soon be able to read Exodus Ch. 16, V. 3. Many are in Devteronomy 28, V. 48. I wish we could be in Hosea 2, V. 9 before it is too late. Most of those who come to church look like those who are described in Jacob 2, V. 2b. All day I see Job. 31, V. 19 and the result is found in Proverbs 30, V. 9. What is written in Amos 2, V. 6 is done in reality. Yes— for an even smaller price. The condition of our neighbours is described in Job 20, V. 19 and Amos 5, V. 12. Many of my boys and girls are in Luke 7, V. 2. I myself am in Job. 30, V. 25-28. How I wish I could find myself in Job. 22, V. 12, and all you, my friends, be found in Proverbs 31, V. 8-9, and Matthew 25, V. 40."

How much I hope that this letter will reach home and that the Lord will really impress upon the friends' hearts the great distress here so that they will really want to help. It is so difficult, not to be able to write straight out and tell everything that we see and experience in this troubled country.

Last winter four boys were captured on the way to Dersim. During questioning, one of the boys said that Anna Varzhoohi, Bessie's mother, had helped him to get away. The police came afterwards to take her but she ran away and hid herself in Mezreh. Six weeks later she returned to Harpoot, and one day two policemen saw her in the street, took her to the police station, and from there to the prison in Mezreh, where she has been held for about a month. I visit her a couple of times a week and got permission by buying fruit and taking it with me and also giving some money to the women in charge of the prison. These prisoners have a terrible life. There are two dark rooms and a little yard where they all live now in this terrible heat. Most of the prisoners are Kurds who know nothing about hygiene and are uncivilised people. Many have small children with them, and when these cry of hunger because they have nothing to live on (as their friends cannot come and bring food) they beat the little ones with their clenched fists on the back, and this makes them cry more. The Kurds are accused of stealing or mistreating people. Some prisoners are Turkish women who must sit there for 10 long years. They are so impassioned that they cannot conduct a conversation for two minutes. They sing and dance and shout, calling for their husbands whom they love—especially one young woman (epileptic) who has killed her husband and thrown him down a well. She is like a wild animal. Every time she hears a man's voice in the street she jumps wildly and climbs over the wall into the street. Then she comes back and tells how handsome the man was, and how he made signs to her. Then she dances a little, while singing and calling to her beloved. Two Kurdish women are lying sick with typhus and two others have scabies. They shout and scream, quarrel and fight every day. Each time the young woman becomes angry, she makes signs indicating that she will cut their throats and put them down a well. It is the very depths of ghastliness, vulgarity, sinfulness and misery. There Anna Varzhoohi has sat in a corner for more than a month, hoping and waiting every day to be released. Suddenly, 10 days ago, the police came and surrounded her mother's house in Harpoot and took the weak 70 year old woman and the five small children to the prison in Harpoot. They sealed the door of the room where they had their few belongings and went their way. At 6 o'clock on Sunday morning a woman came and told me that they were being sent to Ourfa. It was a terrible blow. The poor people. How can they reach Ourfa on foot. They are so weak and the youngest, three years old, was deathly ill a short while ago and cannot walk unaided. A six year old boy is paralysed in one side and the old woman, who has undergone such terrible suffering in her life, has no more strength left. I went immediately to the Vali to ask for a pardon for her. He said—which I found out afterwards to be untrue—that he had nothing to do with her case, but he told me that the order to send her away had come from Constantinople. He assured me that they would not be killed on the way and would be sent in a wagon. He told me that the Commandant was responsible for sending her, so there was nothing else to do but to go to him. First I went down to the prison to see Anna Varzhoohi. I found her in deep despair about her old mother and the children. After talking with her I went to the Commandant. First I went to his home, but when I did not find him there, I went to the Government Building. He gave me a friendly reception and I told him everything. He said he did not know anything about the case, but would investigate it. When he said that, I hoped that the departure could be delayed. In the afternoon I sent a message to the Vali, asking him to delay their departure for a couple of days. He again said that he had nothing to do with the case. On Monday morning I had to go to Harpoot, but I intended coming back early in the afternoon to see the Commandant again. However, when I was approaching Mezreh at about 2 o'clock, I heard the sorrowful news that Anna and her mother and children had been sent away, on foot, in the morning, and without anything. Consequently, I went to the prison to hear more about it. They told me that the old mother and children had been brought there on Sunday evening and had all been in good spirits on Monday morning, when they sent a message to me that my application to the Commandant had had a good result and asked me to continue. I myself was then in good spirits and full of hope, until I came home and found they were gone. Everybody in the prison was very depressed. They said it had been terrible to see them suffering fear and crying. There then followed some days of worry, as I did not know how I could help them. A new Commandant was expected and I decided to go to him as soon as he arrived. We had always wished Izzat Pasha would come because he is a very friendly man and imagine my joy when I went down to Mezreh on Friday evening and heard that he had arrived. I wrote a petition which I intended to bring to him myself on Saturday afternoon, but unfortunately he did not receive people on that day. Then Mr. Ehmann heard about my plan and said that I should not bring the petition personally. He is always very worried, and if I followed his advice I would always sit down and say, "It is impossible." He said that they would not change their intentions, even if I knew she was innocent. But I could not do this when I thought of the five small children and the old mother. So on Sunday morning I tried to get in touch with Izzat Pasha's adjutant but unfortunately did not succeed before evening. Thus another day passed without anything being done, and I was still in great fear that they might be sent further away. When I spoke to the adjutant he said it would be best if I presented the petition myself—as I had thought—saying I should come at 4 o'clock on Monday, which I did. Unfortunately, when Karen-Marie and I reached the house we saw Izzat Pasha leave and get into an automobile, but when he saw us, he got out again and came over and greeted us. I handed him the petition, which he read, and then asked if I knew where they were by now. He promised to do his best for them. I thanked him very much and said goodbye. He got back into the automobile and drove away. I was very glad that I had met him and felt much more calm, knowing that I had done as much as lay in my power. The same evening, when I was on my way to the Garden, the adjutant came again and we had a fresh talk, when I explained everything to him. He was very kind and promised to talk to Izzat Pasha about it. That day an Austrian officer arrived on his way to Malatia. I gave him 20 banknotes to give to Mr. Christoffel, so that he could give them to Anna Varzhoohi. He also promised to look out for them on the road, and if he saw them, to help them. I also wrote to Mr. Christoffel, and asked him to let me know what happened to them. There was nothing else to do but wait. Three or four days later Muzaffer Bey arrived and told me that Anna had been pardoned, and that Izzat Pasha had given orders that she should be allowed to stay in Malatia. My joy was great and I expected a message from Malatia, either from Mr. Christoffel or Anna, after which I would go to Izzat Pasha and thank him. But then news came from somewhere that Anna had been taken away and killed. At last, after two weeks, a letter came from Mr. Christoffel stating that all of them had been sent away in the direction of Marash. It was a hard blow after hoping that they would be released. Again it shows us that we cannot depend on the Turks' word, never mind how kind they are. Now a month has gone and I have heard nothing from them. From Marash the road goes towards Behesni and Adiaman, places where they send the Turkish and Kurdish refugees, and we do not know to which they have been sent. I have not much hope of seeing or hearing from them again. The dreadful exhausting journey in the terrible heat will surely be the finish of them, if they have not already been killed by the soldiers who accompany them. Should they reach one place or another and be set free, they cannot live. They have no money and no way of surviving amongst these wild, uncivilised refugees. Poor, poor people. If I could just have got the older boy Tavit, who is nine years old and a lovely clever boy, whom it would have been a pleasure to bring up.

Because I have not written for a long time, there are many things I must omit, as I can no longer remember details and dates. I will only describe an eclipse of the moon, which took place at the end of July—I cannot remember the date. I woke up and saw that the moon was being more and more overcast by a thick black veil. Suddenly shooting broke out around us—cannon and rifle fire—and continued for two hours, while everything shook and rumbled round about. People who had not noticed the moon thought that the Russians had arrived at least, and that Mezreh was the battle ground. It was rather unpleasant. Not only Mezreh was upset, but also Harpoot and the villages. The Turks thought that devils had collected around the moon, and they were shooting to frighten them away. On August 3rd I came up to the mountains to have a little holiday and have been here three weeks tomorrow. Once a week I go up to Harpoot and spend a busy day attending to all the many different things that are waiting for me, paying wages, giving out work, seeing to the many children, etc. On the 18th I received a big bundle of letters from my American friends. Mr. Jacob had seen them in Constantinople and very kindly brought them here. I had been waiting to hear if I would be getting money for my many, many poor, but no. Instead, they said that the 2,000 liras they had sent was sent in a secure way. The money has still not come. At the same time it is being said that wheat will be dearer. It was down to 230 piastres a kilo, but then it was impossible to find. Now it is already up to 300, but still cannot be had. What is one to do? Just thinking of it makes me ill. What will I do with the many children and poor people? I cannot bear to see them starve to death. No, I will not think about this nor believe it. Our Heavenly Father is mighty and will not allow it. He can send help when we least expect it. That I will believe, and trust in, and continue to take one day at a time.

The German aeroplanes are very active, flying several times a week. In the last week they have been to Erzingan and dropped bombs, so we expect maybe they will be reciprocated by the Russians coming here and dropping bombs. It would not be very nice but if it resulted in wheat becoming cheaper I almost wish they would come.

We still hear about great battles in Flanders. The result is always the same, that the Germans have beaten the enemy and the British have suffered enormous losses. The Germans are also said to be advancing strongly in Galicia. Here they are making great preparations to recapture Baghdad by autumn. When will all this cruelty end? Evil prevails everywhere. I remember the words of the Lord that if these days are not shortened, none of the believers will be able to hold out. We see here how one after the other, those who in the past were members of the congregation, have been drawn away by sin. When the Son arrives, will he find any faith on earth? Immorality flourishes as never before. Even young girls at the age of five are taken off the streets and misused terribly. Now it is so common that it happens in the open. What will be the end of it? It looks so hopeless. But we should not be despondent. Often we think of Abraham's prayer to God about the evil city of Sodom and Gomorrah where, if only three people were found to be virtuous, God would not destroy it.

Here there are still people who belong to the Lord and who have not soiled their garments with sin. With the help of the Lord we would like to help, protect, and keep them in faith.

27 August. We have again experienced the Lord's faithfulness and care, when it seemed like the darkest day of all. The money had stopped and the prices were terribly high. It was time to buy grain, and one kilo was three liras in gold, if we were able to find it. The government took whatever it could and the rest the peasants sowed in the fields. We had not bought any corn yet, and my 600 children were getting thinner and weaker. Many had already died. People were returning from their summer villages, many of them sick, and we had no means to help them. I was almost sick thinking about the future. Imagine then, my great joy, when I received a card from the Consul on Friday, saying that money would be coming to me shortly, to enable me to make some preparations for the winter. I was nearly beside myself

with joy. This is now the third time the Lord has sent money at the last moment, when we stood without anything, but never a minute too late. This should teach me, and all of us who have experienced the Lord's help in time of need, to trust in Him always, and without doubt or fear give ourselves completely over to Him. Praise the Lord, for He is good. Everything looks so bright today. It seems that I can overcome everything, even if I have to work day and night. If only I can help those in need, and not have to say "No," nor to see so many starve to death.

30 January, 1918. Over five months have gone since I last wrote in this book. I am so busy that it has been impossible to find the time to write. Now I have unfortunately contracted scabies from my daily work among the children and the poor, who are all so dirty and infectious that it is no wonder that I have caught this nasty complaint. The treatment lasts for three days, and as there is no need for me to lie in bed, I will use the time to set down what I can remember of my experiences during these months.

While I was up in the Germans' Garden to rest in August, the Mudir, who was living in Dr. Parmelee's house, broke through a window in Mr. Riggs's bathroom and went up into the loft, which was full of all the missionaries' personal effects. When I returned to Harpoot after my holiday Elmas Kuir told me about it. They knew nothing definite but had heard knocking and hammering in the night and in the morning they saw several very large boxes being taken away. I broke the seal on the door and went up with Mr. Pekmezian, where we found everything in an appalling condition. Furniture was broken, suitcases broken into, and the contents gone. There were two cases, one full of Mrs. Barnum's things, and one with Annie's. They were also broken into and everything taken. Mrs. Riggs's bureau, filled with all her personal things which we had put up there, was also rifled. Anything they had no use for had been strewn around on the floor. I went straight to the government, but the Mudir had already left for Constantinople, so I was afraid I would not be fortunate enough to have the stolen goods returned. I asked the government to return the building to us, as this was the only way that the missionaries' belongings could be kept safe. A week later I received an answer that the building was being handed back to me, and the government sent out of the Mudir's and Ser Tabib's families, who had been living in Mr. Riggs's and Dr. Parmelee's parts of the house. When I got the house back it was in a pitiful state. All the shelves and cupboards were torn out. One room had been used to house dogs, another hens, a third had been used as a stable, and all the dirt had been left behind. Mr. Ehmann and I now thought it safest to move all the school things down to the missionaries' house, as they would then be under our protection. Up to now they have opened different places several times and taken away from a third to one half of contents.

On September 23rd I began the removal. Mr. Pekmezian and Baron Garabed came up and helped me. Karen-Marie also came up for a couple of days. I received all the things and Mr. Pekmezian and Baron Garabed sent them all down. I had about 10 women to carry things and also some of my young girls. We had it all moved down in about five days. A lot of things had been stolen—stoves, tables, chairs, and much else. It was a big job and I was glad when it was over.

On September 4th I moved to Baron Harotoone's house with my young girls, after much discussion back and forth. The house is not nearly big enough and I must also keep a part of Kevork Agha's house. Sister Katherina has to have 10 of the girls sleeping in her house, though they spend the day with us and have their meals here. Even though the house is small, and there are some difficulties, we are grateful to have a home to ourselves where we can be together. On October 1st I opened a kindergarten with the help of three of my young girls who have been trained by Miss Harley. We can only take a certain number, as we do not have so much room. We got permission to use the dining room over in the Danish Children's Home. In return we take six of their children into the school without payment. We have 49 pupils, mostly from Syrian homes, some from Turkish homes, and the rest from Armenian. We can only accept those who can pay, otherwise we would have so many that it would be impossible to find room for all of them. Bessie is also going to school. She is the youngest, only 3½ years old, and one of the most clever. She is as tall as a six year old, and no one would take her for a baby. On October 14th Sister Jenny received permission to travel home, but when she applied to the government for permission for Akko she could not obtain it. There followed some difficult but exciting weeks for her. Some said, especially the German missionaries, "Go without Akko," but she always said that this was impossible. While she was waiting for permission for Akko from the government, a telegram came from Mr. Schuhardt saying that she must not go home. This was very hard for her, but she continued to hope. About November 14th Mr. Lederer was leaving here and we went up in the morning to see him go. The Police Director was also there and he called Sister Jenny over and told her that permission for Akko had arrived. Her joy was indescribable. She clapped her hands and jumped. The Turks looked very surprised, as though they thought, "What a foolish woman, rejoicing over that child." No wonder, when they have killed and ill-treated thousands of these people. Another telegram was then sent to Mr. Schuhardt and the permission came through. She left for home on November 30th.

On November 2nd Karen-Marie, Mr. Ehmann, Bessie and I, together with Mr. Christoffel who had been here on a visit, set out for Malatia. We went in a big lorry. The decision to go was so surprising and came so suddenly that I had to make my preparation in the late evening. I was therefore very tired when we left and had a terrible headache. We reached Malatia at 11 o'clock in the evening and longed to get to bed, but this was not possible before 2.00 a.m. First we had to unload the lorry, and then set up our beds. Bessie was exceptionally good and sweet. She did not cry once and everyone was surprised to see how good she was. We had hoped to return on Monday but the soldiers who had come to make purchases could not be finished by then, and we had to stay for two more days. We went with Mr. Christoffel on Monday to visit some rich Turks, in whom he is greatly interested. On Tuesday we went through the market to the Armenian quarter, which now lies in a great ruin. Only a few, very big and fine houses remain standing, as Turks are now occupying them. A large number of trees in the Armenian gardens have been cut down. We also visited a few Armenians who remain for one reason or another. The number is not great. Only 30 women and children of the Protestant faith. There are also a number of Gregorians, but they have all become Moslems. We spoke to some of them, but they have nearly all forgotten Armenian, as they always speak Turkish for fear of anyone hearing them and questioning the sincerity of their conversion to the Moslem faith. It made all the wounds in my heart bleed, everything that has happened in the last year lived again, to think that there are so few real Christians left. On Sunday afternoon we walked up to the mountains. About 20 minutes away from Mr. Christoffel's house, in a cleft between two mountains, a very large and deep hole was dug some years ago. A great crowd of men from Malatia were brought out there and beheaded, their bodies being thrown down into this pit, which was now full with how many thousands we do not know. Around the pit lay many skeletons and bones which the dogs had dragged out. The Turks had poured petrol over the skeletons and tried to burn them but without success. When we stood there and saw this horrible sight, everything came back so clearly. The fear, the torture, the terrible suffering our many friends and brothers and sisters had undergone. We live as in the time of Nero's persecution of the Christians. Oh, if it would also bear the same fruit as then, that new flocks would receive Jesus as their Saviour, and that we, who have already received Him, may be faithful and strong in Him.

Tuesday was my birthday, which I spent in Malatia and celebrated by buying 10 piastres' worth of nuts for my little girl.

On Wednesday we arose at 3.00 a.m. and were on our way at 4.30 a.m. in three large well-loaded lorries, full of potatoes and dried apricots. A couple of times we stuck fast in the bad roads, but as there were many soldiers, they soon had us free again. When we came to the bridge over the Euphrates and the first lorry began to cross it, the bridge broke and one side of the heavy lorry went through. Everything had to be taken off and carried over to the other side. After a couple of hours' delay we were able to drive on again. We reached Mezreh at 7 o'clock in the evening. I enjoyed the journey home more as I had no headache.

29 November. Thanksgiving Day, I celebrated by inviting Karen-Marie to dinner, which consisted of a chicken curry with rice pilaff, and almonds and mulberries for dessert. We had also a party here for our kindergarten children. We had asked each

child to bring boulghour and khurma so that we could cook pilaff and entertain some poor children to food. This was to teach the children to enjoy giving pleasure to others. We had also invited the mothers, but here it is not like home, when the one you invite is the only one who comes. Here, each brought two or three others with them. So the house was packed full and everyone had to sit on the floor close to each other. The Badveli spoke very nicely to the mothers about the children as God's gift to us. Afterwards the children played some of their games and sang some songs to the great pleasure of the mothers. It was a really nice day. Of course my thoughts often went back to previous years, and to our dear friends, who had now safely reached their homes in America.

4 December. The town crier proclaimed that there is an armistice on the eastern front, and hope began to rise again in everyone. The suffering Armenians are hoping for an early return to peace, so that the way to America may be opened and they can leave this troubled land alive. The Turks congratulated each other and told one story after the other. Even the Germans believe that victory is now theirs. They have almost planned their departure from here. All troops are to be moved from the eastern to the western front, to enable an end to the detested British. But one is certain of nothing, because both the Turks and the Germans tell only what they hope will happen, and when something goes against them, they always keep it secret. This is how it was until the other day, when we heard that the peace negotiations had broken down and there was no peace. In the meantime we had heard that the British had taken Jerusalem. This news pleased all the Christians. We have also heard that Beirut is taken, but we do not know if this is true.

24 December. Then came Christmas again without peace, for which we had hoped so much last year. It is well we do not know what the future will bring. We still live in the hope that tomorrow will bring peace. If we knew in advance that we would have difficulties, many would collapse and give up.

On Christmas Eve, Bessie and I had dinner at Karen-Marie's, together with Dr. Asbech, Mr. Fischer, and Mr. Frankel. After the gentlemen had left we sang our Danish Christmas hymns and held a service. Then we exchanged gifts, which were only small and few this year, but we do not think Christmas would be complete without them. At 6.30 we were invited up to Sister Verena's house, where all the Germans were also invited to a Christmas eve party. There were, I think, 27 soldiers, besides all the missionaries, the Ehmann children, and Bessie. There was a lovely Christmas tree, and after the soldiers had sung some Christmas hymns and the Christmas gospel had been read, coffee and cakes were served, and later we had apples, nuts, almonds, and raisins.

On Christmas morning I had a tree for my little girl. There were a lot of gifts because her many friends had been busy before Christmas making different things. Her joy was great and we all felt rewarded when we saw it. Later in the morning there was a

German service and in the evening the soldiers had invited all the missionaries to dinner. We had turkey and salad as a main course, then soup, and this was followed by dessert. For entertainment I had my gramophone brought over, which we played, and Dr. Asbech and Mr. Boler played on the piano.

1 January, 1918. I was here on New Year's Day and received friends who came to wish me a happy New Year. About 50 came, and we served almonds and raisins, figs and leblebi.

On January 8th I went up to Harpoot with Bessie to spend one week, but it became two. There has been talk for a long time that America would declare war on Turkey, and one day the Mutasarrif said to Mr. Pekmezian that as soon as war was declared they would come up and take all the Americans' belongings. So Mr. Pekmezian, Mr. Ehmann, and Badveli wanted everything sent away as quickly as possible. I, myself, would have preferred that everything was left as it was, because everything of value had already been taken, but when all the others voted against this suggestion, it was decided that we should try to save as much as possible. I started immediately sending boxes and books down to Mezreh. We had selected the most valuable books to send. I also tried to send down all the missionaries' private books. I did all this in the morning and every afternoon I had 80 of my children at a Christmas tree party. First they had their favourite meal—kufte—and after that we gathered around the tree. They sang the hymns they had learned and many of them recited verses and whole chapters from the bible. Then one of my young girls, whom I had dressed as Father Christmas, gave out dried mulberries and walnuts. There was only a small quantity for each child, but their joy was great. I had to hold six of these parties to cover all my children.

8 January. In the morning when I was at our prayer meeting, a message came to go over to Digin Annagel's house as quickly as possible, which was surrounded by a big crowd of soldiers. I went over as I was and found poor Maritza amongst the soldiers, who were taking her over to the Kaimakam. She is the daughter of a former Professor Vorperian from our College, who was sent away with his family in the massacre of 1915. He was killed, and his wife and daughter were taken by a Turkish officer who has kept them up to now, in the hope that when peace came he would get a large sum of money from their rich relations in America in exchange for their freedom. But now he wanted to marry Maritza who is only 16 and a lovely girl. She is a strong Christian and she had said all along, "I will not marry him. He is a Moslem, and besides that, he is infected with venerial disease." Then one day he began making preparations for the wedding, which was to take place the same night. Maritza discovered this and there was nothing she could do but run away. So she asked permission to take a bath, which he allowed, and she escaped into a hole in the ground, in which she sat for two weeks, day and night in the terrible stench. She became ill and was brought out and taken to her aunt's, where she had been for two

days before being captured on the 8th. I went with her to the Kaimakam, where she was questioned and a report was written. After that she was to be brought to Mezreh. I got permission to go with her but I had to go home to change first. When I came back she had to be searched, as under questioning she had said that she had poison in her possession which she would take if she was brought back to the man. They asked me to bring her into another room to find the poison, which I did. When we came back and I gave them the poison, another report was written, and the poison was carefully wrapped up and sealed. Then we were sent away with two armed soldiers and another two unarmed ones who walked close to us all the way. Everybody looked at us. We looked like two dangerous criminals with such a guard. We reached the government building, where we were led from one room to another, surrounded by the officer and his friends, who were still trying to get her taken away from me, but they did not succeed. These officers glared at me, but they did not do anything else. We hoped that the matter would be settled that day, but evening came at once, and as they had not persuaded her to return, the court could not force her. The officer then made arrangements so that she should be imprisoned. I went down to the prison with her, but as soon as we reached the door, one of the officers forbade the woman who lives there and supervises the prisoners to let me come in. The other six officers stood at a distance, looking on. Now she has sat there for three weeks and is still not free. He will try to force her back by punishment. When will the sun of justice rise in this country? It later transpired that, if I had not been with her that day, she would have been taken away—but they were afraid of me.

24 January. Sister Maria in Pnuel was taken ill with typhus. She got it through nursing some of their children who happened to have it.

Throughout these five months I have had a great deal of work. Every second day I go regularly to Harpoot, and often stay up there when I have not finished my work in time to reach home. The distress is greater than ever. My house is surrounded daily by a crowd of the poor, who are waiting for me to have mercy on them and give them bread. If we should judge by their apparent need, we should help each one. It is a pitiful sight, which is impossible to describe in any way that would give the friends at home its real meaning. Thin, clad only in a few rags, so dirty that the smell carries a long distance, full of scabies and vermin. As soon as they see me in one place or another, they surround me, all crying and begging.

They take my hands and fall down and kiss my feet. They will not let me go. The result is that I am suffering from scabies. There are not so many people as before. Up until last spring we supported 5,000 people, but when the American missionaries left, this stopped, and we tried to send them all to the villages. A good many left and can live there. We help others, who without our aid, would suffer distress. Here in Harpoot and Mezreh we have 400 children whom we have taken in and cared for. Besides this, we give daily bread to 400-500 people. It is impossible to give bread and help to all who come, as more women and children are continuing to arrive. We hear about those who have nothing apart from what they can find. Women go around where animals are being slaughtered to collect the blood, which they boil. Others collect bones, which they pound down and eat. Entrails of animals are also collected and roasted for food. This is how many people are living. I started this winter greatly worried, as we could only help a quarter of the former number, and I feared many people would die, but now the worst of the winter is over, and deaths have been fewer than I expected. In about a month, those people who have gathered here will be able to leave for the villages, where it will be easier for them to find something to live on. In December it looked again as if we would get no more money, but I still could not believe it. Mr. Ehmann was completely wretched, but I still said that I believed money would come. Just before Christmas we held a meeting at which it was agreed that if no money came we would have to stop, and then came a letter from Mr. Pamle to say that he would be sending 4,000 liras each month. After receiving my letters, he said he would also send 7,000 liras, which we should have had for two months in order that we could end the year without debt. Great was my joy. The Lord's grace and mercy, which has been revealed so often to us in these difficult times, is again shown.

31 January. I had a bath today after the treatment and feel so well in clean clothes. I am attending a prayer meeting at the Ehmanns'.

1 February. Last night I was invited to the Ehmanns' for dinner. The guests were Mr. Christoffel from Malatia, who arrived by airship, two high ranking German officers, Dr. Asbech, and Karen-Marie. After dinner we were joined by the other German sisters.

2 February. We held a meeting today where it was decided that we must cut off the supply of bread to the poor. The 4,000 liras a month is only sufficient to support our children—allowing 60 piastres a month for each child. We will continue the bread distribution this month but must stop on March 1st and only give help in banknotes to those in greatest need.

This week we had two meetings a day with my young girls. The Badveli has spoken to them and had private talks with each one. Tonight I am sitting with Sister Maria who is ill with typhus. The fever has gone down, but she is very weak, and one of her lungs is not good, therefore we are not completely sure that the danger is over.

23 February. Again, three weeks have gone without being able to get anything written down. No matter how determined I am to write at least a couple of lines a day, I never seem to manage it, because when evening comes I am really too tired. It is one of the few things I can postpone without doing any harm and therefore the writing has to suffer.

On Wednesday February 5th, in the evening, just after sunset, when I was going home from Harpoot, I saw some Turkish soldiers as I neared the Tiflis road. They were walking along the road, and they shouted to another man, who was a little way ahead, "He is dead! He is dead!" At first I thought there had been a fight, but two men from the Turkish hospital came with a stretcher, and when they heard that he was dead, they said, "Then we won't touch him. We are afraid." I asked them, "What are you afraid of?" and they answered, "Khanim Effendi, if we carry him home, and no money is found on him, the officer will beat and whip us, and say we have taken the money." They had a long discussion and I said, "I will go with you and search the man, and if the officer says anything, then tell him I was with you, and that he can send for me, and I will come and tell him what I have seen." I went over to the dead man. He had not yet stiffened, so he could not have been dead long. He was an old man, at least 60, very thin, and dressed in wretched rags. All the fingers were missing from one hand. He had come from the hospital in Harpoot and had probably been sent to Tebdil Hana to rest, but he was in such a pitiful condition that he had not lasted longer than 40 minutes from Harpoot before dying on the road. It cut me to the heart to see these soldiers standing around him and not daring to touch him for fear of the officers. While I stood there with them, they said, "Oh, Khanum Effendi. You know what is going on. Tell us about the peace." I told them what I knew and they stood and raised their hands and eyes to the sky shouting, "Allah, Allah." When I left them it was with a heavy heart. I could see before me all these thousands of poor ignorant men, far from their homes, suffering distress and being treated like dogs by the officers. They never hear from their wives, they have no hope, no ray of light comes to them. Ignorance, darkness, distress, and imprisonment fill their lives as soldiers. I called on the Lord, "Oh, have mercy on these thousands of ignorant, suffering souls." The next day I sent someone to see if the dead man had been taken away, but he was still there, and remained until Sunday, nearly four days. This was just outside the town on a public road with people passing. It shows the kind of government we have. No one dares to report a dead man lying on the ground as they would be accused of taking his money, even one in such a pitiful condition as this one who could not have owned a single penny.

Sister Maria has recovered and is regaining strength. February 8th was Karen-Marie's birthday. Bessie and I had lunch with her and in the afternoon all the German missionaries were invited to coffee. In the last month there has been a lot of talk about peace with Russia. I think it was on the 14th when we read in Ajans that a peace treaty was signed. There was great joy all around. The Turks celebrated by going around playing music in the streets, and for two whole nights there was music and dancing. The Germans also made preparations for a party. They raised flags on their houses, though they had not received word by telegram from Germany. At the last moment before the party, they decided to wait for official word. And they had to wait, for no telegram came. At the same time as the news of peace there came word about the death of Abdul Hamid. There was great sorrow about this among the Turks because they all loved him. They wished it had been the present Sultan.

A week ago the Turks said that the Russians had withdrawn from Erzingan and Erzeroum, and the Turks were going back to take them over. When they came to Erzingan they were met by armed Armenian soldiers who opened fire upon them. The Kurds came to the aid of the Turks, the Armenians were overpowered, and 300 of them were hanged. This aroused great anger among the Turks and there were plans made immediately for a massacre of the remaining Armenians. The latter have gone through the old fear for the last week. One of the reasons I am here in Harpoot at this time is because, when I came on Monday, the people were beside themselves with fear. There are no missionaries living here any more, only my visits every other day, and much can happen in the day and night when I am not here. Not that I could prevent a massacre, but it makes a difference, and people feel calmer when I am here. I came up on Wednesday, very slowly, because I had Bessie with me, so it was 10.30 before I arrived. There were many people waiting for me and there was great joy when I finally arrived. How I would like to stay up here all the time. I have about 500 children here and many poor people, and all of the Armenian population needs a missionary. It is impossible for me to accomplish everything in the time I now have, and if it were not for the young girls, I would move back as there are enough people for the work in Mezreh.

21 February (Thursday). Professor Khachadoor came and told me that the Kaimakam and another officer had told him that they had received orders from the government to take over all American buildings and property on March 1st. He wanted to know my reaction and I told him what we have always said, that as long as there is no war between the two countries the Turks cannot take anything belonging to the Americans according to the law. The Professor gave my answer to the Kaimakam, who then said he would send the papers down to the Vali. Now I wrote to Mr. Ehmann and asked him and Mr. Pekmezian to see the Vali about these different questions. Today I received a letter from them saying that there was no change in relations between America and Turkey and that they could not, therefore, touch the houses or belongings. Praise the Lord. He has again helped and my soul is rejoicing. Yesterday, Friday the 22nd, I went around my homes and saw all my children. I was happy to see how nice they are in reality. When I think about how they looked when I took them in, and how little I have to work on them, it is a wonder that they all look so well. I have about 100 still like little skeletons. If they are to survive they must be properly fed, and from where shall I obtain the food? I just do not know. I have a couple with recurrent fever, but no one with typhus, for which I am very grateful. I have three with Noma Gangrene in the mouth, and there

is not much hope for their survival. I used to have 114 with scabies, which were all treated at the same time, but still new cases show up to my great sorrow. It is not easy to look after 500 children, almost without soap, clothes, or fuel.

23 February. Today I had a meeting with Markerid Varzhoohi, when we had to cut off the bread supply to some people, as we have not enough money to continue. Now that the spring is coming, we would like to have as many as possible going out to the villages, where it is easier for them to find work and the means to live. I am trying to get one or more fields and some gardens in which to plant vegetables and different things this summer for my many children. I do not know if it will be possible, but I am hoping so. It would be a great help, and the children could take turns at working there. It would give me a lot more work, as I would have to supervise it, but that does not matter, as long as I can obtain more food for my children.

26 February, 1918. Sunday I attended service at our church here in Harpoot. Badveli Vartan preached on the text, "Come unto Me, all ye that labour and are heavy laden, and I will give you rest." It was a sermon that we all needed. How different is the congregation now from that of 3½ years ago. Then the church was full of men, teachers and professors, and all the young men and girls from the College. Now one only sees poor women and dirty, starving children. The few men are Syrians. The air was so bad that I felt really ill, and that means something, because I have become very used to it by going around the poor houses. All these dirty people took their turn at sitting near the stove, and their dirty damp clothes dried and gave off an indescribable smell. There must be many who pick up infection there, as they sit on the floor and vermin pass from one to the other. I am grateful that I have had typhus and typhoid already, so I don't have to worry about these. But recurrent fever is raging now and the infection is passed on by lice as in the case of typhus. As I have never had this, I am a little bit afraid each time that I may contract it, as I often find lice upon my body. The other day a poor woman came to me with her shoulder out of joint and I put her arm back into place again. When I had finished and was binding up her arm I felt as if I had been sprayed all over with fine sand. It was lice. Before starting I had asked her, "Have you any lice?" and she answered, "I bathed two days ago." Most of the poor are like this this year. We cannot give them soap and other things, so they live in the same clothes until they fall off them. In church I saw a little girl, about eight years old, whom I knew from last year. I called her over to talk to me and as she was terribly dirty I asked her why she had not washed herself. She answered, "It is so cold. I will wait until it becomes warmer."

What we feared last year has now become reality. People lie around in the streets, waiting only for death. Children, who are real skeletons, come to us and will not go away, though we cannot help them as we have no money.

The other day a woman fell down in the street and she lay there for some hours until they called me. I went down with some women and a stretcher on which we carried her to my house. She died one hour later. The other poor women who helped me stood around her and cried and cried. One of them sat down beside her and put her hand on her chest, praying that the Lord would hear her prayer, as she sat beside her dead sister. She called on the Lord for mercy and help, that all this terrible distress would come to an end.

There is literally no work to be found for the poor women. How can they live? They go around and beg, but the Turks are tired of them and give them very little. They are better to the begging children, though they are also very often hard on these. A little boy stood outside a Turkish house and sang his "beggar's song"—and these children will not go away without anything, often standing half and whole hours—suddenly the door opened and a Turkish woman came out with a shovelful of fire which she threw over the boy. Other Turks are milder and give them money or bread. There is now a big crowd of children like this who live by begging. They sleep at night in the ruins of houses and anywhere they can find a hole. Four boys are living like this under my staircase every night, and I am often afraid that the house will be burned down, as they make a fire in the evening and have lighting. The majority of these children are now destroyed. I have tried to take them into the Children's Home, but they run away, saying, "We can live better outside." Many of them steal. I am afraid there is not much hope for them. Many women also live immoral lives as they have no work and are hungry. By living like this, they can find their food. Conditions here are terrible and very often the words come to me, that when the Son of God returns I wonder if He will find any believers on earth. If conditions do not change soon, it seems as if there is no hope for the remaining Christians. This is so terribly depressing, but then the thought comes to me that I must not forget that those Armenians who are left were the ones who did not hesitate to lie to save their lives, whilst all who were faithful Christians are Home with God. But I must not say "all," for God has allowed a little group of true Christians to remain and who are a good influence. It is our hope and prayer that this little crowd will grow. God is mighty, and that is why we hold on, even when everything is dark around us.

3 April. Again we have experienced two very difficult weeks with the thought of a massacre occupying all our minds. The Turks have talked about this for more than a month. The reason is supposed to be that when the peace settlement was made with the Russians, and they withdrew from Erzingan, the Armenian men seized all the cannons and ammunition and started to fight the Turks, killing several hundred Turkish women. Whether this is true or not we don't know, but something has provoked the Turks here, and their only wish—and all their talk—is that the poor women and children who are left shall be killed.

They have approached the Vali, asking him to give orders for a massacre, but he seems to be a fair and good man and has so far refused. However, conditions have become more and more critical and on Friday the 14th a climax seemed to have been reached. A crowd of about 200 women and children were brought from the Peri and Palou area. A few men who had been kept by the Kurds up to now were sent away by themselves. We have not heard of them again. Of course they have been killed. All the older boys were brought here bound and this was enough to convince us that the same terrible things had started again. I was up in Harpoot that day and everybody cried and begged me to stay. But I had to return to Mezreh, where I also have a crowd of young girls, though I promised to return the next day if danger looked imminent. My two men who look after the weaving and whose homes are in Mezreh came back with me that evening. All our conversation was about being ready to die and of the glory that awaits us. How often we experience the truth of Jesus' words, "The Spirit is willing, but the flesh is weak." We all fear the physical suffering which lies ahead, saying time after time how glad we would be if the Lord would take us or if they would simply shoot us. But they do the most terrible things and a deep sigh goes from the heart, "Oh Lord Jesus, my God. You know what is best. Strengthen us, and make us faithful." When I came down to Mezreh I went over to Pompish Yughaper's where a crowd of newly arrived women had collected to hear the details. The women said that when they came here the officers said they could go to their relatives, so, in fear of being sent away again, they all said they had relatives here and came running to us for help.

2 July, 1918. Again, a long time has passed since I wrote anything down. When I last wrote, I mentioned the crowd of women and children who had been brought here, and during this time more have been brought. Yes, now and then, even men have been brought and put in prison. Several rather large crowds of men have been sent away, and from well informed sources we have heard that they have been killed. Recently two Armenians have been shot every other day, all condemned as deserters. One, a strong educated young man, asked permission to speak for two minutes before being shot. This was granted and he said, "I am being shot as a deserter, even though I have paid ransom several times and therefore, according to the law, I am free. I have done my duty." All this of course fills us full of dread when we think of the few who are left. If the war continues much longer, this entire people will be wiped out. If they do not all lose their lives, then the majority of those who survive will be morally dead. We must remember that most of those Armenians who remain are those who were not afraid to lie to save their lives. Yes, many of them even denied their faith. Many sought refuge with their Turkish friends and paid them big amounts of money. One sin led to another and now comes all the other suffering. Hunger has driven many a woman into immorality in order to find bread for herself and her children. They lie and steal, and one can scarcely trust anybody any more. When I was up here one week in May something terrible happened. Opposite my

house lived an Armenian woman and her three children. On a Monday she left with her nine year old son to work for a couple of days in a nearby village. Her other two children, girls of 12 and 6 years, remained at home. On Thursday morning, when I was serving out soup to my children, a girl came and asked me to come down to the road, as a little girl had fallen down a well. I went immediately, along with one of my helpers, and found the child in a deep trench. I got her lifted up. She must have been there since the previous day because she was covered in dried blood from head to toe. I took her to my room and bathed her and found a large hole in her head. She was badly bruised on one side and in one foot, but she was conscious and able to tell me what had happened. She said that a young girl, who was related to them, had come and wanted to take some of their clothes, but the elder sister would not let her. So the girl beat the sister, who then ran away. After that the girl took the clothes and the little girl in her arms, saying they would go to Mezreh. When they reached the trench the girl threw the child into it, after which she stood and threw stones down upon her. I had just got the child fixed up and had gone down to see to some sick children when someone came running to tell me that the child's mother had returned and found the elder sister down in a well in their house. Here in Harpoot there are several underground passages and deep wells, and there was one of these in this woman's house. It was now obvious that the girl had thrown the older sister down there. Then the little sister said that the girl had also taken her there, but that she had said to her, "You won't throw me down the well, Toofanda, will you?" So she had said, "No" and taken her away, throwing her down in the trench instead. When the child was not killed by the fall, she threw stones down on her, possibly until the little one fainted, and she thought she was dead. The same evening that I had taken her in, two men came from the government and questioned the child and us. It is impossible to believe that a girl should kill two children of her family, just to steal a few clothes. Sin has progressed thus far. The girl was found next morning and the clothes were found with her, but of course she denied everything.

All the multitude who were brought here from various places during the deportations have been set free without clothes, food, or houses, and they came immediately to us. Where else should they go? There is no one to help them and we have only very little, so we must cut down on what we have been giving to those who have been here longer. On June 1st, two German officers came from Osmania to buy our handiwork. While they were with me the conversation turned to the missionaries in Mardin, and I said I would like very much to pay them a visit. They immediately said "Come. We will take you with us," and they promised that I would be sent back in 10 days. In half an hour it was decided that I should leave with them on Monday morning. It was then Saturday morning and I now had a busy time setting all my affairs and work in order. I went at once to Harpoot by automobile and was collected again in the evening. I packed on Saturday evening, and on Sunday I was to have gone up to the mountains with the missionaries. Unfortunately I developed a severe headache and had to spend the entire day in bed. Next morning I felt better but very tired. I nevertheless set off, though it was unfortunate that I could not enjoy the journey, as I was travel-sick all the way. How beautiful the scenery was, especially the view from the high mountains over the Mezreh plain with the many green fields, or on the other side, Lake Goljuk surrounded by magnificent mountains. When we reached the lake we stopped as I was feeling rather ill. We went down to the water where I rested for three hours, whilst the two men went shooting in the mountains. It was the first time Bessie had seen so much water, and she was delighted with the little time we spent there. When the men returned we had a meal and set off again at 3 o'clock. When we had been on the way for 1½ hours and had reached a place where the slope down to the river Tigris was most steep, we saw our accompanying lorry that had been driving ahead of us lying in the water in a thousand pieces and all our baggage spread around. There were some Turkish soldiers there, who said that they had sent the driver away, as he was very badly injured. We left our driver there to keep guard until we could send help, and Lt. Gerber drove us on. We went at high speed around the many mountain bends. I never before had driven so fast up and down the mountains, and it was a very narrow road. On one side were the high mountains, and on the other a deep slope down to the Tigris. I felt both sick and nervous, and it did not help having seen what had happened to the other vehicle. After a while we met a group of Turkish soldiers with a horse carrying a man. It was our driver who had had the accident. It was a terrible sight. He was encrusted in dried blood all over and was very weak. We put him into our automobile and drove very quickly to Arghana-Maden where he was put into hospital. Afterwards we proceeded to Osmania and on the way met three lorries and 10 men on their way to the scene of the accident. We reached Osmania at 7 o'clock that evening. I felt terribly tired and rather relieved that we could not continue our journey next day, as all my clothes lay in the river. I used the next day for resting. On Wednesday I travelled on to Mardin, accompanied by Lt. Weibel who wanted to drive the automobile himself, so I felt happy and relieved. It was a terrible journey over the high rocks, bumping up and down in the car. We did not reach Diarbekir until 7.00 in the evening. We left next morning at 4 o'clock and reached the railway Izzat Pasha at 7.30, staying there overnight. We arrived in Mardin next morning to the great surprise of the missionaries who knew nothing of my coming. We stayed there until Sunday evening and every hour was full, as we had so much to talk about. We had not seen each other in the last four years, and these four have contained as much as 20 other years. There are not many Armenians in Mardin—indeed there were not many before the massacre and the few then were killed. Little by little a small flock has gathered who had been left in one place or another after the massacre. The missionaries look after 50 children and give bread to some poor people. They have 1,000 pounds a month, so they cannot do a great deal. A great number of Syrian Christians were sent away and killed at that time. So it is obvious that the Turks wanted to kill not only the Armenians but all Christians. From the German officers' conversation I understand that they expect the Turks to attack the Germans one day, and the officers are prepared to defend themselves in any way. They also say that they know for sure that not a single Christian will survive these times in this country. It is terrible to think of, and we are horrified to contemplate going through these dreadful times again. But only God knows, and if He allows us to suffer, He will also give us strength to endure. My only prayer is that we shall be faithful to the end and always be ready to meet our Lord and Master.

We left on Monday, reaching Osmania on Tuesday evening. They had promised to take me back to Mezreh at once, but when I arrived they persuaded me to stay, which was easy for them as they said they had no car for me. So I remained [in Osmania] for eight days. I had a wonderful time resting in the Garden the whole day. One of the junior officers was an artist and came twice a day and painted Bessie. On the following Tuesday, the two men took me back to Mezreh in their own automobile. The very best experience of the whole journey was to return and be received by all my friends. They had decorated the houses with green branches and as soon as I arrived, people came streaming in to welcome me home, the missionaries, the minister and his family, and many others.

Young men are still coming here, bound hand and foot, and being put in prison. They shoot two every other day, and there are now hardly any left. Many people who up to now have been able to find a living in the villages are being brought here, where they have no possibility of earning anything.

Never before has the price of bread been so high. One oka is ten piastres, and even if one has the money, it is almost impossible to find bread on the market. We are waiting for the harvest with great expectation, as the corn looks promising. We hope, therefore, that the bread will be cheaper. We live in hope.

4 July. Yesterday a great company of German guests arrived—officers and the German Pastor Count Lütticau from Constantinople. They all left this morning for Malatia. We have also heard today that the Sultan is dead, some say murdered.

7 July. There is much talk that there is a revolution in Constantinople. Some say that Talaat Pasha and Enver Pasha have been killed. They say blood is flowing in the streets like a flood. If it is true that Enver Pasha is dead and that Izzat Pasha is Minister in his place, there might be hope for the remaining Christians in this country. Uncertainty about all this is very depressing. Everything is becoming more expensive and it is nearly impossible to find bread.

21 July. We have had a visit from Pastor Lütticau, a lovable man. He held a bible hour for the missionaries in the evening, a meeting for all workers in the congregation the next day, and in the afternoon we were all up in the mountain where we drank coffee and had our evening meal. The next day again he had a public

church service, and in the evening the congregation invited him to a garden party up in Ebenezer's garden. It was so good to listen to him, so full of the spirit, and it was as if every word came directly from our Heavenly Father to us, His suffering and sorrowful children. He won all our hearts and we would have liked to have kept him with us longer. He visited me one day in Mezreh and said he would also like to see my work in Harpoot. So he came up next day and I took him around a few of my homes so that he could see my children. He spoke to them all so charmingly.

22 July. We had a sudden visit from Lt. Gerber and Dr. Weng, who were to leave again next morning, taking Count Lütticau with them. They had lunch with Karen-Marie and their evening meal with me. Lt. Gerber told us that there was a man and a woman in Mosul who had slaughtered 50 children and sold their cooked flesh on the market, and if the Germans had not strongly demanded that an investigation be undertaken, the government would not have done it. The result was that the man and woman were hanged. Lt. Gerber also said that the Germans have sent their troops away, as it was impossible to find provisions. The British had also withdrawn further south. He said that the whole population will die of starvation in the winter as it will be impossible to find foodstuff.

The movement of soldiers is still going on and nearly all have left Mezreh and Harpoot. They are being sent over to the Van area. The officers say that they are preparing for a big offensive against the British who have united with the Persians and are coming up that way. We are happy about the soldiers leaving. Maybe foodstuffs will be a little bit cheaper and there may also be a hope that we will get some of our houses back. This will be a great pleasure, even if they are all in terrible condition, as most of the Armenian children are living in broken-down houses.

We have cut off the distribution of bread this month because I have had several cards in recent weeks from Mr. Fowler saying that he must reduce the amount of money we get from 6,000 liras to 4,000 liras a month, and he is even unable to promise this sum. Of course, it was very hard for us to receive such a message, and we had to cut off the supply of bread immediately. We give three pounds a month in paper money to all the blind, the very old who are completely alone, and the very sick. This takes about 400 liras a month in Mezreh and Harpoot. We know the result will be that many will die—but what can we do?

4 August, 1918. Karen-Marie, Bessie, and I left Mezreh to spend some weeks in Osmania. Earlier, two German sisters had been on holiday there, and because it is a little village with no Armenians, it is exactly the right place for us to have a holiday. This time we travelled in a lorry heavily laden with wheat, wooden beams, and all our luggage on top, so it could only travel very slowly. We did not reach Arghana-Maden before 4 o'clock. There is a copper works there in German hands, and while the wheat, which was for them, was being unloaded from the lorry, we went up to the officers' mess and drank tea with them. They were extremely nice and invited us

to spend a day with them on our way home. We left at 5 o'clock and did not reach Osmania before 8 o'clock. We had been expected the day before and Lt. Gerber had been out with his private car to meet us.

10 August. Lt. Weibel is back from Mosul. He is happy to be here again, saying that the heat in Mosul is terrible. They lie or sit the whole day naked and have to constantly dry themselves as sweat runs down them in streams. He also says that the Germans down there expect the British to take Mosul in December.

16 August. I went with Lt. Gerber part of the way to Mosul where he is being transferred.

17 August. Today I have been with Lt. Weibel on a visit to Arghana-Maden. We had lunch and afternoon tea there.

22 August, 1918. We had a visit from a divisional pastor from Mosul on his way to Mezreh. He held a service and communion here for the soldiers. He spoke about girding the sword of the spirit, but it was a poor sermon. He mostly talked about the Empire and Hindenburg's sword. It was obvious that there was no real spiritual life in him, and this showed up the same evening when he had a heated conversation with Karen-Marie. It was clear that he was a severe bible critic, and the next day it was my turn to try as well as I possibly could to tell him the truth.

On Saturday evening we had all the soldiers here and I played them the gramophone, which pleased them very much.

26 [August] (Monday). We should have been away today. We were packed and ready, and I was sitting in my travelling dress. The automobile came at 6 o'clock, but unfortunately Lt. Weibel has been sick for a few days with severe malaria. We had hoped that the fever would have left him by this morning to enable us to leave but we were disappointed. Today he is worse than ever and we cannot bring ourselves to leave while he is ill. So how long we must wait we do not know.

Here in Osmania there are three Armenian families who have become Turkish. Only one old man has visited us a couple of times, and on these occasions we said we wanted to visit them, but he did not agree. However, yesterday we went and found the house, a miserable cabin, nearly tumbled down. We found the old man with his wife and children. It was hard to see the fear in which they are living. When we spoke in Armenian, they literally shook with fear in case anyone might have heard us. Every time they heard a sound in the street they thought the Turks were coming for them. They said that in the past four years they have only held a service together once or twice. Their hearts were bitter. They said it was the Christians, the Germans, who had killed them. They said that God had left them, so they had denied the Saviour and become Turks. They have no joy nor peace. It was difficult to talk with them but I spoke of God's love—which is as great as ever—and about his longing to give them strength. They said, "No, it is impossible now. We must wait until after the war, when we can go away. Then we will again receive and confess our Saviour. We cannot confess Him now." Then they trembled. Poor, poor people. They had been Protestants and are now so unhappy. How much better for them if, when their faith was strong, they had been killed and gone Home.

Only those who have seen such unhappy people can know what fear and agony they are going through. "Oh Lord God, have mercy on these, your children, who sit and long for You and do not dare to stand up and go to You, because it would bring suffering to their weak bodies. Oh Lord, preserve us faithful to the end." This is my constant prayer.

28 August, 1918. I came home from our holiday in Osmania, which lasted a week longer than expected because Lt. Weibel became very ill with tropical malaria and there was no one to nurse him nor a doctor in the place. As soon as the fever was over we left and had a good journey back. It was a bigger party that returned, as Sister Helena and two men from Arghana-Maden accompanied us. I was very tired and had a bad headache so I went straight to bed.

Early next morning, I got up and packed some things and at 10 o'clock a lorry came to move my belongings up to Harpoot. It took two trips to move most of my private stores.

On Saturday all the company left for Malatia, including Mrs. Ehmann and Sister Katherina. They returned on Tuesday. On Wednesday the automobile was up twice bringing the driver, Mr. and Mrs. Ehmann, and the party from Arghana-Maden to afternoon coffee. I had set my house in order and had made it very home-like according to what my visitors said. At 6 o'clock all of us went down to Mezreh in the automobile and had our evening meal with Karen-Marie, where we had a really pleasant evening.

29 September, 1918 (Sunday). Another month has gone, filled with hope, expectation, and disappointment. All summer it has been said by everyone who knew these things, that this year's harvest would be extremely good, and that wheat would fall in price to one or two liras. This made us extremely happy, not only because bread would be easier to obtain, but because we also hoped that those who have fallen into sinful ways to obtain the means of preventing starvation would come back to the right way. We waited and waited for the price to fall but in vain. Never before has it been so high. One kilo is four liras, 20-30 piastres, and now five liras. Not only is the price high, but the wheat is impossible to obtain because the rich Aghas who have it do not need money now. They therefore bury it, bringing it up later in the season to sell for 10 liras a kilo. This creates terrible conditions, especially for someone like me, who has a family of so many hundreds and must collect enough supplies for one year. To give them soup twice a day I need 300 kilos of wheat. Up to now I have only 48 kilos and all my buying should have been finished by now. It looks as if all roads are closed and sometimes a fear for the future enters my heart,

but I will not give it room. Up to now the Lord has helped wonderfully and will continue to do so in His own way and at His own time. For Him nothing is impossible. I have been busy in the last month, moving my young girls up to Harpoot. On my return from Osmania I had the great joy of having three large buildings returned by the government which had had them for several years. Of course they were in a terrible state, but after two weeks of cleaning, I moved in my many children, who had been spread in 10 different houses. The young girls have also been moved there, because most of them are in the highest class in the College, and will take over the education of the children this year. I am looking forward to the winter as I hope that I can give more time to the children now that I am in Harpoot all the time. At the moment we cannot think of anything else but getting in supplies, preserving meat for the whole year, drying vegetables, preserving wheat, threshing wheat— altogether things we know nothing of in Denmark.

It is terrible to see the many poor people in the streets, especially the many children who are like skeletons, literally naked and dirty beyond description, full of sores and with bad eyes. They sleep in the streets at night and live off refuse that not even a dog could eat. Those who are not too weak to run steal whatever they can find. All the shops here have open fronts and there are also a great number of street sellers. The market is always full of people, so when they can move quickly, it is not difficult to grab goods and then disappear among the crowd. But most of them have gradually become too weak for this. They collect stalks from grapes which they suck. When I was in the market the other day I saw a bigger boy dragging a smaller, nearly naked boy. He held him by one arm and the whole of his bare body was dragged over the stones. I went over to see what was wrong and stopped the bigger boy. He explained that the smaller boy, who was eight or nine years old, had run away from the Turkish Children's Home, and now would not come back without force. The little boy was a typical picture of the Turkish charitable work. A little skeleton wearing only a shirt that did not even reach his hips, black and stiff with dirt. He looked as if he would die of exhaustion after screaming and struggling against the bigger boy taking him back. He had now no more strength left to talk or scream and could only whimper. He was so dirty, full of sores from scabies, and his head was full of the terrible sickness, kael. Blood was flowing from his back and legs from the injuries he had received from being thrown down and dragged along the stones. I said to the bigger boy, "Carry him back to the Children's Home, if he won't come," because after all this terrible treatment the little boy was no longer able to walk. But the bigger boy would not carry him. It demanded too much love and compassion to lift such a dirty poor little soul up in his arms and carry him home. I then gave one piastre to a man who was not much cleaner to carry him to the Children's Home. A crowd of Turkish people had gradually gathered around us and all pretended to feel sorry for the little one.

This is the condition of many children who are without parents, friends, or homes, and who are taken up by the government to be cared for. It is beyond description. I passed another one of these so-called children's homes. In a window sat a girl of about 15, also like a skeleton, so dirty that no one in Denmark has ever seen the like, nor would they be able to believe of their existence. She had unkempt hair and was crying, looking down with pleading and longing eyes on the people in the street. The glance she sent us was such a prayer for help. She had lowered a dirty rag on a piece of string, and a man tied a piece of bread in this rag, which she then pulled up.

These two examples show the fate of those children whom we are unable to look after. That is why we tremble at the thought of expensive times, which seem to get worse and worse. Most of the children here were in a similar condition when I took them in, and how changed they are now. The heart within me thumps with joy when I look at them. I thank God for every single one He has given me, and it is my prayer and complete longing to see these little ones grown into men and women who will serve the Lord.

Today Mrs. Ehmann came and asked me to take in a young woman here in Harpoot for a while. Before the deportations this young woman was a kindergarten teacher with the Germans. She was taken by a Turkish doctor and had been his wife for over two years, but he has now left her and will have nothing to do with her. Last night two Turkish officers broke into the house where she was sleeping in a room with her mother and two young sisters. They wanted to take her and they were both armed, saying that they would shoot her and themselves if she did not agree. The girl managed to knock on the floor, underneath which lived an Armenian woman, who came up to see what was wrong and got away again. This woman succeeded, after two hours, in getting a policeman to come. The girl, of course, cannot continue to live there, as the government will not punish the officers. I told Mrs. Ehmann that the Germans should take her in, as she belonged to them, but she said her husband was afraid to come into conflict with the government and would be pleased if I would take her. He seems to think I can do what he cannot. I have done this before, hidden girls who were in danger, and so far it has gone well. I promised Mrs. Ehmann that if her husband did not really dare and there was no other place, I would take her for a while until the danger was over.

4 October, 1918. It is now certain that Damascus has fallen. The news appeared in Ajans and the Turks are very depressed because their last holy city has fallen into enemy hands. They understand now that it is their end and time after time they say, "It is God's revenge. We have had no right to wipe out a people because a few were guilty."

7 October, 1918. Things are almost happening too quickly for us now. Beirut has fallen and Aleppo is being evacuated. There is much talk amongst the Turks that even Germany wishes peace. Yes, they say that the Emperor will beg Wilson for peace.

11 October, 1918. There are rumours in the last few days that the Turkish government has fallen and that Enver and Talaat Pasha have fled. Izzat Pasha has become Minister of War. If this is really true, every Christian in the country can breathe more freely.

12 October, 1918. I became ill with the "Spanish Sickness," which has appeared here in a bad form. Before I took ill, nearly all my big flock of children had it, and almost all at the same time. There were also sick people in every house and many died, especially the poor who are underfed. Most of my children made good recovery. They were ill for three days, and then the fever left them. I myself had a high temperature, 40 degrees C. all the time, and on the third day I had severe diarrhoea and vomiting, which became worse, like cholera. In the night I was so weak, my heart almost failed. Karen-Marie, fortunately, had come up that evening and gave me more brandy that night than I have ever had in my whole life before, and it helped. It was well that she came because Bessie and my two young girls were also sick and I only had help from a stranger who understood nothing. I was very ill for two weeks, neither eating nor drinking, as my stomach was very bad. I lost 26 lbs. at this time.

While I lay ill there were lots of wild rumours that the Germans would be sent away, and the Americans would be returning. Turkey wanted peace.

17 October, 1918. Peace seems uncertain again. Ajans writes that Wilson has said that because the Germans had plundered and burned cities during their withdrawal from Finland and other places, they were not serious about peace. The Germans here are furious with Wilson. Mr. Ehmann said that Germany has humiliated itself so very much, but America was arrogant and therefore God would punish America and give Germany victory. We hear that Aleppo is about to fall. People are selling everything cheaply and fleeing from there.

20 October. Everyone is coming and saying that the British, French, and Americans have come to Constantinople, and that the Turks want peace, and also Bulgaria. It has been commanded that all American houses shall be handed back within 24 hours, and they are to evacuate the American hospital.

23 October. All the Turks, even the officers, say that the American missionaries who were in Beirut are to come here, but we have had no official news. It is also said that Germany has allied with Russia and if the Turks unite with Britain, then the Germans will enter the north of the country, which will be bad for us.

26 October, 1918. Aleppo has fallen, and the British are moving forward to Aintab. Mosul also seems about to fall. The Turks have received the conditions for peace; (1) Send German military personnel out of the country, and Germans out of Constantinople tonight; (2) Absolute surrender and disarmament of all soldiers; (3) Dismissal of the earlier Cabinet; (4) Surrender of all ammunition. Hard conditions.

30 October, 1918. Aintab has fallen. The Arabs have murdered and plundered. In Diarbekir the Turks are divided—one part wants the war to continue, the other wants to surrender if the British come. It came to a fight in which many Turks were killed. The Turks have also held a meeting here, but everyone has agreed to surrender. There is nothing decided yet about peace. Everything is as expensive as ever. It was written in Ajans that all Armenians should be allowed to travel freely, something which up to now has been strictly forbidden. Also that all Armenian property should be given back. All this is only on paper and will not be implemented so easily.

31 October, 1918. Ajans announces that an armistice has been reached. America and Britain put forward 16 conditions which will be accepted by Turkey. We are very happy, and thank God for the bright prospect. Ajans also said that all German civilians would be leaving. If this is meant seriously, then all our German missionaries must go, and it will be very hard for them to leave. They have begun making preparations to be ready if the word comes.

Today all the buildings have been handed back to me. It was a great moment. It was a strange feeling to walk around in our own houses after they have been in Turkish hands for so long. Of course they were terribly dirty, the windows broken, the doors torn out, and the walls painted over, but it is an old rule that the Christians must build what the Turks pull down. Now that I have got the buildings back I can also open our school, which has been closed for 1½ years.

2 November, 1918. After a month without any automobiles two arrived bringing Mr. Christoffel and Sisters Anna and Mina. They had a very harrowing journey and were in danger of not being able to return. Now that they had reached home in safety they were happy and grateful. Outside the government building they were met by armed Turkish soldiers and the Vali who wanted to search their automobiles and were far from friendly. It must be very difficult for the Germans who at the beginning of the war were treated with so much respect and honour, now to be treated like the Turks' greatest enemies.

3 November, 1918. It has been announced today that the Dardanelles has been opened to the Allied ships sailing through to Constantinople, which is decorated with British and French flags.

5 November, 1918. When I was down in the kitchen today, baking for my birthday tomorrow, one of my girls came running to tell me that an automobile had arrived. I hurried out and to my great surprise saw that it was Lt. Gerber who had arrived with Karen-Marie. He had come from Mosul, leading a great crowd of German soldiers and officers who are on their way back to Germany. He stayed for coffee. Of course, it is difficult for him to return to his country after it has been conquered.

6 November, 1918. Lt. Gerber stayed overnight, driving the automobile into Wheeler Hall, where the driver also slept. A lot of automobiles were expected, so he had to leave early in the morning. All the German missionaries came at noon, except Mr. Ehmann, who had stayed to look after some German gentlemen who had just arrived. I had also invited Badveli Vartan and Mr. Pekmezian who are my good helpers. They all stayed for coffee. The mood was rather depressed because none of them knows if they can stay or not. By evening they all left for Mezreh, except Karen-Marie, who was staying until next day.

7 November, 1918. At noon today I left for Mezreh with Karen-Marie because a lot of automobiles were expected, but they did not arrive. I had a lot of work to do in the Shuga, so I stayed down there that day. In the evening we were invited to coffee by some of the German soldiers. At noon on Friday American effects arrived from Osmania and were brought up to Harpoot in the automobile. I went with them, and also the German Consul from Mosul, who came to my home on a visit. He was very charmed with everything up here, saying that it looked like the centre of civilization! We had a short political discussion. They are all very depressed, not knowing what to think or believe, and the Consul said things do not look well for them.

8 November, 1918. I went down with Bessie to Mezreh today, where we are to stay until Monday. These are very eventful and interesting days. A lot of automobiles come and go daily. Outside Ebenezer there is a long queue of big lorries standing overnight. They have all come from Mosul. People are streaming there to see them. There is also lively trading, as people sell their clothes and few belongings, because it is impossible for them to bring much luggage with them. The soldiers have also brought their own field-kitchen—a complete lorry. As soon as they arrive a fire is lighted, a lamb slaughtered, and very soon they have soup ready. All the soldiers are happy to be going home. They do not seem to be particularly sad that Germany has lost. Many say, "I am not a German," and others, "We will not stay in Germany after the war," but the officers, though glad that peace is near, are sad about the bad result.

8 November, 1918.[*] Yesterday 10 big lorries came from Mosul, and in one there were 10 Catholic Sisters. We thought they would have stayed here overnight, but the leader of the column wanted to go on immediately, so they only had a two hour rest. Karen-Marie invited the Sisters and the officers to coffee. They came and were very

---

[*] Fourth book of diaries starts here.—A.S.

happy and grateful. After coffee, they were able to wash themselves. They bought some knitted clothes, as they felt the cold here so much after the heat of Mosul, and because they had no suitable things to wear. They told us about their departure from Mosul. They had quite a big hospital there. One evening at 8 o'clock, a command came that they were to be ready for departure the next morning. A little later came another order that they were to be ready at midnight. They had to send all of the sick away first and had no time to bring anything with them.

The British had surrounded Mosul on three sides, and if they had not got away in the night, they would have been captured by the British. They left everything behind to the value of millions of marks in medicines, foodstuffs, and other things. The officers told us that when Nazareth was taken, the British came so suddenly that the Germans were asleep. In the morning there was a knock on the officers' door and they said, "Come in," thinking it was one of their servants. But it was the British who were there, telling them to come downstairs and surrender. They also said that in the market in Damascus, 150 German soldiers had been killed in a most cruel way by Arabs. Two Catholic Sisters had escaped from Damascus to Aleppo completely naked. The warm friendship between the Turks and Germans, which existed at the beginning of the war, has been over long ago, and instead, there is hatred in the hearts of the Turks towards the Germans. They say it is the Germans who have destroyed them and their country.

9 November, 1918. Karen-Marie and I went up to Ebenezer to greet the officers. Amongst them was the commanding officer from Mosul, Lt. Col. Riederer. I met him last summer and we were on a tour together on horseback to an old village, which is a Roman ruin. He was a very kind man and I wanted to see him. When we arrived there, we heard one automobile after the other pass, but they did not come up to us. When it was quite dark and we thought that perhaps they could not find the road, we decided that we should go down and guide them up. Outside the wall of Ebenezer there is a large open space, very suitable for the automobiles. When we came down we were received with great joy by the officers, and one returned with us to see the situation. He then went back to bring the other officers and men.

They were busy days for Sister Verena with whom all these people had their meals. This evening Lt. Col Riederer was invited to the Vali's. He told all the soldiers that the latest news from Germany would be published on Sunday morning. Of course, this caused great excitement. Just before noon the Consul visited here. I asked him if the latest news was good and he answered, "The war is finished—but we are also finished. The Socialists rule and Germany will be like Russia." He also said that he believed that we would have peace before Christmas.

10 November, 1918. This morning all the automobiles left. Never before had the population of Mezreh seen such a sight. These enormous automobiles full of soldiers on their retreat, not as victors. Each automobile bore a German flag. Everything is to be left for the Turks, even the automobiles will be given to them.

I returned to Harpoot today because I have a great deal of work. We have just opened the school and I cannot be away, otherwise I would have liked to have seen them leave.

11 November, 1918. The automobiles were called away very quickly to Osmania, the reason being that a panzer train was on its way from Aleppo to Mardin to take the Germans away. The plan was changed later when the British failed to appear.

12 November, 1918. Today 10 big lorries and a column of horses and wagons left, but in their place have come the wagons from Osmania, heavily laden with the officers' and soldiers' clothes from Arghana-Maden and Osmania. A good deal of these must be sold to make the wagons lighter.

13 November, 1918. Bessie and I have come down to Mezreh, as I would like to buy different things from the officers. Last night there was a party for more than 70 soldiers and officers, to which the missionaries were also invited. There was a strange mood the whole evening, because just before the party a telegram from the Soldiers' Council in Germany had been read out. It was pouring today, so they held a day of rest, and there is some doubt whether they will travel further. There is a rumour that the soldiers will rebel and Lt. Weibel is taking it very calmly, saying that if they do he will hand over authority and the soldiers to the Turkish government, who will intern them here. A junior officer, who has been very rough with the soldiers, has now reported sick. The manager of the mines is also very afraid, as he has treated his workers very badly, but he will not let anyone see it, and he is acting over-zealously. When the officers are with us they make fun of it all, call each other "Citizen," and say they will bring each other before the Soldiers' Council. The prospect is not bright for them. They do not expect to reach Germany, but believe they will be taken prisoner by the British. They do not think they can reach further than Sivas in the automobiles, as they have not enough petrol. From there they must go on foot. Lt. Weibel was to hold roll-call at 4 o'clock and drill the troops. The whole column is under his command, and he intended giving them a talk. If they failed to obey him, he would hand them over to the Turks. He had sworn to be faithful to the government and for the time being has no new orders to follow. Of course, we were very interested in how things would go, but he came back confident of victory.

No one had said a word.

15 November, 1918. This morning Column B left. Bessie and I stayed down until they were gone. It is a relief that they are gone, as it took too much of our time and energy for all the many visits here.

We heard today that Mr. Christoffel's niece is dead. A young girl of 22 who had come here. It must be very difficult for him.

Today we have learned from the Turkish Ajans that Kaiser Wilhelm has been to the front to try to assemble soldiers, but he has been unsuccessful and has now fled to Holland, where he will live in a nobleman's castle.

It seems as if the connection with Germany has been broken, as there has been no post for more than three weeks.

17 November, 1918. Ajans announces that Talaat Pasha and Djavid Bey, who had both escaped, have been found and imprisoned in Constantinople. The former is the chief instigator of the bloody massacre and purge of the Armenians.

It is said that 170 warships have arrived in Constantinople to take over Allied interests. The police and the post are also in the Allies' hands.

Hadji Raya, the young Kurdish chief, has fled from here in fear of punishment. Also the many Young Turks who have enriched themselves with ill-gotten gains are in fear.

19 November, 1918. The government wants me to take over all the American buildings, as well as the hospital. They sent a message, asking when I could come, so that they would send a car for me. However, since the hospital is in a very bad condition and nearly all the inventory has been stolen, I will not go back unless it is absolutely necessary.

20 November, 1918. I paid a visit today to Nuri Bey, the "Nokta" Commandant, to see if the government can help me find wheat for bread. He was very friendly and said "Yes" immediately. He gave me 200 grams daily for each child, in all 972, and asked me why I had not come before. It is something new to see the government so kind and obliging when it concerns the Armenians, and this is a big encouragement. I cannot thank the Lord enough for this great help. The wheat, which this year is more expensive than ever, is very difficult to obtain, so my joy is great. I am to get 20 kilos this time, for which I shall pay 6¼ banknotes a kilo. On the market I would have to pay 500 piastres, which is 25 banknotes a kilo.

Some of the town's Syrian grocers and two Armenian bankers have united to collect money so that they can take care of some of the Armenian children who live in the streets night and day. The government has also promised them help. I hope it lasts, but we are happy about what we have got. It is always a help.

We hear that Mosul has been taken back from the British. We thought that the armistice had brought peace, so we do not understand how this could have happened.

Ajans has said that Turks living in Armenian houses must move out in 24 hours, and the houses, fields, and property given back to the Armenians. This is only on paper, in reality it will go slowly and with great difficulty.

28 November, 1918. We have celebrated Thanksgiving Day today. Karen-Marie and Hope came up to spend the day with us. We had given the school a holiday, and in the morning I gave my large group of children pilaff, to their great delight. We had a meeting at 10 o'clock for all the children, their teachers and mayrigs. The Badveli spoke about the different reasons we had to be grateful—and they are not so few. He spoke very well to the children and they were all interested. After the meeting we spent an hour playing together. At the end I stood by the door with two big bags of walnuts, giving 10 to each child. It was such a great joy to see all these children, whom we had taken off the streets in a most pitiful condition of spirit, body, and soul, now so changed. Even for me, who takes care of them, it is nearly impossible to believe that they are the same children.

At 2 o'clock in the afternoon we had dinner—soup, roast, pie, and fruit. I thought a lot about my friends who are now at home among family and friends in America, and also about the many blessed days we had together in earlier years.

29 November, 1918. I went down to Mezreh today, as I had much to do. Tonight I had a long meeting with the German missionaries. The reason for this was that a terrible letter, full of accusations against me and wanting to take over my position, had come from one of our former Professors, the only one who has survived these terrible years. He is living a very bad life, and I have therefore not shared any work with him. He is very angry with me and our Armenian Minister.

I am longing very much for the return of the Americans. It is so difficult to be alone with this great work. The only thing I am afraid of is that Mr. Ehmann, out of fear, will give in to this man and let him have some of the work. On this point Mr. Ehmann is very weak and afraid of what people will say, therefore he will be friends with everyone, even those who would harm the work for God's Kingdom.

20 [sic, 30] November, 1918. I have been down to pay a friendly call on the Commandant's wife, accompanied by Karen-Marie. She gave us a very friendly reception. The Commandant also came in and sat, talking with us about world conditions. He said, "Our country will also become a democracy." He assured us that all roads will be open by the spring, so that people can travel. He is an old friend of the Americans and came to dinner several times before they left. When they went, he sent telegrams to different towns, which meant that they had friendly official receptions and accommodation arranged for them everywhere. It is also well for me to have him here. He can very often help me when I have dealings with the government.

After our visit I went to the bank to see the manager about 30 children they have sent me. They had promised to pay for them, but he now said that they could not. However, he asked me to keep them because I had received help from the government and he had assisted me in this.

3 December, 1918. There is talk of a revolution in Constantinople and that the British have thrown the Germans out. They have got Caesarea Vilayet to live in.

8 December, 1918. It is stated in Ajans that all harbours have been closed by the British. We think that the many German soldiers who passed through here must now remain in the country, maybe even as prisoners.

Censorship is cancelled. Armenian newspapers are also coming here full of reports of the murders from the time of the deportation and massacres.

In one newspaper, there was a terrible accusation against Mr. Ehmann. It hurt us very much because we all know how he worked day and night to save as many as possible. The woman who wrote this was herself helped by Mr. Ehmann during the deportations and this is now his reward. I myself am accused by two of our own men and the only surviving teachers because they have no work. I could not take them in because of their immoral lives and they are furious. The Professor has written a letter full of terrible accusations. I brought it to our meeting and asked for it to be investigated and an answer sent on behalf of the meeting demanding the Professor makes a written retraction. This has been done but he has not yet answered. He and the other teacher are going around spreading evil stories about me and promising money to the young girls to gain their friendship. We are living in terrible times. Lies and injustice rage and rule, and it seems hopeless trying to do anything for these people.

15 December, 1918 (Sunday). When we returned from church this morning, a boy arrived from Mezreh with a letter from Mr. Ehmann telling me that he had been informed by the Vali that all Germans were to leave the country. This came as a terrible blow. Up to now nothing had been said about the missionaries and we had hoped they could stay. How terrible to leave in this deep snow, severe frost, and in the middle of the winter, and what will become of their children and workers? I wish the Americans would come soon.

16 December, 1918. A telegram has come from the Swedish Consul saying he is unable to help the German missionaries beyond having their departure delayed for two months. This is a great relief because we hope that the weather will be a little better and perhaps the Americans will be here by that time. Much can happen in two months. Sister Verena is to leave with them as they all think she could not bear to remain alone. This will mean that Karen-Marie and I will be the only Europeans left here.

27 December, 1918. Now Christmas is over again. We had a pretty nice Christmas, though we did not receive a single card, letter, or Christmas magazine from home, nor could Karen-Marie and I spend it together as in previous years.

In the days before Christmas I was terribly busy. Making Christmas preparations for 900 people is not easy when one must do everything oneself. I stayed up every night until after midnight and was up again at 5 o'clock in the morning. We had a party for all the children on Christmas day. In the morning they got their favourite dish, pilaff, and at 11 o'clock started to collect in Wheeler Hall, which was decorated and had a big Christmas tree in the middle of the room. This was full of gifts—balls, pictures, caps, and scarves—and underneath was a big pile of mulberries, walnuts, raisins, and leblebi. First the children sang and then the Badveli spoke. Then the children stepped forward and recited pieces about Christmas which they had learned by heart. It was a great joy to see these children, now so sweet and clean, healthy and full of life and happiness. What a change from when they were taken in. To see this is reward enough for all the trouble and work of these two years alone. Karen-Marie and Hope came up to the party, and in the evening we had our Christmas food—rice-pudding, chicken, potatoes, and cabbage. After this we lighted the candles on the Christmas tree, and what a pleasure it was to see the joy of the two little ones over the gifts they received. I was busy next day making preparations for the College Girls' Christmas party, which was to take place in the evening. Karen-Marie helped me. They were not given big gifts—a pencil each, some paper to make a notebook, and a handkerchief. I would have liked to have given a handkerchief to every child, but this alone would have cost 40 liras in gold. Because we receive our money in banknotes, it would have cost 240 liras for handkerchiefs of the poorest white material that we would not even have looked at in earlier days. Both parties were nice. Father Christmas was a great success, coming on both occasions to hand out gifts!

I have already experienced the truth of what I learned as a child from Pastor Jespersen in preparation for my confirmation that "when I tried to find joy for myself, it eluded me. But when I tried giving joy to others, it was brought to me, also, on angels' wings."

I have been so happy this Christmas—yes, these last two years, when one would think I would have felt sad and alone. But living to help others fills one with joy and strength from on High, which nothing or no one can take from us. So in spite of loneliness, expensive times, and poverty, Christmas 1918 was a really blessed Christmas.

29 December, 1918. I came down here to Mezreh to spend the last day of the year with Karen-Marie. I am very tired and need a couple of quiet days after the busy time. It is impossible to have them in Harpoot. I must also attend several meetings here, and tomorrow, Monday, I must balance my books. I am returning to Harpoot on Wednesday morning, as I must be home to receive New Year's visitors. It is an old custom, that the American missionaries hold "open house" that day, so I must also do it.

31 December, 1918. The last day of this year, which has, in a way, passed extremely quickly. When I look back, it is with a heart full of thanks to God for His great mercy towards me. It is only by this that I have come through it. The heavy work, the many burdens, and the great responsibility were much more than I could have borne alone. But I have not been alone. "My strength shall be complete in your weakness," and this I have experienced. He shall have all the glory for what I was allowed to accomplish. This has been a year of hope, and now and then a ray of light came from afar to bring it into our hearts. Our hopes were not disappointed, and when I look forward, it is in the full assurance that a brighter time is near. When I now leave this year, it is with the prayer that God himself will close the door, and forgive all my sins, all that was wrong, all that was left undone, and that He will bless all those who can be blessed.

1 January, 1919. Then take my hands and lead me on. I cannot take the smallest step, but where you lead I can walk freely. This is my prayer at the entrance to the New Year. When I know that my Heavenly Father is leading, and my hand is in His, then I go forward in confidence to meet whatever may come to me. I spent last evening at Sister Verena's along with all the German missionaries.

Today I have held "open house," which was an old custom with the American missionaries on New Year's Day. I returned from visiting Mezreh this morning, and immediately people literally streamed in. My room was completely filled until the evening. Even though each guest stayed only a few minutes, sometimes they had to sit on the floor, as there was no room for more chairs. Bishops and priests came, rich and poor. Turks and Christians. It was a rather nice but also very tiring day. There used to be more of us, but now I have to receive the guests myself.

7 January, 1919. The post has arrived here, bringing old letters and newspapers. The latter report that American missionaries have left their own country and are on their way here. Oh, I wonder if it is true? It makes hope grow in many hearts that had almost given up due to the high cost of living. A notice has been put up in the Market, saying that all Armenian women who are married to, or living with, Turks, are free to leave. Now is the time of deliverance for many a poor woman who has been bound these last four terrible years. God be praised! But in what condition will they be? Most of them will have children, others will have their health destroyed, and how will they live? Young, miserable women, who have run away from or been sent away by the Turks, come to me daily and ask me to take them in. But I cannot go on doing this, as I have not enough supplies. Unfortunately this new command is not being obeyed by many Turks, who are furious about it, and forbid their Armenian wives to go, saying they would rather kill them than let them leave. There are also Armenian women who do not want to leave their Turkish husbands and beg them to keep them. This is unbelievable.

12 January, 1919. Several people came and said that a large post had arrived from America. Unfortunately it turned out to be our own letters that we had sent out in 1917, and we were greatly disappointed.

13 January, 1919. A telegram has come saying the American missionaries are leaving New York tomorrow.

14 January, 1919. It is almost too great a joy for me. I had hoped so much during the last months, and prayed about it daily, but to have sudden evidence of its reality is something different.

Oh, how I am looking forward, and thank God I will be allowed, to see the day I can hand over to them my big flock of children. There is great joy among the population who once again are beginning to hope and starting to live. What strange creatures we are. In the last four years, most only wished to die, and now suddenly everyone rejoices in the joy of living.

18 January, 1919. Like all other weeks, this one has been especially busy. Now that I know the missionaries are coming soon, I must have the house in good order, and there is a lot to do. Besides all the daily work, I must move things around, and after that, have all the rooms whitened. Then they must be cleaned and furnished. As most of the furniture is in Mezreh, I must work day and night to have everything finished before they come.

Today I had a letter from Constantinople saying that a Red Cross unit is on the way and will also be coming here, so we must be prepared to receive them.

1 February, 1919. I have received a letter from Constantinople saying that Dr. Parmelee and all the missionaries whose health allowed them, together with 100 or 150 other workers, are on their way from America. Dr. Parmelee asked that a special message should be sent to me about her coming. Of course, my joy is great.

3 February, 1919 (Monday). Sisters Mina and Klara have come on a visit for a couple of days. Karen-Marie and Hope also came on Saturday. It has been lovely to have them, making me realize how lonely is my daily life.

4 February. A telegram came from Constantinople to say that Dr. Parmelee and her colleagues have arrived there and are awaiting the first opportunity to travel on to here. It was a great joy, but also a disappointment, as I had expected more missionaries, but maybe they will come on later. I don't think anyone realizes how much work there is to be done here, or else I think more would come.

One of the German sisters has received a letter from Mrs. Winkel, who was with the big company of soldiers that passed through here from Mosul to Samsoun. She said that when they got near Samsoun they were attacked by a mob of bandits but managed to get away. Just after them came a big column of automobiles, which was also attacked, one soldier being killed, one officer severely wounded, and a captain slightly wounded. Three officers in one automobile were robbed of everything. They had had a very trying journey. The "Spanish Sickness" raged amongst them, and 20 young men died on the road. Poor young men. They left here so full of hope about being in Germany with their families for Christmas. On January 12th a steamer left for Constantinople with the Germans, where they think they will be interned until peace comes. All the sick had to be left behind—37 in all. The Turks say that in Adana Armenians who have arrived from America have killed 3,000 Turks. We do not know if this is true or not. If it is true, it is terrible, but the Armenians are very shortsighted and rash.

Karen-Marie and I have had letters from Mrs. Lange—the first Danish letters in five years—and they contained the happy news that southern Jutland has been returned to Denmark. It came as a big surprise, having heard nothing about it earlier, even though we both had hoped it would happen now that Germany has lost the war. We can well imagine the joy at home.

God be praised and thanked. The glory is His. How good God has been to our fatherland in these heavy years, and now in answer to many years of prayer, has given our beloved country back to us without war.

Mrs. Lange also said that they are now seriously thinking about getting us home. Mrs. Grynhagen and Sister Hansine are preparing themselves to come out here again.

6 February, 1919. Mr. Christoffel has sent a telegram saying he will be leaving Malatia in three days, and he has asked Karen-Marie to come and take over the work. This is completely impossible, as she has our Danish Children's Home here, and there is no one to take over. It has been decided that she and Baron Garabed should go to Malatia to see what can be done, and, if possible, to bring the most promising children here. I will then bring them up to me in Harpoot.

9 February. I came down to Mezreh yesterday on the occasion of Karen-Marie's birthday. All the Germans came to afternoon coffee. I am staying for a couple of days, as I must send up to Harpoot all the missionaries' private possessions, which I had sent down here last year when it was feared that the Turks would confiscate all American belongings.

10 February (Monday). Karen-Marie left this morning for Malatia.

13 February (Thursday). We have returned today from Mezreh in an awful storm, with Hope in front of me, and Bessie behind me on the horse. It was quite a job.

I have received a telegram from Mr. Riggs stating that he reached Constantinople on the 12th and will soon be leaving for Harpoot.

Oh, God be praised! I have also received a telegram from the Danish envoy saying that the Foreign Minister had enquired about Karen-Marie and me.

I now have a very busy time putting everything in order for my friends' return, but the expectation of seeing them again soon makes it easier.

20 February. Karen-Marie is back from Malatia. Her journey there had not been necessary, as everything had been managed satisfactorily. Mr. Christoffel had left with 11 Armenians, without taking leave of the government. He had left behind his possessions in several sealed rooms. A number of children and women were left living in the house, and he had given them provisions for a couple of months. They were all very depressed and disheartened, but Karen-Marie had some meetings with them and had tried to cheer them up, so her journey had not been in vain.

1 March. I received a telegram from Mr. Riggs asking if there was any particular reason why he should leave his travelling companions to come here a couple of days earlier. They expect to be here around the 20th. I only know that Dr. Barton is in the company, but I think there are more. I am happy to know something definite, and I will now continue with the preparations. There is much to be done.

I have attended a meeting to decide about the Germans' work after their departure. Most of it has been handed over into the hands of the Armenians. Sister Verena and Karen-Marie are to supervise. Twice a week both of them will see to the two girls' Children's Homes. Sister Verena will be in charge of the boys' Children's Home, and the school will be looked after by the Armenians.

A very strict order has come to the government that all Turks are to send away all children and young Armenians up to the age of 17, and in recent days we have been besieged by children and young girls and boys. In Mezreh, a home has been opened for such young girls, and Karen-Marie is in charge. Fifty have come so far, without any belongings, and are admitted to an empty house. All they get are two small loaves of bread each, but in spite of this, they are glad to be free and live in the hope that help will soon reach them and brighter times are to come.

I have also opened a woollens workshop for such girls who come. Apart from giving them bread I am unable to do anything further. I have also opened a home for young men who come to me for help. Up to now they have been living among the Kurds but are now running away. These young men have suffered greatly and are happy and thankful for the little we can give them. Everyone must work, as I am against giving help to those who are able to work. However, it is often hard to find work for so many people, but it must be done.

Quite a number of men who have been soldiers have also been set free and have returned in a very sickly condition, hardly able to walk. They also come to me, asking for help for themselves and their families. Everybody comes to me. They do not just ask for help, but demand it. It almost drives me mad sometimes. From morning till evening there is a crowd outside my door. As soon as the door opens, they all shout at once. So it is impossible to speak to one of them. I am besieged by the poor people in the streets, in the church, and in the house. I am longing for the Red Cross to come. I hope workers will also come to take a share of the burden.

9 March. The other day a woman came from the town and asked to speak to me. She had been sent by the women in Harpoot to tell me that all Turks are in a state of agitation recently, holding meetings and making plans, saying they will put an end to the Christians, before the Americans and British come. They wanted me to try, one way or another, to send a message to Constantinople. This is impossible as it would be very dangerous if the Turks found out. A lot of very imprudent things are being written in the newspapers about the Armenians' independence and so on. This infuriates the Turks who now understand that their country has lost, and they do not want to give up the Armenians whom they took at the time of the massacre and have used as slaves. This puts an end to their comfort, when they have no man or maid servants. All this makes them angry and their hatred flares up. The future again looks dark and threatening. People in Constantinople and the port towns, who are under British protection, forget that we are in the inner part of the country, far away from the railway and help, and anything might happen before help could reach us.

We have heard that Mr. Christoffel is in prison at Sivas. The government here is doing all that it can to send the Germans away as quickly as possible, and I had to send telegrams to different places to have permission to allow them to remain. It sounds incredible that a Danish woman missionary must work to get German missionaries out of prison, and so on.

Karen-Marie, Bessie, and I were invited for dinner at Commandant Vehib Bey's last Friday. He has always been especially kind to the Americans. He has a lovely young wife, who does not look Turkish, and she is also very kind. We spent the whole afternoon with them and they would not let us leave until 5.30 p.m.

Rumours are circulating that Mr. Riggs is returning to investigate the condition of the Armenians. This has also appeared in the Turkish newspapers, and the Turks, who so far have been looking forward to his arrival with pleasure and expectation, are very infuriated, and it is said that plans are being made to attack him. We have heard this from different sides. For many years here in Harpoot, we have had a very dangerous enemy, both as regards our work and the Armenians. During recent years he has been a member of the Parliament, and when he left for Constantinople last autumn, he was captured by the British and has now died in prison. Recently he said, "It is obvious that my end is near, and I cannot escape the Great Judgement, but one thing I will try to fulfil—to take Mr. Riggs's life." He is supposed to have sent a message to one of the worst and most clever of robbers here, Hadji Raya. It has been said for a long time that he is gathering Kurds together to attack the missionaries when they arrive.

All this fills me, and all of us, with anxiety. Tomorrow I will have to go down to Mezreh to see what can be done. Maybe I will go to Vehib Bey and discuss it with him. We cannot send letters or telegrams, as it is dangerous. If there is real danger, something has to be done quickly, as they are already on the way and expected in 10 days. Maybe I will have to go out to meet them. At least I can stop them in Diarbekir or even reach Mardin before them. It mars the pleasure. I had so much to do before they arrived, which I will have to give up, if I am to go. This is an insecure country. We are always surrounded by danger and uncertainty, but with God's eternal arms under, over, and around us, nothing can happen to us without His will. We rest in this, and it is our strength.

10 March (Monday). Today I went down to Mezreh to discuss the rather threatening situation with the leading men. Everyone is talking here about the planned attack by these dangerous robbers against Mr. Riggs. This afternoon I spoke to Mr. Pekmezian, who is also anxious. We decided to go and see the Commandant and talk to him, and set-off at 5 o'clock. I told him what I had heard every day for more than a week. He said it could not possibly happen, as the government had strict orders to honour all who came and to protect them. I said I did not fear the government, but these robbers who are planning without the government's knowledge. I also told him that I had considered travelling out to meet and warn them. However, he said he would telegraph Mardin and order both the military and civil government to give help and protection, and also to let Mr. Riggs know of the plot against him. The Commandant told us that a very important member of the Young Turks was with him in the afternoon and had told him that they were collecting men to defend themselves when the British came. So the rumours are not without substance. This Commandant has always been a good friend of the Americans, so I am sure he will do what he can. Besides this, he is also afraid for his own life, because he will be held responsible for what happens here.

I am now happy and more calm, and I am glad that I do not have to leave, as it would have been very difficult, and who knows if I could have reached there before they left.

11 March (Tuesday). Our Police Commissioner came to visit me today. He is also an old friend of the Americans, and especially of Mr. Riggs. I told him also of my fears and misgivings. He also said that these men can do nothing but are like mad dogs, because they know they are condemned.

15 March (Saturday). Today I had a telegram from Constantinople saying that Miss Riggs, and more new workers, also Dr. Parmelee, are there, and will soon be leaving for Harpoot. Thank God that workers and help are coming. I am especially glad that Miss Riggs is coming.

16 March (Sunday). Mr. Ehmann has received a message from the government, that they are all to leave on Friday, March 21st. We still hope that Mr. Riggs will come before they go, because they would like to hear about the road and the conditions. I have now taken over all work and funds. Mr. Ehmann has also given me their important papers and belongings to take care of.

23 March (Sunday). It has been a busy week. I have been in Mezreh nearly every day, transacting business with Mr. Ehmann. Added to this I have made the last and most necessary preparations for our friends' arrival. The other day I had a letter from Dr. Barton in Constantinople, which said he was coming here with others, and they will bring 50 hospitals, each with 100 beds. A doctor and two nurses will come for each hospital, many new workers, and our old missionaries. I am looking forward so much.

I just received a letter from Mr. Riggs in Constantinople saying he will come as soon as possible. He has been delayed by having to go to a harbour in the Marmara Sea, where the ship was being unloaded. It is good to hear from him and to know he is coming.

Now our German friends have gone. They left at noon on Friday, in clear weather, but cold with a strong wind blowing. A lot of people assembled to bid them farewell. At one stage, when the room was full of people, someone came and said that Mr. Riggs had arrived, and we all ran out. There was a terrible crowd, but it was not true, and we were all disappointed. There had been a moment when the sorrow that the Germans were leaving had been forgotten at the thought of Mr. Riggs's arrival. Up to now Mr. Riggs and party have not arrived. I do not know where they are, and I am expecting them every day.

16 March (Sunday evening). I have received letters from some of my friends telling me the sad news that my precious and beloved Miss Blædel has gone to her Heavenly Home on January 9th, after only a couple of days of illness. This is a hard blow, almost harder than I can bear. How empty my life will be without her letters, without her love, and intercession. How blessed it has been to know her—my beloved little mother at home, who always carried us in her heart, and loved us as her children. The first thing I did, when the post came, was to see if there was a letter from Miss Blædel. How loving and understanding she always was. Words cannot express what she has been to me. How often I have trembled at the thought of the bad winter and the bad sickness at home, and have had fears and misgivings, but each time we had word from home, with nothing special being said about our precious friend, and I rejoiced that we still had her with us. How I have looked forward, as soon as conditions allowed it, to come home, and see, and be with her, to love her, hug her, do something for her, and tell her everything. Now that she is not there any more how empty it will be without her. How difficult it is, that we have not been able to write to her, which I would have liked so much to do. We have not

been able to write much these last years, and I suppose she only got a few of my weekly cards and letters. How I would have liked to have made her happy here on earth. But I know I am selfish, and I should be happy to know that she is Home with God, and today I feel that. We will not wish her back. She has heard the blessed words from our precious Saviour, "Enter thou into the joy of thy Lord, Thou hast been faithful over a few things. I will make thee ruler over many things." She has now seen and talked with Him whom we love, face to face. The veil has been lifted and everything has been made new. Now she will no longer suffer in her weak body. The tears are now wiped away, and there is only light, joy, peace, and love, and God's glory for her forever. Oh, God be praised. "Oh, thank you, dear Lord Jesus that you have conquered death and Satan, and you want those who love You to be where You are, that they may see Your glory." May my beloved little mother's death help me still to look upward and set my longing and aspiration upon the Heavenly. So I must live every day as if it were my last, and always be prepared to meet my Saviour. May my life always be, to the end, what she would have wished it to be.

I have in the last year called her "Mother" and that is what she truly has been. A faithful, precious mother. Blessed be your precious memory. "Oh God, my Father, preserve me faithful to the end that I may partake of Your Glory and meet You and Yours."

21 April, 1919. It is Easter Monday and so much has happened in the last weeks. It is impossible now to remember everything, but I will briefly write down the most important.

Several weeks passed without my hearing anything definite from Mr. Riggs and his party, which we expected. On March 28th I received a telegram from Ourfa from Mr. Jacob, saying, Mr. Riggs and party had reached there on the 27th. Then I began to expect them and had everything ready to receive them, but one day followed another without their arrival. At last on April 10th at 3 o'clock in the afternoon I got a telegram. The latter had taken two days to arrive, so I knew they could come at any time. It was well that I had everything finished. I went over and told my young girls about it, and asked them to practise the different hymns. Karen-Marie came up at 6 o'clock, saying that they expected Mr. Riggs that night, as the authorities had received a telegram saying that the party had left Arghana Maden at 3 o'clock that afternoon. Now we were completely certain, and everyone was wild with joy. There were a few last minute things to do before they came, and by the time I had finished them, they had still not arrived. It was pouring with rain, and completely dark, and I could not imagine how they would reach up here if they came. We waited until 10 o'clock, by which time we thought it would be impossible for them to come, so we started to prepare for bed. As I turned off the lamp, I heard loud knocking at the gate, and a man asking for me, saying he must see me personally, as he had brought a letter from Mr. Riggs. It was not long before I had it in my hands and was reading it.

Mr. Riggs said it was impossible for them to come up to Harpoot in the dark and through the deep mud. We dressed immediately and rode down to Mezreh on our donkeys in the darkness and rain, reaching Emaus at midnight. It was nice that we had him safely here without danger. We went to bed at 1 o'clock, but no one was asleep as the joy was too overwhelming. This can only be understood by someone who has held a lonely position with heavy burdens and great responsibility. Before 6 o'clock in the morning, people were already starting to stream here to meet Mr. Riggs, and we could hardly get him freed at 7.30. He had to say, "I can't see you now. I must leave for Harpoot." Then he got out of the automobile and we sped away to Harpoot where all my large family was eagerly waiting. When we arrived at the house the bells started to ring, and my boys burst into a song, which had been specially composed for them, as we got out of the automobile. Then one of my small girls, dressed in white, stepped forward and bade our guests welcome, presenting each with a bouquet of flowers. After that the children began to sing another song, and when we reached the door, the girls from the College sang, "Crown Him! Crown Him! King of Heaven's Son." Everywhere was beautifully decorated and the big crowd of children filled every empty space. There was no doubt about the joy. Some of them cried, some of them laughed, and Mr. Riggs was embraced by our Minister and several others. As soon as we had finished lunch people began to pour in, and the room was crowded with guests all day.

On Saturday afternoon I had invited all the College graduates to come and meet Mr. Riggs. I had decorated the College Hall, and it was rather nice. Everybody came, except two, and we were altogether about 70 people. First Badveli Yeghoian bade everyone welcome, and then he read passages from the bible and offered a prayer. Some hymns were sung, which were especially suitable and lovely:

The cross it standeth fast—Halleluya!

The wind of hell hath blown.

The world it's hate hath shown.

Yet it's not overthrown.

Halleluya for the cross!

Mr. Riggs spoke, and told us of the Armenians in America, which filled us all with joy. Then there was an opportunity to ask questions, which Mr. Riggs answered. It was a lovely afternoon to which we will all look back with pleasure. Sunday, Mr. Riggs must again receive visitors. The Vali and a lot of other government officials came. On Monday we had a party with all our children. It was the most beautiful of all. The hall was completely full of children. I had made uniforms for 36 of my best boys, who were lined up on each side of the entrance, and when Mr. Riggs and Mr. Wroman arrived, the children clapped their hands. Then all our small "soldiers" began to sing their song. Mr. Riggs gave a talk, our senior woman teacher read a lovely essay, another woman teacher read a beautiful poem. The children and young people sang several hymns, and Bessie sang a "welcome" song. She looked sweet, standing there singing:

A welcome, oh a welcome, a welcome be to you.

A welcome, oh a welcome to all, both warm and true.

Love has brought you to this place,

Love is shining in your face.

A welcome, oh a welcome, a welcome be to you.

A welcome, oh a welcome to all, both warm and true,

May your life be sweet and true

May His kind face rest on you

Each day we have been invited out for dinner and we have made more promises to come to other places. Yesterday was Easter Sunday, and it was truly a blessed Easter. We felt as never before that life has won over death, justice over injustice, truth over lies, and good over evil. Praise and thanks to God were sung from the heart. The few churches that are left have been handed back, and even though they have been stripped of everything, doors and windows taken away, and the walls falling down in many places, they were completely full of people. We have no church bells here in Harpoot, but they have one in Mezreh, where the church was opened for the first time. When the Armenian Sharagan was sung the tears rolled down everyone's cheeks. There were five services in the day, and each time there was a "full house." Oh, thank God for Easter, that brought us life!

Today Mr. Riggs and Mr. Wroman have gone out to some villages to investigate conditions there. I expect them home tonight. I have just received a message that three gentlemen arrived in Mardin on Saturday, so I expect them here tomorrow or Wednesday. I am making preparations again today, as we must give them a "welcome" party when they arrive.

Some busy weeks have now followed. Many Armenians came daily to see Mr. Riggs, and hear about their relatives in America, and what their future possibilities were. We are invited out every day by Armenians and Syrians for meals. People started streaming in from the villages, and every day I was taking in children, young women and men, who up to now have been living like slaves in Turkish houses. We intend visiting the villages several times a week to investigate and see what we can do. In the three weeks since Mr. Riggs's arrival, loans have been made of hundreds of liras to young Armenian men, so they can buy oxen and commence farming. We have also bought tools to enable other young men begin handiwork, or we give them money to rent shops, and we hope that in a year or two most of these young men will be self-supporting. Yes, even be in a position to give work to many others.

3 May (Saturday). I have today received a telegram saying that Dr. Barton and several other gentlemen will be here tonight. Mr. Riggs, Mr. Wroman, the Vali and the Commandant have gone out in an automobile to meet them.

4th May (Sunday). We had the table laid for dinner and decked with flowers. We had "killed the fatted calf" and the food was ready. The doors and gates were decorated with greenery, and the children all assembled to greet the arrivals at 6 o'clock—and nobody came! We waited and waited, looking out over the plain, but there was nothing to see, so I knew they would not come before morning, and we went to bed. At 2.30 a.m. I was awakened. A man had brought a telegram from the party, saying they were spending the night in Kezin Khan and would arrive here next morning. I arose early next day to have everything ready at 7 o'clock. We had another wait, like yesterday, until around 9.00, when we saw the automobile approaching Mezreh, so it was another hour before they came. Finally only one automobile arrived with Mr. Riggs and Dr. Barton. They had gone directly to the church in Mezreh where Dr. Barton had preached. The rest of the party would not arrive until about noon. Dr. Barton was received with song from my large flock of children, who all beamed with joy. Dr. Barton is an elderly, very imposing man, with a happy, loving, and very attractive face. He reveals in his attitude and demeanour that he is a man of dignity and influence. He was very happy with his reception and regretted that the other gentlemen were not with him, as he would have liked them to have seen the children and have heard their songs. So I said the children would assemble again when the others came. The other automobile arrived at 12.30 with four gentlemen. Dr. Dodd, the missionary from Caesarea who has lived there for 30 years; Dr. Bartlett D.D, sent by the Sunday Schools' Organisation in Canada to travel through the country, to take pictures and stories of children's lives and suffering; two young men, Mr. Fornsworth who is also travelling through, and Mr. Means, who is to stay here and take over the work of the different industries. The children also gave all these a welcome in song. It was especially solemn when the young college girls started to sing, "All hail the power of Jesus' name," and everyone, including the guests, joined in heartily.

After they had time to wash and change, we had dinner. It was a solemn meal with these, our best friends, after two years of loneliness during which we had not heard from them. We then had a service in the church at which Dr. Barton preached. He said that the American people had suffered with, and were ready to do all that they could for, the Armenian people. He said the dark time had now come to an end and brighter times would come, but if the Armenians were to be a strong people, they must set their belief in God, who alone can make them so. They must follow God and do His will. The church was completely full, even the windows and entrance, and I think that the hope of better times, which had been extinguished in most hearts, began to rise again.

At 4 o'clock I had a meeting for all my children to which I invited all the guests. Dr. Barton, unfortunately, could not come, but the others came and Dr. Bartlett spoke to the children. One could see, as he stood up on the platform, that he was a great friend of children. He said that he had been sent by the children of Canada to see the children here and to tell them that those in Canada loved them and were working to help them. Then he sang "Jesus loves me" in English and the children sang the chorus in Armenian. After the meeting I took all the children out to the playground, where Dr. Bartlett took pictures of them.

6 May. This afternoon we had a "Hantess" welcome meeting for our guests in Wheeler Hall. All the Americans were there. The Hall was nearly full of people, women and children, and the few men who had been allowed to live.

Mr. Riggs introduced the others to the meeting, and Dr. Barton, Dr. Bartlett, and Dr. Dodd spoke. Our Badveli translated and also spoke briefly but very well in English to our guests. British and Armenian hymns and songs were sung. It was an extremely nice occasion and everyone was very happy and thankful for it.

This morning Dr. Barton, Dr. Dodd, and Mr. Riggs paid another visit to the Vali. The first occasion had been an official visit, but this time it was to express their feelings with regard to the Armenians. They said they would hold him personally responsible for seeing that the Armenians were treated with justice and their property given back. They said, "We cannot hold you responsible if a Turk kills an Armenian, but you will be responsible for seeing that such a Turk is caught and punished. You are not responsible for what happened four years ago, but for what happens now." The Vali is two persons, one is friendly and polite to foreigners, the other hates foreigners and Christians. But he has now been given a clear message. Dr. Barton said afterwards, "I talked to him like a father."

7 May. Our guests left this morning. Mr. Riggs and Karen-Marie were to accompany them as far as Malatia. They wanted me to go with them, but I was so tired after the very exhausting days, when I had so much to see to and do in the house without any efficient help in the kitchen. I had to arrange rooms for the guests, with all the necessary washing and cleaning, and then there were all the different functions to arrange and supervise. From morning till evening many visitors had come, and every day the hundreds of poor came for help. On Tuesday morning I had taken in 63 new children. I had also to take the guests around, show them the work of the last two years, and tell them its history. Every minute there were a hundred things I should do.

They were all very surprised to see how much work I had. They had not known how great it was. They voiced their thanks and pleasure many times, and it did my heart good. But God alone shall have the glory.

There have been some blessed days and I will always remember them with happiness. I am so glad that I have learned to know these people personally. They said they had not seen such great work in other places, and they promised to send as much help as is needed. Time after time Dr. Barton said, "You must have help at once, and then you must go away at once, for a long and good rest."

9 May. Mr. Riggs returned suddenly this afternoon. I had not expected him so soon. They had had a good journey, being received by Turkish government officials as soon as they neared Malatia. The Mutasarrif [of Malatia] was very friendly towards them. He had only been there two weeks, and said he could not do as much as he would like to, as the Vali in Mezreh, who is his superior, is a Young Turk, and he said, all who are sitting in the government are murderers. He himself is a Kurd, and is full of hopes about an independent Kurdish control. He is no friend of the Turks, but he must be very careful. Karen-Marie enjoyed the trip very much.

10 May. I have handed over the industries section to Mr. Means—the woollen work, weaving etc. This is a great relief, as it took a couple of hours every morning. Of course I must help him a bit at the beginning—explain, give advice, etc.—but the responsibility is not upon me any more. The money situation is very bad, and complicated. At the moment paper, gold, silver, and nickel is being used, and the value changes every day. Suddenly today we hear that nickel cannot be used any more, and another day we hear the same about silver. There is terrible chaos, and it is very difficult work to keep accounts.

14 May, 1919. Sister Verena, Karen-Marie, Mr. Riggs, and I went today to Hoghe. Mr. Riggs and I were to investigate conditions and see if it would be possible to open a Children's Home there. We left at noon and reached our destination after an hour's drive in the automobile. It was a lovely trip, everything so fresh and green, and the air so clean. There were marvellous birds flying around us, and the mountains were extremely beautiful with a soft, delicate blue sheen upon them, and the tops covered with snow. The Armenians in Hoghe streamed to meet us as we arrived, and we went in to the house of the sole Armenian man surviving there. He has not returned as an Armenian, but has changed his name and become a Moslem. The women looked well and were quite well-dressed. There were about 60 young men who had been taken by the Turks four years ago to work in their fields. These are now about 18 years old and able to support themselves. Several of them have got their fields back from the government, and we gave them money to buy oxen to plough their land. We also found a rather big and good house belonging to a young Armenian girl, which we can use for a Children's Home. Up to now, a Kurdish chief has been living in it. Elsewhere, hundreds of Armenian houses have been knocked down and are lying in ruins. All the women work like slaves in Turkish homes.

We were invited to dinner by the village Agha, the chief man. He was very friendly and obliging, and told us how much he had helped the Armenians. We came home about 6 o'clock.

18 May, 1919. We were all invited down to Sister Verena's for the evening.

22 May, 1919. The other day when we were down at Sister Verena's I became ill very suddenly, with dizziness, vomiting, and diarrhoea, and could not return home that evening. I was driven up next day and was really sick for the next couple of days. Now I am better again. Mr. Riggs was worried and sent a telegram to Constantinople saying "Miss Jacobsen sick from continuous strain. Please send workers at once."

Mr. Riggs and I have been down in Mezreh where we had a meeting with Sister Verena, Karen-Marie, and Kuchukian Effendi, concerning their Children's Home. We decided that their children should have the same ration of food as ours in Harpoot, and what this will cost them extra, we will pay.

Notices have been put up in the streets telling of a massacre in Smyrna. Greeks there have killed Turks. The Turks are very upset and furious that "Christian dogs" have killed their "true faithful" brothers. This could have a bad result here.

26 May, 1919. We should have left this morning for a village called Perchenj, where we were to visit Armenians, hold a service for them, and I was to conduct a women's meeting. But just after our morning meal someone came and told us that the outer door of the office was open. When Mr. Riggs went to investigate he found to his horror that his little safe was gone. There was then great confusion, with children starting to bring papers they had found flying around in the mountain. Shortly afterwards the safe itself was found there, broken open and empty. Mr. Riggs went to the police, who came, walked around, and wrote everything down. They questioned different people. A lot of valuables, jewels and papers, belonging to the Armenians, which I had kept for the last two years and had handed over to Mr. Riggs on his arrival were all in this safe, along with gold money, and were all taken.

We left at noon. We were invited to dinner by a Turkish Agha, but before that a rumour had gone around that he would poison us, and many came and asked us not to go to his house. But we know there are always rumours and we cannot believe them all. We went there and the man gave us a very friendly reception. It was a meal of 12 courses which we ate heartily and without harm. We talked with him about the village and the Armenians. He said he had killed no one, and had helped them much in the last years. It is true that he is the Turk in Perchenj who has treated them best. This does not say much, as all Turks in Perchenj are very hostile and have done all they can to make the lives of the Armenians as hard and sad as possible. After dinner we went to an Armenian house, where some children came and we held a service for them. There were not many, as the Turks would not give them freedom to come. During the service I sat by the window and every minute a stone came through it and struck my back.

After the service we went around to see some houses and gardens to see if we could open a Children's Home there, but we decided against it because the Turks were so hostile. The night before our arrival an Armenian woman had been attacked by a Turk in her own house. He had broken in and beaten her so badly that she had a big wound in her head. Next day she went to the authorities in Mezreh, but, of course, they did nothing, even though they say they should report everything and they will have their rights. The man who had beaten her had said, "as long as you live, we will always hear the Armenians say, 'Give us our children, houses, and land.' You are the one who encourages them." He had hoped she was dead. We returned home in the evening. It was a lovely journey. Everything looked fresh and green. The weather was cool, and the mountains were marvellous, with the soft blue sheen over them.

30 May, 1919. It has been a very hard day. My dear Arshaloois has died suddenly in an accident. We left happily this morning in a big lorry, packed full of bedclothes and some food, and some of the smallest children of the "family" who were to spend the summer in Hoghe. Arshaloois had promised me to go out there with the children and supervise them, and also conduct meetings for the Armenians in the village. There are quite a few women, and about 60 young men there, who were taken by the Turks four years ago when they were about 14 years old. Arshaloois is especially suited to this, as she is a serious, faithful Christian girl, educated, clever and a real personality, and I was sure she would do a good job and bring great blessing. The people in this village are longing, very much, to hear God's word. Arshaloois sat in the front with Bessie and me, and as we neared the village there was a rise in the road, and Mr. Wroman went at full speed to surmount it. The lorry lurched and Arshaloois fell off it. As soon as it was possible to stop I jumped off and ran, trembling, back to her. I found her lying deathly pale, and it was a terrible moment. When she saw how distressed I was she said, "Don't be sad, I am well." I was afraid she would die before I could do anything for her. The lorry could not drive all the way up to the village, so I ran as fast as I could to get help. At last I met some big Turkish boys on the outskirts of the village and they returned with me. I took a padded quilt, laid Arshaloois on it, and we carried her into the village. It was a dreadful journey for her, she suffered so terribly, I was afraid she would die before we got there, but we reached the village and an Armenian family, the only one in the village, gave me a room in their house and bedclothes. I cut the clothes from Arshaloois and found her in a terrible condition. The lorry had gone over one hip and there was profuse bleeding. I had nothing with which to bandage her, and her heart began to weaken. The only thing I could find to give her was some spirits which I gave her by mouth, and with which I cleaned the wound. Mr. Wroman drove as quickly as the lorry would go back to Mezreh for medicine and a doctor.

Her suffering became greater. I had to turn her from one side to the other, and I could see that she would die. I said to her, "Arshaloois, I think the Lord will take you Home in a short time. Are you sorry for that Arshaloois?" She answered, "No, Miss Jacobsen. I am not sorry for that, I am glad." She was very cold and pale with her lips blue, and a cold sweat on her brow. She became weaker every minute. When she had lain for a while we began to sing "Hisous ashkharks em lkadz." She sang the first verse, all through, with a pause after each word. She would not let me move from her bed. She suffered much, because she could not breathe and I had to turn her every two minutes. It was a terrible torture for her. Then she said, "Give my love to all the young at home, my friends." Then she began to call, "Jesus, come soon." She recognised me all the time and understood everything I said to her. After three hours of suffering she died. I had just set her in order and was washing my hands when Mr. Wroman and Dr. Michael came. It was then 4 o'clock. They had brought her some clean clothes in which I dressed her and packed her in her bedclothes. After that the women and the children from the village came and I had a short service with them. How strange it was that they had waited and were longing for her, and then she was not allowed to work among them. But it made them think seriously and showed us that death can come when you least expect it. I had to go and make arrangements with some Kurds concerning the house I was to have for my children. Two Kurdish Effendis were living in it and said they would not move out. The house belongs to a young Armenian girl. I talked with the Kurds for a very long time. One said he would leave the house next morning, not because the government said so, or because the Americans wanted it, but because a lady had asked him! "We Kurds have also ladies, and we know how to behave." He was quite French in his style! I thanked him very much for his kindness and said that I trusted his word. He said, "When we Kurds make a promise we keep it. We are not like the Turks, who say, "Tomorrow," and then let people wait for weeks and months." After I had seen him, I had to see the Turkish baker there, and make an arrangement with him to get bread for my children. After all this we went home.

It was a heavy journey back. I dreaded having to bring our beloved Arshaloois home as a corpse. When we reached the town, everyone came running. They had heard about the accident and expected to hear that she was better. It was a hard blow when I told them she was dead.

31 May. Today we buried our dear Arshaloois. I covered the coffin with white and all her many friends sent roses. It is just the time for roses now, so everything was beautiful. We assembled in the church, where the Badveli spoke really perfectly about her life, giving a true picture of her as a child, a pupil, and a teacher. He has known her the whole time. He said she had risen up and gone to her calling in Hoghe with joy, and had fallen on the road, but the Lord had considered her work accomplished, as she had gone to it so willingly. Who will now take her place? Mr. Riggs spoke so well about the Home, up there, with many mansions, which is

waiting for us, and advised us always to be ready. She was ready, when the Lord suddenly called her. He talked about the day before she left, how she had conducted a service for the young, and had talked to them, as if she knew it was for the last time. She had chosen several hymns about Heaven, and going Home there, as if she could not stop thinking about it. Baidzar read a farewell to her from her friends. Several beautiful Armenian hymns were sung, and a funeral march was played as the young girls carried her coffin to the cemetery. After it was lowered into the grave we sang the hymn, "When the roll is called up yonder, I'll be there" and before parting we sang, "There is no night there." It was very solemn, and we were happy to know she was Home with God, where everything is bright and glorious. But she will be much missed here by her friends, and in the work, where she played such a necessary part.

1 June, 1919. Placards have appeared again in the market telling people to wake up and be ready, otherwise their women and children will fall into the hands of the Christian dogs! Also the holy mosques will be taken and used by the infidel dogs! "Do you wish that? This will happen if you do not stand with a weapon in your hand and be ready to defend yourself against the enemy."

The weather is very heavy and thundery and has rolled all day, with rain and hailstones as large as birds' eggs falling all afternoon. The water collected in the streets and flowed in streams down the mountain carrying everything with it on its way. When the weather was at its worst Badveli Yeghoian rang Mr. Riggs twice, asking him to come down to Mezreh as soon as possible, because everyone was very afraid. Police were going around collecting young Armenian men, and he said he was sure the final persecution had started, which the Turks had often threatened. Mr. Riggs put on his raincoat and hat and walked down to Mezreh. When he reached it he was completely soaked and his hat was not recognisable. He went to the Badveli's and found two other men there. He asked what had happened, but could not get an answer, they were so scared. Mr. Riggs then went to Vehib Bey and asked him what was wrong. He also asked him to stop all these evil rumours, saying, "It will be bad for you if the Armenians are kept in this fear." Vehib Bey said that some of the "Young Turks" were furious over what had happened in Smyrna and had put up these notices in the Shuga, but when the Commandant had heard about them, he had given orders that they were to be taken down immediately. One placard had been overlooked and had not been taken down until the morning.

At noon two young Armenians were taken down to the government building for questioning because an Armenian woman—a bad woman—had been found drowned in a well, and the young men had been seen with her on the previous day. The placard that was overlooked, and the bringing in of these two young men, had set the whole of Mezreh beside themselves with fear. The Commandant assured Mr. Riggs that nothing would happen.

Mr. Riggs returned at 6 o'clock and told the true story, and everyone was calm again.

8 June, 1919. Arrival of ACRNE workers.

9 June, 1919. Last evening about 6 o'clock we had a call from the hospital to say that an automobile had arrived and 17 others would soon reach Mezreh. We put our coats and hats on in a hurry and Mr. Riggs took us in his automobile half way to Khankeoy and there we waited until it became dark. Suddenly we saw the automobiles' lights a good distance away, and it was not long before we were all out of the automobiles and greeting each other. Karen-Marie, whom we had met on the road, was also with us, and we two went with Dr. Parmelee in her automobile, reaching Harpoot about 9 o'clock. It was around midnight before they were ready to go to bed. They were a lively flock, most of them young people, all talking at the same time.

17 June, 1919. There have been some busy days, with several meetings of the Harpoot Unit every day. I have been appointed to nearly all Committees, and I must give some time to each of the new workers every day. All the time I have three or four, or more, around me in my office. Everybody asks questions and it is not easy to fit them in to all the work. My work has been divided and each of the newcomers has a part. I do nothing else but instruct them. I must also find young girls who can translate for them, as none of them can speak Armenian.

Today, Mr. Riggs, Mr. MacDaniels, Dr. Parmelee, and I have had a Committee meeting at which it was decided to take over all the boys from the Armenian Children's Home in Mezreh. After that we had another meeting with Karen-Marie, Sister Verena, Dr. Michael, Harotoone Effendi, and Derderian Effendi, at which we decided the arrangements for salaries.

It is a great pleasure for me that our helpers who have had so little during these last years—yes, even suffering want—will now have their salary increased so well that they can live without trouble.

A young man has been shot in the stomach in Perchenj while he was watering his garden and has died. The Turks are very evil minded.

20 June, 1919. The Harpoot Unit has held a meeting to decide the future of Professor Khachadoor and Baron Antreas. I gave them [the Unit] the letters I had received from them, and after they had been read, everyone was furious, and said that no discussion was necessary. Mr. Riggs thought Baron Antreas was not so bad, and wanted him to come forward to the meeting and defend himself. It was decided that he should come next morning. I was not present. He would not talk, so they asked him questions, and he did not manage very well. After two hours they all voted to dismiss him. It has also been decided that Mr. Wroman, Miss Riggs, the Badveli, and

I should go to Malatia to investigate the conditions there. We are leaving on Saturday. Mr. Riggs and Mr. Means are to go to Arapkir on the same mission, and are leaving tomorrow.

26 June. We have returned from Malatia today. We left here Saturday morning and arrived in Malatia in the evening. We went to Mr. Christoffell's Home for the Blind. On Sunday we had a morning service in the Protestant Church, if it can still be called that. It was taken by the government at the beginning of the war and used as a stable. It has been returned in that condition. But, at least, we could be together there, and we had a blessed meeting. It was the first time in four years that the Armenians in Malatia had had a service in fellowship.

Miss Riggs and I held a women's meeting at noon and there were many present. We held our evening service in the Catholic Church, which was almost full of people, nearly all women, with only about 10 men. In between the services we met different men and talked with them about conditions in Malatia. Monday, all day, was occupied in the same way. We found conditions there very poor. So much need and no work; everyone was very despondent. There is not one of the survivors in the whole big town who is able to stand up and be a leader of the lost sheep. In the streets hundreds of people are lying, suffering from hunger, dirty, sick, and full of scabies. The German Blind Home was also in a pitiful condition: No food, no clothes, no money, and no one to take care of the children and the blind. Baron Khoren and Digin Makrouhi who are the leaders have not taken care of the others. It has been said that there are 6,000 children in Turkish homes and in the surrounding villages. This may be an exaggeration, but there are undoubtedly many. We left on Tuesday morning, and many cried and asked me to do something to help them. We did not reach home until 5 o'clock. We had so many punctures on the bad road.

It is said that all the peace treaties have now been signed. God be praised and thanked that we have been allowed to see this day.

10 July. There have been busy days since we came back from Malatia. A couple of days later Mr. Riggs and Mr. Means returned from their trip to Arapkir, and we had a meeting of the Harpoot Unit to enable Mr. Riggs to give a report on his tour and we gave one on ours. Mr. Riggs was sure that the distress in Arapkir was greater than that in Malatia, but when we gave our report about Malatia, it was decided that it was greater there. So it was agreed that two of our workers should be sent there as soon as possible. If it were possible we would also send some to Arapkir but it is impossible at the moment.

Now we have meetings every day, and because I am on nearly all Committees, I have been sitting at meetings almost from morning till evening. It was decided that I should go with Miss Moore and Miss Greene to Malatia, and start the work there. We are to leave Saturday the 12th. On Monday the 7th, 18 large automobiles arrived, fully loaded with goods, for the hospital and our children. It was a splendid sight, so many automobiles, so many things, so many men. We have not been used to seeing this. Last time it was with things for the war and only meant for destruction. Now it is for our many small children, whom the Turks did everything to kill. It must surely have annoyed many a Turk to see what came on this day. But I was delighted and praised and thanked my Heavenly Father, who has now made possible what I have longed for during many a dark and long day. Our children are happy. The automobiles are driving back and forth between Mezreh and Harpoot, and when they are empty, we fill them with children who are then given a ride.

29 July, 1919. We left for Malatia in the morning of Saturday the 12th. Many travellers came with us. They had to pay, as only those of the party could travel free. Badveli Vartan, Bessie, and I were in the first car, which was driven by an American engineer Mr. Derver. It was quite a sight when the 18 big cars drove out from the hospital through the market and on to the road. When we had driven part of the way, we were stopped by some Turkish officers who asked permission to drive with us for a while. They were in pursuit of a runaway soldier who had taken some important papers. They came with us and when we reached Khankeoy we stopped while they investigated all the cars, but they did not find the soldier. We stopped at Tutloo Keoy and had a meal and then proceeded to Keumer Khan. There is a very broad river bed with deep sand. We crossed over well, but one of the other cars sank down in the sand, and it took a lot of work to get it over. Others sank as well, and we were delayed for three hours. We finally got clear and went on to the bridge over the Euphrates which was in a very bad condition. The Armenians who were travelling with us on the way back to their homes had tears in their eyes, remembering what they had seen at this place four years ago. A short distance on the other side of the river two cars fell through a bridge, and there was another delay of a couple of hours. It was getting dark by then, but we drove on without stopping, reaching Malatia at 11 o'clock in the evening.

We held a service next morning in the Protestant Church, and during our stay held a meeting every evening, and two every Sunday, which were attended by many. On the last Sunday evening we had a service of Communion for the first time in four years.

It was terribly hot while we were there, and it drained my energy going back and forth in the burning sun. But there was nothing I could do, as the Armenian quarter was at the other end of town.

I spent the first week seeing the women and trying to find houses we could use as Children's Homes. On Thursday afternoon we paid a visit to the Mutasarrif's wife. She was rather young, about 20, and dressed like a doll. It was difficult to find something to talk about with her. On the same evening we visited the Mutasarrif in his garden. He was an elderly man and was very friendly. He came and visited us on Saturday evening. I told him then that the object of our visit was to help those in need, both Christian and Moslem. I told him that we had invited many of the unhappy Kurds, who were lying in the streets, suffering from scabies and other illnesses, but that they would not come. I asked him if he could help me to collect them, and he said, "Yes" he would "with pleasure."

Next morning, Sunday, I was scarcely out of bed before one of the young people came and said that some sick people were waiting for me. I went down and found several patients, Turks, with chronic illnesses, sitting in the yard. I told them that I could not help them. They said that a man was going around saying that an American doctor had come to the town and would treat all the sick, free. I said it was a misunderstanding, that I had promised to collect all the little sick children and treat all those who have scabies. All day long crowds of sick came, on horseback, in wagons, or carried on the backs of friends, and I spent all the time talking to them and giving them good advice. I had no medicine, so I could give them none. In the afternoon a soldier came with 25 miserable little children, whom he had gathered up in the streets. They were the most pitiful I have ever seen. I talked to them and promised them something nice, sending immediately for bread and fruit to win their hearts. We put big kettles of water on the fire for baths and after that my two nurses came with scissors and started cutting their hair.

Next day soldiers came with two big crowds of children and grown ups, both men and women, all in an indescribable condition. They all shouted and cried, and when I asked them why they cried, the children answered, "I want my mother." This showed me that the soldiers had collected every Kurd they found, without telling them where they were going or why. No wonder they were afraid, being taken to the "Christian dogs," whom they themselves have ill-treated and killed. I told them that nothing bad would be done to them, but they would be helped to become well. I said that those who had parents and wished to leave could go, and a crowd of them immediately ran away. About 50 remained, to whom we gave bread and soup, and then began bathing and cutting hair. More of them ran away that evening, but the rest stayed until the cure was finished before also running away. Every time I went through the streets and saw them they smiled at me. At least we had shown them that we would do them no harm.

In the last week we took over the big Armenian Children's Home with 400 people. It was in a pitiful condition. Everyone had scabies, and there were no clothes or food, so I had my hands full in the last days.

I got some houses, and made a Children's Home for girls under 13, one for boys over 15, and one for girls who came from Turkish homes. We also started a weaving industry, hand work for the poor, and a lot of other things. It was sad to see those few men who have survived the massacre. How they have changed to resemble the men who protected them. They look completely like Turks and would not even speak Armenian until they were completely sure that no Turk could see or hear them.

There were those who spoke Armenian, but still kept their Turkish name and wore white around their hats. When we asked for the reason the answer was always the same, "We are afraid."

On Saturday Mr. Bishop and Miss Nyves came for me. We left Malatia on Monday morning but did not reach Mezreh until evening as we had engine trouble on the way. It was good to be home again.

30 July, 1919. Today at our Unit Meeting it was decided that I should pay visits to the children in the Homes in the different villages before I leave here for Denmark.

31 July (Thursday). Today I have arrived in Keghi where we have 120 children. We have a house with three rooms, and the Protestant Church. This is in a very bad condition with big holes in the roof and no doors or windows.

2 August, 1919 (Saturday). I have returned from Keghi this evening, where I spent two lovely days. Oh, how it did my heart good to see these many children so well and so happy. I had a meeting with them and told them about Jacob's dream. They sang many of their favourite songs, recited their verse, some even whole chapters, from the bible. I spent my time writing down some of my children's histories—how terrible they are. I could hardly bear to ask them about their experiences, as I could see how nervous they became, and sometimes, when they talked about the deaths of their families, they cried. But I did it to tell the friends at home what these little souls have gone through of suffering and persecution. Maybe it will be a blessing and help in the work.

4 August (Monday). Today we arrived at Sursuri Vank where we have about 120 children, and 16 big boys who plough our fields and take care of the garden. There are also 10 of the young girls from the School who are spending a holiday here. It is really wonderful here. The Vank lies on the side of a little hill, so we can see the whole plain with Mezreh and the surrounding villages, with Harpoot up on the mountain.

6 August (Wednesday). We left Sursuri this morning to travel to Mezreh on a donkey, and by automobile from Mezreh to Harpoot.

We had our Unit meeting this afternoon. I had some lovely days in Sursuri. The first night I went down to sleep in the church, and I thought I would sleep well, but, alas, as soon as we were in bed and everything was quiet, the sandflies began to bite. They got through the net, and Bessie and I tried to sleep with the sheet over us.

Appendix[*]

Maria Jacobsen left Harpoot in the autumn of 1919. In a letter dating from that period, she wrote about those terrible years, "When I look back over these last years I see our loving Heavenly Father's guiding and protecting hand. My heart is especially full of thanks and praise for His marvellous goodness in the last one and a half years—a time so hard, only God knows how hard, but also full of blessing. It is wonderful to dwell in the shadow of the Almighty: to know that His eyes are always open, and His hand always outstretched to help His children, and not only to know it but to experience it in a marvellous way in one's life and work."

After a time in Denmark, Maria travelled to the U.S.A. in October 1920, where she toured until the autumn of 1921, reporting on the massacre of Armenians, and what she had seen and experienced of distress and terror among these persecuted people.

In 1922 Maria again journeyed on a mission of aid. This time she went to Lebanon where thousands of Armenians had fled, amongst whom were many orphaned children.

The first home she set up for these children soon became too small, and in 1928 the K.M.A. purchased the place that was named the "Bird's Nest," and here she continued her work until her death in 1960.

On Maria's death, on April 6th, 1960, Pastor Oluf E. Paaske—a missionary at the Bird's Nest from 1948-63 wrote the following obituary:

Mama's (our dear Maria Jacobsen's) long working day is ended. The Lord has called her Home to the rest that awaits every faithful servant, when the race is run and the furrow ploughed to the end.

Mama had been very feeble for a long time and was confined to bed a week ago. By Sunday it had dawned upon her that God's time had now come, and the morning of Eternity was about to break. Quicker than we thought possible, Mama lost contact with us, and most of the time lay in a daze, which gradually lapsed into unconsciousness. Sometimes when Mama seemed more alert, we had a short devotional period, but on Tuesday evening it was clear, even to the least experienced among us, what was about to happen. The message "Mama is dying" went quietly around the Bird's Nest. Many of the children, maybe all, asked the Lord Jesus to be near

---

[*] This appendix was provided by the KMA.—A.S.

Mama—and He was. The long night passed, and on Wednesday morning, April 6th, all the Danes and many Armenians gathered around Mama's deathbed in stillness and prayer. At 10 o'clock in the morning Mama drew her last breath, and we united in a prayer, in both Danish and Armenian, and gave thanks to the Lord for all that He had given us through her.

It was my task to go down to the children and tell them that Mama had now gone home to Jesus, and that they must give thanks to Him for all that He had given them through Mama.

Out here, as the friends know, we had to make the funeral arrangements quickly, and by 3 o'clock on the same afternoon, Mama was prepared for burial. Those children and colleagues who wished it had the opportunity to file past the open coffin which stood in the large room of the Missionaries' House. Afterwards we sang a hymn and had a period of prayer before the coffin was closed and borne on strong arms down to the Church, followed by all the children.

In the Church we spread a large Danish flag over the coffin. This was Mama's heartfelt wish. We then read together a word from the Bible, sang a hymn, and said the Lord's Prayer. All through the night the lights from the Church shone out in the darkness.

The same evening, and again this morning, we have had a large and touching crowd of people on visits of condolence, which is the eastern custom. There were several hundred, the head of the County, the Mayor, and other important officials, but also long queues of ordinary people, to whom Mama had been a blessing and who now wished to show their gratitude. To the great pleasure of both Armenians and local Arabs here from Djoubeil, it was arranged that Mama would be buried in the Bird's Nest. Just inside the main gate lies a little triangular garden, up to a high wall, and here we prepared Mama's last resting place. After a discussion with our men I had them make a strong burial chamber of concrete under the Garden earth. They worked far into the night to finish it, and this morning the children have been busy bringing green branches and thousands of wild flowers with which to decorate the roof of the little chamber and its surroundings.

This afternoon people began to assemble. The funeral was announced for 3.30 p.m. through the newspapers, and by cards and notices posted up. But a great many people were informed verbally, and as the clock struck one hour before the time, the whole Church was packed with people. Most of them, naturally, were Armenian, but there were also people of several different nationalities and faiths.

The service began with our choir of 60 boys and girls singing, "Deep River," which Mama's sister had taught them and which Mama loved. Little did anyone think it would be used on this occasion. The children excelled themselves today, singing without a conductor, and joining together themselves in this beautiful tribute to Mama's memory.

The American Pastor Eder read a passage from the scriptures in English, and then Dr. Puzant Hadidian, who is married to one of Mama's two foster-daughters, spoke on behalf of the family, plainly and simply, and with a smile between the tears.

The next speaker was Father Sempad, a young Armenian-Gregorian priest, who is an "old-boy" of the Bird's Nest, having come in his time as an infant. He spoke on behalf of thousands of boys and girls, all Mama's children, whom only God in Heaven could number. He spoke so, that there was scarcely a dry eye, least of all his own, which made the deepest impression.

Three verses of the hymn "For All the Saints" were then sung, then the Moderator of the Armenian Protestant Church and head of the Theological School in Beirut, Pastor Aharonian, spoke so strongly and dynamically that he carried the whole congregation with him. He was followed by the old Armenian Church's Archbishop of Lebanon, Khoren Paroyan, who represented the Catholics (as head of the Armenian Church) and who spoke for all the people. He offered thanks and homage on behalf of the martyred ones, beautifully expressed and full of meaning, ending with the words from 2 Tim. 4, V. 7 "I have fought a good fight, I have finished my course, I have kept the faith, henceforth there is laid up for me a crown of righteousness, which the Lord, the righteous Judge shall give me."

After another three verses of "For All the Saints" the old venerable Pastor Hadidian gave the blessing, and the great mourning procession moved out to the grave, led by boys and girls bearing crosses and wreaths, then the coffin, borne high on outstretched arms over all the heads. This was followed, and all were pleased and touched to see it, by Archbishop Khoren, supporting the old feeble Protestant Pastor Hadidian under the arm. Here by Mama's coffin they were just Armenians, and all differences in faith were laid aside in mutual respect.

At the grave the Arab parish official raised a great voice in a glowing speech of praise in Arabic, and finished by saying how suitable it was that Mama should be buried after the manner of the ancient Phoenician kings, as she deserved, and that her resting place and memory should be held in reverence for a long time.

The burial service was conducted in Danish and after the Danish custom, the coffin was carefully placed in the narrow grave chamber. While it was being bricked in, the Archbishop and his priest sang an Armenian burial hymn, and then old Pastor Hadidian once again lifted his hands and his spirit in prayer. So ended Mama's funeral: a solemn ceremony for a tired worker who has entered in to the joy of her Lord.

Tonight lights burn over Mama's grave with its many lovely flowers and wreaths. A light in the dark night and a symbol that she, herself, was a light in the darkness, lit by Him who is the source of light, and borne Home to still more beautiful radiance before His throne.

Glossary

Abour	(Arm.) Soup
ACRNE	American Committee for Relief in the Near East
ABCFM	American Board of Commissioners for Foreign Missions
Agha	(Tur.) Landowner, lord
Ajans	Official Ottoman news agency
Arabadji	(Tur.) Wagon driver
"Buzlük"	(Tur.) A natural ice cave near Harpoot
Badveli	(Arm.) Reverend
Baedael, Bedel	(Arab.) Military exemption tax
Bairam	(Tur.) Muslim religious festival
Baron	(Arm.) Mr.
Bingbashi, Binbashi	(Tur.) Military rank of Major
Boulghour	(Tur.) Cracked wheat
Capitulations	Concessions granting certain rights to foreigners in the Ottoman Empire
Chaush	(Tur.) Sergeant
Charshaf	(Tur.) Women's outdoor overgarment
Churuk	(Tur.) Rotten, inferior, frail
D.M.S.	Danske Missions Selskab (Danish Missionary Association)
Digin	(Arm.) Mrs.
Gavur	(Pers.) Infidel, non-Muslim (used as a derogatory term in Turkish)
Gurush, grush	(Tur.) A unit of currency (*piaster*)
Hantess	(Arm.) School play, show, ceremony
Hayrik	(Arm.) Father
Kaimakam	(Arab.) Head official of a district (*kaza*)
Kavass	(Arab.) Messenger of an embassy or consulate
Kavoorma	(Tur.) Preserved meat
Kelek	(Tur.) Raft made of inflated animal skins
Khanum	(Tur.) Mrs.
Khaterdji	(Tur.) Muleteer
Khodja	(Arab.) A Muslim cleric
Khurma	(Pers.) Date (fruit)
Kufte	(Pers.) Meatball

Kuir	(Arm.) Sister
Kurban Bairam	(Arab.) Muslim Festival of Sacrifice
Leblebi	(Tur.) Roasted chick peas
Mayrig	(Arm.) Little mother
Mejidie	(Tur.) A unit of currency
Merkes	(Arab.) Administrative centre
Mohadjir	(Arab.) Emigrant, refugee
Mudir	(Tur.) Administrator, official
Mutasarrif	(Tur.) Head of a sub-province (*sanjak*)
Naephar	(Arab.) A private soldier
Oka, Oke	(Tur.) A unit of weight, approx. 2.8 pounds
Onbashi	(Tur.) Corporal
Para	(Tur.) Money
Piaster	See *gurush*
Pilaff	(Pers.) Boiled rice with stock
Pompish	Title given to wife of an Armenian Protestant minister
Ser Tabib	(Pers./Arab.) Head doctor
Shalvar	(Tur.) Baggy trousers
Sharagan	(Arm.) Church hymn
Shuga	(Arm.) Market
Tabur, tabor	(Tur.) Battalion
Tebdil Hana	(Tur.) Sanitorium
Vank	(Arm.) Monastery
Varzharan	(Arm.) School
Varzhoohi	(Arm.) Female teacher
Vali	(Tur.) Governor of a province (*vilayet*)
Yeghpair	(Arm.) Brother
Yuzbashi	(Tur.) Captain
Zaptie	(Tur.) Gendarme

Index